WITHDRAWN
UTSA LIBRARIES

INTRODUCTION TO SOCIAL PSYCHOLOGY

 **SOCIOLOGY SERIES**
John F. Cuber, *Editor*
Alfred C. Clarke, *Associate Editor*

INTRODUCTION TO
Social
Psychology

JOHN T. DOBY

Emory University

NEW YORK

APPLETON-CENTURY-CROFTS

Division of Meredith Publishing Company

Copyright ©, 1966, by

MEREDITH PUBLISHING COMPANY

All rights reserved. This book, or parts thereof, must not be used or reproduced in any manner without written permission. For information address the publisher, Appleton-Century-Crofts, Division of Meredith Publishing Company, 440 Park Avenue South, New York, New York 10016

656-2

Library of Congress Card Number: 66-11456

PRINTED IN THE UNITED STATES OF AMERICA
E 27020

To

ROSE, MARY, and NANCY

FOREWORD

THE GREAT PROBLEM, I think, in introducing thoughtful students to social psychology lies in giving them a perspective on the whole array of human social behavior and at the same time a context in the broader world of history and contemporary society. One must likewise report the recent empirical research—biological, psychological, and sociological—which constitutes the cutting-edge of the new science into the future. That a book can succeed in doing all this is a marked tribute to its author. But it is more than that. It is a reminder of the newly achieved maturity of the social sciences, the actual stuff of daily human social behavior that interests us; for abstractions have no more and no less a function than they have in the physical and in the biological sciences, namely to keep us constantly reminded of the general principles that transcend individual cases, but lead us back again to the better understanding of each individual case. I believe that the book makes good on this score also.

One of the things that I like best about this book is that one cannot decide whether the world of "biosocial" response is a derivative from biological realities or from sociocultural realities. The fact is that the same phenomena described here by Professor Doby arise directly from the biological nature of man and from the nature of the institutional setting in which biological responses appear. The context is historical, cultural, social from the largest contours right down to the structure and function of the small cooperating or competitive group, the understandings and misunderstandings between groups based on economic, sex, racial, or other factors which are both liberating and binding.

Such a presentation must altogether transcend the controversial attempt of psychology or sociology to compete with, or detract from, the other. Human social behavior is the important theme, and the methods of interpretation are inevitably drawn from a half-dozen different biological and social sciences. The results will be as unitary as is the initial conception; and that it succeeds here, is as evident at the initial as at the terminal point. I would count the young man or woman very fortunate who could pursue, throughout his or her psychological and sociological studies, an approach as free as this from petty academic partisanship. Fortunately the trend represented by Professor Doby's book is now beginning to be well defined. Several of the recent textbooks of social psychology have made much of this capacity of the observer to transcend academic clichés. This is all to their credit, and it means that the present book, instead of being a lonely pilgrim out of touch with the vanguard nearby, is in thorough contact with the contemporary trend.

At the same time, the peppering of the pages with significant new research gives the student more than a sound general framework. It gives him some of the excitement of real and concrete efforts, and the definite findings emerging from these methods develop a sense of *science* as the category of human effort within which human social responses must be classified.

If well taught, the student will get a broad range of information, a wide familiarity with research method, and the challenge of understanding human nature more and more fully.

GARDNER MURPHY

Menninger Foundation
Topeka, Kansas

PREFACE

IN THIS BOOK I have emphasized the unity of knowledge in social psychology rather than its diversity. My motive derives from my pedagogical belief that it is best to *introduce* the student to a field by giving him a confident and systematic introduction to its major problems and intellectual issues rather than surveying it in broadest outline. Too broad an *introduction,* especially one which attempts to include conflicting views, assumes a maturity of interest and experience of the beginning student that in the opinion of this writer is unrealistic and self-defeating.

Once a student has been positively motivated by a stimulating introduction to a field, then, it is appropriate in advanced courses to expose him to more diverse views, conflicting theories, and an increasing scope of data. By this time he should have the maturity of judgment that comes from cumulative experience with the data and thinking in a discipline. In other words, this book is not eclectic nor is it meant to be a reference source. It is instead an effort to organize the major problems and data of social psychology into a reasonably unified scheme.

This text focuses throughout on the behavior and behavioral properties of the individual, first, as a member of a species and second, as a member of sociocultural systems. It is intended for the junior-senior level of college and assumes that the student has had introductory psychology and introductory sociology. Different instructors may wish to place different degrees of emphasis on Chapters 11 and 12 (A Perspective For Analyzing Human Behavior and Principles of Experimentation), depending upon how much background their students have in these areas. If they already have considerable background in statistics, then, these materials may be given less emphasis. Mastery of these materials is not absolutely essential to the learning of subsequent research, but it is very helpful.

I believe that it is an aid to the student if he is given in the beginning an overall picture of the organization of the text and the author's reasons for taking up the various parts of the book in the order given. Therefore, a brief statement on this is in order.

Part I introduces the student to the field of social psychology. It examines the interrelations of the field to general psychology and general sociology. It attempts to provide the student with a relatively integrated theoretical orientation to man in environment, rather than the customary segmental treatment of personality, culture and collective behavior. Furthermore, the author assumes that accurate learning and understanding of the theoretical materials in a field are closely related to an adequate knowledge of the research procedures and the assumptions underlying these procedures.

Following the introduction to the data and to selected methods of research, the student is introduced to an analysis of human behavior as a species phenomenon. The aim here (Chapters 3 and 4) is to provide an evolutionary context for the understanding of the development of human behavior. A general theme throughout the book is that biological and physiological potentialities are, in regard to behavior, latent structures and functions whose specific contributions to social psychological behavior are joint outcomes of biological, physiological, and social processes. The social system, or society, is conceived as the evolved behavioral and cultural means through which the biological potentialities of the species are constantly being released.

Since the biological and physiological bases of behavior are important in social psychology, and since students often engage in naïve "biologizing" about behavior, the necessary elementary concepts of biology and genetics are presented in Chapters 3 and 4 in order to permit a better understanding of their relationships to behavior.

In Parts III and IV, the concern is with the behavior of the individual in a behavioral environment. That is, we tend to react behaviorally to things in the world in terms of our perceptions. The stimuli of our phenomenal worlds are definable in terms of meanings and significances and include the behaviors of other people and their cultural systems. The behavioral environment is built up gradually as the result of an interaction between the perceiver and what is perceived. The person or the organism is guided by perceptions which vary in strength or magnitudes as a function of prior interactions. This is the general theme that runs throughout Chapters 5 through 10—behavior is a function of one's perception and conception of his behavioral environment, and changes as the perceptions and conceptions change. It, of course, becames important to identify the variables which are related to these perceptions and conceptions. The approach in this book has been to conceptualize these problems in terms of operant conditioning theories.

Finally, it has been my observation, and research supports it, that the social environment is cumulative and reflects through time both continuity and change. This suggests some interesting connections between the elements of social systems and the behavioral elements and characteristics of the individual actors. This general set of problems is treated in Chapters 9 and 10.

In the preparation of this book, many individuals have contributed in one way or another to the intellectual background of the author. In this regard, I wish to mention first my major Professor, the late Professor Thomas C. McCormick, Chairman, Department of Sociology, University of Wisconsin. Secondly, I am much indebted to the writings and thinking

PREFACE

of Dr. Gardner Murphy in the field of social psychology from my graduate school days to the present. In addition, Dr. William Bevan read Chapter 5 and made many valuable suggestions, Dr. Benjamin L. Wycoff read Chapter 7 and provided helpful guidance and Dr. Henry Sharp, Professor of Mathematics, read Chapters 11 and 12 and provided many helpful suggestions. Finally, Dr. Gardner Murphy and Dr. John F. Cuber read the complete manuscript and contributed many valuable comments.

I am indebted to the Literary Executor of the late Sir Ronald A. Fisher, F.R.S., Cambridge, to Dr. Frank Yates, F.R.S., Rothamsted, and to Messrs. Oliver and Boyd, Ltd., Edinburgh, for permission to reprint Table 2 from their book *Statistical Tables for Biological, Agricultural, and Medical Research*.

I wish to express my personal appreciation to Mrs. Jerry Bailey for typing and editing the complete manuscript.

J. T. D.

Emory University

CONTENTS

Foreword by *Gardner Murphy*   vii

Preface   ix

Part I

INTRODUCTION

1. The Nature and Importance of Social Psychology   3
2. The Data and Level of Analysis of Social Psychology   31

Part II

MAN AS A SPECIES: BIOSOCIAL BASES OF HUMAN BEHAVIOR

3. Evolution and Culture   49
4. The Release of Human Potentialities   73

Part III

MAN AS A SOCIOCULTURAL ANIMAL: THE INDIVIDUAL AND THE GROUP

5. Perceiving and the Social World   113
6. Social Judgment   148
7. Learning and the Social World   167
8. Some Effects of Social Learning on Behavior   199

Part IV

SOCIAL INTERACTION: GROUPS AND ORGANIZATIONS IN CONTINUITY AND CHANGE

9. Social Interaction: Groups and Organizations 247

10. Behavior and Social Change 285

Part V

SOME METHODS OF ANALYSIS

11. A Perspective For Analyzing Human Behavior 323

12. Some Principles and Methods of Experimentation 341

Appendix: Tables 1 and 2 389

Name Index 395

Subject Index 399

Part I

INTRODUCTION

1

The Nature and Importance of Social Psychology

•

1. *What is Social Psychology?*
2. *The Importance of Studying Social Psychology*
3. *Basic Units of Analysis of Social Psychology*
    (a) *Sociological Considerations*
    (b) *Psychological Counterparts of Status and Role*
4. *Applications of Social Psychology*
5. *General Approach*
6. *Summary*

1. WHAT IS SOCIAL PSYCHOLOGY?

THE HISTORY OF SCIENCE reveals a continuous but an uneven line of growth and development. Its pathways, while reflecting a glowing history of successful problem-solving, also generate many new problems. Often these unsolved problems pile up and the progress of science is slowed until the body of science is revitalized by bold new concepts and theories.

Medical science was stymied until Pasteur demonstrated the fruitfulness of the new concept of the microbe as a disease-producing agent, and, likewise, was the study of physics until Einstein revitalized it by his concept of relativity.

While psychology and sociology each often claims the whole domain of human behavior as its individual bailiwick, the history of these two disciplines reveals basic differences in their approaches to the understanding of human behavior.[1] These differences have generally been

---

[1] See, for example, Howard Becker and H. E. Barnes, *Social Thought from Lore to Science*, 2nd ed. (Washington, D.C., Harren Press, 1952) and Edwin G. Boring, *A History of Experimental Psychology*, 2nd ed. (New York, Appleton-Century-Crofts, 1950). One recognizes, of course, that as these disciplines have matured, differences in basic assumptions have diminished. For a recent statement of current differences see Arnold Rose, *Theory and Method in the Social Sciences* (Minneapolis, University of Minnesota Press, 1954), pp. 220-227.

the result of varying approaches to the types of problems posed for different levels of behavior being analyzed by the two disciplines. One has emphasized one level of abstraction and the other, another. Some differences have stemmed from differing definitions of what are the significant problems. For example, in the early history of psychology, psychologists tended to emphasize the physiological bases of behavior and minimized social and cultural experience, while sociology tended to minimize the physical bases and emphasized social processes and conditions. Such differences earlier led to extremes like McDougall's concept of instinct and LeBon's "group mind" concept. These efforts, while stimulating in some respects, are marred by the error of borrowing concepts which are appropriate for one field and using them in another field without establishing their theoretical and empirical relevance and validity for the new application.

For instance, the informed student today knows that the old "instinct theory" of behavior was an application of biological concepts to psychological and social behavior. That is, they postulated an *innate* tendency to perceive, feel, and purposively react to a situation. In the beginning of the development of the theory the so-called instincts were conceived as nonspecific. But in time their proponents began to apply the label to any kind of consistent and habitual behavior. Thus they extrapolated physiological and biological concepts to account for psychological and social behavior which today is more satisfactorily explained by principles of learning. These writers were almost wholly investigators with psychological leanings.

However, as an instance of the other extreme, one finds certain sociological investigators (for example, Sumner, Ross, and LeBon) who became interested in individual behavior; and, not having adequate psychological concepts, they often engaged in naive psychologizing about the behavior of individuals. The student will soon learn that both these types of early investigators simply did the best they could with what they had. That is, if one of us had been living then and had been interested in the same problems, we would have done no better, if as well. The reason is quite simple when one realizes that the adequacy of scientific explanation in a given field is related to the maturity and state of development of the *theory* in that particular field. Thus, the quality and precision of the explanations within any field of science improve in time by means of research.

In order to comprehend what social psychology is, the reader must consider some of the difficulties which early investigators encountered which eventually led to the current general conception of social psychology. The early investigators who used a sociological approach generally attempted to "explain" individual behavior almost entirely from situational and social influences which often ignored or explained away as irrelevant psychological processes such as the functioning of perception, learning, and motivation. At more or less the same time, early researchers with a psychological approach (example, William McDougall's psychology of instinct as the major motivating factor in life) engaged in a rather one-sided effort to account for social influences upon the individual by assuming that such influences were not real and could be explained by means of inherent psychological processes alone. This approach ignored even the common-sense observation that individual behavior varies with group membership. It also ignored, or was unable to cope with, the problem of variation in individual behavior between societies with major differences in the culture patterns within and between the societies. The difficulties with such an extreme psychological approach become apparent when one takes into account the fact that if the whole of social life were a result of independent psychological or physiological processes, then, since man represents one biological species, his social behavior should exhibit a rather high degree of uniformity in time and space, except for changes or differences produced through biological evolution. Biologists tell us that man has *not* changed biologically in any significant way in the last 50,000 years; therefore, it is quite obvious that one cannot take this absence of change and use it to account for change in something else. Sorokin aptly criticizes this extreme psychological approach and the preceding extreme sociological position as follows:

> A and Non-A $= f(E)$, that is, the most opposite phenomena are the result of the same cause. Such an equation is logical nonsense; it contradicts the fundamental principle of science,—the uniform connection of cause and effect. It admits that the same cause may have the most different and opposite results. Under such a premise, the very conception of regularity and causal or functional relation is destroyed.[2]

In other words, these early approaches not only mixed levels of abstraction but also ignored the joint or reciprocal effects of many factors. As a matter of fact, it may be asserted that to a very great extent modern social psychology emerged out of a reaction to these two extreme approaches to individual behavior, the purely sociological and the purely psychological. It would perhaps be more accurate to say, out of a reaction to the sociological and psychological conceptions of that time.

It took some time for psychologists and sociologists to learn that each had important concepts which the other needed in his effort to understand the psychological behavior of the person. Among the first American writers to recognize this fact was James M. Baldwin, who emphasized

[2] Pitirim A. Sorokin, *Contemporary Sociological Theories* (New York, Harper & Row, Publishers, Inc., 1928), p. 534.

a genetic approach to the study of social behavior; logically, this led him to consider early childhood influences in the formation of personality. Thus, Baldwin as far back as 1900 noted that

> The society into which the child is born is, therefore, not to be conceived merely as a loose aggregate, made up of a number of biological individuals. It is rather a body of mental products, an established network of psychical relationships. By this the new person is moulded and shaped to his maturity. He enters into this network as a new cell in the social tissue, joining in its movement, revealing its nature, and contributing to its growth. It is literally a tissue, psychological in character, in the development of which the new individual is differentiated. He does not *enter into it* as an individual; on the contrary, he is only an individual when he *comes out of it*—by a process of "budding" or "cell-division," to pursue the physiological analogy. Society is a mass of mental and moral states and values, which perpetuates itself in individual persons. In the personal self, the social is individualised.[3]

C. H. Cooley[4] later with almost graphic clarity called attention to the falsity of the antithesis *society* vs. *the individual* by noting that a *separate* person is an abstraction unknown to experience, and so likewise is society itself when regarded as something apart from persons. His idea of the self in terms of what he called the "looking-glass self" called attention to the role of social interaction in the formation of self-attitudes. However, the specific mechanisms by which self-attitudes are formed were only vaguely implied in Cooley's work. Here G. H. Mead went further with an aim for determining the working mechanisms in the formation of the self. The concepts which he emphasized were the *significant symbol, language,* and *role-taking.* While Mead's formulations were on a philosophical level rather than an experimental level, they had a great influence on conceptions regarding social interaction.[5]

Such contributions eventually made their impact upon theories about conditions and factors by which persons influence one another in specified ways. One of the most influential of these contributions was the conceptual system of Thomas and Znaniecki,[6] which emphasized the necessity of differentiating the scientist's definition of the situation being observed from the definition of the person who was behaving in the situation. In fact, the situation as defined by the scientific observer al-

---

[3] From F. B. Karpf, *American Social Psychology* (New York, McGraw-Hill Book Company, copyright 1932), p. 285. Used by permission.

[4] C. H. Cooley, *Human Nature and the Social Order* (New York, Charles Scribner's Sons, 1902).

[5] G. H. Mead, *Mind, Self and Society* (Chicago, The University of Chicago Press, 1934) and G. H. Mead, *The Philosophy of the Act* (Chicago, The University of Chicago Press, 1938).

[6] W. I. Thomas and F. Znaniecki, *The Polish Peasant in Europe and America*, 5 vols. (Boston, Badger, 1918-20).

ways comes after a knowledge of the situation as defined by the actor, if one is to understand correctly the meaning as the actor himself intended it. The major concepts used by Thomas and Znaniecki toward this end were the interdependent concepts of *social value* and *individual attitude*.

Thomas and Znaniecki went a long way toward showing how the group influenced individual behavior. The method they employed was the culture case study. The student will learn later in this text that scientists have particular preferences or tastes as to how they like to receive scientific information. As a consequence of the success of the experimental method in physics, this method seems to enjoy a higher status today partly because of the power and clarity of the method, and partly because of psychological reasons of its users, who are victims of conventional modes of reasoning. The reader must bear in mind that scientific method evolves by change just as science evolves by change. Nevertheless, it would help if more propositions about the influence of social behavior upon the individual could somehow be subjected to experimental tests. Most people today do not need to be told that groups influence the behavior of individuals; however, they do need to be shown *what* the specific effects are and *how* they are produced.

In an effort to improve the situation Sherif [7] in 1935 studied some specific relationships between social norms and perceptual processes. He demonstrated that the communication between individuals in regard to an ambiguous stimulus resulted in a common judgment regarding that stimulus. While it is a common observation that group norms have power over individual group members, the importance of Sherif's experiment was to bring this effect into the laboratory and to demonstrate *how* the "group effects" process operated. That is to say, Sherif grounded the group effects process in the familiar psychological processes of perception and learning.

One of the clearest and simplest examples of the effect of social interaction on perception and cognition is afforded by Piaget's studies of language, judgment, and reasoning of children. He discovered that children think that everyone's understanding is the same as theirs. When differentiation does occur by young children between themselves and others, it occurs step by step through the acquisition of rules of behavior based upon the understanding of the reciprocal nature of social roles. This reciprocal understanding is very difficult for young children to acquire because of their difficulty in distinguishing between abstract and concrete relationships and ideas. For example, there is no necessary connection between a symbol and the thing it stands for. The validity of a symbol rests only on the agreement of the people who communicate

---

[7] Muzafer Sherif, *An Outline of Social Psychology* (New York, Harper & Row, Publishers, Inc., 1948).

with each other by using it. The more limited a person's experience is in relation to the possibility of a given object being known and understood in terms of *other* symbols, the easier it is for him to come to believe that his understanding is necessary and right. Piaget found that children could not conceive of calling a cow "a horse," for example, because then it would not have horns—and cows have horns. The following quotation from one of Piaget's interviews with a child further illustrates this tendency:

> (A child is being questioned.) Could the sun have been called "moon" and the moon "sun"?—No.—Why not?—*Because the sun shines brighter than the moon.* . . . But if everyone had called the sun "moon," and the moon "sun," would we have known it was wrong?—*Yes, because the sun is always bigger, it always stays like it is and so does the moon.*—Yes, but the sun isn't changed, only its name. Could it have been called . . . etc.?—No. . . . *Because the moon rises in the evening, and the sun in the day.*[8]

Thus one is forced to note the great dependence of the personal beliefs and understandings of children upon the shared symbols or consensus of meanings held by the group of which the child is a member. Another example, only this time derived from adults, should put us in a position to state more clearly what we mean by social psychology. Common-sense observation and scientific observation are full of examples which show that the behavior traits of a person vary with his interdependence and interrelationship with other persons in groups. For instance, reports from the study entitled *The American Soldier* [9] of World War II provide ample evidence of how attitudes vary with rank and position in the army structure. Speier in the study just cited showed that ". . . the difference between opinions on the same subject matter expressed by groups high or low in power, privilege or prestige will increase as the subject matter is more closely and directly related to the status characteristics and relations of the group." [10] T. N. Newcomb concludes that this fact, together with that of systematic changes of attitude as one ascends the scale of rank, makes it abundantly clear that one's attitudes are not only properties of single persons but also properties of parts of social systems.[11] Obviously, then, we are in need of

---

[8] Eugene L. Hartley and Ruth E. Hartley, *Fundamentals of Social Psychology* (New York, Alfred A. Knopf, Inc., 1952), p. 110, taken from J. Piaget, *The Child's Conception of the World* (New York, Humanities Press, Inc., 1929), pp. 81-82.

[9] Robert K. Merton and Paul F. Lazarsfeld, *Continuities in Social Research: Studies in the Scope and Method of "The American Soldier"* (New York, The Free Press of Glencoe, Inc., 1950).

[10] *Ibid.*, p. 124.

[11] Theodore Newcomb in John Gillin, ed., *For a Science of Social Man* (New York, The Macmillan Company, 1954), p. 241.

a concept which reciprocally relates the behavior of the individual to the system or systems of behavior of the groups of which he is a member. Such a concept seems to be provided by the notion of the social role of the individual. The preceding introduces three terms which need some conceptual clarification in order to insure the meaning intended here. These are *systems of behavior, group,* and *social role*. Actually, they represent three different but interrelated levels of abstraction of human behavior.

By system of behavior is meant those accepted patterns of social behavior which originate through social interaction (and subsequently regulate interaction) and are symbolically transmitted through the learning process from one population set to another.[12] Although these patterns may change, and often do change rapidly through time, they are nevertheless cumulative in nature and possess a continuity which serves to regulate and standardize human interaction to a relative degree.

The concept of *system of behavior* or *social system*, as we will designate it from here on, implies that the participants are not *all* expected to do the same thing. The system provides the coordination, control, and integration which make possible the attainment of goals and the overcoming of conditions which would not be possible through individual action alone. If one wishes to obtain a real feel for this distinction, then he should observe medical practice in a hospital, the production process within a factory, or the administrative operation of a large staff.

A social system is composed of several elements. Among these are *social positions, social and technical norms,* and *social relationships.* There are, of course, other properties to a social system, such as knowledge, skills, communication networks, and shared goals. However, for our purposes just now, it will be sufficient to consider a social system in terms of the three elements of *positions, norms,* and *relationships.*

As was pointed out earlier, the participants in a social system are not expected to do the same things. No one person acts at any given time and place in terms of all of the culture he knows; he could not do so if he wanted to. Social behavior is organized and integrated in terms of social positions. That which is expected of a particular person depends upon the social position which he occupies within a particular group. Thus *social positions* result from the functional differentiation within a social system. The fundamental characteristic of the system is the prop-

---

[12] The advanced reader may wonder if this usage of system of behavior or behavioral system is similar to the meaning generally assigned to the term *culture*. The answer is yes. The reason I did not use the term *culture* is because I am reserving it for later use in a broader sense to include all the cumulative *products* of social interaction, and not just *behavior patterns* as here used; for example, the inclusion of artifacts.

erty of *reciprocity* and *interdependence*, that is, the parts of the system are organized into a network of *mutually* interacting relationships.[13]

The reciprocal or *relational* aspect of a social position can be more clearly understood when we note that any particular social position is composed of two parts, one part consisting of *obligations* and the other of *rights*. These two parts are designated as *role* and *status* respectively. A doctor's *role* consists of what others can legitimately expect of him when he is occupying that position. The doctor's status consists of what he can legitimately expect from others when he is occupying that position. Thus what is role from the point of view of one member is status from the other's point of view. Social behavior would hardly be possible without a shared view of the role properties by the actors. This latter characteristic is what we mean when we speak of the relational property of the concept of position and its two elements, status and role.

It should now be clear that a social system is principally an organization of roles into a system of relationships for the attainment of human motives and ends. A social relationship may be said to exist when two or more people are in interaction. The interaction may vary all the way from the most casual or transitory exchange to such relatively permanent and sustained relations as marriage or a business partnership.

Once two or more people form a set of relationships for the attainment of common goals we say that a social *group* exists. The behavior of the group is principally regulated by the status rights and role obligations of the members of the group. A person generally has as many different roles in a group as there are people to whom he relates. This constellation of role relations of one person to many others by virtue of occupying a particular social position is what Merton calls a "role-set." [14]

A role refers to a behavior pattern as a functional part of a social position. It is interesting to note that the other members of one's role-set may have differing evaluations of one's role performance. This suggests that there exist standards by which role behavior is evaluated. This brings us to a consideration of one of the central concepts in sociology, namely, the concept of *social norm*. A norm does not describe actual behavior but it is instead an ideal or standard by which actual behavior is defined, judged, or evaluated. Norms are not perceived by persons; they are conceived.

---

[13] The basic distinctions of position, status, and role which I have made follow the distinctions of Talcott Parsons and Edward Shils, eds., *Toward a General Theory of Action* (Cambridge, Mass., Harvard University Press, 1951), pp. 47-275. For two somewhat different views the student might read Ralph Linton, *The Cultural Background of Personality* (New York, Appleton-Century-Crofts, 1945), and T. R. Sarbin in Gardner Lindzey, ed., *Handbook of Social Psychology*, Vol. 1 (Reading, Mass., Addison-Wesley Publishing Co., Inc., 1954).

[14] Robert K. Merton, *Social Theory and Social Structure*, revised edition and enlarged edition (New York, The Free Press of Glencoe, Inc., 1957), pp. 368-371.

Norms do not define the minute details of action but provide a boundary range for determining the degree of acceptability or nonacceptability of behavior. Thus norms are abstract patterns of evaluation.

When a person learns a social role, the pattern of behavior then becomes a part of his personality and exists in latent form until the proper stimulus situation arises and the behavior pattern then becomes manifest. Since the role is socially derived, it is also a part of the social system. In other words, as the person learns to meet his own needs, he necessarily learns at the same time to meet some of society's needs. Thus the concept of social role is a bridging concept, that is, one which connects the personality system of the individual with the social organization of the society.

Our interest in the concept of role is primarily from the point of view of assessing the influence of *role behavior* upon the person performing the role. This interest in roles should not be confused with the study of roles from the point of view of how a social system or group *maintains* its system of behavior: this is primarily a sociological analysis of roles. On the other hand, these two kinds of role problems are interrelated; however, we distinguish them here to call attention to our principal interest, namely, the influence of *role behavior* upon the person.

Sociologists define a role as the behavioral obligations necessary to the performance of a given status. For example, suppose the status is that of a mother. Then, the role consists of the set of behavior patterns which are characteristically expected of mothers in that society.

Role behavior, on the other hand, refers to the *actual* behavior of specific individuals as they take roles. Furthermore, role behavior involves a personal motive on the part of the individual as he takes a role. That is, he takes the role primarily for immediate personal satisfaction. But since the role is a reciprocal pattern of behavior, it is perceived in terms of a frame of reference or context which is shared with others. Thus, irrespective of his personal motives his behavior is to a large extent defined for him by others in the group. For example, a first baseman in a baseball game does what he does to a large extent because of his position in relation to the other members of the team. In reference to this reciprocal nature of roles Linton says about the individual,

> He takes the bait of immediate personal satisfaction and is caught upon the hook of socialization. He would learn to eat in response to his own hunger drive, but his elders teach him to "eat like a gentleman." Thus, in later years, his hunger drive elicits a response which will not only satisfy it but do so in a way acceptable to his society and compatible with its other culture patterns. Through instruction and initiation the individual develops habits which cause him to perform his social roles not only effectively but largely unconsciously. This ability to integrate into a single configuration

elements of behavior some of which serve to meet individuals needs, others to satisfy social necessities, and to learn and transmit such configurations as wholes is the thing that makes human societies possible.[15]

The reader is no doubt saying to himself by now that he thought that this particular section of the chapter was supposed to tell what social psychology is, not to develop a part of the field. He is right, and we have now supplied sufficient background to enable the formulation of a working definition. Recall that all through the foregoing discussion the concept of inter-individual action has been stressed. Since this is a rather clumsy expression, we prefer to use the term *social interaction* instead of *interindividual* action, and will from here on use the term *social interaction*, but in the sense of interindividual action. Thus the unit of study in social psychology is the covert and overt behavior of the individual as this behavior is influenced directly or indirectly by other persons, groups, cultural products, and institutions. While no definition is complete and satisfactory to all, this one gives the general meaning of the term *social psychology* as we intend to use it here.

2. THE IMPORTANCE OF STUDYING SOCIAL PSYCHOLOGY

It seems obvious that, if students know the significance of a field of study, they can more easily and effectively organize and relate the data to personal goals and interests and thus facilitate learning. Some people are indeed motivated to learn for the sake of learning, but they are rare, although commendable in spirit. But for most people some more mundane reason is necessary.

Why study social psychology? Socrates gave one good reason over two thousand years ago: "Know thyself!" From the definition of social psychology given in Section 1 above it is obvious that the main interest of this science is human nature as localized in the person.

As the methods of modern science in general advance the depth and scope of human knowledge, it becomes increasingly apparent that the various fields of knowledge are all interrelated. Thus today to be a good chemist a man needs also to be a good physicist and biologist. To understand and treat successfully physical ills, a physician must also have a good knowledge of human nature. There is apparently no final distinction between physical and mental illness. The wonder today is that man ever thought there was. The answer to this problem is itself an interesting study in historical sociology. Physical science has already aided man

---

[15] From *The Cultural Background of Personality* by Ralph Linton (Copyright, 1945, D. Appleton-Century Company, Inc.). Reprinted by permission of Appleton-Century-Crofts.

tremendously in his understanding and control of problems of the physical world. We make no claims for science as a panacea for human problems; in fact, we know that it is not. However, it has been and is one important means of human progress and cultural development. In the Western world, the first great strides in scientific progress were made in chemistry, physics, biology, and medicine. More recently, anthropology, psychology, and sociology have emerged to transform man's notions of his own nature and characteristics. As these fields grow in knowledge, man's ability to control the problems which stem from his own nature and culture likewise grows. Such problems are too numerous to mention. Some are personality conflict and mental disorders, group conflict and prejudice, crime, war, poverty, and the whole gamut of problems of personal and social adjustment which derive from cultural and social change, all of which have in common certain basic characteristics of human relationships. The scientific understanding of man in society contributes greatly to man's means of solving problems in connection with human adaptation. Obviously, then, in a modern complex society it is important if not necessary that each participant in so far as possible have a more adequate and efficient understanding of himself and the factors which affect his personality. To aid the student in this endeavor social psychology offers at least four objectives:

(1) It is a basic science which is concerned with understanding the individual as a person rather than an organism. Its importance in contrast to general psychology is that it focuses on the interaction of the internal processes with the social processes responsible for human behavior as it is recognized in daily life, whereas general psychology is more concerned primarily with the internal processes of the organism *per se*. A human offspring without human interaction (if such could exist) is a physiological bundle of potentialities but not a human personality.

(2) The student after becoming acquainted with the basic concepts and theories of social psychology is himself better equipped to understand man and his behavior. Obviously, the student must first learn exactly what the psychologist means by his concepts and theories before he can ever accurately understand what the psychologist can tell him *about* man and his behavior.

(3) It provides the student with a general introduction to the methods and procedures used by the psychologist in the deriving and testing of his concepts and theories.

(4) It affords the student with a practical and realistic interpretation of the basic and more important findings of the social psychologist.

Such are the major objectives which the student should expect to achieve from an introductory course in social psychology.

3. BASIC UNITS OF ANALYSIS OF SOCIAL PSYCHOLOGY

SOCIOLOGICAL CONSIDERATIONS

Social psychology seeks to understand the development, modification, and change in the behavior of individuals, primarily as this development and change is influenced by social interaction. Thus, social psychology studies the psychological processes of the individual as they are primarily influenced or affected by social and cultural experiences. The major psychological processes with which social psychology is concerned are learning, perception, cognition, and motivation.

The social psychologist in his study of human behavior is somewhat like the geologist in his study of the earth, that is, many of the factors responsible for the *present* behavior of human beings and the characteristics of this behavior are factors which have already acted or are acting upon the person or persons under observation. This is a very important fact, since it means that the social psychological investigator is handicapped in his effort to disentangle the antecedents to social psychological outcomes. The physical scientist is often aided by being able to arrange his experimental situations in what appear to be very unreal ways, but nevertheless *ideal* for experimentation. As Spence says, "Although nature may abhor a vacuum, fortunately the experimental physicist did not." [16]

The social psychologist is often concerned with the observation of human behavior in terms of a more or less natural environment and uses the controlled experiment to check the validity of his observational studies. The physicist's vacuum and the psychologist's natural environment type of experiment imply that there are different levels of observation of behavior, and hence different levels of conceptual abstraction and description.[17] That is, one may be interested in coal in terms of its atomic structure, in terms of chemical compounds, in terms of its relation to synthetic products, or simply as a fossil fuel. Here we have a range of abstraction running all the way from physical chemistry to manufacture and distribution of synthetic items for consumers to direct consumer consumption, each representing a different level of conceptualization and perspective. Consequently, in the discussion of units of analysis in social psychology it is also essential that one make clear the level of abstraction with which he is primarily concerned.

First, it should be obvious that psychological concepts and principles are derived from psychological data or variables, that is, processes and

---

[16] Kenneth W. Spence *et al.*, *Learning Theory, Personality Theory, and Clinical Research: The Kentucky Symposium* (New York, John Wiley & Sons, Inc., 1954), p. 2.

[17] This notion of levels of abstraction and observation will be developed in detail in Chapters 2 and 11.

acts of thinking, conceiving, interpreting or perceiving, motivation, imagination, and so on. In other words, we are interested in the behavior system of the organism rather than his biochemical system. Such delimiting of interests in science is not only legitimate but necessary. Such analytical compartmentalizing does not, of course, imply that any one level of abstraction is any more important than any other. We would like to leave the matter by saying that in respect to behavior we (and other animals, for that matter) live in a world of things, objects, and relationships rather than a world of stimuli in the purely sensory sense. In addition, man has inherited a language system which implies a dualism of mind and body, that is, the Cartesian mind/body dualism. Therefore, in order to preclude the possibility of being misleading, we must add that these *things, objects,* and *relationships* are what they are for man, or any other creature, by virtue of the structure of the nervous system, endocrine system, general physical and skeletal system, emotional state, past experience with similar objects, and—in the case of man—his culture.

As we have indicated, there are many physical variables which affect indirectly the problem of order and meaning for an organism. But the specific effects of these physical factors, such as the structure of the nervous system, the condition of the body chemical system, and so on, can only be assessed by data derived directly or indirectly from *these* variables, not from the psychological acts of the organism. On the other hand, the totality of conditions or factors in a person that makes a given object or experience what it is for that person at a given time is his personality. This, of course, refers to the most fundamental of all operations in the human organism, namely, the *joint* operation of physiological and psychological processes. When we speak of viewing the human organism as a whole, this implies that it must be viewed as functioning in its environment. Therefore, the *behavior* (B) of the person is a joint function of the personality (P) and the environment (E), or $B = f(P, E)$.[18] It is the task of the researcher to determine the specifics of P and E and their joint relationships. Many of the known specific factors included under these two general concepts will be considered in place in later chapters. Just now, we need to specify more sharply the *units* of analysis of social psychology.

Are we to consider the more simple forms of behavior of individuals such as reflex action, motor behavior, molecular action, and the like, or shall we be concerned with total behavior *acts,* such as choosing a marriage partner, voting, answering a questionnaire, or performing a role in a group? Following Krech, Tolman, Lewin, and others, we designate the former type of behavior as a "molecular" unit, and the latter a "molar"

---

[18] Kurt Lewin, *A Dynamic Theory of Personality* (New York, McGraw-Hill Book Company, 1935), p. 79.

unit.[19] It is with the latter type of unit that we shall be concerned in this book. Thus the basic level of behavior, which we shall consider, is the *acts* of individuals. And these "acts" will be viewed primarily in terms of a *context* of social behavior.

We have succeeded thus far in identifying the general level of analysis to be considered, but we have not specified any particular concepts by which the foregoing level of analysis may be carried out. At the present level of development of social psychology such a specification is no easy task. First, the concepts to be employed, if they are to be useful in social psychology, should provide a reference to the *interaction* between the individual's past experience and the norms and processes of social groups. Two such concepts in current usage that seem to meet the foregoing requirement are the concepts of *attitude* and *role*. Both of these concepts are difficult to define with satisfactory precision. In the first place, we know attitudes only indirectly. That is, they are inferred from the overt or observable actions of individuals. Thus, if we hear someone making derogatory remarks about some ethnic group or some religion, we infer that he has a negative attitude toward the group or the religion. Again, it is important to note, however, that the observer *infers* the attitude from the overt actions of the person toward the object of the alleged attitude. While the attitude is inferred from the overt action, it is assumed that the overt action closely corresponds to an inner psychological state to which the term *attitude* refers.[20] The existence of an attitude may or may not be the result of first-hand contact with the *object* of the attitude. While it is assumed that the attitude is learned in either case, it may be learned through personal experience or through cultural contact or vicarious experience. Hartley has demonstrated that attitudes are not necessarily the result of personal contact.[21]

In a study in which three *imaginary* groups—the Danireans, the Wallonians, and the Pireneans—were included in a list of races and nationalities, subjects responded essentially the same to these nonexistent groups as they did to other actual groups, with coefficients of correlation ranging from .78 to .85. For example, people who disliked Negroes and Jews also disliked the fictitious Danireans and Wallonians, and vice versa. From such data, it is clear that one important source of attitudes is that they are learned from other people, rather than through contact with the group or object toward which the attitude is directed. Of course, with

[19] David Krech and Richard Crutchfield, *Theory and Problems of Social Psychology* (New York, McGraw-Hill Book Company, 1948), p. 31.
[20] Common-sense observation often suggests a divergence between an alleged attitude and overt behavior, but more careful and systematic observation will reveal that in such apparent cases there is more than one attitude operative, and hence a different attitude from the assumed one is dominant at the moment.
[21] Eugene Hartley, *Problems in Prejudice* (New York, The King's Crown Press, 1946), p. 26.

respect to the foregoing fictitious people, the response of the subjects represented a *generalization* of an existent attitude.

Thus it seems that attitudes affect one's perceptions, that is, the foregoing nonexistent groups were perceived as a part of the subject's category of out-groups. One might argue that the nonexistent Wallonians could be confused with the Walloons of southern Belgium, assuming that the test subjects had such knowledge, although no such argument could be made for the other two. It should also be clear now by implication, at least, that attitudes provide a partial basis for further or subsequent organization of behavior. Also, from the functional point of view this implies that one's attitudes and behavior are correlated. As Adams points out, an attitude also includes an affective component, that is, ". . . an object is also what we feel about it, as well as what we know or do about it." [22] As a working definition of the concept of *attitude*, we offer a modified version of Faris' conception of the term: An attitude is a learned conscious or unconscious conceptualization of an object, person, or situation, which defines its potential or actual relation to the activity or well-being of the person holding the attitude.[23]

With this working definition of the concept of attitude, let us return to a consideration of the concept of role. As with the concept of attitude, the term *role* meets our requirement of an *interaction* reference. That is, roles exist as a part of the social system and as a part of the personality of the persons who have learned them. For example, the members of a society have a conception of the minimum obligations of the role of mother. Likewise, any particular mother has a general conception as to what society expects a mother to do, as a mother; and she also holds an *attitude* toward motherhood. Group action is largely organized and sustained through a system of interlocking roles. That is, the reciprocal action of persons is to a significant extent determined by the social roles they perform as members of a group. Newcomb defines a social group as an aggregate of people who share norms about certain things and whose social roles interlock.[24] The reciprocal or interacting characteristic of the concept of role in respect to the individual and the group should be clear by now. But this is not the only interacting aspect of the concept in which we are interested. There is interaction between the person *himself* and his role, that is, the interaction of role and self.

---

[22] Donald K. Adams *et al.*, *Learning Theory, Personality Theory, and Clinical Research: The Kentucky Symposium* (New York, John Wiley & Sons, Inc., 1954), p. 77. Hereafter referred to as the Kentucky Symposium.

[23] Robert E. L. Faris, *Social Psychology* (New York, The Ronald Press Company, 1952), p. 200. Some people may object to the idea of something which is unconscious as being a conceptualization; nevertheless, we recognize degrees of conceptualizing.

[24] Theodore M. Newcomb, *Social Psychology* (New York, Holt, Rinehart and Winston, Inc., 1950), pp. 491-92.

In social psychology it is at this latter level of interaction that we are most interested.²⁵ Such a conception permits the treatment of problems at a level of complexity which jointly involves the previous learning of the person in relation to structures in his environment. These environmental structures may be physical objects, such as automobiles, buildings, and so on, or they may be intangible objects such as social acts, beliefs, and roles.

The formulation of a psychological definition of role requires a broad picture assuming first a general understanding of the concepts of culture, society, and personality. The generally accepted definition of culture, following Linton,²⁶ is that *culture* is regarded as an organization of learned behaviors together with the tangible and intangible products of behavior which are shared by and transmitted among the members of a society. It is these organized and standardized actions of persons which make possible human social interaction. A *society* is simply an aggregate of people who share and enact a given culture. Thus, it is the culture which gives direction and orientation to the members of society. Linton and others have shown

> . . . that a society can neither endure through time nor function successfully at any point in time unless the associated culture fulfills certain conditions. It must include techniques for indoctrinating new individuals in the society's system of values and for training them to occupy particular places in its structure. It must also include techniques for rewarding socially desirable behavior and discouraging that which is socially undesirable. Lastly, the behavior patterns which compose the culture must be adjusted to one another in such a way as to avoid conflict and prevent the results of one pattern of behavior from negating those of another.²⁷

To a very large extent a society achieves those three conditions by organizing its activities into statuses and roles.

Sociologically, we have already indicated that the term *status* refers to the expected rights associated with a social position or function and its related evaluation or rank. More concretely, a status is usually designated by a single term such as mother, father, doctor, teacher, and so on. Thus, the place in a particular social system or group which a particular individual occupies at a given time is his status with respect to that system or group, though one individual may, of course, occupy more than one latent status at any given time. We also saw that the term *role* is used

---

[25] Theodore R. Sarbin, "Role Theory," in Gardner Lindzey, ed., *Handbook of Social Psychology*, Vol. 1 (Reading, Mass., Addison-Wesley Co., 1954), p. 223. See also George H. Mead, *Mind, Self and Society* (Chicago, The University of Chicago Press, 1934), Part 3.
[26] Ralph Linton, *op. cit.*, p. 32.
[27] *Ibid.*, p. 24.

to designate the obligations or behavior patterns necessary to validate a particular status. Thus status is a positional or structural concept and role an action or behavioral concept.

While status and role are conjoined, they are not the same. As Linton points out, every status is linked with a particular role, but the two are not the same. In addition, each status is not just linked with one general role, but it is linked with a cluster of roles, one for each person with whom the status occupant's *position* puts him in contact. Roles are learned on the basis of one's statuses, either current or anticipated. As an example of the latter, when an individual learns the duties and qualifications for, say, a medical doctor, he is then awarded the degree; and the rights and privileges are automatically ascribed to him. Thus the reciprocity of social behavior is made possible through the organization of the social functions in a society into statuses and the accompanying roles which define the actions to be performed by the persons occupying those statuses. This is a major source of much of the observable order which exists in society.

It should be evident from the foregoing argument that the personality can be conceived in terms of the resulting psychological organization of an individual's experiences as a participant in a sociocultural system. This was the purpose for considering the interrelation among the concepts of society, culture, and personality.

Psychological Counterparts of Status and Role

Let us examine the psychological attributes of status and role. We have already shown that sociologically status refers to the cultural differentiation of a system of rights and duties into a hierarchy of ranks within a social system. Role is the cultural pattern or patterns which validate the functional requirements of a status.

The psychological counterparts of status and role are *self-esteem* and *social habit*. We often hear the first idea, self-esteem, expressed with some derogation by the statement, "just because he occupies a high position, he thinks *he* is worth it." Social habit refers to the individual response patterns which develop from the occupancy of a particular social status and the performance of the related configuration of roles.

Let us consider with some detail self-esteem. Self-esteem refers to *one's own* evaluation of his performance in a status irrespective of the status. *Esteem* refers to others' evaluation of one's performance irrespective of the status. It is not unusual for people who occupy a high status to have very high regard for someone who occupies a very lowly status because of the pride, honesty, quality, and integrity of the low status person's performance.

The converse is also true. That is, a person of high status may be viewed by other high status persons and by low status persons as being unworthy of his position as judged by his performance. In such a case, the man would have high status but low esteem. An example of such a person would be a doctor who practices abortions or a university professor who is for "hire" by "interest groups" for propaganda purposes.

It makes an interesting and important social psychological study to compare a subject's self-esteem evaluations with the evaluation of him by others who are his peers. The effects of wide variations between the two sets of evaluations are very severe, and a study of the conditions which produce the discrepancies and the accompanying adaptive responses is very important.

Equally important is the fact that the evaluations very often correspond to an amazing degree. This suggests a certain objective capacity on the part of some to "see themselves as others see them," or perhaps others see them as they see themselves but not *because* of the way they see themselves.

It is interesting to note how the members of a group or an organization respond to discrepancies between self-judgment and the judgment of others to whom they are related.

Sometimes the discrepancy is clearly conveyed by the members concerned to each other. The result is, of course, considerable conflict in adjustment. Sometimes sham judgments are communicated and a pretense of mutual acceptability is maintained. This allows for a state of accommodation to exist among the members. Many other modes of response could be described, but this is sufficient to show the essential difference between the sociological meaning of the concepts of status and role and their psychological counterparts.

We may now interpret and summarize. *First*, it has been shown that status and role refer to the overt observable parts of a system of social relationships, and esteem and social habit are the respectively related psychological attributes of the personality system. Thus, one important difference between status and role on the one hand and esteem and social habit on the other is that the former is more observable and social in nature while the latter is more covert or potentially hidden in nature. *Secondly*, status and role are socially *prescribed* as minimum elements of an external system and a person's performance is judged in terms of the *norms* for the position within the system. The element of esteem represents a subjective or judgmental evaluation of a person's observable role behaviors and role attitudes. Social habit refers to the person's characteristic ways of role performance under given conditions.

Sometimes the prescribed role is validated with great fidelity by the status occupant, but frequently the performance departs sharply from the cultural prescriptions. The concept of social role and its related concept of norm and the concept of social habit provide analytical means by which comparisons can be made between individual behavior and the role specification.

Some elaboration of this distinction should make clear the intended meaning. For example, as Stouffer's research has shown, the socially *prescribed* role, say, of a student proctor may be to dismiss a student observed cheating and then report him to the proper authorities.[28] This may be called part of the social role of a proctor. But if the student proctor is a fraternity brother, roommate, or close friend of the student caught cheating, then the proctor may *perceive* that his role is to take away the notes, but let him finish the examination and not report him for cheating. Thus, the socially prescribed role may be one thing and the person's perception or interpretation of his *self* in relation to that role may be something else. Therefore, it should be clear that a psychological definition of status and role requirements is made in terms of *individual expectations* and *perceptions* of behavior in a *self-other* context. Thus, psychologically, status is conceived in terms of *the expectations* of the occupant of the status. That is to say, the person learns (a) to expect or anticipate certain actions from people in certain functions and (b) that others have certain expectations of him. These expectations and perceptions become organized into concepts which serve as a shorthand representation of the function in general. This generalized definition and evaluation of the function then becomes the verbalized status. The terms "teacher," "doctor," "mother," and so on, are examples of status in a sociological sense, while the accompanying individual *mental image* and *concept* of these is status in a psychological sense. Thus, the sociological concepts of status and role, as here used, refer *primarily* to the social system, while their psychological counterparts—esteem, social habit, role perceptions, role expectations, and role performance—refer to the personality.

We are now in a position to conceive of human behavior in a context of social interaction. That is, we have established conceptual reference to a set of internal factors and to a set of external factors and have indicated that human behavior is a *joint* function of these two sets of factors. Presently, it is necessary only to refer to these two sets of factors in a categorical way and to label them collectively as social systems and social groups on the one hand and the personality system on the other. The specific factors of each set, and how they interact with each other, will be dealt with in subsequent chapters. So far, we have identified only attitude, habit, and self-esteem as examples of personality variables, and status and role as examples of variables of the social system. Other interacting concepts will be derived in place in subsequent chapters.

It is a general psychological principle that human behavior is rela-

---

[28] Samuel A. Stouffer, "An Analysis of Conflicting Social Norms," *American Sociological Review,* Vol. 14, Number 6 (December, 1949), pp. 707-717.

tional in nature rather than discrete. That is, the individual perceives, judges, remembers, and so on, in terms of relations among component parts. Thus, for example, a series of concentric circles by themselves are perceived as concentric circles, but when presented in the presence of other patterned stimuli appear considerably different. Such differential effects, whether due to the presence of other internal factors or to other external factors, operate not in a simple additive way but in a functionally related manner. This principle applies to both the internal and external stimuli. That is to say that while there is a relational element between stimulus and response in human behavior, this relational element is a derivative from the *interplay* of an internal context and an external context.

It should be clear that the units of data in social psychology and the concepts used for ordering and classifying these data are primarily relational in nature. Thus this text emphasizes the interdependency of the factors of response determination. However, we wish to post one note of warning before we leave the subject of units of analysis. That is, we do not want the student to get the impression that social psychology is the primary field concerned with the study of the *social* interaction of human beings. As a matter of fact, by definition, *social* interaction is the primary subject matter of sociology. This fact becomes obvious, of course, when we recognize that *inter*actions mean action of a reciprocal nature, and this presupposes communication of some sort between persons. Social psychology is primarily concerned with properties of individual behavior whether of the sort which involves only *action* or *inter*action or both.

This section on units of analysis is meant only as an introduction necessary to provide the proper orientation to the data to be presented on social psychological behavior in later chapters. The specific concepts to describe these data will occur in place in these chapters. Just now, it is perhaps pertinent to ask what are the practical uses of social psychology? One can perhaps say that the primary function of all science is to enable one "to know" and that its ultimate function is to allow one "to do." We turn now to a consideration of what applications a knowledge of social psychology affords.

4. APPLICATIONS OF SOCIAL PSYCHOLOGY

Britt in discussing the value of social psychology in his book *Social Psychology of Modern Life* notes that

> More and more, outstanding persons are realizing the benefits to be derived from the study of psychology. Thus, the engineers who attended the Economics Conference for Engineers a few years ago specifically recom-

mended that executives, in order to learn more about their men, take courses in psychology and human relations—courses presented on a factual, scientific basis. Similarly, when a newspaper correspondent asked a former chief of the Division of Foreign Service Personnel of the State Department, "What are the requirements for a young man who wishes to enter the foreign service?" he promptly replied: "A man must have a sound education. In addition to general subjects, a knowledge of social psychology and sociology is very important. A man must have an inquiring mind and the ability to analyze people and situations." [29]

When one considers the tremendous effect of social attitudes, social values, beliefs, and systems of social organization upon individual behavior, then the question "what are the applications of social psychology to the problems of modern living?" is superfluous. As Robert Lynd has so aptly said: "Inasmuch as every individual grows up in [a] culture among other people, such things as perception, memory, reasoning, and the other psychological processes are socially conditioned and can be fully understood only in their specific social setting." [30] In other words, the human mind is largely a social product.

The particular concrete applications with which the social psychologist concerns himself depend to a large extent upon the special concerns of his society at the moment. They may, for instance, be problems of learning or adjustment in the school and community on the part of children. Rates of juvenile delinquency or mental disorders within a community may register a significant upturn and thus become an object of study for social psychology. As one final example, we cite the important problem of the relation and frequency of individual creativity to varying types of social environments both within and between societies.

Before we proceed to a more precise distinction between social psychology, general psychology, and sociology, we feel that we must first clarify the general approach and plan of the content to follow in this book.

5. GENERAL APPROACH

It should be obvious that whatever is the approach which philosophers and scientists alike take during any age, time, or place toward an understanding of nature—be it man's nature or any other aspect of nature—their study will contain both implicit and explicit assumptions regarding

---

[29] S. H. Britt, *Social Psychology of Modern Life*, rev. ed. (New York, Holt, Rinehart and Winston, Inc., 1954), pp. 3-4. The first statement, *i.e.*, the Engineers Conference, was cited by Britt from *The New York Times*, July 2, 1939. The statement from the State Department official was cited from the *Washington Star*, Aug. 20, 1939.

[30] R. S. Lynd, *Knowledge for What?: The Place of Social Science in American Culture* (Princeton, Princeton University Press, 1939), p. 162.

this nature.[31] The more explicit the assumptions are, the more precise the thinking in relation to the problems to be analyzed.

> The ramifications of the assumptions we are willing to make are sometimes more extensive than we realize. The effect seems to be greater to the degree that our metaphysical assumptions remain implicit. An unawareness of basic assumptions can lead to contradictions if, basically, the assumptions were contradictory. Regarding the place of man in the universe, should a social scientist conceive of his object of inquiry as a thing, like other things in the universe, or should he ascribe to man a "human coefficient" that makes him different from other things in the universe? . . . It should be clear that one's research methods will be partly contingent upon the answers given to these questions.[32] As Burtt has so aptly stated it, "We inevitably see our limited problem in terms of inherited notions which *ought themselves to form part of a larger problem.*" [33]

An attempt will now be made to make explicit some of the inherited notions or propositions about man's behavior which we intend to use as guides to the ordering and interpreting of the data in this text.

Biologically speaking, man is classified as belonging to the class labeled mammals, of the order of primates, and of the family called Hominidae or man. We shall consider in some detail the significance of man's biological and physiological characteristics to his behavior in a later chapter. Just now it is sufficient to say that man's biological nature constitutes the *foundation* upon which his most unique and distinctive characteristic rests: the capacity for *conceptual symbolizing* or *conceptual* thought. The *first* proposition may be stated as follows: Man is a social animal whose sociability is dependent upon culture and social interaction.

Aristotle observed over 2,000 years ago that man is a *social* animal. However, the adjective *social* needs some interpreting, since animals in general exhibit various *biosocial* reactions, such as the group life of ants and bees or the simple family life of the anthropoid apes. This kind of sociability is primarily a biological inheritance from generation to generation and is the outcome of biological evolution.[34] Man's sociability is a result of his *own* domestication: man created culture, and culture, in a certain sense, created man. To borrow a phrase from Professor Gordon Childe, "Man makes himself!"

Although the bees have a very elaborate social life, their patterns of social behavior are genetically determined and transmitted. Man also

---

[31] See, for example, E. A. Burtt, *The Metaphysical Foundations of Modern Physical Science*, rev. ed. (Garden City, N.Y., Doubleday & Co., Inc., 1954), pp. 15-35.
[32] Roy G. Francis and John T. Doby et al., *An Introduction to Social Research* (Harrisburg, Pa., Stackpole Books, 1954), p. 5.
[33] E. A. Burtt, *op. cit.*, p. 28. Italics added.
[34] Kingsley Davis, *Human Society* (New York, The Macmillan Co., 1949), p. 31.

has an extremely elaborate social life, but his patterns of social behavior are symbolically transmitted from one generation to the next through the learning process. Thus, in the words of Professors Woodruff and Baitsell:

> The obviously unique characteristics that set man apart from the rest of the animal kingdom are the capacity for conceptual thought which is synonymous with true speech, the development of *cumulative* tradition, and its chief consequence, the continuous development of *tools*. These are mutually interdependent and collectively are responsible for the dominance of man on the earth. His position above the beasts is based largely upon the fact that he alone possesses a genuine culture. . . . Although these cultural processes are an addition to, and are dependent upon, the hereditary biosocial endowment, they are something more than merely an elaboration of it. They are essentially untrammelled by the limitations of the slow process of organic evolution, which is dependent upon germinal variations and natural selection. Apparently there has been no significant changes in the societies of insects for some thirty million years since the Oligocene period; compare this with the evolution of human society during a few thousand years.[35]

The cumulative growth of culture which represents the collective problem-solving efforts of man throughout the ages gives each new generation something of an edge over the preceding generation. That is, the person of ordinary intelligence during current times can perform some tasks that the most extraordinary man of a few centuries back would have considered impossible. Thus, as a culture grows and becomes more complex through time, the performances of particular individuals at a later date become progressively more skillful as compared to those of their predecessors. But it does not necessarily follow as a consequence that man's problems of adjustment and adaptation today are thereby easier and less complicated. As a matter of fact, this culture-bearing characteristic of man seems to produce something approaching a paradoxical state in respect to his adaptation. On the one hand, it has enabled him in large measure to conquer famine, infectious diseases, gravitation, the hardships of climate, the control of energy, and so on; yet, on the other hand, it has produced the specter of mass destruction of civilization by atomic war and new strains of bacteria and viruses with greater pathogenic powers. The greater pathogenic power of the bacteria and viruses is apparently attributable to their becoming somewhat immunized to the antibiotics through natural selection. Thus, while modern man is a much better problem-solver than his ancient relative, he is also

---

[35] L. L. Woodruff and G. A. Baitsell, *Foundations of Biology*, 7th ed. (New York, The Macmillan Co., 1951), p. 620. Similar points had been made earlier by sociologists Cooley, Thomas, and Mead and the psychologists Baldwin and James. Italics added.

a much better problem-maker or producer of problems than his ancient kin, although we do believe that his problem-solving activity is gaining relative to the gains of his problem-making behavior.

This brings us to the *second* proposition, that ". . . any given behavior is a product of inseparable . . . hereditary and environmental influences but also that in order to change any given behavior one must change the environment so that hitherto untapped biological potentialities can come into operation." [36] This idea also assumes that changes may occur through variations in the germ cells and natural selection, but random variation is likely to cancel any practical long-run effects. Finally, it assumes that human biological evolution is presently and continually occurring and that the possibility exists of man's culturally influencing its direction.

The significance of this second assumption is considerable when we realize its implications, namely, that the potentialities inherent in the last great evolutionary change of man are still being realized and are yet to be fully realized. Thus, in speaking of man's evolution, Howells says, ". . . whatever the course by which [man] reached his high mental powers, he thereupon found himself unburdened by physical specializations, and was able, because of his *generalized* nature, to turn his hand to the most complicated of pursuits." [37]

In a very broad sense, we are now in a position to present the general point of view to be represented in this text. *First,* the data to be explained in social psychology, that is, the dependent variables, derive from observations of the behavior of individuals as individuals, whether as members of groups or not. The study of group behavior and group structure *per se* belong primarily to the field of sociology. The social psychologist indeed is greatly interested in groups, but primarily as independent variables rather than as dependent variables.

Second, our approach to the dependent variables of individual behavior will be through the use of interaction concepts such as social roles, attitudes, and social norms or values. They include such problems as the effects of social factors on perception, learning, and motivation. That is to say, we will be studying the psychological processes of learning, perceiving, and motivation with an aim toward understanding how these are affected through variations in the social stimulus world.

Third, the evolution of physical man and society is assumed to be two different and theoretically separable aspects of the biological foundations of human nature. The evolution of society or social change occurs through sociological and psychological principles, and as such is independent of biological *heredity* for direct transmission and change. This

[36] Arnold Rose, *op. cit.,* p. 222.
[37] William Howells, *Mankind So Far* (Garden City, N.Y., Doubleday & Co., Inc., 1946), p. 13. Italics added.

fact allows for a rapidity of change limited only by the stabilizing demands of the social system and man's physical and mental heritage. This area of man's nature is the most dynamic of all, since it deals with man's culture and social organization; as such it is the source of the content of the individual's personality. The independent variables here are ideologies, values, institutions, and groups on the social side, and the processes of heredity and biological evolution on the physical side.

Fourth, the reader should recall that in the second major assumption about the nature of man it was emphasized that man, by means of varying his environment through culture building, is able to release or bring into operation hitherto untapped biological potentialities. We wish to be perfectly understood on this point, and, therefore, we disclaim immediately any implication in the preceding toward "acquired biological characteristics"; nor do we necessarily imply that by varying his sociocultural environment man can *produce new* biological potentialities.[38] Instead, we are told by the biologists that man has made no known *significant* biological changes in 50,000 years or more. Yet, on the other hand, he has within the last few centuries made fantastic strides in the evolution or change of his social order. Therefore, we must assume that, since no significant biological changes are known to have occurred in man for thousands of years, the biological potentialities for an atomic age existed in man during the Stone Age. From the foregoing point of view it thus follows that the period from the Stone Age to the Atomic Age has been one of bringing into operation "hitherto untapped" but existent biological potentialities. This implies the very important question of the relationship of different types of social systems and social conditions to rates of cultural expansion and growth, and thus the *development* of human potentialities.

Since these biological potentialities exist only in the individual members of the human species and the range of variation of potentialities between individuals is great, then it follows that in order to achieve effective realization of these potentialities the social order should be flexible and variable enough to allow for effective individual release.[39] Hence the study of the human personality as an organization of activity produced through experiences of interaction in a social process becomes a paramount consideration in social psychology. The study of the mere interaction with other persons is not sufficient. The social system itself has a distinctive character, and its social organization becomes a part

---

[38] This, of course, does not rule out the possibility that man-made environments may affect the genetic process. For example, man-produced increases in concentration of radiation might conceivably *affect* heredity. See, for example, H. J. Muller, "How Radiation Changes the Genetic Constitution," *Bulletin of the Atomic Scientists,* Vol. 11, No. 9 (November, 1955), pp. 329-339.

[39] Howard Becker and H. E. Barnes, *op. cit.,* pp. 141-153.

of the individual and provides a basis for his personal organization, in much the same way as organized language is incorporated into speech habits of the person and thus provides a means of communication.

Fifth: The fifth and last point is a consideration of method rather than theory. To learn only the concepts and general conclusions within a given field is dangerously insufficient. To do so means that the learner has to accept on faith all too much of what he reads; and he consequently becomes to some degree a slave to printed words, since he is deprived of an effective means of evaluating their validity and reliability. Thus, progress in thought is stifled, since the learner was not concomitantly provided with an adequate set of analytical tools and techniques to go along with the substantive ideas he was expected to learn. It is, therefore, our aim to include, as an integral part of the discourse of this text, an explanation and demonstration of the major elementary methods and techniques used in developing the concepts and principles of the text.

6. SUMMARY

Early psychologists, following the biological discoveries that man is an animal which is closely related in the evolutionary series to other animals, attempted to explain individual behavior by resorting to data on the behavior of lower animals. For instance, during the first two decades of the twentieth century the concept of instinct, which apparently had some use in regard to the insects and perhaps some other lower animals, was widely used in human psychology.[40] On the other hand, Gabriel Tarde (1843-1904), a French sociologist, and Edward A. Ross (1866-1951), an American, were emphasizing the role of society in regard to individual behavior without adequate psychological concepts to account for society's influence. But as time moved on, both psychologists and sociologists arrived closer to a common meeting-ground in the newly developing field of social psychology.

More and more scholars were beginning to realize that it is fruitless to search for the elements of human behavior in the physiological nature of man. As Ellsworth Faris, Jr., has pointed out, "The heart of the difficulty . . . lies in the assumption that biological individuals constitute society."[41] At present, most writers seem to agree that a more sound and fruitful approach is to regard the physiological mechanisms of man as providing the physical bases for energy and potential action; but the primary guiding and directing of the action they consider to be the

---

[40] Thus, in 1908 one of the first textbooks in social psychology written by William McDougall, a psychologist, was based on the notion of instinct. A little earlier during the same year Edward A. Ross, a sociologist, published a text on social psychology which put the psychology of society in contradistinction to the psychology of the individual.

[41] Robert E. L. Faris, *op. cit.,* pp. 32-33.

result of a joint functioning of a physiochemical process of organization within the central nervous system joined with the processes of social interaction within society. The basic concepts which guide the social psychologist today are concepts which relate to those processes of learning, perceiving, and motivation within the individual. Two such interacting concepts are attitude and role. A working definition was given for each of these. Attitude was considered to be a learned conscious or unconscious conceptualization of an object, person, or situation, which defines its potential or actual relation to the activity or well-being of the person holding the attitude. Role was viewed first in relation to status as a sociological concept which refers to elements of the social structure. Thus status was sociologically defined as a person's defined rank and legitimate rights in a group as these are socially defined. It is obvious that, if social behavior is to be efficient and avoid confusion, there must be some common understanding of a person's position in respect to those of all others in the group. Role is the more dynamic and concrete aspect of status; that is, it refers to the socially prescribed or expected behavior of a person occupying a given status.

The concepts of status and role were also defined in terms of their psychological referents. Thus status, which is given or acquired by one's possessing or achieving of certain rights and values, was defined as a person's self-esteem in a social group. Role, on the other hand, would be the person's conception of his expected actions in relation to others in the group and his social habits deriving from his status.

Following the definition of the units of analysis, certain applications of social psychology were suggested to give the student some concrete and practical understanding of its value. Thus it was pointed out that, since so much of an individual's life is involved in a culture with other people, an understanding of how people's behavior is socially conditioned is a *sine qua non* in modern society.

Finally, then, a general statement was made concerning the overall approach of the text. This is briefly summarized as follows: *First,* it was pointed out that man is a social animal whose sociability is dependent upon culture and the processes of social interaction. *Secondly,* it was assumed that any given human behavior is a product of inseparable hereditary and environmental influences, and that in order to change any given behavior one must modify the environment so as to release existent biological potentialities. Following these two general propositions regarding human nature, the overall approach of the text was pictured in terms of five organizing principles. *First,* the data to be explained in social psychology are conceived to be the covert and overt actions of individuals. *Second,* the approach to the explanation of this behavior is to be through the use of *interaction* concepts such as role, attitude, and social norms. That is, we will be studying the psychological processes of learning, perceiving, and motivation as these are affected by varying stimuli in a society defined in terms of social processes. *Third,* the evolution of physical man will be sketched with an aim toward noting the contribution of man's physical characteristics to his behavior and adaptation. Also to be considered are the relationships of the evolution of man's society and culture to the development and organization of the behavior of the person; and the subsequent perpetuation of the society through the socialization of the individual members. *Fourth,* we assumed that the personality in social interaction is the dynamic agent of social evolution or change; hence comes the need to study the development and organization of the personality in different sociocultural environments. Such a study should aid in an understanding of the processes of creativity, leadership, and the relationship of adjustment of personality to types and qualities of different social systems.

Finally, the need to present concomitantly both data and the techniques by which data are analyzed and conclusions drawn was emphasized as necessary for sound and efficient learning.

Further References

1. E. P. Hollander and Raymond G. Hunt, Editors, *Current Perspectives in Social Psychology* (New York, Oxford University Press, 1963).
2. William W. Lambert and Wallace E. Lambert, *Social Psychology* (Englewood Cliffs, N.J., Prentice-Hall, Inc., 1964).
3. Gardner Lindzey, Editor, *Handbook of Social Psychology,* Vol. 1, Chapter 1, "The Historical Background of Modern Social Psychology," by Gordon W. Allport (Reading, Mass., Addison-Wesley Publishing Co., Inc., 1954).
4. Edward S. Sampson, Editor, *Social Psychology—A Book of Readings* (Englewood Cliffs, N.J., Prentice-Hall, Inc., 1964).

2
The Data and Level of Analysis of Social Psychology

●

1. *Introduction*
2. *Conceptual Level of Analysis of Social Psychology*
3. *The Data and Problems of Social Psychology*
4. *The Relation of Social Psychology to Psychology and Sociology*
5. *Summary*

1. INTRODUCTION

WHEN USING COMMON-SENSE LANGUAGE AND DESCRIPTION, the speaker generally assumes that his terms and their referents are also the terms and referents of the listeners or readers. While such an assumption is hazardous, even for everyday communication, it is a requirement in respect to scientific language and description.

It is true that precise use of terms and their referents is essential to all communication, but the purpose of scientific communication is so different from common-sense description that some word of warning must be issued to the student in respect to maintaining a clear connection between one's terms and the specific referents of these terms. This point is too fundamental to pass over with the simple statement that common-sense communication and description differ from scientific description. What we wish to show is how they differ and the significance of this difference for our purposes.

The *first* difference which we wish to note is that when one uses common-sense description he is generally satisfied when his explanations and observations agree with past experience and are logically consistent with his beliefs and feelings. The discerning student will note immediately that the danger of this approach is that it assumes the validity of the premises. Therefore, with the common-sense approach one is psychologically and logically unconcerned with maintaining a clear connection between one's terms and their referents. It is unnecessary because the validity of the premises is not questioned or, when it is questioned, it is ascertained within a limited and *ad hoc* framework.

On the other hand, scientific description and explanation *questions* all its premises and assumptions. That is, scientific propositions must be logically consistent and also empirically verifiable.[1] In order to meet the latter requirement it is absolutely necessary that one's terms and their referents be kept clear and precise.[2]

A *second* distinction between scientific and common-sense observation which is relevant here is that the scientific observer is primarily concerned with the establishment of general laws as principles based on empirical observation and testing. This leads us to recognize that science is systematic and that one scientific law cannot contradict another and each be true. Such interdependency of theory and fact, and the interrelatedness of one area of theory with another, need not concern the layman or common-sense observer at all in his everyday communication. Yet, on the other hand, in the field of science, the establishment of a system of general laws and concepts is its primary aim.

In distinguishing between scientific concepts and common-sense concepts, it is not intended to derogate common sense and eulogize science. Instead, the purpose of noting this distinction is to avoid the confusion which results from failing to so distinguish. Common-sense description is concerned with what is taken to be direct experience or observation, whereas scientific description is intended to get beyond so-called direct experience and observation. Galileo's contribution to the law of falling bodies affords a good example of the point in question.

> In Aristotelian and medieval physics, a distinction was made between "heavy" bodies, like rocks, that fall to the ground, and "light" bodies, like smoke, that ascend to the heavens. This is the language of the "man in the street." . . .[3] Herbert Dingle has written: "The undying glory of Galileo's contribution to thought is that, though only half-consciously, he discarded

---

[1] This does not refer to certain types of scientific laws and constructs that are used principally as heuristic devices of which truth is mainly a matter of definition or semantics. The student is invited to examine Rudolf Carnap, "Remarks on Induction and Truth," *Philosophy and Phenomenological Research*, Vol. 6 (1946), pp. 590-602. Also, Alfred Tarski, "The Semantical Conception of Truth, and the Foundations of Semantics," *Philosophy and Phenomenological Research*, Vol. 4 (1944), pp. 341-376.

[2] This, of course, raises the difficult problem of the language of science, that is, operational definitions and their related mathematical variables. See Chapter 11.

[3] This is a common-sense or direct observation formulation, and it is true in that framework. It has no scientific value, since it does not allow one to explain other facts, that is, it is too specific.

the everyday common-sense world as a philosophical necessity." In his theoretical system, all bodies fall with equal acceleration to the ground.[4]

One can appreciate the purist's criticism of jargon in scientific writing. But at the same time one would also appreciate his realizing the necessity and purpose for introducing technical words into the language of science. It should also be realized that when these words are retranslated into ordinary language, they do *not* actually carry the same meaning as before. The less abstract levels of a new theory must yield insights which agree with common sense. Oskar Morgenstern has stated the basic point which we wish to make with great force and clarity:

> . . . new theory also shows clearly a feature that must be expected in any true mathematization: the mathematical theory must *first* yield the same insights which can be obtained from common sense. Thereafter it will give results which go far beyond common sense, results which common sense could never even guess at. When this happens, some of the new results may be translatable into ordinary language, but, for still others, this will become impossible. They will remain in mathematical symbolism. When that point has been passed, a higher state in the development of a science has been reached. It is *only* attainable by means of mathematics. Game theory has already entered this phase of development. . . .[5]

A simple example from Richard von Mises will illustrate the difference in word usage by the scientist and the layman. *Work* in the ordinary language sense means the exertion of strength. One of the simplest scientific definitions of work is

> . . . "the scalar product of the vectors of force and displacement" . . . this scientific definition of work is . . . applicable to [simple] activities . . . of a mechanical nature . . . it is hardly possible to say that the correct measure of the work performed by the musician is the product of the force applied by the fingers of the musician and their displacement. Again, when we speak of the work involved in writing a book, painting a picture, or attending a patient, we are even further from the scientific meaning of the word "work."[6]

The point is that the meaning is relative to the situation and the *purpose* of the situation; and ordinary language describes ordinary situations,

---

[4] Quoted from Philipp Frank, *Philosophy of Science* (Englewood Cliffs, N.J., Prentice-Hall, Inc., 1957), p. 45.

[5] Oskar Morgenstern in James C. Charlesworth, ed., *Mathematics and the Social Sciences*, A Symposium, sponsored by the American Academy of Political and Social Science (Philadelphia, American Academy of Political and Social Science, 1963), pp. 22-23. Italics added.

[6] Richard von Mises, *Probability Statistics and Truth*, 2nd rev. ed. (London, George Allen & Unwin, Ltd., 1957), p. 5.

but the scientist is not referring to such situations irrespective of their apparent similarities. If the common-sense and ordinary language understandings were sufficient for all purposes, then the scientist would *not* have a problem to explain.

The *third* and last distinction between scientific knowledge and common-sense knowledge, with which we are concerned here, is the necessity in science for making explicit the level of abstraction which one's data represent. This, of course, is desirable and necessary in common-sense reasoning, but the point is that it is seldom if ever honored. The following example should suffice to make clear the meaning and importance of making explicit the level of abstraction involved in one's argument so as to avoid the error of mixing levels of abstraction. For example, take the question: What explains the fact that man is a language-speaking animal? Does this mean why one speaks English or German, or does it mean how is it that man speaks at all? If it means the latter, then common-sense reasoning might explain or answer the question by referring to the biological level of abstraction. That is, by noting that no other animal has a language, and since man does, then his language trait must be a result of his biological differences. But this explanation as *stated* is false. It is false, since we know that a child who is reared in isolation and does not hear other people speaking will not speak a language.[7] In other words, a certain biological structure for speech is *necessary*, but not *sufficient*, to explain the language trait of man. That is, biology provides the physiological raw materials for the capacity for speech, but actual speaking is a function of social and psychological factors as well.

We are now in position to make our point, namely, the data which have been obtained from one level of observation cannot be used to explain behavior on another level unless one is able to show that there is a relationship between the two levels. To state the idea in its most elementary form, one would note that sociological laws are derivable only from social facts, biological laws are derivable from biological facts, and psychological laws from psychological facts, and so on. The reader may be tempted to say, "So what? This is obvious." The answer is that it is obvious only to those who are carefully trained and who have had experience in research. For example, it is common practice for students to try to explain different forms and levels of *human* social organization of different societies by referring to biological concepts for

---

[7] This is borne out by studies on the deaf and studies on extremely isolated children. See Kingsley Davis, "Extreme Social Isolation of a Child," *American Journal of Sociology*, Vol. 45 (1939-40), pp. 554-565; also, "Final Note on a Case of Extreme Isolation," *American Journal of Sociology*, Vol. 52 (1946-47), pp. 432-437; also, Marie K. Mason, "Learning to Speak After Six and One-Half Years of Silence," *Journal of Speech Disorders*, Vol. 7 (1942), pp. 295-304.

an explanation. This is an example, *par excellence*, of mixed levels of abstraction.

The error of mixing levels of abstraction should not be confused with the highly desirable process of subsuming a less general proposition or hypothesis under a more general or higher level hypothesis from another area of data. This becomes possible when the deductive system from which the first proposition is derived becomes conflated or fused into a unified system with the deductive system of the second proposition. For instance, this could happen through the highest level hypotheses of chemistry becoming subsumable under the highest level hypotheses of the deductive system of physics. But to attempt to fuse or conflate *before* the two deductive systems are unified in *fact* would be to err by mixing levels of abstraction.

Enough has been said about levels of abstraction in general. Let us turn now to the task of specifying the level with which we are primarily concerned.

2. CONCEPTUAL LEVEL OF ANALYSIS OF SOCIAL PSYCHOLOGY

A few words of warning are in order for those (and we all are to some extent) who are inclined to view new or different data through yesterday's concepts. There is no better warning than the excellent paper by Donald K. Adams on "Learning and Explanation," from which I quote freely: [8]

> What concerns me here is an epistemological (grounds or basis for the validity of knowledge) [9] fallacy that has had a paralyzing effect upon American psychological thinking ever since Watson popularized it. This is the widespread belief that our perceptions of "physical" situations and objects are somehow in better epistemological status than our perceptions of other people's psychological situations and objects; that seeing a cat's situation as frustrating is less secure *in epistemological principle* than seeing his physical environment as made of wood or glass. This is simply not so. The only test we have in either case is intersubjectivity. This test may be less frequently or less easily satisfied for psychological situations (although even this is questionable), but when it is satisfied they are just as objective . . . as are physical ones. For psychologists (and I might add sociologists, as well) [10] especially it is important to realize that the *epistemology* of values is neither different nor separable from that of things.[11]

[8] Donald K. Adams, *Learning Theory, Personality Theory and Clinical Research: The Kentucky Symposium* (New York, John Wiley & Sons, Inc., 1954), excerpted from pages 66-79.
[9] Remark in parentheses added.
[10] Remark in parentheses added.
[11] Adams, *op. cit.*, p. 71.

Frequently, it is claimed that some data are subjective in a different way in that they are described by probabilities rather than certainties. But it will be shown in Chapters 11 and 12 that the probabilities with which we are concerned are to be described in terms of statistical frequencies, and a statistical frequency of 40 percent is no more *subjective* than one of 100 percent. It just occurs less frequently.

The claim that data are not objective unless they are directly physical and tangible is to betray a seventeenth-, eighteenth-, and nineteenth-century concept of the meaning of physical. Adams has derived three uses or meanings of the term *physical* which are appropriate for our consideration, since the distinctions he makes will assist the reader in properly orienting himself toward the data of this course:

> A generation or two ago it might have been supposed that "physical" meant "material," but in a period when Einstein's equation $E = MC^2$ appears in mass-circulation slick-paper magazines, this is rarely what is meant. When mass is energy and energy may be a local deformation of space, when the particle—is it the pi-meson?—that holds the atomic nucleus together, and thus gives "matter" such permanence as it displays, has itself a duration of a tiny fraction of a millionth of a second, the concept of materiality ceases to be physically meaningful. However, let us call this Meaning 1. . . .
>
> The application of the seventeenth-century criterion of materiality, simple location, is a special case of what Whitehead has called the fallacy of misplaced concreteness. . . .
>
> Consider what a psychologist means by "physical" when he talks about a physical (sometimes, to be sure, a physiological) model or a physical correlate. The word seems always, except for an occasional atavistic naivete, intended to mean something like "comprehensible to the physical principles and theory current at the time of writing." Actually, it is more likely to mean "comprehensible to the writer's remembered high school or college physics and haphazard impressions of developments since then." In either event it does not mean the same thing on 13 March 1953 that it meant on 9 August 1935 or on 21 November 1912. And we may be quite sure that it will mean something still different by this time next year. . . . Let us call this Meaning 2.[12]

Physical in the sense of Meaning 2 is not very precise. Thus in much psychological writing the phrase "comprehensible to the physical principles and theory current at the time of writing" means comprehensible in terms of currently accepted notions about the "physiological" or "neurological" basis for behavior. In addition, Meaning 2 with its dependence on present or current interpretations of physical principles is both dogmatic and chameleon-like in nature. Otherwise, one is forced to make the most dubious assumption that all the great physical prin-

---

[12] *Ibid.*, excerpted from pp. 66-68.

ciples have been discovered. Upon analysis of Meanings 1 and 2 it becomes clear that *physical* is being used in a normative or evaluative sense. And further, the basis of meaning for physical is drawn from traditional views of the term where the scope of information and interpretations are less than the present scope of facts and theories.

As Adams notes:

> When one looks back over the developments of the last 50 years of physics and considers that the rate of discovery appears to be increasing logarithmically, one wonders why we are so timid about our constructs or *should insist that they be reducible to the physics of today or even of 50 years hence*.[13] Our constructs may be good physics or bad physics, but that does not depend on their intelligibility in terms of present-day physics. It depends rather on their adequacy to the data of behavior—*all* the data, *all* the phenomena, that we have at a given time.[14]

Careful reflection by the student upon the preceding paragraph will reveal that a *third* meaning of physical is implied. This meaning is neither based on materiality (Meaning 1) nor the current interpretation of "scripture" "with its dependence upon the calendar" (Meaning 2). "In this *third* sense, 'physical' simply means 'explanatory.'"[15] In this sense an argument on the street corner is no less physical than the street and the surrounding buildings. The frustration and anxiety of an individual is no less natural and hence physical than the individual's body. The criterion with which we are here concerned is whether the event or phenomenon under consideration is subject to explanation within the general framework of science. If it is explainable and hence predictable by established scientific procedures, then one phenomenon is on no less secure epistemological grounds than any other, irrespective of the differences in the nature of the phenomena.

Much the same difficulty inheres today in connection with the use of the words "natural" and "normal."[16] In conclusion, it should be pointed out that "physical" and "natural" will be used in this text in the sense of Meaning 3 above. This we believe avoids the bifurcation or splitting of nature into two parts with its implication that some processes such as "knowing," "interpreting," and so on, are not natural processes, but something outside or beyond nature, and thus beyond science.

The preceding considerations suggest the following orientation or approach to the ordering of the data of social psychology. *First*, it is

---

[13] Italics added.
[14] Adams, *op. cit.*, p. 68.
[15] *Ibid.*, p. 69.
[16] For a good discussion of the uses of natural see Howard Becker, *Social Thought from Lore to Science*, 2nd ed. (New York, Dover Publications, Inc., 1952), pp. 423-427.

necessary to again remind the reader that scientific observations are not necessarily direct observations of material objects and their properties. The observations to which the scientist refers need not be observations in the ordinary sense of immediate experience and generally are not. The observations may be traces on a photographic film, holes punched in a tape by an electron counter, responses to a questionnaire or a Rorschach plate, or the number of trials in a learning maze. In other words, the "observing" may be done by a machine or a recording instrument with the scientist acting as inspector and interpreter.

Secondly, any data whether of a direct or indirect source which relate to the scientific problem at hand, and are manageable within the scientific framework and procedure, are to be viewed as part of the data of the scientific field under consideration.

Thirdly, the concepts which guide the data-gathering process by providing a point of departure or point of view in psychological research should be free from an actual or implied mind-body dualism. It should also be added that the nature and characteristics of the data determine the nature of the descriptive and explanatory principles to be used in research, rather than tailoring the data to the concepts. That is to say, the concepts and theories evolve from the requirements of the data rather than the data being selected or fitted to existing concepts.

Fourthly, the data necessary for scientific explanation consist of two types of data, which are being labeled as the problematic data and the explanatory data.[17] By the problematic data we refer to the general category of data describing the problem to be explained. By the explanatory data we refer to those classes of data which are presented to account for or to explain the problem.

In respect to operational variables or specific factors the idea expressed in the fourth point above is called the dependent variables and the independent variables—the *dependent variable* being defined as the problem or the variable to be accounted for, and the *independent variable* being defined as the variable which accounts for the phenomenon described by the dependent variable. The question of the explanation or *how* the independent variable accounts for the effect will be discussed in Chapter 12.

We are now in position to make a relatively explicit statement describing the general field of study of social psychology. Social psychology is the study of the effects of social interaction and the sociocultural environment on psychological behavior and processes. That is to say, the dependent variables of social psychology are the ordinary psychological

[17] John T. Doby *et al., An Introduction to Social Research* (Harrisburg, Pa., Stackpole Books, 1954), pp. 101-103. Cf. C. G. Hempel and Paul Oppenheim in Herbert Feigl and May Brodbeck, eds., *Readings in the Philosophy of Science* (New York, Appleton-Century-Crofts, 1953), pp. 320-321.

THE LEVEL OF ANALYSIS OF SOCIAL PSYCHOLOGY 39

variables of learning, memory, motivation, and perception, while the independent variables are the specific factors within the social and cultural environment which affect the dependent variables. This, of course, raises the question of the relation of social psychology to general psychology and general sociology. This question will be treated in Section 4 below. Right now we turn our attention to a consideration of the data and problems of social psychology.

3. THE DATA AND PROBLEMS OF SOCIAL PSYCHOLOGY

As conceived in this text, the explanatory data or independent variables of social psychology are derived in broadest outline from social and cultural processes which in turn derive from processes of social interaction. The problematic data are derived from the response system of the individual or groups of individuals. Such acts as perceiving, conceiving, learning, and motivation are examples of response fields in which we shall be interested.

At this point in the text both these sets of processes will appear to the student as very abstract and will perhaps have little meaning. They will be given concrete, and where possible, experimental meaning in Parts III and IV of the text. At this point it is sufficient for our purposes to state that by social processes we are referring to those relatively standardized behavior patterns which channelize and organize the human population from generation to generation. These processes regulate the relations between the sexes, kinship groups, classes, racial and cultural groups, as well as relations within groups, such as husband-wife, parent-child relationship, and so on.

In other words, the data of social psychology are derived from those factors and processes of the social world which help determine and/or condition the *behavioral system* of the human organism. Thus one notes that if a child is born in a preliterate society, his intellectual development will not include abstract mathematics and science, since these would be absent from the culture of the society. This is related to the fact that the process of increasing intellectual development in general in a society proceeds parallel with the process of social development.

The specific data necessary to the solution of some given social psychological problem are necessarily determined by the *purposes* of the investigation and the *nature* of the problem under investigation. For example, if the investigator is a minister who is checking on the character of one of his church members, then the data will consist of much material deductively arrived at from certain religious or theological assumptions. On the other hand, if the minister's purpose is to explain why or how the man behaves as he does, then his data are likely to be derived from certain social and psychological categories.

One way of gaining a clearer picture of the data at this stage in the course is to have some notion of the problem areas in social psychology. A few examples of these should help give a clearer picture of what the field is about. Consider the field of language as one source for a set of independent variables; then such questions as the following become very significant. How does language relate to perception? What is the relationship of language to measured intelligence? What is the relationship of language to thinking? To illustrate the last question Poul Anderson points out:

> The Indo-European languages have a structure based on substantives and actions (nouns and verbs). They draw an unreal distinction between what a "thing" *is* and what it *does*, and compound this confusion by separating its qualities from the "thing" itself—as if "heaviness" had some separate existence apart from the class of heavy objects.
>
> In scientific theory, if there is reason to suppose that some action is taking place, it becomes all too natural to imagine that there must be some*thing* [18] which acts—if you think in Indo-European terms. For instance, classical physics had cause to believe in electromagnetic undulations: or, strictly speaking, in certain phenomena describable by wave-type equations. It was therefore a linguistic (not, be it noted, a logical) necessity to postulate an "ether" which could undulate. This ether became more-or-less identified with absolute space. But the substantive concept of space or of time is due merely to the fact that in the Indo-European languages "space" and "time" are substantive nouns.
>
> Newton's contemporary, Leibniz, recognized the self-contradictory character of the "absolute space" concept. . . . He pointed out, for example, that the only way to detect it would be to find something which was absolutely at rest—but this particle or ether or what-have-you would, by definition of motion, be moving with respect to everything else! His suggestions lay fallow to Poincaré's day, and not till Einstein did anyone base a complete physical theory on the insight. This is not a matter of Leibniz being an obscure figure like Mendel. Is it too much to suggest that his acute analysis was neglected because the structure of Western language made it difficult to understand? [19]

The foregoing suggests that the concrete nature of the language conditioned thought in a way which resulted in the conceiving of a purely abstract idea in terms of a thing or substance. In other words, the language structure contributed to a reification of the concepts of time and space. Language also affords an excellent opportunity for the study of the effects of past learning upon subsequent learning, and also upon

---

[18] Italics added.
[19] Poul Anderson, "How Social Is Science?" *The Saturday Review* (April 27, 1957), pp. 10-11.

human perception; for example, Rosenzweig and Postman's study on frequency of usage and perception of words.[20]

Another important problem area is the relation of group and class membership to levels of achievement motivation or aspiration. Another is the relationships between group experience and group organization to the socialization or personality development of the child. This, of course, includes comparative studies of the differential effects of different cultures on personality variables.

A considerable amount of knowledge is available on the effects on behavior of physiochemical deficiencies and changes. Deficiencies and serious degrees of change in physiochemical processes of the body may seriously affect the organization and functioning of the personality. It is also true that severe behavioral stress interferes with the physiochemical processes of the body. It is also known that social disorganization within a community is correlated with a high rate of personality disorders. However, the nature of these latter relationships is presently not clear. It would seem that the study of the effects of various types of social life upon physiological and psychological variables would be most fruitful toward understanding these.

It is not our purpose here to try to point out the so-called most important problem areas in social psychology. Instead, it is desired to give the beginning student sufficient orientation to allow him to recognize social psychological data from other types of data. This brings us to the question of the relation of social psychology to the disciplines of psychology and sociology.

4. THE RELATION OF SOCIAL PSYCHOLOGY TO PSYCHOLOGY AND SOCIOLOGY

Social psychology, psychology, and sociology are each related in that each is concerned with describing and explaining human behavior. However, each has a somewhat different perspective and orientation, and each is primarily concerned with different aspects or problems of human behavior. Perhaps it would be more accurate to say that the research problems posed by each discipline are different, although in this connection it should be pointed out that what is considered an important problem in a given field changes with the accumulation of research results. The important problems of social psychology of tomorrow are probably buried among some obscure facts in the field today. This should provide us with sufficient caution and warning against drawing any sharp and inflexible boundary lines among the fields.

While there is *not* any inherent difference among the fields, there is

[20] M. R. Rosenzweig and L. Postman, "Frequency of Usage and the Perception of Words," *Science*, Vol. 127, Number 3293 (February 7, 1958), pp. 263-273.

a difference in the kinds of problems which the researchers formulate in their respective areas. That is to say that in practice or in terms of what social psychologists, general psychologists, and sociologists *do*, then there are some discernible differences.[21]

These differences can be most readily portrayed by noting the level of abstraction of the data in the respective fields and the units of analysis of each. The units of analysis of a physiologist, for example, are determined by his problems. If the problem is the relation of nutrition to digestion, then the researcher will vary nutrition under controlled conditions and observe its effect on various indices of digestion. If he is a psychologist, then, he will observe the same nutritional variables but in relation to different *dependent* variables. That is, instead of his dependent variable being digestion it would be some index of sensory behavior, thinking, learning, and so on.[22]

The foregoing should illustrate the point that the level of abstraction of the problems in a given field and the related data or units of analysis are actually the basis by which one field is delineated from another. One may ask, what are the units of analysis of the three fields in which we are concerned? To attempt to specify such in any specific and definitive sense would be foolish. It is foolish because the history of science is replete with examples of so-called *basic* units of analysis of one day turning out later to be subordinate to some smaller but previously unknown unit. Efforts to conceptualize the basic unit of matter in physics afford a good example. It is also foolish from another point of view, namely, that the establishment of so-called basic units of analysis is an empirical problem, and *not* a matter of *a priori* determination. On the basis of existing empirical research in the three fields, one can roughly differentiate them by distinguishing the broad areas of behavior studied. However, it is not claimed that the resulting distinctions are definitive or that there is not any overlapping. The differentiations are made more for the purpose of indicating the conception of social psychology in this text and the relation of these other fields to this conception. The following table, while considerably oversimplified, nevertheless conveys the general conception of social psychology and the related disciplines of psychology and sociology.

[21] Departmental organization in the colleges and the resulting competition for public recognition and financial backing for staff and research, in other words, vested interest, leads to claims of hegemony by specialists in a given field.

[22] This formulation should not be interpreted as meaning that all laws in psychology are of the independent-dependent variable type, that is, S-R type laws. There are also correlational laws such as the R_1-R_2 type. The opinion represented here is that they mainly differ in purpose and in concern for *specifying antecedent conditions in a causal sense*. See Gustav Bergmann and Kenneth W. Spence, "The Logic of Psychophysical Measurement" in Herbert Feigl and May Brodbeck, eds., *op. cit.*, pp. 103-119. Also, from the same volume, Carl G. Hempel and Paul Oppenheim, "The Logic of Explanation," pp. 319-350.

TABLE 2:1

	INDEPENDENT VARIABLES	DEPENDENT VARIABLES
Social Psychology:	Social and cultural stimuli. Belief systems, roles. Systems of interaction.	Individual behavior. Psychological processes such as perceiving, motivation, cognition, and learning. Personality. Responses. Psychological correlates of social structure.
Sociology:	Psychophysical processes in group members. Physical environment. Sociocultural environment.	Group interaction, organization and processes. Social continuity and change. Decision making, leadership. Social order.
Psychology:	Constitutional and physiological factors (heredity, hunger, sex, rest, fatigue, etc.). Physical and social stimuli.	Acts, responses of individuals as individuals. Sensation, emotion, abilities.
Psychological Sociology:	Psychological processes.	Group behavior and interaction.

The question of the theoretical interpretation or linking of the independent variables to the dependent variables *via* hypothetical constructs and/or intervening variables will be discussed in Chapter 12 under the heading of scientific explanation. Presently, we are only concerned with conveying to the student a general picture of what social psychology is about. Thus, by way of general conclusion it may be said that social psychology is primarily the study of the effects of social interaction and social systems on the psychological behavior of the individual, especially the development and change of the individual's behavioral system as a result of learning.

The most important idea in the foregoing conception of social psychology is the theoretical combining of psychological properties with the person's social environment. The reason for doing so should be obvious to even the casual observer. Social interaction is influenced by such psychological properties as drives, motives, habits, previous learning, emotional states, and interests. Conversely, the social environment within which a person acts contributes to one's psychological characteristics. Irrespective of whether group behavior or individual behavior is conceived of as the dependent variable, in the social psychological sense, the two kinds of behavior are interdependent. Consequently, the conceptual units of analysis must be *interacting* concepts rather than parallel concepts. That is, the conceptualizing is based on the *relationships* among the actors rather than simply the behavior of a person. To borrow a phrase from Robert R. Sears, we are seeking dyadic laws rather than monadic laws.[23] And this leads us to the question of how are such laws derived? Chapters 11 and 12 are primarily concerned with questions of this nature. If, at this time, the student does not feel that he has sufficient introductory background in scientific reasoning and elementary statistical techniques to enable him to proceed without an introduction to these, then, he should read chapters 11 and 12 next. This text assumes that the student has had a course in elementary statistics so that he can make appropriate use of the "t" statistic, the F ratio, chi-square, and elementary measures of correlation and association. If this is not so, then, the student should study carefully chapter twelve next. If the student has had a course in elementary statistics, then, chapter twelve may be reviewed in order to assist the student in practice research assignments in the course.

5. SUMMARY

First, a distinction was made between scientific data and description and common-sense data and description. The purpose of this was to show the necessity for maintaining a precise connection between one's terms or concepts and their empirical referents. Another reason for such precision relates to the aim or purpose of pure science, the primary purpose being the establishment of general laws and concepts which explain or account for empirical observations. Thirdly, the necessity for making explicit the level of abstraction of one's data was emphasized in order to avoid the error of mixing levels of abstraction in scientific explanation.

Next a discussion of the conceptual level of analysis of social psychology followed, in which it was emphasized that one's problem and its related data determine the concepts and explanatory principles. The adequacy of concepts is assessed in terms of their capacity under a minimum number of assumptions to account for and include all the

[23] Talcott Parsons and Edward A. Shils, eds., *Toward a General Theory of Action* (Cambridge, Mass., Harvard University Press, 1951), p. 468.

data and their theoretical integrating power. The data were conceived in terms of two categories—problematical data and explanatory data.

The next question was what are the data of social psychology? This was answered by pointing out that social psychology is a study of the effects of social systems and social interaction on those psychological processes which are in any way affected by learning. This led to the notion that the units of analysis would necessarily have to be units of an *interacting* nature rather than a parallel nature.

Further References

1. Sigmund Koch, ed., *Psychology: A Study of Science* (New York, McGraw-Hill Book Company, 1959-1963), Vol. 3, *Formulations of the Person and the Social Context,* Chapter by Solomon E. Asch, "A Perspective on Social Psychology," pp. 363-383.
2. Koch, *ibid.*, Vol. 6, *Investigations of Man as Socius,* Chapter by Muzafer Sherif, "Social Psychology: Problems and Trends in Interdisciplinary Relationships," pp. 30-93 and Chapter by William W. Lambert, "Social Psychology in Relation to General Psychology and Other Behavioral Sciences," pp. 173-243.
3. Neil J. Smelser and William T. Smelser, eds., *Personality and Social Systems* (New York, John Wiley & Sons, Inc., 1963).
4. Pitirim A. Sorokin, *Society, Culture and Personality* (New York, Harper & Row, Publishers, Inc., 1947).

Part II
MAN AS A SPECIES: BIOSOCIAL BASES OF HUMAN BEHAVIOR

3
Evolution and Culture

•

1. Introduction
2. The Concept of Biological Evolution
3. The Concept of Culture
   (a) Introduction
   (b) Adaptation
   (c) The Definition of Culture
4. The Evolution of Response Complexity
5. Presumed Biological Prerequisites to Culture
   (a) Introduction
   (b) Some Physical Bases for Culture
       1. Accommodative vision
       2. Bipedal locomotion
       3. Manipulation
       4. Carnivorous-omnivorous diet
       5. Cortical control of sexual behavior
       6. Vocal communication
       7. Expansion of the cerebral cortex
6. Summary

1. INTRODUCTION

THAT ALL THINGS *change* AND *evolve* is now one of the basic ideas contained in man's intellectual storehouse. In respect to the history of ideas it is not old. It is slightly more than a century ago, in 1859, that Darwin's work, *On the Origin of Species,* was published. It is just over two hundred and ten years ago that Jacques Turgot delivered his famous discourse at the Sorbonne entitled "On the Successive Advances of the Human Mind." It was only during the eighteenth century that a reasonably clear idea as to the unity and continuity of history began to emerge. In other words, the idea that culture is cumulative and that its future states are significantly determined by its present conditions and processes is indeed very recent.[1]

It is quite appropriate to begin Part II with a discussion of evolution and culture. This is true for two important reasons. *First,* the evolution of man the organism has made possible his capacity for creating culture. *Secondly,* once culture emerged and assumed its own evolutionary form, it in turn largely determines man's *behavioral* characteristics. It is here assumed that biological evolution is continuing and likewise is cultural evolution. Let us now examine how these two *interacting* systems of evolution function.

2. THE CONCEPT OF BIOLOGICAL EVOLUTION

The enormous variability and bountifulness of nature have long been observed. One corn plant yields several ears of corn, and hundreds of grains per ear, each of which is capable of producing another corn seedling. Fish produce thousands of eggs at one spawning and these may result in only a very few that grow to maturity. And so it is with man; many more offspring are born than mature. Potentiality is always greater than manifest functioning. From nature's bountifulness in producing offspring, an exceedingly important factor in the adaptation and survival of a species is the wide range of *variability* of characteristics among the offspring. The greater the range of variability of characteristics, the more likely it is that a type will occur whose characteristics are more fitted to the demands of the environment.

In the long run the environment tends to produce selection from among the varieties within a species. Those that are poorly adapted are eliminated, and the remainder vary around a general type represented by their parents. Thus, those who survive are a selected group, and their descendants receive and transmit the favored variations. In other words, there is a gradual but progressive shift in type to eventually new types and new species. Generally, the variations or mutants are only slightly dissimilar, but sometimes the changes are drastic and the biologists speak of *lethal* mutations. Mutations range all the way from very minute to sudden and drastic changes. Some of the changes have increased adaptive capacity and hence species survival value. On the other hand, others are deleterious and maladaptive.

We may summarize the discussion thus far by saying that one of the important factors in the evolutionary process is increased genetic *variation* or *mutation* within a species.

Different forms of life seem to have achieved their own way of fitting into the environment. The insects are particularly noted for their ca-

[1] See Howard Becker and H. E. Barnes, *Social Thought from Lore to Science,* 2nd ed. (Washington, D.C., Dover Publications, Inc., 1952), pp. 463-475.

pacity to adapt and survive by mutation. On the other hand, other forms of animal life, particularly mammals, have evolved over a long period of time a very complex *nervous system,* thus enabling a new form of adaptation, that is, the ability to make *new* responses within the lifetime of the organism, hence to *learn.* Thus we find that through the process of evolution certain species are characterized by the elaborate development of certain organs or systems within the organism. The duck's foot, the hawk's eye, and man's nervous system are cases in point. The less highly developed the nervous system, the more the organism depends upon genetically determined responses for adaptation. Survival in a changing environment is then a function of *mutation* and *natural selection* or what we referred to a few paragraphs ago as environmental selection.

The more highly developed the nervous system, the more effective is the process of learning and the less the organism depends upon genetically built-in response patterns. It should now be clear that there is constant change occurring within a species through the *hereditary* process. It should also be clear that some hereditary outcomes are better suited than others for coping with the demands of a changing environment. Those hereditary mutants that are advantageous to adaptation lead to the survival of their kind and hence the eventual development of a new type of organism. This process is what Darwin called *natural selection.*

Following Howells, we will now define biological evolution as a combination of hereditary processes and processes of natural selection.[2]

We have indicated that the evolutionary process functions through a combination of heredity and natural selection. Two important results from this process are an *increasing complexity* and an *increasing variability* in the forms of life. We have mentioned the fact of the increased complexity of the nervous system of many forms of animal life and hence the importance of learning as a new mode of adaptation as opposed to tropisms and instincts. In a discussion of evolution this fact can be misunderstood. For example, it should *not* be assumed that the traits which have been learned or acquired within one's lifetime are genetically transmitted to the offspring. The habits learned by the parents of any animal are not inherited by the offspring. They have to be learned.

We need to make a distinction between germ cells and body cells. Changes that occur in the germ cells produce changes both in the germ cells and body cells of the offspring. Changes in the body cells alone do not produce new characteristics in the offspring. It is possible that certain types of radiation in the environment can cause changes in the germ cells and thus affect the hereditary outcomes.

[2] William Howells, *Mankind in the Making* (Garden City, N.Y., Doubleday & Co., Inc., 1959), p. 19.

It was noted earlier that one of the results of the evolutionary process was increasing complexity of the body structure of animal life. We particularly emphasized the increasing complexity of the nervous systems of certain types of animals. In fact, it is generally recognized that, as one proceeds up the evolutionary scale of development of animal life, say, from the *protozoa* to the *primates,* the ability to learn more quickly and to learn more difficult things increases. It seems that as complexity of animal life increases, a premium is placed on learning as a mode of adaptation. This is particularly striking in man, who stands at the head of the primates.

For all animals, other than man, the results of their learning are not cumulative from one generation to the next. Each generation has to learn all over again and through *direct* experience. However, in the case of man a new dimension is added. The results of his learning have become organized and are transmitted in *cumulative* form from each generation to the next. This is not a form of biological transmission. It is social transmission. The results of man's learning have become organized into a new system of adaptation called *culture*. This system provides an almost limitless potentiality, flexibility, and variability. This mode of adaptation is dependent upon biological evolution but functions by dynamics which are of its own nature. Let us consider now in detail the concept of culture.

3. THE CONCEPT OF CULTURE

INTRODUCTION

The evolution of human behavior through systems of culture constitutes a third type of evolution. We discussed briefly biological evolution or the emergence and development of life. Of course, prior to this, and still continuing, is cosmic evolution, or the evolution of matter and the universe. We will not discuss the evolution of the universe, except to say that it is assumed that it is still evolving, and, as for that matter, it is assumed that all three forms of evolution are proceeding at the same time.

It has been estimated that the appearance of atoms and the formation of matter into stars and planets occurred approximately five billion years ago. Life appeared on earth at an estimated 2.5 billion years ago, and the first man-made tools appeared sometime between 500,000 and 800,000 years ago. *Modern* man as a biological form appeared around 30,000 to 35,000 B.C.[3]

---

[3] *Ibid.*, pp. 205-213.

Adaptation

Before we present a working definition of culture as a system of human adaptation, it would be well to specify the meaning which we are assigning to the term *adaptation*. Adaptation is the response of living organisms to outside or environmental influences—that is, responses which promote survival, health, and reproduction are adaptive responses. The reaction of the body and the blood stream to invasion of the body by bacteria illustrates the body's remarkable defense reaction to infection. Dobzhansky points out that "In general, every living species reacts adaptively to the external stimuli which occur frequently in the environments in which this species has evolved. Thus the human species had for countless generations to deal with the danger of sunburn, but it did not encounter X-ray burns until very recently." [4]

When we speak of a system of social adaptation, the focus is not on individuals as individuals but on *populations* of individuals. Neither is the focus particularly on the avoidance of death. If so, then wars are highly maladaptive. One could argue that today they are very much maladaptive; but the point is that when they are fought, they are fought for the maintenance and perpetuation of the population and its sociocultural system. In other words, the conceptual emphasis of adaptation is on the survival and perpetuation of populations. When one refers to the *mutual* adaptations of members to one another, this is sometimes called *integration*.[5] This is simply a form of internal adaptation, or intra-adaptation.

The Definition of Culture

The foundation of every society is a population of individuals. This provides the raw materials from which the society, as such, develops. However, for it to develop, the population must persist in interaction through time. Unless there is persistence in interaction, the integration of forces cannot take place, and hence the population aggregate cannot be transformed into a society. For example, a crowd or audience may interact and have much in common, but unless the interaction persists, the necessary differentiation and integration of parts cannot occur and therefore societal characteristics cannot emerge.

Given a population in interaction, the interaction in time will become patterned and organized into a system of shared behavior which becomes relatively self-perpetuating. This cumulative system of shared

---

[4] Theodosius Dobzhansky, *Evolution, Genetics, and Man* (New York, John Wiley & Sons, Inc., 1955), p. 14.
[5] Harry C. Bredemeier and Richard M. Stephenson, *The Analysis of Social Systems* (New York, Holt, Rinehart and Winston, Inc., 1962), p. 54.

behavior and ideas which are transmitted from the current members of a population to the new members is called *culture*. The transmission mechanism is not through the germ cells as in biological evolution, but is through language or symbolic communication and the learning process.

What determines which interaction patterns persist and become shared and transmitted? The answer is that a new form of natural selection determines the developmental patterning and trends. What is the new form of natural selection? Obviously, behavioral responses are transmitted through learning. No child is born with response patterns to write, speak, or do arithmetic. These are learned. Let us assume that the members of a population are interacting and that they evolve a new form of behavior. What determines whether the new form will persist? Two basic conditions determine the persistence. These are: (1) When the behavior patterns consciously or unconsciously contribute to the adaptation and integration of the group, i.e., those patterns which tend in the long run to have group survival value, they will persist. (2) Those responses that are rewarded or positively reinforced by the group members will persist.

Sometimes responses are also rewarded or only rewarded by outside groups who become aware of them. When this occurs, this further reinforces and maintains persistence. This spread of behavior patterns from one group to another is called *diffusion*.[6]

We have in effect derived two concepts to help account for cultural change or evolution. These are *invention* and *diffusion*. Obviously, discovery and invention are starting points in any effort to understand cultural evolution or change. But it is not appropriate at this point to discuss the details of the processes and conditions which these concepts involve. Suffice it to say that all we are attempting to do just now is to point to the dynamics which produce cultural evolution. This is all we did in discussing biological evolution, where we found that it was governed by heredity and natural selection. But many books could be written in explaining what is known about how each of these processes functions. It is not intended to imply that as much is known about cultural evolution as is known about biological evolution, but a great deal more is known than space will permit one to discuss here.[7]

Let us now summarize the discussion about the concept of culture. Culture is a form of adaptation peculiar to man. It is obviously based on the existence of biological properties necessary for its development. But it differs from biological mechanisms of adaptation in the way in which it is acquired, transmitted, and changed.

[6] Ralph Linton, *The Study of Man* (New York, Appleton-Century-Crofts, Inc., 1936), Chapters XVIII and XIX.

[7] In addition to Linton, *op. cit.*, see Paul Bohannan, *Social Anthropology* (New York, Holt, Rinehart and Winston, Inc., 1963), Part 6. See also Raymond Firth, *Elements of Social Organization*, 2nd ed. (London, Watts & Co., 1956), Chapter 3.

Biological adaptation is a form of natural selection of organic characteristics which have species survival value. Cultural adaptation is less a state of man's increased correlation of his physical characteristics with the *demands* of the external environment than it is man's derived solutions to and increased cumulative *control* over nature, including man's own nature. Consider two examples: first, the history of man is characterized by an increasing control over the sources of energy; and secondly, man has likewise increased his control over the attitudes and thinking of his fellows by methods of communication which extend around the earth with electronic speed. It can be said with a good deal of validity that man through culture is gaining rational control of the forces which release human potentialities and thus man has begun "to make himself."

Culture consists of the established or customary patterns and standards for behavior and social organization that exist within a society. Culture is the derived system of human solutions to *recurring* human events, experiences, and conditions.

Some elaboration of the foregoing phrase "established or customary patterns and standards" is in order. It is not easy to define culture. In the first place, it encompasses the total evolution of the results of human creativity. In the second place, it refers to materials, ideas, and products of ideas that have social meaning and utility; hence, it constitutes a system of social organization which differentiates and integrates human interaction and provides guides to behavior and motives to conform.

The phrase "solutions to recurring human events, experiences, and conditions" also needs some elaboration. The important point to recognize is that unless the event or experience does recur, it cannot have adaptive or adjustment significance for the population. Death is an event which occurs with a regular frequency in a population and every society has elaborate bereavement practices, funeral and burial rites for the dead. These function to console and restore the stability of the remaining family and relatives who have had their lives disrupted and shocked by the loss of a loved one. This does not mean that unique or nonrepeating events are of no consequence for the development of culture. Such events are significant for disrupting and perhaps contributing to the altering of existing patterns. It does mean, however, that the general framework and pattern of culture evolves around the recurring problems of human living that are common in time to human groups.

Finally, we concluded that (1) culture was transmitted through time by means of symbolic communication or language and becomes a part of the behavioral makeup of the participants through the learning processes; and (2) it changes through processes of invention and diffusion from other cultures.

The diffusion of culture elements from one culture to another is an important and complex problem itself. The receiving culture defines the meaning and use of the diffusing element. The more similar two cultures are, the more likely a new element will diffuse to one and retain the form, use, and meaning it had in the culture where it originated.

After World War II certain American ideas about the rights of women diffused to Japan, but the scope of application of these rights was defined differently by the Japanese.

An interesting example of the diffusion of a cultural product where its meaning was radically redefined is the diffusion of the metal axe head to the Polynesians. They used the axe heads by stringing them on a cord and wearing them as necklaces. Therefore, whether an axe is an axe in the sense of a chopping instrument depends upon the culture. This suggests something which has been implicit in all our discussions of culture, namely, that cultural meanings are symbolically determined and are quite arbitrary in nature. The concept of *symbol* is so important in the understanding of human behavior that some discussion of its meaning and significance is important. This we shall provide in the next section.

4. THE EVOLUTION OF RESPONSE COMPLEXITY

The principal ideas in the following discussion follow closely those presented in a paper by Leslie A. White.[8]

In the previous discussion of adaptation it was indicated that behavior has evolved from the simple to the complex, the most complex currently being found in man and resulting from processes of learning rather than inheritance. On the other hand, the simplest form, the simple reflex response, is most typically represented by one-celled animals. Of course, lower forms of animal life than man possess the ability to learn. The point which we wish to convey is that animals depend more and more on learning as they evolve up the phylogenetic scale of development. Thus we note that the one-celled protozoa adapt entirely by reflex-type responses, the chimpanzee by reflexes plus a considerable stock of learned responses, and man relies primarily upon learned responses.

It very well may be that all forms of life are capable of developing *conditioned* reflexes and some may define this as learning. This point is of no interest here. What is of interest from the point of view of evolution is the fact that learning as a means of adaptation becomes more and more prominent as one goes up the scale of animal development.

White, in discussing the evolution of responses or what he calls "mind-

---

[8] Leslie A. White, "Four Stages in the Evolution of Minding," in Sol Tax, ed., *Evolution After Darwin*, Vol. II (Chicago, The University of Chicago Press, 1960), pp. 239-253.

ing," notes that an organism may react positively (+), negatively (−), or neutrally (○). "That is, it approaches, withdraws, or does nothing, depending upon the meaning that the object has for it."[9] It is, of course, in the case of man particularly important to define what we mean by a negative response. In man and certain other animals aggressive behavior is not withdrawal behavior, but it may be considered negative from the point of view of feeling or emotion. This complexity in the variety of meaning involved is not important for the moment. What we wish to emphasize just now is that there are *levels of response* complexity.

The simplest type of reaction, says White, is the simple reflex. In this type of response the meaning which the stimulus has to the organism is determined by the intrinsic properties of *both* the organism and the stimulus structure. For example, the physiological structure of the human eye is such that it will contract when a beam of light is focused on it. Thus the reaction of the eye is a function of its intrinsic properties in conjunction with the properties of the light wave.

White illustrates this response relationship as follows: Let the symbol O refer to organism and the symbol S denote the stimulus. The simple reflex is then indicated as shown in Figure 3:1.

```
0 ─────────────────────────── S
```

FIGURE 3:1. The Simple Reflex.
After Leslie A. White.

At this level of response the behavior of the organism is *mechanically* determined by the interaction of the intrinsic properties of both the organism and the stimulus.

The next type in the evolution of response levels is the *conditioned* response or reflex. Pavlov's classic experiment with the dog and the electric bell well illustrates this response configuration. The general characteristics of the experiment are well known. A hungry dog salivated when he smelled food and he was indifferent to the sound of the electric bell. But, when stimulated by the food odor and the bell simultaneously for a number of times, the sound of the bell alone became sufficient to evoke the salivation response.

White diagrams this type of response as follows:

Thus the process of conditioning is represented in three phases. In the first, or *a*, phase of Figure 3:2, the situation is the same as in the first type or the simple reflex. In the *a* stage the stimulus is not conditioned. There is simply an intrinsic relationship between food and organism. This, of course, does not imply that an object of food for one organism is necessarily such an object for all organisms. This would vary with the

[9] *Ibid.*, p. 240.

variation in the intrinsic properties of the organism. A worm, for example, could hardly crack a walnut, but a squirrel feasts on them.

In phase b the S_1 of phase a is paired along with S_2, the sound of the bell. The organism, O, relates by association S_2 and S_1 as a consequence of their already being related in time and space. Thus S_2 through its relationship to S_1 becomes capable of evoking a response of salivation in the dog. When the relationship between S_2 and the dog, O, has been established, S_1 may drop out. Thus we are left with c, which is a direct relationship, similar in form to a.

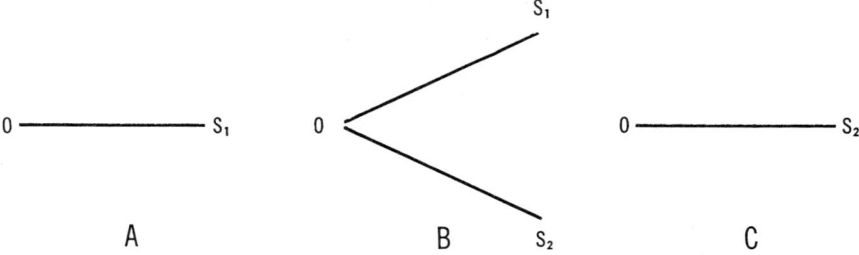

FIGURE 3:2. The Conditioned Response. After Leslie A. White.

The conditioned reflex is similar to the simple reflex, but they are not the same. It is true that the conditioned reflex grows out of the simple reflex, but the relationship between organism, O, and the S_2 stimulus, the sound of the bell, is *not* dependent upon their intrinsic properties. S_2 could just as well have been any other stimulus. In other words, it was not S_2 itself which was important, but the *relationship* in time and space between S_1 and S_2. As White stated the idea ". . . the salivary-gland-meaning of the electric bell is in no sense intrinsic in the sound waves that it emits." [10]

The third type or level of response we have designated as *sign* behavior. White does not specifically label type 3 and it is easy to see why he did not. It is extremely difficult to label with a single term and still convey the desired meaning. The point we wish to emphasize in the third type is the increased control which the organism has over its choice of responses.

A type 3 response is probably best illustrated by the behavior of chimpanzees. Again we draw from Professor White's discussion, in which he illustrates the third type by the example of a chimpanzee using a stick to knock down a banana which is suspended from the roof of his cage beyond the reach of its hand. Another example is the throwing of coconuts and clods as weapons by certain of the larger monkeys, particularly the Pigtail monkey.

[10] *Ibid.*, p. 241.

EVOLUTION AND CULTURE

Type 3 is illustrated by Professor White as follows:

In Figure 3:3, O = chimpanzee, E_1 is the banana, and E_2 is the stick. Note that E_1 and E_2 are concrete things that are physically nearby in the immediate context.

Professor White in contrasting response type 3 with type 2 notes four important distinctions. *First*, the third type is like the second type (conditioned reflex) in that the *organism* is related simultaneously to two things or events in the external world. *Secondly*, in the case of type 3, the two things which are related are significant to the organism from the start to the finish of the type 3 action. *Thirdly*, the relationship between the banana and the stick in type 3 is determined from experience and learning and is directly established, whereas in type 2 the sound of

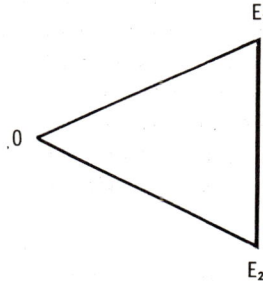

FIGURE 3:3. Sign Behavior. After Leslie A. White.

the bell and the odor of the food were indirectly related within the biochemical and neurological system of the dog. And, finally, the relationships established in type 3 are determined by the organism, whereas the relationships established in type 2 are *not* established by the organism but by its relationship to other factors, the experimenter, or circumstances such as chance association. These four points lead Professor White to make two important distinctions: (1) Either the organism principally determines the response configuration which it executes, or (2) it does not. That is, the organism initiates and revises responses, or it mechanically responds like a plant which turns toward the sunlight. In type 1, the simple reflex response, the organism alone does not determine the response. The response is a joint function of intrinsic properties within the organism and the stimulus. The organism has no alternative. The worker bee, for example, responds the way it does because of the structure of its body and the nature of the stimulus. As White says, "It is something that it undergoes as well as something that it does." [11]

The organism also plays a subordinate role in the response process in type 2 behavior. "The dog has nothing to say about how he shall

---

[11] *Ibid.*, p. 242.

respond to the sound of the bell; this is determined by the experimenter. . . . Here, also, the organism has neither initiative nor choice." [12]

The situation is quite different with type 3 behavior. Here the organism itself plays the dominant role in response formulation, revision, and execution. As White puts it, "It is the chimpanzee who decides what to do and how to do it. He has initiative, alternatives, and choice. He may use the stick to reach and knock down the food, or he may, as they sometimes do, use it to pole-vault ceilingward and snatch the food when it comes within his reach. Or he may decide to build a tower of boxes from whose summit he can reach his prize." [13]

In type 3 the response is still determined by the intrinsic properties of the organism and the intrinsic properties of the stimulus situation, but the organism plays the *dominant* role in that it is capable of formulating response alternatives and it also has control over their execution.

The type 3 response level represents a considerable increase in complexity over that of types 1 and 2, but the organism is restricted to learning through direct experience. That is to say, an organism responding at the level of a type 3 response cannot *create* an environment, but it can use constructively elements of the existing physical environment. It is doubtful if one would ever observe a chimpanzee with a stick *searching* for bananas to knock down. That is to say that such tool implementation as that exhibited in a type 3 response is apparently used in connection with the *immediate* visual environment rather than environments outside the visual range of the organism.

This form of behavioral adaptation is limited in that the experience of one organism cannot be transmitted to another without the other having to *observe directly* the event or behavior being transmitted. In other words, the chimpanzee will have to provide direct examples for the other chimpanzees if they are to learn what he has learned. The chimpanzee who has learned to knock down bananas with a stick cannot construct a hypothetical banana-knocking-down exercise and thus provide a symbolic example for teaching other chimpanzees. To be able to do so would facilitate the process of learning among organisms of a given type and it would also allow for the accumulating of experience within and between generations. This latter, or the means for accumulating experience, is of great significance in facilitating the adaptation of a species. It is precisely these aspects of symbolic experience and cumulativeness of its results that characterize the type 4 response.

A type 4 response configuration may be illustrated by human speech as diagrammed in Figure 3:4.

O is the organism, this time a human being; E_1 is a banana; and E_2 is the *word* "banana." The situation is like a type 3 response set in that

[12] *Ibid.*, p. 242.
[13] *Ibid.*, p. 243.

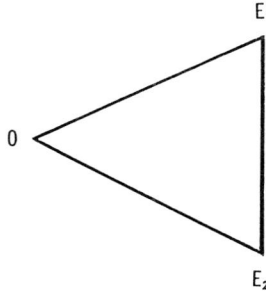

FIGURE 3:4. Symboling Behavior.
After Leslie A. White.

there is a simultaneous or near-simultaneous relationship between the organism and the two external things or events. Also, as in type 3 the relationship is determined by the organism itself.

In type 3 the *intrinsic* properties of E_1, the suspended banana, and E_2, the stick, were such as to enable the chimpanzee to perceive a functional connection between the two in regard to his goal of obtaining the banana as food. In type 4 there is no intrinsic relationship between the object banana and the combination of sounds in *banana*. The word "banana" as the name for that particular fruit is arbitrary. It is a *symbol* which stands for the concrete object.

Type 4 or symboling behavior affords an extraordinarily efficient mode of adaptation and is characteristic only of man. White defines symboling as meanings that cannot be comprehended with senses alone.[14] Symboling is the communication of meanings by means of symbols. The meaning of the symbol is arbitrarily determined. The symbol 5, for example, is a conventional means for conveying the idea of the number of digits on the normal human hand. The physical form of the symbol is arbitrary and the meaning given it is entirely determined by man himself. That is to say, the physical form of 5 could have been in any other shape so long as all concerned agreed upon the form to represent this given meaning. Thus the *meaning* of a symbol and its physical structure are two different matters. A symbol must have some physical form in order for man to experience it. It may be a spoken word, or it may be a written word which represents a sound combination, or it may be an object such as a crucifix. The principal idea is that the meaning of a symbol is derived from the interaction of human beings and the resulting meaning is social in nature, that is, it is a shared meaning. It has significance because it provides a vehicle for a common understanding or meaning among the members of a group or a society.

[14] *Ibid.*, p. 249.

The combination of sounds *by* and *buy* are vehicles for transmitting a great variety of meanings. Their particular or specific meanings are determined by the behavioral context. As Professor White says, "Holy water is not the same kind of thing, from the standpoint of human experience, as mere H_2O; it has a distinctive quality, or attribute, in addition to hydrogen and oxygen in molecular organization."[15]

The distinction between meanings which are the result of the *interaction* of intrinsic qualities within the organism and the stimulus, and meanings which are wholly determined by the organism, is a distinction worthy of additional elaboration. Failure to note this distinction has led to a confusion of what we have called "symbols" with "sign" or what we designated as a type 3 response.[16] For example, some investigators have labeled as symbolic behavior the chimpanzee's behavior in conditioning experiments using colors and geometric figures that come to be identified with food or electric shock. Some chimpanzees were taught to use different colored poker chips to purchase bananas from an automat. These acquired connections and relations were labeled by the researchers as the learning of symbols. It is much more appropriate to label them as "signs" since the chimpanzees did not determine the meaning of the objects.

> The red circles and the blue poker chips have indeed acquired a meaning which is not inherent in their physical structure and composition, just as holy water or the combination of sounds *see* has acquired a meaning. This is the similarity. But there is a fundamental difference also. It is not the rats and apes that have determined the meanings which the red circles or the blue poker chips have acquired, and, what is more, *they are incapable of doing this.* Only man is capable of freely originating such kinds of meanings and of bestowing them upon things or events. The apes and rats can *acquire* meanings for things, but they cannot originate or determine them.[17]

A sign is a behavioral or physical property of an organism or an event which enables an observer to anticipate some subsequent event or consequence. For example, a dog's snarl or growl becomes a warning sign of danger and a wagging tail a sign of friendliness. Thus the meaning of a sign is established through experience and the mechanism of the conditioned reflex.

The meaning of the symbol is freely created and bestowed. That is to say, symbols are created to convey certain intended meanings. Once

[15] *Ibid.*, p. 249.

[16] For a more detailed discussion on the concept of symbol see Leslie A. White, "The Symbol: The Origin and Basis of Human Behavior," *Philosophy of Science,* Vol. 7 (1940), pp. 451-463. Also, Leslie A. White, *The Science of Culture* (New York, Farrar, Straus & Giroux, Inc., 1949); Susanne K. Langer, *Philosophy in a New Key* (New York, Mentor Books, 1948).

[17] White in *The Evolution of Man,* p. 250.

the symbol has been accepted as denoting a given meaning, then its mere presence is sufficient to evoke the meaning. For example, the symbol *chair*, after it is learned, is sufficient to evoke the appropriate meaning associated with the physical object which the word *chair* denotes.

The discussion of symboling behavior or the type 4 response concludes our presentation on the evolution of response levels. In closing this section it should be noted that the progression of response development from the simple reflex to the symbol constitutes a form of evolutionary development. The simplest form of animal life exhibits the simple reflex, but only man possesses all four of these response levels.

It is hazardous and difficult to attempt to compare the learning ability of organisms among orders, classes, and phyla. However, it does seem quite clear that evolution has resulted in the development of animals with an increased potentiality for and dependence upon learning. Man has carried this form of adaptation to its most elaborate form. In fact, he has developed it to such an extent that he is now literally capable of rationally making himself. He can through the use of technology alter his environment; he can even alter himself.

> Man makes himself . . . in two senses, and the two senses imply a contrast between folk society and, at least, modern civilization. Man is self-made through the slow and unpremeditated growth of culture and civilization. Man later attempts to take control of this process and to direct it where he wills.[18]

Redfield is saying that during many years of the development of human culture, it shaped and directed man in its earlier forms as now, but that the cultural influences then were relatively unconscious and unplanned. The forces of change and development are now more rationally planned and developed.

We indicated in the very beginning of this chapter the idea that man through his present culture largely shapes the *future* state of his culture and hence himself is an idea that is only a few centuries old. This suggests that cultural evolution occurs at an increasing rate of change. This is unquestionably related to the improved adaptive capacity provided by man's type 4 response (symboling) capacity. From the capacity to create symbols to represent experience, ideas, and systems of ideas it was possible to create an alphabet and number systems. These in turn became the vehicles for describing, probing, and analyzing nature. The result was man's increased control over nature and himself as a part of it. Obviously, the growth of human culture has produced new problems

---

[18] Robert Redfield, *The Primitive World and Its Transformations* (Ithaca, N.Y., copyright, 1953, by Cornell University. Used by permission of Cornell University Press), p. 113.

some of which are awesome to contemplate. But we will not digress into a discussion of the nature of the road to "progress." Suffice it to say that the development of a written language and mathematics made it possible to record experience and thus free a tremendous amount of human energy from the task of conserving and remembering experience. In other words, it enabled man to change from a state of almost total orientation to the past or tradition to a new state of orientation toward the attainment of future goals.

Redfield in commenting on the late V. Gordon Childe's book, *Man Makes Himself*, says,

> . . . Childe writes of the long historical development of tools and institutions wherein man, once a being not yet human, came to be the creature that he is now. The "making of man" with which Childe is concerned is unplanned. It is that making of man in which a future is made that men do not foresee or strive to bring about. . . . In the early and very much longer part of his history man did not see himself as maker of either his future world or of himself.[19]

In other words, man's cultural evolution has been until very recently a blind, unconscious force. As a conscious force it appeared in modern civilization. Redfield says:

> The West invented progress and reform. The East today is in revolt; there is a great purpose to change things. The intentional making over of society is a conception of civilized man, perhaps only of modern man. May we not say that there was no Utopia prior to *The Republic?* But there have been many since, and most of these since the Renaissance.[20]

The change in orientation and perspective from one of tradition orientation and primary concern with immediate problems to one of long-range orientation and planning for the future is related to the growth of culture. That is, it was not possible for man to observe that by his own actions he could affect his future states until culture developed sufficiently for man to note its cumulation and growth. The rate of change during the 340,000 years surveyed by Childe was so slow in a relative sense that the pace and direction of change were not perceptible by man. The pace became quickened by the development of an alphabet and mathematics. It should be noted that these are examples *par excellence* of a type 4 response level, namely, symboling. Of course, spoken language or speech is also symboling behavior.

Since man is the only species which possesses a culture, it is significant

[19] *Ibid.*, p. 111.
[20] *Ibid.*, pp. 111-112.

to ask: what are his biological properties which relate to the development of the cultural form of adaptation?

5. PRESUMED BIOLOGICAL PREREQUISITES TO CULTURE

Introduction

It is necessary to say "presumed biological prerequisites to culture" at this stage in our knowledge of the relationships between the biochemical action of the brain and behavior. However, these assumptions are not mere guesswork. They are more at the level of educated guesses. Many times it is observed that a given brain process is related to behavior, but what is needed in addition is to know *how* it is related and *what determines* the relationship. For instance, Gerard comments that memory traces are more easily fixed in some individuals than others.[21] But what is the relationship between this fact and behavior? Certainly, poor memory fixation leads to discontinuities in behavior, but overfixation may be expected to lead to unimaginativeness and the absence of creativity, that is, robot-like behavior.

It is certainly important to study the dependence of behavior on the brain, but the other side of the coin is also very important if one considers the possibility of manipulating the neural structure itself. Such a possibility raises the general question of the effect of culture on the neural structure. How does experience function to release latent biological capacity? Also, how may cultural knowledge be applied to control genetic outcomes? New knowledge in the biochemistry of genetics suggests such possibilities.

Let us look now at some of the general properties of man the organism and try to relate these to the evolution of culture.

Some Physical Bases for Culture

The basic processes of metabolism and the chromosome and gene functioning of the most primitive organisms and the very advanced are fundamentally alike.

The major changes in evolution have come in the ability of organisms to *interact* with the environment. In this respect man transcends all other animals. The principal reason for his great flexibility in adaptation derives from the fact that he has culture. Obviously, a given form of adaptation by a species is not possible unless the species possesses the biological and physiological capacity for the behavior. Since man is the only animal which has evolved a culture, what are the biological prop-

[21] J. N. Spuhler, Editor, *The Evolution of Man's Capacity for Culture* (Detroit, Wayne State University Press, copyright, 1959), p. 19. Quotations reprinted by permission of the Wayne State University Press.

erties that he possesses which appear to favor the development of culture as a mode of adaptation? This asserts a gap between human behavior and nonhuman behavior. As J. N. Spuhler says, ". . . there is a gap between cultural behavior and noncultural behavior." [22]

In the discussion to follow, I wish not only to specify some of the physical prerequisites to culture but also to stress the gradual changes in the evolution of all animal forms which have enhanced adaptability. In this way, we will emphasize not only the gap between the human and the nonhuman but also the *crossing* of the gap from nonhuman to human.[23]

Recall that in Part 2 of this chapter we showed that the fundamental processes which produce or make possible a given form of adaptation are genetic mutation and selection. In this way populations that survive accumulate genes which are favorable to survival in the environment. It is here assumed that the physical characteristics conducive to the formation of culture in the population of men slowly emerged over millions of generations in the hominoid line. We can see a glimpse of the process by noting how a human offspring or infant becomes human in the processes of physical maturation and learning of the culture of its groups. The infant receives from its parents the genetic resources or raw materials necessary for the prevailing mode of adaptation of the species. These genetic resources determine, assuming proper nutrition and care, the physical properties necessary to enable the child to *interact* with socialized human beings and thus the new offspring acquires the prevailing patterns of culture.

Spuhler identifies seven evolutionary conditions, though presented here in a much oversimplified manner, that are prerequisites to culture and he indicates that these conditions were ". . . interdependent and roughly synchronous." [24]

(1) *Accommodative Vision*. Vision is the primary sense of all vertebrates. It is the major means of their mobility.

> Visual behavior is one key difference between the nocturnal, mostly solitary Prosimians, and the diurnal, more social Anthropoidea. The difference between these two is perhaps the largest gap in nonhuman Primate social behavior. With upright, or sitting-up posture, vision in the Anthropoidea

---

[22] *Ibid.*, p. 1.
[23] There are several good basic sources for piecing together the argument of this section. Two of these are Anne Roe and George G. Simpson, *Behavior and Evolution* (New Haven, Yale University Press, 1958); Theodosius Dobzhansky, *Mankind Evolving* (New Haven, Yale University Press, 1962). However, in my opinion the best single summary is Spuhler's *The Evolution of Man's Capacity for Culture*. The basic argument in this section is borrowed from Spuhler.
[24] Spuhler, *op. cit.*, p. 4.

gained strict control of manipulation—it became super*vision,* a guide and control of fine manipulation.²⁵

The two-way relationship between the evolution of keen vision and delicate manual manipulation has been emphasized. Spuhler, quoting from Polyak, says: ". . . vision itself [became] more refined and the intellectual absorption and mental utilization more complete and lasting as the skilled movements became more complex and more efficient." ²⁶ Thus we see that change in one system stimulates change in correlated parts of other systems.

(2) *Bipedal Locomotion.* It is not just bipedal motion which is significant, but *upright* bipedal motion. The upright posture freed the hands of man for the handling of tools and the manipulation of elements in the environment. Howells emphasizes that man's distinctive upright position is importantly related to the evolution of his foot.

> This foot has a completely nonopposable great toe and two solid arches, one across and one from front to back—features which mark it off distinctly from other primates. It also has a big heel as the hinder part of the long arch, and none of the bony structure of the foot bears upon the ground between the heel and the broad region of the ball. The bones of the arches are all compactly fitted together, enabling them to bear the weight of the body and to transmit it forward from the ankles to the toes. This is what makes it possible to take long and effortless strides, which an ape with his flabby foot cannot do. . . .²⁷

The structure of the human arch has aided man in achieving complete uprightness in body posture.

(3) *Manipulation.* Monkeys have a fair degree of skill in manipulation with their hands. But man, whose hands are continuously free, since they are not used in locomotion, has achieved the highest use of his hands.

> . . . the arms and hands—under the guidance of binocular vision with good accommodation—are principal organs for interaction with the immediate physical environment. Getting food, eating, grooming, fighting, making, using, and carrying tools, these manipulations, accompanied by a rich flow of sense data including those from the more developed proprioceptive arm- and-hand muscle sense, enlarge the flow of information to the brain which in turn fosters development of association areas for storage of past experi-

---

[25] *Ibid.,* pp. 4 and 5.
[26] S. Polyak, *The Vertebrate Visual System* (Chicago, The University of Chicago Press, 1957) as quoted in Spuhler, *op. cit.,* p. 5.
[27] William Howells, *Mankind So Far* (Garden City, N.Y., Doubleday & Company, Inc., 1946), p. 72. See also revised edition, entitled, *Mankind in the Making,* 1959, p. 89.

ence with the hands and guides and initiates new hand movements. The neural delay required when some extra-organic tool is interposed between stimulus and response probably had much to do with the first ability to use symbols and the start of language. The co-adaptation of the *hands, senses,* and *association areas* in precise manipulation seems a first basis for the subsequent development of human intelligence.[28]

(4) *Carnivorous-omnivorous Diet.* The fact that man is omnivorous, that is, eats both animal and vegetable foods, increases his range possibilities for food hunting and collecting. This in turn stimulates the growth of a communication system, since hunting of large animals was dangerous and required group effort. Spuhler points out that man's carnivorous diet had significant implications for the social organization of early hominoids. The killing of large animals afforded a large supply of calories in highly concentrated form. Such concentrated stocks of food were more easily stored in a central shelter place than low caloried and more bulky plant food. Also, the hunters needed tools to kill the animals and the use of tools to attain *future* goals requires a considerable degree of conceptualization.[29]

(5) *Cortical Control of Sexual Behavior.* In most mammals sexual behavior is seasonal and corresponds to periods of female ovulation. In such mammals, copulation is induced by an increase of gonadal hormones in the blood stream and their resulting stimulation of the brain. In such animals gonadectomy can prevent copulation. However, in man and the chimpanzee sexual behavior is strongly under the control of cortical influences and is not prevented by gonadectomy.[30] This means that neural pathways may be acquired by means of learning and sex behavior would then be a function of learning as well as hormonal activity.

It should be clear that a prerequisite form of adaptation for culture is the change from biologically built-in blueprints for behavior or neural pathways to neural connections built up in the association areas of the brain. This, of course, allows for the involvement of learning and symbol behavior.

The fact that the human female is capable of sexual activity over a continuous period throughout most of her life span may have aided in the transition of the hominoid family from a social unit where sex and reproduction were predominant to one where economic and social functions are dominant.

(6) *Vocal Communication.* Human speech is of tremendous impor-

[28] Spuhler, *op. cit.*, p. 6. Italics added.
[29] *Ibid.*, p. 6.
[30] C. S. Ford and F. A. Beach, *Patterns of Sexual Behavior* (New York, Harper & Row, Publishers, Inc., 1951).

tance as a preadaptive capacity necessary to culture. Spuhler's comments on speech are important enough to warrant quoting in detail:

> Human speech is an overlaid physiological function. It uses a set of body parts of quite diverse primary action. Consider the muscles used in speaking. Most of our coordinated muscular movement involves corrections and adjustments from proprioceptors. But the laryngeal muscles lack proprioceptors, and feedback control of speech comes by way of the ear and the 8th cranial nerve. When we talk, the voice box, tongue, and lips must work together smoothly and precisely. The 10th nerve controls the adjustment of the vocal cords and the 5th nerve the movement of the lips. Both of these involve branchial muscle while the 12th nerve moves the tongue with somatomotor muscle. The neurological basis of speech is not clear, but it is clear that the only place where the motor organs and steering apparatus of speech are wired together is in the cerebral cortex. Perhaps handtool manipulation in group activities like hunting coordinated by vocalization may have helped to make the connections.
>
> Although the larynx is homologous in all primates its position in the throat differs in man. The larynx of quadrapedal primates from the lemur to the chimpanzee is in close to slight contact with the soft palate. This is why chimpanzees cannot make long, resonant sounds. As a consequence of upright posture and flexion of the craniofacial base, the larynx in man is moved down the throat away from contact with the soft palate, and an oral chamber is formed which makes possible resonant human phonation.
>
> This is not to deny a rich variety of vocal production to the chimpanzee and other primates. The position of the larynx, however, is one reason why attempts to teach chimpanzees English have failed. Unfortunately no one has tried seriously to teach a chimpanzee to learn to speak using chimpanzee "phonemes." [31]

(7) *Expansion of the Cerebral Cortex.* In the past considerable emphasis has been placed on brain weight relative to body weight in man and primates in general. The general conclusion has been that among primates and with man in particular the brain is larger relative to body size than among mammals in general. Recent data indicate that the brain weight in modern man is just about what would be predicted from the knowledge of the relationship between brain weight and body weight among primates.[32] In other words, the general conclusion is that the size of the frontal lobes and the over-all brain size in man is not extraordinary as compared with other higher primates.

The size is important, but relatively speaking, what seems to be the most distinguishing feature of the human cerebral cortex is not its over-all size but the complexity of its structure. Particularly important is the increase in the number of interconnections within the brain. This greatly

[31] Spuhler, *op. cit.,* p. 8.
[32] *Ibid.,* p. 9.

increases the possibility for learning. In this regard Spuhler says, "The distinctive feature of the human cerebral cortex is not so much in overall volume nor in relative size of the frontal lobes, but rather in the way that the projection areas are connected with association areas, especially in the temporal lobes, and in the way the whole thing works." [33]

These seven assumed prerequisites to cultural adaptation did not occur full-blown as discrete forms of development. Instead, they gradually emerged over vast periods of time involving, at least, over a million years. Evolutionary changes are, of course, still taking place. In fact, Spuhler argues that hominoid evolution has speeded up and suggests that selection for a new type of environment—a cultural environment— has had a lot to do with it.[34]

Man has been able from his very beginning to dream and imagine better worlds to come. But only now has he come to possess the power and the means to actually translate into reality his highest aspirations and ideals. In this regard George Wells Beadle, President, American Association for the Advancement of Science, in 1955 said:

> Man's evolutionary future . . . is unlimited. But far more important, it lies within his own power to determine its direction . . . an opportunity never before presented to any species on earth. . . .
> To carry the human species on to a future of biological and cultural freedom, knowledge must be accompanied by collective wisdom and courage of an order not yet demonstrated by any society of man.[35]

It seems quite evident that before such "collective wisdom" can be achieved, the gap between existing potentialities of the great mass of the members of a society and their current level of attainment will have to be significantly narrowed. This raises the important question of how to more effectively release heretofore untapped human potentialities. For the social psychologist this raises questions about the relationship of the quality and quantity of varying types of experience to behavioral development. It also poses the important problem of how to create a social system which will more effectively release and utilize superior biological potentialities. In addition, there is the important question of the relationship of experience to the biochemistry of behavior.

Many of these questions will be considered in the next chapter, which deals primarily with some of the relationships between biological and physiological potentialities and experience.

[33] *Ibid.*, p. 9.
[34] *Ibid.*, p. 10.
[35] Quoted from an undated pamphlet of the American Association for the Advancement of Science, p. 12.

6. SUMMARY

It is estimated that life began on earth approximately 2.5 billion years ago and the first man-made tools appeared sometime between 500,000 and 800,000 years ago. The best current estimate is that modern or Cro-Magnon man appeared around 30,000 to 35,000 B.C.

Biological evolution is defined as a combination of hereditary processes and processes of natural selection. The hereditary process provides a wide range of variability of physical characteristics among the offspring. The greater the range of variability of characteristics, the more likely it is that a type will occur whose characteristics are more fitted to the demands of the environment. Different forms of life seem to have achieved their own way of fitting into the environment. The insects are particularly noted for their capacity to adapt and survive by mutation. Other forms of animal life, particularly mammals, have evolved a very complex nervous system, thus enabling the emergence of a new form of adaptation, namely, the ability to make new responses within the lifetime of the organism, hence to learn.

This form of adaptation has been developed to its highest state in man. The results of man's learning have become organized into a new system of adaptation called culture. This system provides an almost limitless potentiality, flexibility, and variability. It depends upon biological evolution but functions by dynamics which are of its own nature.

The evolution and persistence of cultural patterns are determined by behavioral variation or invention and by social reward or reinforcement.

The evolution of behavior in terms of differing levels of complexity of response was considered and four response levels were derived. These were: the *simple reflex,* the *conditioned reflex, sign behavior,* and *symboling.*

Following this, the biological prerequisites to culture were discussed. Seven prerequisites were identified. These were: (1) accommodative vision, (2) bipedal locomotion, (3) manipulation, (4) carnivorous-omnivorous diet, (5) cortical control of sexual behavior, (6) vocal communication, and (7) expansion of the cerebral cortex.

Further References

1. Walter B. Cannon, *The Wisdom of the Body* (New York, W. W. Norton & Company, Inc., 1932).
2. Earl L. Count, "The Biological Basis of Human Sociality," *American*

Anthropologist, Vol. 60, 1958. Also in Bobbs-Merrill Reprint Series, No. A-44.
3. Theodosius Dobzhansky, *Mankind Evolving* (New Haven, Yale University Press, 1962).
4. Harry F. Harlow and Clinton N. Woolsey, Editors, *Biological and Biochemical Bases of Behavior* (Madison, The University of Wisconsin Press, 1958).
5. G. A. Harrison, J. S. Weiner *et al., Human Biology—An Introduction to Human Evolution, Variation and Growth* (New York, Oxford University Press, 1964).
6. William Howells, *Mankind in the Making* (Garden City, N.Y., Doubleday & Co., Inc., 1959).
7. Frederick S. Hulse, *The Human Species—An Introduction to Physical Anthropology* (New York, Random House, Inc., 1963).
8. Wilder Penfield and Lamar Roberts, *Speech and Brain Mechanisms* (Princeton, N.J., Princeton University Press, 1959).
9. Anne Roe and George G. Simpson, *Behavior and Evolution* (New Haven, Yale University Press, 1958).
10. Michael Scriven, "Explanation and Prediction in Evolutionary Theory," *Science,* Vol. 130, Number 3374, 28 August 1959.
11. Homer W. Smith, *From Fish to Philosopher* (Boston, Little, Brown and Company, 1953).

4
The Release of Human Potentialities

•

1. *Introduction*
2. *Biological Potentialities*
    (a) *The Elements of Genetics: Introduction*
    (b) *The Elements of Genetics: Some Basic Concepts*
        1. Somatic Cells and Germ Cells
        2. Genotypes and Phenotypes
3. *Cultural Potentialities*
    (a) *Introduction*
    (b) *Service's "Law of Evolutionary Potential" of a Culture*
4. *The Release and Development of Individual Potentialities*
    (a) *Intelligence and Experience*
    (b) *Creativity and the Release of Potentialities*
5. *Summary.*

1. INTRODUCTION

THE PRINCIPAL TYPE of biological evolution considered in Chapter 3 is what is commonly called phylogenetic evolution. That is, the unit of study is the population, the species as a whole, which evolves and differentiates into new kinds of populations. This can be illustrated by the primates. There are two major divisions of the primates. These are the lower primates or Prosimians, of which the "lemurs" are good examples, and the higher primates or Anthropoidea. The latter contains apes, monkeys, and man. The Anthropoidea are divided into several families, but for our purposes we shall divide them into three categories. These are commonly called New World monkeys, Old World monkeys, and apes and man or Hominoidea.

This classification is crude, but it well illustrates our general idea of specialization and divergence of types. The study of phylogenetic or specific evolution then consists of tracing the differentiation or radiation *within* a species to determine how, when, and why each of the specialized types diverge into new lines.

However, the three types of primates which make up the suborder Anthropoidea can be viewed in another way. Each of these three types can be viewed as representing three distinct *levels* of evolutionary development, levels in the sense of constituting *new and higher forms*. This latter is what Sahlins calls *general evolution*.[1] The former or phylogenetic evolution which we discussed in Chapter 3 he calls *specific evolution*. These two concepts, specific and general evolution, will have great significance in helping to understand the argument of this chapter.

We turn now to a more specific statement of the meaning which we wish to assign to these terms.

Specific evolution results in more specialized adaptation. Certain of the New World monkeys have a very specialized tail in that they generally use it as a "hand." This serves as an extra safety device to prevent falling from the trees. Some of the New World monkeys, the marmosets, are small and look like squirrels. In general, the New World monkeys are not as large nor as fierce as the Old World monkeys. They also have a more restricted range of adaptation.

The Old World monkeys range widely over Africa and much of Asia. They are larger than the New World monkeys and are less adapted to trees. In fact, many have descended from the trees and range widely over nonwooded areas. This suggests that relative to the New World monkey they have enlarged their span of control over their environment.

Let us next take a brief glance at the third category of Anthropoidea, the Hominoidea. These are the apes and men. There are many distinctions which set this category off from the other two, but the most important distinctions have to do with locomotion and uprightness of body position. These differences are, of course, related to physical differences in the pelvis, leg, and foot. Men, of course, walk upright as true bipeds. The anthropoid apes fall in between, that is, they are neither quadrupedal nor bipedal. Chimpanzees and gorillas can stand up well, but they cannot walk well.

I have attempted to convey in this all-too-sketchy description of the three categories of Anthropoidea that they well illustrate *both* specific and general evolution. The elaboration and differentiation of various types *within* a category illustrate what we mean by specific evolution. In terms of adaptation, specific evolution leads to accommodation with the environment. Sometimes the species becomes overspecialized and is then

---

[1] Marshall D. Sahlins and Elman R. Service, eds., *Evolution and Culture* (Ann Arbor, The University of Michigan Press, 1960), p. 12-22.

unable to cope with sudden or radical changes in the demands of the environment.

The development of the various types of Old World and New World monkeys would be specific evolution. However, if one focuses on the fundamental changes which have occurred *among* these three classes of Anthropoidea, we will see the emergence of not only new forms but also *higher* forms. Thus we see that among the primates man is more highly developed than the ape, the ape more highly developed than the monkey, and some monkeys more highly developed than other monkeys. And so it is with life in general; "a man is more highly developed than a mouse, a mouse than a lizard, a lizard than a goldfish, a goldfish than a crab, a crab than an amoeba. All of these are contemporary, no one is ancestral to the other; they are present termini of different lineages."[2] But what are the criteria for determining which is higher on the evolutionary scale and which is lower? One answer to this question has already been suggested in Chapter 3. This was White's four types of responses, namely, the simple reflex, conditioned reflex, sign behavior, and symboling behavior. These four response levels represent a scale of complexity in terms of increasing control by the organism over its environment. The simple and conditioned reflex levels would more appropriately characterize the small New World monkeys, and sign behavior as well as the simple and conditioned reflex would be exhibited by the chimpanzee. Man, of course, exhibits all four types, but is principally known for his symboling behavior. It is also worth noting that response levels 3 and 4, that is, sign and symboling behavior, correlate with an evolving higher organization of the nervous system and this is reflected in the growing independence of the use of the hands.[3]

Specifically, how does the evolving from one response level to another indicate a higher form and thus an example of general evolution? Sahlins answers this question in terms of an organism's capacity to transform energy into a higher state.[4] In other words, given two organisms of roughly equal size and assuming that each has trapped an equal amount of energy, then the one which is able to transform the energy into a higher state would seem to represent a superior level of life. This transformation of energy to higher states should result in a further freeing of the organism from environmental control, and this in turn should increase the range of adaptation over a greater variety of environments. General evolution then seems to be the way in which *higher* forms of life emerge.

To summarize: Following Sahlins' ideas, specific evolution is species

[2] *Ibid.*, p. 18.
[3] For an effort to relate evolutionary concepts to brain functioning see the chapter by H. W. Magoun in Sol Tax, ed., *The Evolution of Man* (Chicago, The University of Chicago Press, 1960), pp. 187-208, Vol. II of *Evolution After Darwin.*
[4] Sahlins, *op. cit.*, p. 21.

modification, the radiation of life "along its many lines." When improved adaptability results from specific evolution, it is relative to a particular environment or a given adaptive problem. General evolution, on the other hand, transcends a particular environment in that it affords greater energy utilization and transformation and thus greater "all-around adaptability."

What is the significance of the concepts of specific and general biological evolution for the cultural evolution of man? In the first place, cultural adaptation is a new means of biological adaptation peculiar to man. It emerges from man's symbolic capacity and evolves like life in both a specific and general sense.

From the point of view of biological potentialities, the most important consideration is the *modal* frequency of genes of a given type in the population. If there is a minute frequency of gene carriers of high ability, this will not significantly affect the population. However, a large relative frequency of genes of a given type will affect the genetic pool within a population and in turn in combination with natural selection effect population differentiation. Thus gene frequency determines dominance, and dominance in a population determines genetic equilibrium.

The same is true in regard to cultural evolution. The appearance of a cultural genius or two will not significantly affect the culture of his time unless a significant portion of the population can grasp and accept his contributions. In other words, the presence of an invention or innovation does not assure that it will become a part of the fabric of the culture of the population any more than the presence of a mutation assumes that it necessarily becomes a characteristic of the population. Just as genetic mutation and evolution are significant only as they affect a species population, it is also true that cultural evolution is significant only to the extent that it alters the structure and functioning of the *system of culture* of a population. We now come to a very important question. What are the interrelations between the genetic pool within a population and the cultural processes and elements which release in varying degrees genetic potentialities of the population? The remainder of this chapter will be devoted to an effort to answer this question. At this time we will offer a tentative answer, but the evidence for the answer will be given in subsequent sections of the chapter. An answer is given now only to provide a guide to the analysis and discussion later.

Recall that we earlier argued that a significant measure of the improved all-round biological adaptability of a population was a change in its capacity to trap energy from nature and to transform it into a higher state than before. Let us for the moment apply this idea to cultural evolution. Suppose that a given human population or society possesses the cultural means to extract energy from coal and oil, that is, fossil fuels. This yields a certain energy potential and adaptive capacity. Now suppose that this same society either combines existing elements from its own culture or borrows them from without and comes up with electrical or atomic energy. This then gives them an additional as well as a more efficient energy resource. And in turn it provides the means for the control over many other societal problems which were before not subject to control. The net result is an increase in the division of labor of the society, that is, specialization and its concomitant increase in organizational efficiency. Obviously, not every increase in the division of labor in a particular organization results in improved organizational activity or adaptation. Our generalization is not in respect to any concrete corporation or group, but to the overall cultural system of a population. And yet, the generalization also has a certain degree of validity for subunits within a given society. For example, General Motors Corporation can solve both scientific and engineering problems which no local car dealer could even undertake. The point is: As a greater amount of human knowledge is harnessed by coordinating and integrating the efforts of a greater number of specialized people, the result is to *increase problem-solving power*.

To summarize: (1) The interaction of the processes of invention and diffusion provides the *source* for the increase in the cultural potentiality of a population. (2) The application of the results of invention to improve the social organization of a society or population is the principal means for the *release* of the biological potentialities of the population. An example of the latter would be the changing of the economic organization of a society from a focus on agricultural activities to one focused on industrial organization.

Before we begin the detailed discussion of the relationships of experience to the release of potentialities, we should first make clear the meaning we wish to imply by the concept of biological potentiality. To this end we now turn our attention.

2. BIOLOGICAL POTENTIALITIES

A full treatment of the meaning of biological potentialities would require a semester course or two in genetics. Obviously, an effort to accomplish such by a section in one chapter is hazardous, to say the least. There are so many mistaken and erroneous notions about genetics among the general public and also among most college students that some specification of the interrelations of genetics and behavior is necessary.

Let us begin by considering some of the elements of genetics.

The Elements of Genetics: Introduction

The modern theory of biological inheritance is generally labeled the gene-chromosome theory. In this section we will summarize some of the fundamental concepts of the theory.

The gene hypothesis was formulated in biology in order to explain the persistence of certain well-defined characteristics through two to three generations. It was first confirmed by a series of experiments conducted by Gregor Mendel (1822-1884). His experiments consisted of crossing different varieties of garden peas and observing the distribution of the characteristics of the parental varieties among the hybrid offspring. The results of these experiments were published in 1865. However, Mendel did not label the hereditary determiners *genes*. This name was given the units which control heredity by the Danish geneticist Wilhelm Johannsen some years after Mendel's death.

The fundamental idea which Mendel formulated was that inheritable characteristics are transferred from parent to offspring indirectly through genes, which segregate into the germ cells (reproductive cells) according to certain laws which we shall mention later. Thomas Hunt Morgan, an American, later showed that these genes were localized in the chromosomes of the cell nucleus, each gene occupying a specific position on a specific chromosome.

We are concerned with providing a genetic perspective which will help the reader understand our later analysis of the effects of experience on behavior.

The Elements of Genetics: Some Basic Concepts

We shall turn now to a discussion of the elements of genetics.

Human beings normally possess twenty-three *pairs* of chromosomes located in the nucleus of human somatic cells. Of these pairs *one* is called the *sex* chromosome and is designated X and Y and the remaining twenty-two pairs are called *autosomes*. Autosomes are those chromosomes which are alike in females *and* in males. The twenty-two pairs of autosomes are designated in order of size from the largest, or pair number one, to the smallest pair or number twenty-two. The two members of an autosome pair are the same length and are made of the same genetic material. Therefore they are said to be *homologous* to each other. The pair of sex chromosomes is heteromorphic, the X being approximately five times as long as the Y.

In the case of human beings each individual by means of fertilization receives *two* sets of twenty-three different kinds of chromosomes, one set with the egg from the mother, the other set with the sperm from the father. Therefore, all cells derived from a fertilized egg or *zygote* contain two sets of twenty-three chromosomes or a total of forty-six chromosomes. It was thought, until recently, that the human being possessed two sets of twenty-four (or forty-eight) chromosomes, but improved counting techniques have shown that there is a total of forty-six instead of forty-eight.

The single egg cell cleaves by repeated division into consecutively two, four, eight, sixteen, and so on, more cells. Biologists have shown that the cytoplasm (protoplasm) of the original unfertilized egg is not identical in all parts of the egg. Therefore the cleavage of the egg, which separates its different areas by breaking up into different cells, leads to a *differentiation* of the cytoplasmic contents of the cells. This results in identical genes being present in the nucleus of each cell and the nucleus being surrounded by different cytoplasmic environments. This raises the question of whether differential cellular substance affects genic action. This question is raised here only to call attention to the fact that the term "environment" is a very relative and expansive term. In other words, the environmental context is relative to the process under consideration. In the first stages of genic action the nucleus of the cell is environment to the chromosomes, and the cytoplasm is environment to the nucleus, and the other cells are environment to each other and so on to the social environment of man, which provides nutritional and health supports and/or interferences. Thus man's environment consists of a series of interlocking materials and processes.

Somatic Cells and Germ Cells. The somatic cells make up the tissue and organs of the body. The germ cells are formed in the gonads (testis and ovary). The somatic cells which make up the body house the germ or sex cells. The germ cells provide the basis for reproduction and give rise to new individuals and of course the soma cells of a given individual cease with death. While the genes are present in every body cell, they are also present in the reproductive cells; but it is the reproductive cells which transmit the hereditary characteristics.

In somatic cell division each chromosome separates lengthwise into two separate halves forming two daughter cells with the same content and forty-six chromosomes, like the mother cell. This type of cell division is purely multiplicative in nature and is called *mitosis*. It increases the number of cells without changing the chromosomal number or content. This type of cell division does not concern us and will not be discussed further.

The germ cells (sperms and eggs) are produced in a different and more complicated manner. Since the basis of heredity is determined through the functioning of the germ cells, we shall focus on the cell division of the reproductive cells. In the gonads a mother cell with twenty-three pairs of chromosomes goes through a dividing process by which the daughter cells (sperms or eggs) receive only *one* member of each pair of the chromosomes. This type of cell division is known as *meiosis*.[5]

Briefly each sex cell, male or female, goes through a maturation period

[5] A detailed description of this process is uncalled for here. For the student who is interested in the details of the process he should read a *recent* introductory textbook on genetics.

before it is ready for fertilization. During this maturation period the chromosomes join in pairs, a process called *synapsis*. Then the chromosomes of each pair split lengthwise so that each synaptic pair now forms a synaptic group of four chromosomes known as a *tetrad*. The tetrads then separate into two *dyads* each consisting of two chromosomes. This in essence completes the first division of the meiotic process. In the second or final meiotic division each dyad divides and goes to a different daughter cell, so that each mature reproductive cell or gamete has only twenty-three single chromosomes without their corresponding partners. The fact that the partners of each pair separate independently of the other pairs is known as *independent assortment*. Hence, for any given mother cell, there are 2^{23} or 8,388,608 equally possible types of germ cells as far as whole chromosomes are concerned. However, this large number of possibilities is only part of the picture since it ignores the exchange process which earlier occurs during synapsis.

To summarize: The reproductive cells are produced in the gonads. In the gonads during the formation of germ cells a mother cell with twenty-three pairs of chromosomes goes through a dividing process by which the daughter cells (sperms or eggs) receive only one member of each pair of the chromosomes. This type of cell division was called (reduction division) meiosis. Thus the segregation of the genes into the germ cells is explained by the segregation of the chromosomes during meiosis. This genic segregation results in each gamete receiving one complete set of genes. Each sperm or egg has a set of twenty-three *single* chromosomes. However, when a sperm fertilizes an egg, the resulting zygote then has twenty-three pairs of chromosomes. A reproductive or germ cell with one set of twenty-three chromosomes is called a *haploid* set. An individual resulting from the union of two germ cells has two sets of chromosomes and is said to be *diploid*. Thus a halving process (meiosis) precedes a union process (fertilization). The number of chromosomes remains constant throughout generations, but the genes and chromosomes are thoroughly randomized or shuffled in each generation. Since after synapsis there are twenty-three pairs of chromosomes, there are 2^{23} or over eight million gametes in each sex; and, since these combine at random at fertilization, the possible number of different types of zygotes from one parental pair is astronomical.

The genetic potentialities fuse in the fertilization process with the formation of a zygote. The development of the zygote into an embryo and later into a fetus and then an infant and finally an adult involves a delicate process of interaction between nature and nurture. One of the clearest formulations of the problem of the interrelation of heredity and environment was initially made by the Danish geneticist Wilhelm Johannsen. Johannsen stated that the genotype plus the environment makes the phenotype or the individual. Let us examine in detail the meaning of the foregoing statement.

Genotypes and Phenotypes. The term genotype refers to the genetic constitution of the individual. The genes through their molecular structure and functioning serve as the mechanisms of heredity. The detailed structure and composition of the gene in terms of some of its currently identified molecules like *DNA* (deoxyribonucleic acid) and *RNA* (ribonucleic acid) need not concern us.[6] Recent experiments clearly show that the gene is a structure which is composed of smaller structures and therefore the ultimate unit of genetic organization consists of some subunits of the gene. Nevertheless, we shall speak of the gene, for purposes at hand, as if it were the basic unit on the chromosome. We can do this since our concern is not with the molecular and cytologic functioning of the genes and chromosomes. Our concern is to provide an elementary genetic perspective which will help the reader understand and prevent misinterpretation of the later analysis of the effects of experience on behavior.

Returning now to the concept of genotype which is defined as the fundamental hereditary constitution, or gene complex, of an organism, let us take a closer look at its functioning.

It is presumed that the genotype of a person is relatively constant throughout one's lifetime. Let us concentrate on one pair of genes in order to more clearly illustrate the role of genotypes. It was earlier shown that each individual by fertilization receives two sets of chromosomes—one set from the egg and the other set from the sperm. All cells derived from the fertilized egg contain two sets of genes, each gene of one set having its counterpart, its so-called *allele,* in the other set. Every gene has a certain location or *locus* on a chromosome. Conceiving of a pair of genes as consisting of two alternate forms of the gene of the locus under consideration, then we can designate one as A and the other as A'. That means that the form A gene has a certain effect (say, normal pigmentation) and the form A' has a different effect (say, lack of pigmentation). The two alternate forms of the gene, A and A', are called the *alleles* of this particular chromosome locus. Assuming that A is located on chromosome 1 and A' on chromosome 1', then the transmission of these genes from parent to offspring follows the rules of chromosome transmission.

Given the two alternate gene forms A and A', an individual may assume one of three possible types with respect to this gene locus. These types are AA, AA', or A'A'. These are the *genotypes* of individuals with

[6] For the student who has had some chemistry and is interested in this a good source is Bernard S. Strauss, *An Outline of Chemical Genetics* (Philadelphia, W. B. Saunders Co., 1960).

respect to this locus. The types AA and A'A' are called *homozygotes*, because the two member genes are of the same form. The genotype AA' is a heterozygote.

Assuming that each gene form or allele has a separate and distinguishable effect independent of that of the other allele, then there will be three distinguishable types of individuals. For example, AA individuals would all have normal pigmentation, while the A'A' individuals would all have abnormal pigmentation. The offspring of AA' individuals when married to each other would have a percent who would be normal and a percent who would be abnormal. These percents may be equal though not necessarily. The percentage of AA' type offspring in a population would depend upon the relative frequency of the A and A' genes in the population. The individuals produced by these three genotypes are the three *phenotypes* corresponding to the three genotypes.

Phenotypically speaking, it often happens that the heterozygote AA' is indistinguishable from the homozygote AA. When this occurs, it means that the allele A is *dominant* over A', or A' is *recessive* to A. In this case, AA and AA' will be of one phenotype and A'A' of another, and in such a case, there are only two phenotypes. When there is dominance, the capital letter A is used to denote the dominant allele and the lower case *a* to designate the recessive allele.

Each of the three genotypes AA, A*a*, *aa* may be a male or a female. We will not discuss the genetics of sex determination except to note the traditional interpretation given to the twenty-third pair of chromosomes, the X and Y pair. Males and females all have twenty-two pairs of autosomes, but they differ in the X, Y pair. An individual with two X-chromosomes (denoted by XX) is a female; XY indicates a male. In the female all her eggs will contain an X, hence the female is *homogametic*, that is, all the gametes are of one type. Since the male is the XY type, half of his sperm will contain an X and half a Y; thus the male is *heterogametic*. When an X sperm fertilizes an X egg, the child will be a female; when a Y sperm fertilizes an X egg, the child will be a male, XY. The average result is approximately half boys and half girls. Since the egg is uniformly X-carrying and the sperm are of two types, it is the sperm that determines the sex of a child. Figure 4:1 below is a photograph of the 23 pairs of human chromosomes.

The actual process of sex determination is far more complex than the foregoing implies. For example, maleness and femaleness do not always follow the traditional XX and XY relationships. Individuals may have a Y-chromosome and two X-chromosomes and be normal females provided they have two sets of autosomes.[7]

Returning now to the matter of dominant and recessive genes: The fact that a certain type gene is dominant means that any two allelic genes

---

[7] For a detailed discussion of sex determination see Theodosius Dobzhansky, *Evolution, Genetics and Man* (New York, John Wiley & Sons, Inc., 1955), pp. 261-268.

RELEASE OF HUMAN POTENTIALITIES

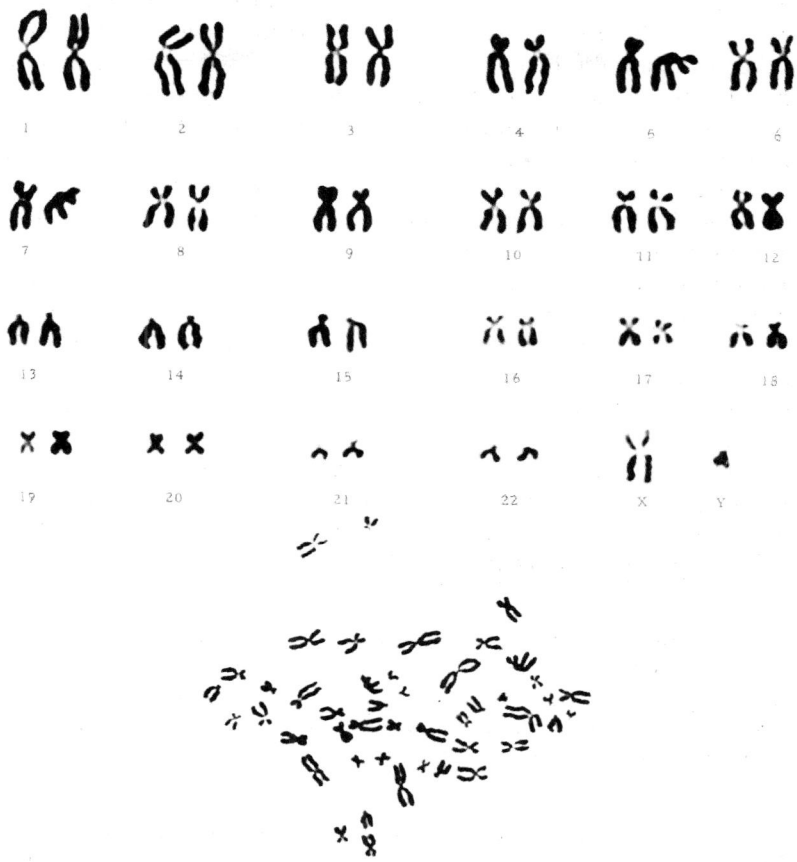

FIGURE 4:1. Normal Karyotype. (Wrights Stain. x 1950)

which a child receives from its two parents do not express themselves equally. If a child has received the gene A for brown eyes from one of the parents and the gene *a* for blue eyes from the other, the genotype of the child with regard to eye color will be A*a*. Such a child will have brown eyes because the gene for brown eyes is dominant over the gene for blue eyes. Brown-eyed people of the genetic constitution AA and A*a* look alike. They are "phenotypically" the same with respect to eye color. Nevertheless, the A*a* type can produce a blue-eyed offspring, namely by mating with a blue-eyed *aa*, or a brown-eyed A*a* partner.

In spite of the fact that we have linked single genes to specific characteristics such as eyes or eye color, this is an oversimplification. The student will find in any textbook on genetics that there exists no simple connection between most observable characters of a human being and a single gene. Most characters come about by the complex interaction of a number of genes and the cytoplasmic environment of the chromosomes. For example, there is no gene for the eye or for even a part of the eye. In other words, there is no one-to-one relationship between genetic units in the chromosomes and the different tissues and organs of the individual. Genic functioning is dependent upon the biochemical and physiological environments, and these are also dependent upon the genotype. Thus there always exists a delicate balancing of genetic qualities with environmental factors and conditions. Consequently, it is meaningless to speak of whether the genotype or the environment is more important in the formation of the phenotype. There is no organism without a genotype, and there is no organism without an environment to sustain it. The question is: What are the interacting effects of given genotypes in given enviroments?

It is probably correct to say that the genotype sets the developmental limits in the sense of the potentialities of the organism. More specifically, we might best express the situation by saying that the genotype provides the biological potentialities, and the environment the opportunities—for good or bad. The following quotation from Dobzhansky and Holz expresses more precisely what we wish to say:

> Genes produce not characters but physiological states which, through interactions with the physiological states induced by all other genes of the organism and with the environmental influences, cause the development to assume a definite course and the individual to display certain characters at a given stage of the developmental process.[8]

This section is ended with the conclusion that potentialities are genetically determined, but their release, in whatever degree, is a function of the stimulation and engagement of the biochemical and physiological functioning of the organism with its environment. In the case of man we are particularly interested in the interaction of human potentialities with the sociocultural environment. For example, even the human eye will be blind unless it is stimulated adequately by light waves, and the human personality as ordinarily understood cannot develop and does not even exist apart from society.[9]

---

[8] T. Dobzhansky and A. M. Holz, "A Re-Examination of the Problem of Manifold Effects of Genes in *Drosophila Melanogaster*," *Genetics*, Vol. 28 (1943), p. 301.

[9] See Kingsley Davis, "Extreme Social Isolation of a Child," *American Journal of Sociology*, Vol. 45 (January, 1940), pp. 554-564; and by the same author, "Final Note on a Case of Extreme Isolation," *ibid.*, Vol. 50 (March, 1947), pp. 432-437.

We have briefly surveyed the concept of biological potentialities and indicated that these are released and developed through their interaction with environmental forces and in the case of man primarily sociocultural forces. Therefore, it follows that the extent and degree of release of biological potentialities is not only a function of the amount of the biological potentialities which exist but also a function of the quality and quantity of sociocultural stimulation.

Assuming that the *proportion* of people with very great ability is roughly the same from generation to generation, then the absolute number of people with great ability is, of course, a function of the size of the total population of a society. As the population increases (and it increases geometrically), then the absolute number of very able people would concomitantly increase. One would expect very few cultural giants, other conditions being equal, in a small population, but in a population of several millions there may be a large number. It follows that the larger the number of cultural giants or geniuses, the greater the probability of their interacting with one another and the likelihood of invention or cultural contributions occurring is increased by the impact of great minds on other great minds. As an interesting exercise the student might wish to make a hypothetical comparison of the social organization of a community of geniuses with a community having a normal distribution of abilities and skills. What differences would there be in problems relating to the division of labor, social control, and deviant behavior?

The significant point to be emphasized is the *joint* functioning of biological and sociological factors. It makes no difference how high the quantity and quality of biological potentiality; these potentialities cannot unfold or develop without stimulation from outside forces. Likewise, if adequate biological potentialities are not present, it makes no difference how ideal or efficient are the sociocultural forces, since no amount of stimulation can produce development beyond the potential of the organism. Thus again it is clear that it is futile to think of heredity and environment in terms of which is the more important. Both are necessary and the research problem is to determine the interrelations and joint functioning.

Since a person's environment, particularly human social organization, can be changed during one's lifetime, but one's genetic potentiality cannot, then it is feasible to focus on means of improving the social organization as a means to more efficiently releasing and transforming one's biological potentialities into manifest characteristics. This raises the important question of the meaning of cultural potentiality and the conditions under which cultural change occurs. We turn next to a consideration of this question.

3. CULTURAL POTENTIALITIES

INTRODUCTION

We have already shown that man is a product of two interacting kinds of evolution, biological and cultural. The latter has also come to be an important determinant of natural selection.

Hudson Hoagland has pointed out that

> There is a suggestive analogy between biological evolution through mutations of genes, on the one hand, and social evolution through novel ideas, on the other. For example, a creative scientist is one who has many ideas and who is free to test and develop them. Many of these he discards as worthless, but some withstand the rigor of experimental testing and may constitute valuable advances.[10]

For a good idea to actually lead to social advancement in a society, it must be communicated to other members of the society and become a part of the society's social organization. In this regard Hoagland says:

> There is environmental selectivity to favor not only the rare gene mutation responsible for biological progress, but also social environmental selectivity to favor new ideas contributing to social progress. Like mutant genes, an idea may be before its time—that is, the social climate may not be right for its acceptance.
>
> Many ideas are harmful and may even be lethal to the individual and to society, especially when they become institutionalized. Here one might mention as examples the institutions of slavery, of ritual human sacrifice, of racism, of Nazism and other rigid authoritarian political systems, including various forms of chauvinistic nationalism. Just as mutant genes may be lethal for a species and lead to its extinction, so ideas in the minds of men may produce a catastrophe, such as a nuclear war, which could in time, if the arms race continues, be lethal to the human species. The nation-state is a relatively recent social invention, and its primary function has been to give security to its nationals. It became obsolete in 1945 with the advent of nuclear weapons, although few people are aware that this has happened. If its sovereignty continues to be uncontrolled by enforceable supranational law, it may, in our post-1945 environment containing nuclear weapons, produce its own destruction, along with widespread genocide. Thus, ideas and the institutions they generate may be considered related to social evolution as genes and their phenotypes are related to biological evolution, and selective processes operate upon both. Societies are built by ideas, and, within limits, the more new ideas there are competing with each other for social acceptance, the more effective social evolution is likely to be. Free-

---

[10] Hudson Hoagland, "Science and the New Humanism," *Science*, Vol. 143, No. 3602 (January 10, 1964), p. 111.

dom of individuals to express and develop many ideas is necessary for progress in social evolution, just as mutations must be screened by natural selection for the development of an improved or a new species of plant or animal. In the case of social evolution the impact of ideas is measurable in years or at least in centuries, while in biological evolution the time scale for mutant genes to establish new forms is measurable in millions of years.[11]

The genetic structure of an organism sets the potential limits to behavior. The visual capacity of the hawk, for example, is greater than that of any man. This difference in visual capacity is due to a difference in genetic structure. The potential limit of a species changes as the genetic structure changes, and we have already learned that change in the genetic structure is a function of genetic mutation and the reshuffling of the genes by independent assortment from generation to generation.

Thus far we have spoken only of physical or *potential limits* to behavior. We have not said anything about central tendencies and the upper and lower limits about these for *actual* behavior. It is here assumed that the behavioral performance of an organism, and in this case man, never exactly equals his potential. In other words, it is assumed that the potential energy of the human being exceeds in varying degrees his consumed energy. At this stage of our knowledge, the potential behavioral capacity of a person is only a hypothetical construct. That is, we cannot, as of now, specify its properties so that they can be observed and measured.

However, it is known that the *demonstrated* behavioral performance limits of individuals and populations do change through time and experience. Some of the changes in actual performance levels are almost fantastically large and they occur off and on over large parts of a person's lifetime. To be sure, they slow down with aging and in time even begin to decline with age. The point is that one of the major sources of evidence for assuming that behavioral potential always exceeds performance is the fact that performance levels of persons can be significantly changed by practice and experience.

We can better appreciate what is meant here by the phrase "release of potentialities" if we think of the following example. Suppose a woman among the Arunta (or Aranda) natives of Australia gives birth to identical twin boys and that she keeps one and rears it in the Arunta culture, and the other twin is taken immediately to the United States and reared in an ideal family situation. Assuming that each child possesses average or above average biological potentiality, then what difference could be expected by the time each is of age twenty? This, of course, assumes that both live to this age; and this is much less likely for the one who remains in the Arunta culture. The differences in the behavior

[11] *Ibid.,* pp. 111-112.

patterns would reflect what we mean by release of potentialities. The Arunta-reared boy could probably count to five or six and his American brother would know some calculus. On the other hand, the Arunta-reared brother could perform hunting feats that his American-reared twin could not. Thus we see that biological potentialities in man are general in nature and the demands of culture and social organization of the society largely determine the specific behavior patterns and skills which the individual acquires.

The second source of evidence which supports the proposition that development is less than its potential is the fact that the performance levels of *populations* change through time. For example, athletes used to aspire to reach the four-minute mile. This limit has now been broken by several people. The new aspiration is to run a mile in three minutes and fifty seconds and in time this will be accomplished, thus establishing still a newer level. It is also a matter of historical observation that persons of ordinary ability in any current generation can perform tasks which in some instances not even the most extraordinary person in generations of the past could do. Since such significant changes in the levels of performance can and do occur *within* the life span of a particular generation, then the change in level would have to be a function of nonbiological factors, since no significant biological changes had occurred.

What are these nonbiological changes which affect changes in human performance levels? They are changes in the culture of a society which provide the general knowledge and skills which in turn determine performance level in conjunction with a person's motivation and ability to learn. In other words, they are cultural means for releasing unreached biological potentialities.

For example, the achievement of such a physiological feat as running a mile in less than four minutes was aided and made possible by improved knowledge of nutrition, methods of physical conditioning, and conserving and timing of energy release. This statement does not detract from the importance of the runner's genetic potentialities. The new speed record could not have been achieved had the physical potential not been there, but neither would the potential have become manifest without new cultural means for conditioning and transforming it into behavior. The foregoing discussion allows us to state a very important conclusion. *Biological potentialities consist of physiological states which are genetically determined, but the transformation of these physiological states into behavioral characteristics is a function of social and cultural conditioning.* It follows from this that significant change in the performance level of members of a group or a society depends upon the development of new knowledge or cultural change and the correct application of this by the members concerned. It may be that such knowledge already exists. If so, then the problem becomes one of disseminating it and training the members who need it. Assuming that the required knowledge does not exist, then the problem becomes one of deriving *new* knowledge and perfecting its development and means of application. This raises the question of the meaning of cultural potentiality and the conditions which affect its change.

Service's "Law of Evolutionary Potential" of a Culture

In Part I of this chapter it was shown in some detail that general evolution provided a better possibility for adaptation and survival under conditions of change than specific evolution. The reason for this is that general evolution provides a high probability for the emergence of new types; in other words, it allows for species "radiation." This radiation of types increases the probability that one of the types will possess characteristics which meet the demands of the changed environment. Thus general evolution results in higher forms of life which exhibit greater "all-around" adaptability.

Julian Huxley has stated the preceding idea as follows: " 'the further a trend toward specialization has proceeded, the deeper will be the biological groove in which [the species] has thus entrenched itself.' " [12] Or again " 'there is no certain case on record of a line showing a high degree of specialization giving rise to a new type. All new types which themselves are capable of adaptive radiation seem to have been produced by relatively unspecialized ancestral lines.' " [13]

Thus Huxley is saying that the more biologically specialized a species becomes, the more this decreases its potential for adaptation to a significantly changed environment. What is the point of Huxley's idea in regard to cultural evolution? The point is that his notion of increased biological specialization and its concomitant reduction of overall adaptability is also helpful in understanding aspects of cultural evolution.

This particular similarity between biological evolution and cultural change or evolution has been suggested by other writers as long as a half century and more ago.[14]

Let us examine more closely the applicability to cultural evolution of what Huxley was talking about. First, he says that the more biologically specialized a species becomes, the less its chances of giving rise to a new type and hence its reduced potential for increasing its general adaptability. The converse of this is also true; namely, that the new types

---

[12] Sahlins and Service, *op. cit.*, p. 96, quoting Julian S. Huxley, *Evolution: The Modern Synthesis* (New York, Harper & Row, Publishers, Inc., 1943), p. 500.

[13] *Ibid.*, p. 562.

[14] For example, Thorstein Veblen, Lewis H. Morgan, and Leon Trotsky each noted the tendency of so-called backward societies to skip over whole stages of development by borrowing from the culture of some advanced society.

that have been produced which have shown improved general adaptability have been produced by relatively unspecialized types.

These ideas apply in regard to culture and have been applied in the following way. *First*, it has been noted that a society which is less highly developed has more potentiality for subsequent development than a more highly developed society. By this it is meant that a backward society may borrow the best ideas from several more advanced societies, combine these ideas in new ways so as to advance at a faster rate than the currently most advanced societies, and, as a consequence, leapfrog *ahead* of the currently most advanced of these societies. The point is that the more backward society is more motivated to experiment with change and to seek change than is the more advanced society.

Secondly, the converse of this is also true; namely, the more advanced a society is and the more it occupies the pinnacle of power among societies, the less potentiality it has for growth and change.

The reasons for the above two conditions are very interesting; we will at this point note only a few, but will discuss them more fully later. Just now we will examine the reasons for the highly limiting potential for change of the most advanced society at a given point in time. *One* of the major reasons derives from the great efficiency of the existing modes or ways of doing things. The fact that existing practices work and work well serves to "blind" the users to the possibility of alternative means which might work better. The utility of the present method may be such as to preclude any motivation for even pondering the possibility of alternatives. A *second* reason derives from the number of different uses which a cultural element or system comes to have. For example, our number system which uses the base ten is so intricately involved as a part of household finance, industry, and business that this fabric of cultural grooves constitutes a virtual web from which it is almost, if not actually, impossible to wholly escape. To be sure, some highly specialized people can use other-based systems, such as the binary system, but they have to do so within the framework of their own operations because to do otherwise would assume that others also used their system. A rather humorous recent example of resistance to change is afforded by the group which tried to organize against the telephone company to prevent their utilizing the more flexible number switchboard designations instead of letters. Among the arguments given was one which contended that the assignment of numbers in lieu of the letters previously used "dehumanized man!" Just how the assignment of a number rather than a letter affected anything other than habit is not known. This is an example of what one would call an irrational reaction to change.

A *third* factor which limits the potential for cultural and social change in an advanced society which occupies the pinnacle of power or enjoys its protection might be indicated by the question: "Where do you go from the top?" Under such conditions there is a great tendency for complacency, and this is probably related to the difficulty in setting goals which are beyond where anyone has ever been. The current American-Russian so-called moon race appears to be a case in point. That is, most Americans, and probably Russians also, have a difficult time visualizing what it is all about. This is quite different from a society's setting production goals which are based on goals already achieved by some other national competitor. It is difficult to keep running at a hard pace when one thinks he has won the race. Instead, the tendency is to try to stabilize and coast on one's previous success. The deception lies in a society's time perspective in regard to the notion of winning—that is, one may be a winner today and a loser tomorrow.

Let us now take a brief look at some of the reasons for the greater potential of a relatively backward society for cultural evolution.

First, there is the matter of goals. Societies which are behind in their development relative to the technological achievements of other societies have the accomplishment of the more advanced societies as goal targets. Thus the achievements of a more advanced society may serve to stimulate the efforts of others. This kind of goal-structuring occurs *within* a society as well as between societies. For example, the various states within the United States compare their achievements and failures with those of other states. Often the leaders of a particular state will use the relatively low position of their state in some area, say education, as a means of encouraging the people of the state to make the necessary sacrifices to permit improvement.

Secondly, a society which is backward or behind relative to some societies has by this very fact a powerful incentive to attain new ideas for speeding its development. It is particularly not embarrassed by the thought of importing ideas from other societies. Thus, for example, a society whose agricultural system is based on primitive conceptions and techniques may skip a whole series of stages which were gone through by the societies which currently have the most advanced agricultural systems. Such bursts of development can and do occur because it is possible for one society to extract or import the best ideas available from a number of societies and combine these into new and still more advanced forms. This explanation for the growth potential of backward societies was initially most explicitly formulated by Leon Trotsky and he labeled it the *Law of Combined Development.*[15] Trotsky emphasized the great potentiality for rapid change and growth of backward societies and pointed to the process of the diffusion of ideas from an advanced society to a backward society as the principal means by which a less advanced society can skip certain historic stages which the advanced

---

[15] Sahlins and Service, *op. cit.,* p. 100.

society from which they imported the ideas went through. Thus the emphasis on diffusion calls attention to an important aspect of the evolutionary process in culture which does not have a similar counterpart in biological evolution.[16] It is the relative lack of constraint in regard to the adoption of new ideas and the freedom to combine these in new and novel patterns which enable less advanced societies to oftentimes forge ahead of advanced ones.

We are now in position to summarize all we have said regarding the evolutionary potential of a culture by quoting Service's *Law of Evolutionary Potential*, which says: The more specialized and adapted a form in a given evolutionary stage, the smaller is its potential for passing to the next stage. Another way of putting it which is more succinct and more in conformity with Part I of this chapter is: Specific evolutionary progress is inversely related to general evolutionary potential.[17]

The essence of Service's "Law" is that general evolution is not linear. That is to say that the improvement in the *general* adaptability of a culture does not continue at the same rate through time. Service calls this aspect of his general law of potential the *phylogenetic discontinuity of progress*. In other words, an advanced form of culture does not normally produce the next stage of advance; the next most advanced stage normally begins in a different line. Service also states an obvious corollary to the foregoing form of discontinuity. He calls it the *Local Discontinuity of Progress*. That is, since species tend to occupy a given territory continuously and if successive stages of advance in general cultural forms are not likely to go from one culture to its descendants, then *successive* stages of progress are not likely to occur in the same locality.

Service points out that while no one before had explicitly formulated these laws, Veblen and Trotsky had employed similar ideas.

> Veblen's analysis of Imperial Germany makes considerable use of two ideas reminiscent of the above discussion. One is that Germany became more efficient industrially than her predecessor, England, because of "the merits of borrowing"; the other is that England, conversely, was finally less efficient than Germany because of "the penalty of taking the lead." Later, Trotsky, in his *History of the Russian Revolution* formulated the idea somewhat more aptly. He used one particularly luminous phrase: "the privilege of historic backwardness." In the context of his discussion this means that an "underdeveloped" civilization has certain evolutionary potentials that an advanced one lacks.[18]

[16] *Ibid.*, p. 100.
[17] *Ibid.*, p. 97.
[18] *Ibid.*, p. 99.

RELEASE OF HUMAN POTENTIALITIES

In this regard, Professor Service quotes Trotsky as follows:

> Although compelled to follow after the advanced countries, a backward country does not take things in the same order. The privilege of historic backwardness—and such a privilege exists—permits, or rather compels, the adoption of whatever is ready in advance of any specified date, skipping a whole series of intermediate stages.[19]

In regard to existing economic and technical resources an advanced country has a greater potentiality for the development of new forms than a less advanced society, but the point is that throughout history such societies have not *continued* to achieve to the limit or near limit of their economic and technical capacity and as a consequence of "underachievement"[20] have fallen behind other one-time less advanced societies. Thus the explanation of the lack of evolutionary potentiality of an advanced society seems to depend to a significant extent upon the factors and conditions which explain "underachievement."

Odum saw underachievement as one of the central characteristics and problems of an advanced industrial society. He contended that the great complexity of a highly advanced society tends to generate such a multiplicity of goals that overall progress is slowed by the inability of even the most advanced society to simultaneously develop an increasingly great number of goals. A backward society does not have the problem of developing at the same time a large number of goals. Such societies may objectively have a great number of needs, but they do not have formulated a large number of goals; therefore, they can concentrate on a very few national goals at a given time, and, in time, forge ahead in special areas of even the most advanced societies. Russia decided after World War II to concentrate on heavy rockets and as a consequence developed for awhile a superior technology to the United States in the fields of rocket propulsion and space satellites.

In fact, it seems that the less advanced societies seem to concentrate their resources in the area of producing producer or capital goods and in the area of military production. Therefore, in time, they become military threats to the more advanced societies and hostilities grow. In regard to this point a fundamental question of all mankind arises. Would the less advanced societies be less militaristic and expansionist in national policy if the more advanced nations cooperated with the less advanced societies in making possible their maximum internal development? The current experience of the United Nations in Africa in aiding the de-

---

[19] *Ibid.*, pp. 99-100.
[20] Howard W. Odum, unpublished work memorandum, "Notes on the Changing Structure of Contemporary Society," November 12, 1948.

velopment of these underdeveloped nations seems to suggest an affirmative answer.[21] Certainly Red China's militaristic and expansionist policies today seem to be related to their efforts to advance economically and technically. At the same time, their aggressive behavior toward other nations is certainly not conducive to obtaining economic aid from these societies. Thus a vicious circle arises, namely, underdeveloped countries respond militarily to the greater competitive and containment powers of the more advanced nations, and the more advanced nations are then threatened by the military advances of the less advanced nations. Therefore, the real problem is how to bridge the period of transition of the less advanced nations.

One may ask if the militaristic and expansionist policies of advanced nations are not an exception to the foregoing generalization. For example, were not the Dutch, English, and Spanish wars of the sixteenth century an exception? Space will not permit a detailed answer, but instead of being an exception, these wars appear to be a special case of the above general rule regarding competition and conflict over the economic resources for development when a nation does not itself possess the necessary resources. Granted these societies were at that time considered advanced and relatively equally advanced. But each was pursuing a mercantilist policy of economic expansion. Hence, each was a competitor to the other, and there were no institutional systems in existence to regulate such competition between nations. There is still today a struggle for influence among the most advanced nations—for example, France, Germany, Britain, and the United States. But among these advanced nations there has developed a rudimentary common culture which provides the basis for general trust in each other's motives and this trust allows for the creation of such a relatively noncompetitive structure as the Common Market, that is, noncompetitive to the member nations.

Evolution, whether biological or cultural, has, as we have seen, an irregular but normal, as Service says, "leapfrog" effect which makes backward forms potentially more effective than advanced forms in the course of moving into a new form. But an advanced culture, like an advanced biological species, can and does exercise dominance over lower forms. This leads to conflict of which the recent world scene affords many examples. We have indicated several times before that each new evolutionary form, whether biological or cultural, is more complex than the preceding form. This evolving complexity has had an important effect on competition. If we look back in time at the development of human

---

[21] Obviously, one of the complicating factors to the maintenance of peace is the factor of the concentration of power in a society. If central power is concentrated in the hands of one or a few people who have no real checks on their actions, then they may become overambitious and reckless in their use of this power.

RELEASE OF HUMAN POTENTIALITIES

culture, we note that the earlier the form, the smaller the population unit associated with it and hence the cultural operations involved were on a smaller scale. For example, the beginnings of industrialization in Europe and the United States reflected a relatively simple technology, and the industrial units were small family operations.

Professor Service very aptly points out that there is an important connection between the amount of capital needed to finance an industrial undertaking and the type of organization necessary to obtain and administer the capital.[22] For example, the small structure of the basic industries in the early industrialization of the West made it easy for private financing. But there is no private source of funds in the United States or elsewhere which could have financed the T.V.A., the construction of atomic energy, current rocket programs, or education for the masses. Consequently, these enterprises were financed by pooling national resources through taxation.

It would perhaps have been possible for several major industries in the United States to have pooled their resources and produced atomic energy, but this would have eliminated competition as we know it and hence the only difference in this hypothetical collective endeavor and that which the federal government did would be the personnel who controlled the enterprise. This is an extremely important point, if we recall that highly specialized forms have a limited potential for the development of new forms. Thus we have the situation in the advanced technology of the United States where many of the cultural forms are too complex and expensive to be financed by private sources, but our commitment to an older form or means of financing makes it difficult for the acceptance of new means of organization which are compatible to the demands of the new era and as a consequence advancement is slowed except in times of crises.

Professor Service has expressed this same idea as follows:

> The new areas cannot industrialize with small beginnings, as did the West, and then proceed through the original stages of growth, creating capital in the process. They will begin with the latest and most advanced of the known technologies and attempt to create the complete industrial complex at once, skipping whole epochs of our development. This requires a huge capital investment. The economy, therefore, must be socialistic; the government rather than private persons provides most of the capital by necessity. It also means that if capital is not otherwise available to the government it must be extracted from the subsistence-oriented peasantry, as happened first in Russia and is now happening in China. The significance of this situation is that the extraction of capital must be forced. This is the most important *internal* cause of the police state, of despotic government.[23]

[22] Sahlins and Service, *op. cit.*, p. 114.
[23] *Ibid.*, pp. 115-116.

In a sense this is the penalty which these societies have had to pay for late industrialization. England, for example, which was the earliest country to industrialize, was able to obtain much of her needed surplus capital by a colonial policy of mercantilism. In a very real sense the satellite countries of the Soviet Union serve the industrialization of the Soviet Union in a similar way.

The law of evolutionary potential which states that a highly advanced and specialized type of culture has less evolutionary potential than a less advanced culture does *not* mean that an advanced society must necessarily fall behind. It simply means that it will fall behind unless it overcomes the conditions which control its reduced potential. If it does not fall behind, then it will prove an exception to the principle and the exception will then become the problem to explain. The laws of gravity explain the anchorage of man to the earth, but this does not prevent man from developing principles of aerodynamics to control gravitational forces and soar into outer space. The point is: If man is to control the effects of gravity on his efforts to fly, then he must develop the principles which would enable him to manipulate the interfering effects of gravity. Likewise, if an advanced society is to control its loss of evolutionary potential to develop new forms, then it must develop the necessary principles to manipulate this potential. For example, potential consumption in the United States is manipulated by creating consumer demand through advertising. This is planned consumer demand. This manipulation is based on the insatiability of human appetites and the infinitude of human aspiration.

Technically speaking, Service's Law is more a statement of an empirical relationship. That is to say, it describes an observation to the effect that the "more specialized and adapted a form in a given evolutionary stage, the smaller is its potential for passing to the next stage," but it does not contain an explanation of this relationship. What we have done in the last few pages is to provide a theoretical interpretation to Service's Law. We will now summarize this interpretation.

Let us look first at the theoretical reasons for the limited potentiality for the development of new forms by a highly developed and specialized culture.

1. An advanced society, particularly one which occupies the pinnacle of power or enjoys such protection, has great difficulty in choosing long-range goals for its future development. The tendency is to be complacent with being at the top.

2. The success of the present system discourages experimentation with alternatives by blinding the users to the need to consider other methods.

3. In an advanced society the network of vested interests in the status quo and existing ways of solving problems will not react favorably to major change except in the fact of grave crises. This is one reason why

major changes can be made in such societies during great crises such as depressions or wars.

4. Advanced societies tend to generate a very great variety of goals and obviously the greater the number of goals to achieve, the slower the overall rate of advance. Hence one of the major problems of an advanced society is to select an optimum number of national goals to pursue at a given time at an optimum rate of speed. To phrase the idea differently: The great multiplicity and diversity of goals in an advanced society tend to slow the overall rate of achievement relative to less specialized societies unless the advanced society can solve the problem of selecting and focusing on major goals for the future.

Now to summarize the theoretical reasons for the great potentiality for the production of new cultural forms by a backward society.

1. The backward society has the achievements of the advanced societies as goal targets to surpass. Thus the backward society has its goals set for it.

2. Their strong motivation to improve and catch up makes it easy for them to import new ideas from many advanced societies and combine these ideas in their own way. With new combinations comes the possibility of producing new and more advanced forms.

3. The backward society can profit by the errors of the advanced societies and, by selective borrowing of ideas, skip whole stages which the advanced society went through.

We have purposely focused until now on the question of releasing *cultural potentialities* since it is principally through the process of cultural change that a society obtains the resources for releasing biological potentialities. Thus the overall improvement of the achievement or adaptation of a human population is dependent upon cultural evolution and the engagement of the members of the population in the results of this evolution.

The improvement of the average performance of a population relative to other populations is only one measure of improvement. This we will call phylogenetic cultural improvement. We can also look at the question of *individual* improvement in performance. After all, the ultimate test of a new cultural or social technique is the effect it has on an individual member of the population. This brings us to the important question of the relationships of experience and previous learning to subsequent adaptation, performance, and behavior in general.

4. THE RELEASE AND DEVELOPMENT OF INDIVIDUAL POTENTIALITIES

In Section 3 we dealt with the evolution of the cultural and social systems of man as a species. In this section we will be dealing with some effects of these systems on the development of the behavior of individuals. Hence our concern here is with phenotypes. It will be recalled that a set of genes provides the physical basis or potentiality for a given phenotype, but that the development of the phenotype necessitates the interaction of the organism with environmental factors and conditions. Thus the genotype sets biological limits to phenotypic variation. But "As Sinnott, Dunn, and Dobzhansky point out, however, it is impossible to know the entire range of possible phenotypic variation for any genotype because to know the entire range would require that the genotype would have to be exposed to not only all existing environments but also to all possible environments." [24] This principle of genetics says that, given a certain genotype, then its range of variation is determined by the range of environmental stimulation. Thus in respect to variability the environment is considered primary. This principle applies all the way from such sensory functions as vision to the expression of such complex skills and operations as mathematics, music, and art. Actually, this interaction between genes and environment applies at all levels of functioning.

When we talk about the relationship of experience to the development of behavior, we must be very clear about specifying the level of experience with which we are concerned in specifying a connection with development. The problem of delineating or fixing the level of experience in question is extremely complicated because the context of interacting factors is wide indeed and the separation of factor effects is extremely difficult.

Gerard says:

> The problem of fixing experience is universal; the mechanisms involved are highly particular. The mitotic dealing of genotypes and the environmental sieving of the resulting phenotypes, which helps produce species of well-adapted organisms, is patently different from the residues left by activity in neurons and synapses, which underlie learning and well-adapted behaviors. The formation of antibodies or adaptive enzymes at the molecular level is different from the differentiation of muscle or bone at the cellular level, the callousing or wrinkling of skin . . . at the organ level, the acquiring of percepts and skills and memories at the individual level, or the establishment of customs and edifices and languages at the social level. Yet even here some commonalties exist.[25]

[24] J. McV. Hunt, *Intelligence and Experience* (New York, copyright ©, 1961, The Ronald Press Company), p. 41, quoting E. W. Sinnott, L. C. Dunn, and T. Dobzhansky, *Principles of Genetics* (New York, McGraw-Hill Book Company, 1941), p. 331.

[25] Ralph W. Gerard, "Becoming: The Residue of Change," in Sol Tax, ed., *The Evolution of Man* (Chicago, The University of Chicago Press, 1960), pp. 255-256.

The title of Professor Gerard's chapter to which we have just referred describes very aptly the level and system of behavior to which we are now turning our attention. This title is "Becoming: The Residue of Change." It is through contact with environments and by means of the processes of learning and learning how to learn that man "becomes." And, in becoming, an internal behavior structure develops which comes to have a certain autonomy of its own, a continuity, but it also grows and changes. This is an aspect of the nature of all life.

Experience is fixated through learning, but learning is cumulative and this implies change, which in turn implies the expression of different responses to an identical stimulus.

Let us look now at some of the research on learning how to learn. Much of this kind of research has focused on the relationship between the development of intelligence and experience.

Intelligence and Experience

The sources of data for assessing the effects of varying degrees and kinds of stimulation upon the development of the IQ are: (1) from the studies of identical twins reared apart, (2) from studies of the effects of training upon performance by control and experimental groups, and (3) from repeated testing of the same subjects.

H. H. Newman assembled data on twenty pairs of identical twins reared apart.[26] Out of the twenty cases studied there were four pairs in which the differences in schooling between twins of a pair differed by more than a year or two. ". . . in each of these four cases the better educated twin had a distinctly higher rating on *all* the tests." [27]

The difference in IQ among the four pairs with more than two years' difference in education between the members of a pair was 24, 19, 17, and 15 points. In the remaining sixteen cases of separated twins, in which the differences in education were two years or less, they showed an average difference in IQ which was slightly less than that of one-egg twins reared together. Thus it appears that small differences in education do not significantly affect the development of ability, but large differences in education do significantly depress its development.

The fact that twins are reared separately does not mean that they will necessarily have significantly different IQ's. The important factor is the degree to which the different environments differ psychologically.

"In 1942, . . . Goodenough and Maurer reported individual growth-

---

[26] H. H. Newman, "How Differences in Environment Affected Separated One-Egg Twins," in Theodore H. Newcomb and Eugene Hartley, eds., *Readings in Social Psychology* (New York, Holt, Rinehart and Winston, Inc., 1947), pp. 1-6.
[27] *Ibid.*, p. 2.

curves in intelligence in which changes of from 20 to 50 points of IQ appeared during the course of nine years." [28] These changes are not always increases; they are sometimes decreases. Directors of custodial institutions in which life is monotonous and care is limited have reported as commonplace the contracting of the IQ year by year.

Professor Gardner Murphy reports a case in which he had personal knowledge and which is of interest because of his knowledge of the facts and because of the range of change in IQ over a period of ten years.[29] The boy first came to the attention of a clinical psychologist as a consequence of difficulties in nursery school. He had very little contact with other children except to occasionally engage in aggressive behavior toward them, and his intelligence appeared to be quite limited.

His life history revealed a mother who could not spare any time for him and who turned him over to a nurse for care. The nurse in turn did not want to be bothered with small children, especially troublesome ones, so she restricted her relations to impersonal handling of the boy.

The child's intelligence quotient was 65 at the time of first testing, and it was recommended that he be sent to an institution. This was not done and arrangements were made instead for psychiatric visits. After a while the child gradually developed confidence in himself and others, and he soon acquired warm friends and interesting activities to perform. Following this, Murphy reports that his IQ began to rise. "It went to 80. It went to 95. It went to 110. When last tested it was 150, and the child has made a good general adjustment, at the age of fourteen, after ten years of very attentive care." [30]

Obviously, this child had a high genetic potential, but his development of this potential had been thwarted by improper and inadequate environmental stimulation. The notion of genetic potential implies a limit beyond which development cannot go. Consequently, children cannot be pushed beyond their potential capacity. The point is that measured IQ or current performance attainments cannot be taken as reliable or valid measures of potential. In fact, they are not measures of potential at all. They are only rough indicators of the current development of these properties.

It is assumed that there is a set of genes which along with nutritional provisions and the environmental stimulation together determine the somatic cerebral structure and its physiological functioning. The quality of the cerebral structure and its functional properties are extremely important as physiological resources for behavior development. The evidence which we have already cited, and this hardly scratches the surface

---

[28] Hunt, *op. cit.*, p. 23.
[29] Gardner Murphy, *An Introduction to Psychology* (New York, Harper & Row, Publishers, Inc., 1951), pp. 352-354.
[30] *Ibid.*, p. 353.

of the data available, clearly shows that experience is also necessary for the development of behavior patterns, and especially for the development of those complex organizing- and information-processing skills so necessary for problem-solving activity.

Harlow in 1949 demonstrated how learning sets (learning how to learn) are acquired in monkeys.[31] He showed that in the beginning or early phases of a learning experiment problems were learned slowly by trial-and-error processes, but the learning of the solution to one problem facilitated the learning of the solution to other related problems so that in time the once slow and ineffective process became converted into an amazingly rapid and efficient process. This illustrates what we mean by the phrase "learning how to learn." It also suggests the great importance of *what* is learned. That is, if the strategies learned are inefficient strategies, then the performance by the subjects will be poor. This suggests that if two subjects are of equal genetic ability and motivation, but one has acquired very efficient learning sets and the other has acquired inefficient or inadequate sets, then the one with the superior "sets" will appear to be superior in potential when in fact he is not. We have already in Chapter 3 referred to the potential danger of rigid overorganization of experience in that such might interfere with the formation of new combinations or insights. The same can be said about sets. While invention and insight depend upon previously organized processes, if these are rigidly organized they could interfere with the construction of new insights.

This is not an appropriate place to discuss theories of brain functioning, even if the author were competent to do so, and he is not; but it is appropriate to cite a brief passage from Newell, Shaw, and Simon on their theory of neural functioning, which seems congruent with the behavioral theory presented here:

> The picture of the central nervous system to which our theory leads is a picture of a more complex and active system than that contemplated by most associationists. The notions of "trace," "fixation," "excitation," and "inhibition" suggest a relatively passive electrochemical system (or, alternatively, a passive "switchboard"), acted upon by stimuli, altered by that action, and subsequently behaving in a modified manner when later stimuli impinge upon it.
>
> In contrast, we postulate an information-processing system with large storage capacity that holds, among other things, complex strategies (programs) that may be evoked by stimuli. The stimulus determines what strategy or strategies will be evoked; the content of these strategies is already largely determined by previous experience of the system. Ability

---

[31] Harry F. Harlow, "The Formation of Learning Sets," *Psychological Review*, Vol. 56 (1949), pp. 51-65.

of the system to respond in complex and highly selective ways to relatively simple stimuli is a consequence of this storage of programs and this "active" response to stimuli. The phenomena of set and insight that we have already described and the hierarchical structure of the response system are all consequences of this "active" organization of the central processes.[32]

The foregoing quotation emphasizes neural functioning as primarily an information-processing system with a very large memory capacity. In addition, the writers postulate an ongoing intrinsic organizing activity of the brain.

This neural interpretation is compatible with the general emphasis in this chapter on the interaction of internal processes and external processes. It also helps us to understand the acquisition or learning of complex strategies which have already been worked out and developed by others. This is to say that the behavioral strategies or programs which comprise the related actions of several people may be acquired in one cumulative form or gestalt by any one person and thus psychologically become the property of an individual. For example, the first baseman on a baseball team not only perceives and conceives what he is supposed to do and to whom he is supposed to do it, but he also knows what all the other players are supposed to do. That is to say, he has acquired a working picture of the entire game and can therefore assume the role of any player.

Viewed in the foregoing way, interaction serves two functions: one, an external or outward *adaptive* function; and, two, it functions internally as *organization*. Thus, by viewing interaction as adaptive coping with the environment *and* neural organization, it is then logical to conceive of intelligence as a problem-solving process. Thus Einstein's problem-solving skills in mathematical physics contributed to an increase in man's adaptive capacity by his contributions to atomic physics. These contributions were highly creative and highly adaptive.

Hunt comments that "A conception of intelligence as problem-solving capacity based on a hierarchical organization of symbolic representations and information-processing strategies deriving to a considerable degree from past experience, has emerged from several sources. These sources include observations of human behavior in solving problems, the programming of electronic computers, and neuropsychology." [33]

Jean Piaget, a Swiss social psychologist, has derived a similar view of intelligence after more than thirty years of observing and studying the development of intellectual functions and logic in children.[34]

[32] A. Newell, J. C. Shaw, and H. A. Simon, "Elements of a Theory of Human Problem Solving," *Psychological Review*, Vol. 65 (1958), pp. 151-166.
[33] *Ibid.*, p. 109.
[34] In my opinion the single best interpretation and summary of Piaget's recent works is found in Hunt, *op. cit.*, pp. 109-307.

Piaget conceives the interaction between the organism and environment as an adaptive function which involves two complementary processes, namely, inner organization and outer adaptation. These he calls *assimilation* and *accommodation*. These are broadly inclusive concepts. Assimilation to Piaget includes not only the conditioned reflex but also what is known in general psychology as "stimulus generalization" and "response generalization." The process of assimilation results in the formation of behavior patterns which Piaget termed *schemata*.

Accommodation involves the functioning of the schemata in coping with the demands of the environment and this in turn modifies existing schemata.

The infant in Piaget's view is born with biologically ready-made reflexive schemata which

> become progressively transformed through differentiations and coordinations into the logical "organizations" (or operations for information-processing) of adult intelligence. . . . The picture of the development of intelligence which emerges from the observations and experiments of Piaget and his collaborators is one of continuous transformations in the "organizations" or "structures" of intelligence. At birth the only "organizations" available are the congenital sensorimotor schemata, reflexes or instincts. The first period of intellectual development, the *sensorimotor*, lasts from birth until the child is roughly between 18 months and two years old. The reflexive sensorimotor schemata are generalized, coordinated with each other, and differentiated to become the elementary operations of intelligence which begin to be internalized and which correspond to the problem-solving abilities of subhuman animals. During this period, the child creates through his continual adaptive accommodations and assimilations . . . such operations as "intentions," "means-end" differentiations, and the interest in novelty. On the side of constructing reality, the child also develops the beginnings of interiorized schemata, if not actual concepts, for such elements as the permanence of objects, space, causality, and time.[35]

Piaget conceives of the intellectual development of the sensorimotor period as taking place in six stages. The reflexive schemata to which we have just referred constitute the first stage. It is not necessary for our purposes to describe the remaining stages except to say that he conceives of the six stages as ending with the beginnings of symbolic imitation, that is to say, the period when the child begins to repeat adult words. This is the period in which according to Piaget's conception genuine intelligence emerges. By genuine intelligence Piaget means the development of formal operations such as logic, information processing procedures, symbolic capacities and skills. The development of these behavioral structures and operations presupposes the existence of neuro-

[35] Hunt, *op. cit.*, pp. 113-114.

logical capacities to symbolize and the encountering of these capacities with the social environment. Thus the content of neurological organization (mind) is principally a social product. Consequently, the structures comprising intelligence are constantly changing as a consequence of the "accommodation" and "assimilation" involved in a person's encounters with his environment.

The general ideas which we have developed in this chapter on the interacting relations between biology, culture, and experience are congruent with Piaget's general framework. It also coalesces with the somewhat simpler, neurological conception by Newell, Shaw, and Simon mentioned earlier.

In summary, Piaget conceives intelligence as a changing phenomenon, the change being primarily a function of the interaction of past experience (as expressed through neural schemata) with new experience, thus modifying existing schemata. Thought processes are conceived to originate through a process of internalizing actions. Hence early action and experience are very important in conditioning subsequent development of intelligence. He also conceives that intelligence increases as thought processes are loosened and developed from their bases in perception and action.

This latter point is very important since it suggests the possibility of viewing creativity as the development of *new* operations for problem-solving. Recall that we have already defined intelligence as a problem-solving process. Therefore, creativity would be viewed as the development of improvements in the processes of problem-solving. From the standpoint of a given human population improvements in the problem-solving processes or creativity would result in an increase in its measured average intelligence assuming that the new operations were diffused among the population. If increasing intelligence is the liberating of thought processes from their concrete bases in perception and action, then this implies that central neural processes such as thought and conceptualization tend to become increasingly autonomous. This should result in increased powers of imagination which in turn would further liberate thought processes.

Let us further examine the process of creativity.

Creativity and the Release of Potentialities

We have defined creativity as the development of new processes and operations for problem-solving. The development of the new forms would be somewhat dependent upon the old forms in that the new forms would, to some extent, be new combinations of old forms. Accordingly, it would be appropriate to compare and contrast the characteristics and conditions of individuals with differing outputs of creativity.

Let us examine some of the recent work on this problem.[36]

We first note that several qualities other than IQ enter into the definition of giftedness. High IQ does not necessarily go with high imagination, and high imagination is necessary for creativity. Getzels and Jackson quote Thurstone as follows:

> To be extremely intelligent is not the same as to be gifted in creative work. This may be taken as a hypothesis.
>
> It is common observation in the universities that those students who have high intelligence, judged by available criteria, are not necessarily the ones who produce the most original ideas. All of us probably know a few men who are both creative and highly intelligent, but this combination is not the rule.
>
> The confusion between intelligence and creative talent is common. For example, Quiz Kids are often referred to as geniuses. They would undoubtedly score high in memory functions, including incidental memory and rote memory. But it is doubtful whether they are also fluent in producing original ideas.[37]

Our earlier discussion of creativity and intelligence viewed the two as being related in a very special sense. That is to say that we saw intelligence as a problem-solving process and creativity as the capacity of the individual to reconstruct and improve his problem-solving skills by producing new forms. This statement implies that manifest intelligence can be increased through creativity. On the other hand, Thurstone's statement says that intelligence and creativity are not the same. Thus we appear to have a contradiction. How can we resolve it?

In the first place, all people with normal intelligence are capable of being creative, that is, they may produce new ideas. Thus creativity is not an attribute of only those in the upper end of the IQ spectrum. In fact, as Thurstone says, they usually are not. Consequently, if IQ as currently measured correlates poorly with creativity, then this could be a function of the way in which IQ and creativity are measured. It is well known that historically the interest in measuring IQ has been primarily concerned with predicting the learning performance of school children. Hence the cognitive qualities considered have been conditioned by our concern with academic abilities and achievements. These qualities have centered around the learning and recalling of materials provided by someone else. There is not much attention to or emphasis upon dis-

[36] It is suggested that for details the student consult Howard E. Gruber, Glenn Terrell, and Michael Wertheimer, eds., *Contemporary Approaches to Creative Thinking* (New York, Atherton Press, 1962) and Jacob W. Getzels and Philip W. Jackson, *Creativity and Intelligence: Explorations with Gifted Students* (New York, John Wiley & Sons, Inc., 1962).

[37] Cited by J. W. Getzels and Philip W. Jackson, *Creativity and Intelligence* (New York, John Wiley & Sons, Inc., 1962), pp. 7 and 8.

covery and invention. If the IQ concept were broadened to include these qualities, then it would be appropriate to include measures of creativeness and IQ as defining properties of unusually high ability.

Getzels and Jackson point out that

> The student with a higher IQ who is doing poorly in school and the student with a lower IQ who is doing well appear too often for the IQ to stand as the only predictive measure of intellectual ability or as the sole criterion of giftedness. Moreover, it is commonly observed that many children who are very high in intelligence *as measured by IQ* are not concomitantly high in such other intellectual functions as creativity, and many children who are very high in creativity are not concomitantly high in intelligence as measured by IQ.[38]

The table below shows the results of comparing the school achievement of high IQ but low creative subjects with high creative but significantly lower IQ subjects.

TABLE 4:1

Means and Standard Deviations of IQ and School Achievement for Total Student Population and Experimental Groups [39]

		TOTAL POPULATION (N = 449)	HIGH IQ (N = 28)	HIGH CREATIVE (N = 24)
IQ	$\bar{X}$ (mean)	132.00	150.00	127.00
	s	15.07	6.64	10.58
School	$\bar{X}$	49.91	55.00	56.27
Achievement	s	7.36	5.95	7.90

Note that despite the 23-point difference in mean IQ between the "high creatives" and the "high IQ's" the achievement scores of the two groups are nearly the same with the highly creative group being slightly higher but with both the experimental groups achieving significantly higher than the total population. The difference was significant at the .001 level.

How can we interpret the results in the foregoing table? What do they mean? There are several ways which we could argue about these results, but space will permit but one argument.

First, let us note that there is high achievement between both the high IQ group and the high creativity group. This suggests that there may

[38] *Ibid.*, p. 3. Italics added.
[39] See J. W. Getzels and Philip W. Jackson, *Creativity and Intelligence* (New York, John Wiley & Sons, Inc., 1962), p. 24.

be important cognitive functions which are related to learning that are not measured by IQ tests but that are measured by the creativity tests. Getzels and Jackson also make this point. In addition, Getzels and Jackson suggest that the customary explanation of low achievement by high IQ and high achievement by low IQ subjects as being due to motivational factors is not an adequate explanation. Their data indicate that the so-called motivational factors are not causes but are themselves inextricably related to one's general *cognitive style* and that cognitive style and motivational structure can only be separated for analytic purposes.[40]

This interpretation is in harmony with our whole emphasis in Section 4 of this chapter. This emphasis was upon the function of schemata or the content and the logical organization of the meanings of previous experience as major determinants of information-processing, interpreting, and correlating as these are organized and mediated by central neural processes. Thus the previous "sets" which one has learned, and the flexibility of one's cognitive operations, seem to be a more significant index to problem-solving and learning skills than motivational indexes.

Crutchfield quotes from Emerson's essay, "Self-Reliance," regarding the antipathy of conformity and creativity: "The virtue in most regard is conformity. Self-reliance is its aversion. It loves not realities and creators. . . ."[41]

Thus it is suggested that blind conformity involves loss of self-reliance and that a loss in self-reliance weakens a person's creative powers and trust in his own thought processes. The loss of reliance on one's thought process would lead to loss in contact with reality. Therefore, factors which determine a high degree of self-reliance are significantly related to creativity. Studies of creative persons have revealed that they are low in conformity.

If one views the flexibility of cognitive style as being a function of the imaginative capacity of subjects, then it might be useful to look at the process and content of the imaginative productions of the two groups. In this regard Getzels and Jackson comment as follows:

> With respect to process, the high creatives tend to free themselves from the stimulus, using it largely as a point of departure for self-expression; the high IQs tend to focus on the stimulus, using it as the invariant for communication. For the high IQ, the issue is essentially one of conserving what others give to him. If the picture stimulus is of a man in an airplane, he must tell a story about travel; if the picture stimulus is of a man in an office, he must tell a story about work. For the highly creative, the issue is essentially one of constructing what he wants to give. With respect to the con-

[40] *Ibid.*, p. 28.
[41] Richard S. Crutchfield, "Conformity and Creative Thinking," in H. E. Gruber, Glenn Terrell, and Michael Wertheimer, eds., *Contemporary Approaches to Creative Thinking* (New York, Atherton Press, 1963), p. 120.

tent . . . the fantasies of the high creativity adolescents contain at once more wit and more violence. They seem more expressive of impulses from within that are frequently inhibited, and descriptive of experiences from without that are often denied. The high creativity adolescent has a more playful—or if you will, more experimental—attitude toward conventional ideas, objects and qualities.[42]

One of the major variables which Getzels and Jackson found that seemed to be related to the greater flexibility of imagination and resourcefulness of the high creativity group as against the high IQ group was parental security. There seemed to be a greater insecurity among the parents of the high IQ group than among the high creativity parents.[43] This was also supported by the interview data in the study.

Could it be that parental security is related to child security and this in turn related to a sense of freedom to seek new experience and to construct new ways of actively dealing with one's environment? If so, then parental and child security are important conditions relative to creativity.

We now conclude the section on the release of potentialities through the development of intelligence as a problem-solving process and the development of creativity as the principal means of liberating intelligence. At this point the reader must recall Section 2 of this chapter which dealt with biological potentialities as setting the potential physical limits to the development of behavior. In addition, it should also be recalled that Section 3 dealt with cultural potentialities, and that these through experience and learning determine the content and actual level of development of behavior. That is to say, biological factors and cultural factors come together through social interaction and we recognize the releasing and developmental effects of social interaction through developmental changes in intelligence and creativity.

With this general picture of the development of behavior we are now ready to examine the effects of social and cultural experience on such major psychological processes as perception, learning, and motivation. We shall look first at perception, which is the subject of the next chapter.

5. SUMMARY

In this chapter we have viewed the evolution of human potentialities as a function of two forms of evolution, *general* and *specific*. By specific evolution we meant the interplay of nature and nurture in producing the great varieties and elaborations on the themes of life. Specific evolution produces the divergences within a species. On the other hand, gen-

---

[42] Getzels and Jackson, *op. cit.*, p. 42.
[43] *Ibid.*, p. 65.

eral evolution produces new and higher forms of species. We applied these concepts to both biological and cultural evolution.

We saw biological evolution as a function of genetic mutation and environmental selection. The corresponding processes of cultural evolution were invention and diffusion as sources of social and cultural change and social selection, acceptance, and experience as the environmental sifting and winnowing of the new elements.

Following this, we examined the genetic transmission of biological potentialities by a discussion of the gene-chromosome theory of heredity. The evolution of cultural potentialities was considered by an analysis and application of Service's "Law of Evolutionary Potential."

Recall that the concepts of biological potentiality and cultural potentiality were applied in respect to species or populations as wholes. We next connected these concepts by propositionally relating them to two major psychological processes within the individual. These were the processes of intelligence and creativity. The development of these processes was viewed as the releasing of individual potentialities.

It was shown that intelligence was developed and released through a process involving the individual in interaction with other individuals. Intelligence was defined as a problem-solving process and creativity was defined as the construction and development of new forms of problem-solving.

Further References

1. J. McV. Hunt, *Intelligence and Experience* (New York, The Ronald Press Company, 1961).
2. Ching Chun Li, *Human Genetics* (New York, Blakiston Press, McGraw-Hill Book Company, 1961).
3. Ludweg Von Bertalanffy, *Problems of Life* (New York, John Wiley & Sons, Inc., 1952).

Part III
MAN AS A SOCIOCULTURAL ANIMAL: THE INDIVIDUAL AND THE GROUP

5
Perceiving and the Social World

●

1. *Introduction*
2. *Some Effects of Experience on Sensory Perception*
3. *The Role of Learning in Perception*
4. *Behavioral and Cultural Influences in Perception*
5. *The Perceptual Process and Social Norms*
6. *Some General Perceptual Findings*
   (a) *Figure and Ground Factors in Experience*
   (b) *Change in Perceptual Organization*
7. *Summary*

1. INTRODUCTION

IN CHAPTER 3 of Part II it was shown that the dependence of organisms upon learning as an important means of adaptation increased with increases in the level of complexity of animal life. The more primitive an organism, the more likely it is to reveal immediate and highly uniform reactions to certain environmental patternings. The more highly developed an organism is, the more complex are its responses and the longer the period of development of the response skills. For example, in man vision is a very complex skill that develops gradually through the years of infancy and childhood. How much of this capacity is a function of the unfolding of innate properties through natural maturation and how much, if any, is due to environmental stimulation and conditioning?

In our discussion in Chapter 4 of the effects of environment on intelligence we noted how difficult it is to separate the effects of hereditary factors from the effects of experience. Obviously, if genetic factors and environmental factors are involved as *necessary* factors, then the outcome property cannot develop unless *both* sets of antecedents (hereditary factors and environmental factors) are present and in sufficient degree. Therefore, if the dependent characteristic or outcome cannot emerge, it would be impossible to observe the relative effects of heredity and environment. However, it is not necessary to experiment with the independent variables on an "all or none" basis. We can vary in amount the variable in which we are interested and note the effects of this variation on the dependent factor or outcome.

It is well known, for example, that a newborn infant does not initially show any clear indication of any response to a bright object held before his eyes. After several weeks he begins to look at the object. Is this the result of growth, experience, or both? That is to say, does the change in response occur as a function of the use of the eye or through natural maturation independently of use? Certainly, if environmental factors are to affect development, the organism must have some kind of sensory contact with the environment in order to experience it. Aside from being able to see and feel only what our sense organs and nervous system will let us sense, we also, of course, can see and feel only that which comes into contact with the sense organs and the nervous system. Therefore, we view perception as jointly depending upon biological properties of the organism and upon the physical patterning of the external world. This joint functioning of the sensory processes and central neural processes with the external patterning of the environment results in a stored-up and organized way of looking at the world. It is argued here that perceptions are the end-products of a slow process of construction through manipulation of and experimentation with the external world. This assumes that perceptions are stable and orderly but that they tend to change with the differential effects of subsequent experience. Thus learning plays an important role in the view of perception presented here, and, likewise, perception plays an important role in the learning process. Perception affects subsequent learning by providing the perceiver with a conception of himself and the world.[1] Thus through experience he evolves a system of organizing and interpreting information, which, of course, in turn structures the learning situation.

The fact that species and organisms can and do adapt implies that they have an inherent capacity for experiencing. After repeated experiencing of a stimulus pattern, all organisms become capable of increasingly refined and complex discrimination as well as capable of elaborating and correlating sensory signs and, in the case of man, symbols also. Perceptual elements become specific as well as enriched by differential reinforcement, that is to say, the arrangement of the environment so that one stimulus reinforces (confirms) and another one does not. The rewarding or punishing effects of a stimulus serve to heighten discrimination and sensitivity and thus enable perception to occur.

[1] No attempt is here made to rigidly distinguish between conception and perception. To be sure, semantic distinctions can be made, but it is difficult to make a scientifically meaningful distinction.

The resulting patterns of perceptual discrimination condition the way the individual views the world, and, as indicated earlier in the chapter, this in turn greatly affects subsequent learning. Thus the intent here is to relate the structure of perception to past experience. In doing this, we are viewing perception as a complex interactive process composed not only of present stimulus input and receptor function but also of motivation (which has stimulus properties too) and past experience. The building up of new perceptions through new experience seems to be a gradual process of pattern discrimination and reinforcement.[2] The clarity and consistency of a percept varies with the relevance or significance of the events in the behavioral environment to be perceived, and with the probability of occurrence of these events.[3]

Fundamentally, perception is concerned with the adjustment of the organism to the world about it and to stimuli and stresses arising from within the organism. In discussing perceptual learning, Professor Gardner Murphy says:

> . . . we suspect that that garden variety of learning that offers the classical basis for our vast system of social rewards and punishments is a matter of instilling in the individual a new way of perceiving the environment. Some things, originally neutral, he comes to see as desirable; others, originally neutral, he comes to see as undesirable. The affect may range from abject horror to the mystic's sense of unutterable joys, and the connections formed may range from the simplest nonsense-syllable kind of connection to the profoundest creative integration. Through all this, I believe, runs a central theme: the perceptual field comes to take on a structure in which the acceptable, the good, the satisfying, tends to take the dominant position.[4]

We have described perception as an interactive process involving stimulus properties, sensory and cortical functions, and past experience. Keeping in mind the interacting nature of perception, we offer the following general definition of perception as a guide to the use of the concept in this book. Perception is an awareness and an interpretation of a stimulus.[5]

From a social psychological point of view the interest in perception

---

[2] Harry F. Harlow, "Recovery of Pattern Discrimination in Monkeys Following Unilateral Occipital Lobectomy," *Journal of Comparative Psychology*, Vol. 27 (1939), pp. 467-489.

[3] Egon Brunswik, *Perception and the Representative Design of Psychological Experiments* (Berkeley, University of California Press, 1956), esp. Part Two. Also, Harry Helson, "Adaptation-Level as Frame of Reference for Prediction of Psycho-Physical Data," *American Journal of Psychology*, Vol. 60 (January, 1947).

[4] Gardner Murphy, "Affect and Perceptual Learning," *The Psychological Review*, Vol. 63 (January, 1956), p. 14.

[5] For an excellent survey and analysis of the concept of perception see William Bevan, "Perception: Evolution of a Concept," *The Psychological Review*, Vol. 65 (January, 1958), pp. 34-53.

centers around two general problem areas. The *first* problem area concerns the matter of the effect of existing perceptions upon subsequent learning. This general problem divides into two particular problem areas: (1) The first type of perceptual response connection is the *transfer* of a previously learned set of responses to a new set of stimuli. This is largely a process of defining and abstracting relevant elements from the new stimulus in terms of the person's existing response sets. This appears to be a process of *stimulus generalization.* This concept refers to the fact that when a response has been developed to a given stimulus or stimulus pattern, the same response will also occur to similar stimuli without any reinforcement for such occurrences. The mechanism by which this occurs is not specified. (2) The second type of perceptual response connection is established through *association* as a function of external reinforcement (that is, some external cue informing the respondent of the correctness of his response).[6] An example would be a person's increasing the loudness of his voice while speaking to a man wearing a hearing aid. The respondent associates a hearing deficiency with the hearing aid and he notes that the wearer of the aid speaks louder than normal; therefore, he speaks louder.

The *second* major interest of social psychologists in perception concerns the relationship of *past experience* to perception. By this is meant the gradual building up of patterns of discrimination based upon the exploring of one's environment and the patterns of feedback from the environmental events.

In summary, we may say that we are interested in the effect of perception upon learning and of the effect of learning on perception.

Let us examine first some of the evidence which suggests that experience affects perception.

2. SOME EFFECTS OF EXPERIENCE ON SENSORY PERCEPTION

Riesen provides some interesting data on the effects of limited experience or sensory deprivation on vision.

Riesen first points out that studies on human patients operated on at advanced ages for congenital cataracts reveal that such patients cannot, at first, identify an object or describe its shape, but that they are able to distinguish light and colors. However, over a period of months and sometimes years, they do develop the ability to discriminate simple geometric figures, read letters and numbers, and, in rare cases, to identify complex patterns such as words, drawings, and faces.

---

[6] For a detailed analysis of perceptual learning as response transfer and association see Joachim F. Wohlwill, "Definition and Analysis of Perceptual Learning," *The Psychological Review,* Vol. 65 (1958), pp. 283-294.

Riesen also points out that these cases of congenital cataract do not provide clear-cut evidence of how disuse affects the development of visual behavior. The difficulty in interpretation derives from the presence of uncontrolled variables. He identifies three such variables which need to be taken into account in order to clarify the results described above. These are: (1) the degree of the patient's previous blindness, since he was not in total darkness, (2) the limit that is imposed on his potentialities for improvement by the fact that the eye operated on lacks a lens, and (3) the circumstance that in all these cases there appears to be another visual handicap—jerky movements of the eyeballs known as spontaneous nystagmus.[7]

With these difficulties in mind Riesen decided to set up a controlled experiment to determine the effects of disuse on normal eyes. The chimpanzee was chosen because its behavior, like man's, is dominated by vision and because of its intelligence and obedience.

The experiment which we are about to describe was conducted by Dr. Riesen in 1945 at the Yerkes Laboratories in Primate Biology, which were then located in Orange Park, Florida. The laboratories have now been moved to the Emory University campus in Atlanta, Georgia.

Two newborn chimpanzee infants, a male and a female respectively named Snark and Alfalfa, were housed in a completely darkened room. During the first sixteen months the only light these infants experienced was an electric lamp turned on for intervals of 45 seconds several times daily for their routine care and feeding. They were tested for visual perception at the age of sixteen months and both showed extreme incompetence. Both failed to show any visual responses to complex patterns of light until after they had spent many hours in illuminated surroundings. They did not respond to play objects or their feeding bottles unless these touched their bodies.

After the sixteen-month period of darkness, Alfalfa was placed on a limited light schedule until the age of twenty-one months and Snark until thirty-three months. When Alfalfa was finally placed in a normal daylight environment, she finally after many months developed normal recognition of objects, began to blink in response to threats, and ceased to be startled by a touch. Snark, who was continued on a relatively unlighted environment, was much more retarded. Between the ages of twenty and twenty-seven months, while still on rationed light, he learned after many hundreds of trials to tell the difference between contrasting signs, differing in color or pattern, which indicated either food or a mild electric shock. His visual acuity, as measured by ability to discriminate

---

[7] Austin H. Riesen, "Arrested Vision," in David C. Beardslee and Michael Wertheimer, eds., *Readings in Perception* (Princeton, N.J., D. Van Nostrand Co., Inc., 1958), pp. 306-307.

between horizontal and vertical lines, was much below that of animals raised in normal lighting.

At the end of thirty-three months Snark was placed in a normally lighted chimpanzee nursery and later out of doors with chimpanzees of his own age. It was expected that he would acquire normal visual behavior. He did improve slightly at first, but eventually lost his initial improvement until finally his reflex activity began to die away. Dr. Riesen asks:

> What is the explanation of this deterioration? Had the development of his eyes been permanently arrested by the absence of light? There had been no previous evidence that stimulation by light is essential for the normal growth of the primate retina or optic nerve. It was a surprise to find that, while the eyes of these chimpanzees remained sensitive to light after 16 months in darkness, the retina and optic disk in both animals did not reflect as much light as normal chimpanzee eyes do.[8]

So it appears that the physiological effects of the lack of light may be part of the explanation for Snark's loss of visual function, but it is not the whole explanation. Stimulation of the retina and the optic nerve by *visual patterns* is also essential to normal visual development. Riesen designed other experiments to test the effects of patterned stimulation. These are described next.

In these experiments three other newborn chimpanzees, two females and a male, were put into the darkroom. Debi was raised for seven months in complete darkness, including the time of her feedings and other care. Kora was raised for the same period on a ration of an average of one-and-a-half hours of light daily, but the light, admitted through a white Plexiglas mask, was diffuse and unpatterned. Lad was given one-and-a-half hours of patterned light daily: he could observe the edges of his crib, the variations in pattern introduced by movements of his own body and the moving of other persons in the room.

At seven months the three subjects were moved to a normal daylight environment and tested for visual performance. Lad's visual performance was not different from that of chimpanzees raised normally. Kora and Debi showed the same kinds of retardation as had Snark and Alfalfa, with certain minor exceptions. Kora did not develop the blink response to a moving object until six days after her removal from darkness, and Debi not until fifteen days. It took Kora thirteen days and Debi thirty days to acquire the ability to pursue a moving person with their eyes, and they did this by a series of refixations instead of following smoothly as normal animals of comparable age do.

[8] *Ibid.*, p. 308.

In another study an infant chimpanzee named Kandy was put in the darkroom for only the first three months of life. After she was removed to normal daylight surroundings, her progress was essentially the same as that of Debi and Kora. There were three interesting differences: (1) Kandy showed a convergent squint (cross-eyes), which cleared up in a little less than two months; (2) she did not have spontaneous nystagmus; (3) she required twenty-four days, as compared with thirteen or fifteen, to develop consistent avoidance of the black and yellow shock-disk. The last difference suggests that Kandy learned more slowly because of her younger age, that is, the development of visual discrimination was a function of maturation as well as learning.

These experiments by Riesen demonstrate that vision if it is to develop normally must be put to use, but they also demonstrate that during the first few months visual development is advanced by growth factors which are entirely independent of practice. Normally reared animals, for example, do not blink in response to the movement of objects across the visual field until they have reached the age of two months.

Riesen also cites an experiment which shows that the *maintenance* of normal visual functions in higher primates depends on a complex set of interrelated hereditary and environmental factors. In reference to the environmental factors it was shown in an experiment with a chimpanzee named Faik that a normal chimpanzee with normal vision can lose his ability to utilize vision if kept in a darkroom for certain periods of time. Faik was raised in the normal light of the laboratory's nursery until the age of seven months. At that time he showed excellent use of vision. Then from the age of eight to twenty-four months he was kept in the darkroom. He lived an active life filled with tactile, auditory, olfactory, gustatory, and kinesthetic stimulation. His general state of health remained entirely satisfactory. When Faik was returned to daylight living quarters at twenty-four months, he had lost all ability to utilize vision in his interplay with the environment. He no longer recognized the feeding bottle and failed to look at objects or persons, either stationary or moving. More than this, he possessed a strong spontaneous nystagmus and was even unable to follow a moving light in a darkroom until the fifth day after he was put back into a lighted environment.

Faik showed pallor similar to that of Snark and Alfalfa in his optic disks. His recovery of vision has been slow and is still only partial. Riesen concludes by saying that explanation of his case, and that of Snark, remains a challenge to further research.[9]

The development of visual discrimination involves both the structure of the eye and the central nervous system. The studies of Riesen suggest the importance of stimulation in the development of visual ability and

---

[9] *Ibid.* Freely quoted from pp. 309-311.

its maintenance. It is logical to assume that this may also be true of higher mental processes such as perception and thinking.

It is generally agreed that the organization of perception depends upon experience and the orderly dynamics of brain functioning. It would be interesting to test to what extent, if any, orderly brain functioning is dependent upon neurological stimulation by patterned external stimuli. This would be particularly important during the early years of maturation, but it is assumed that it would also apply in varying degree throughout the life span.

It is well known that once the brain is stimulated, its activity continues for some time after the stimulus has been removed. This phenomenon is known as *perseveration*. Murphy states that this continuation of activity after removal of the stimulus

> . . . is almost certainly connected with the slow dying-down of brain activity. There are big individual differences in perseveration, and they seem to be connected with the fact that one person can turn to a new activity at the drop of a hat, whereas another can only slowly drag himself along.[10]

One of the most interesting inherent features of brain behavior is the *rapid adaptation* of the responses of the brain stem reticular system to external stimuli (roughly the base of the brain connecting the spinal cord). For example, everyone is familiar with the disruptive effects of new noise and the subsequent fact that in a very short time a person has adapted to the new noise so that it no longer bothers him. Herbert Jasper, in describing research results on such adaptation, notes that

> An initial startling stimulus is always far more effective than the same stimulus repeated or expected. For example, if a sound is administered to a sleeping animal, the animal will be awakened on the first administration of the stimulus. If the subject is allowed to go to sleep again and the same sound repeated, it may be again awakened with the characteristic changes in the electrical activity of the cortex. If this is repeated many times, however, sometimes only 10 or 12 times, this stimulus loses its effectiveness for arousal, and the animal sleeps right through the stimulus. Then, however, if the stimulus is changed, for example, if instead of using a 500-cycle tone, one uses a tone of 100 cycles, then the animal will be awakened as though to the first sound stimulus. . . . This seems to be a kind of learning process, in which the animal learns to ignore a repeated stimulus, the response to which has become extinguished, but to be alerted by a novel stimulus.[11]

[10] Gardner Murphy, *An Introduction to Psychology* (New York, Harper & Row, Publishers, Inc., 1951), p. 162.
[11] Herbert Jasper, "Reticular-Cortical Systems and Theories." Reprinted with permission of the copyright owners, the Regents of the University of Wisconsin, from Harry F. Harlow and Clinton N. Woolsey, eds., *Biological and Biochemical Bases of Behavior* (1958, The University of Wisconsin Press), p. 55.

The experimental result cited by Jasper is a scientific demonstration of a well-known observation that monotonous stimuli tend to lose their capacity to hold our attention or to arouse us. It is cited here to call attention to the fact that common everyday experiences are constantly conditioning and reconditioning our neural activity.

We will conclude the discussion of some effects of experience on sensory perception by noting briefly some research on delayed sensory feedback and its effect on behavior.

Riesen's experiments on the effects of experience on vision and perceptual discrimination clearly show that neurological mechanisms *and* experience affect response integration. Some would argue that

> . . . an understanding of human learning requires first of all some degree of understanding of the neuromotor regulatory mechanisms underlying behavior patterns and skills. Only when we understand something of the nature of response integration can we hope to specify how integrated patterns become reorganized with experience, i.e., how learning occurs.[12]

It is not the intention here to discuss the matter of the neurological basis of response integration. For our purposes, this is not necessary. We are not concerned with *how* human behavior is learned. Instead, we are concerned with the effects of a learning experience on the subsequent behavior of the learner. However, we do wish to point to some research findings on the effects of a sudden lack of continuity in the accustomed environment of a subject on response integration. In so far as the writer knows, Karl U. Smith's work at the University of Wisconsin affords one of the better—and probably the best—illustrations of behavioral disturbance due to disruption of sensory feedback.

Experiments using disruption of spatial patterns and auditory patterns as means for studying perception have been in use for a long time. We will note an example of spatial displacement through visual inversion in a later section in this chapter.

If a subject speaks into a microphone and the sound of his speech comes out several seconds *after* he speaks, we have the phenomenon of delayed sensory feedback. The usual method for producing delayed auditory feedback is to prevent the subjects from hearing the sounds of their own speech for a specified delay period, and following this to play back the speech to the subjects.

Smith used videotape recorders to systematically analyze the effects of delayed visual feedback. He describes the procedure as follows:

> The subject sits or stands before the monitor of a closed-circuit television system, watching the image of his own manual movements on the monitor

[12] Karl U. Smith, *Delayed Sensory Feedback and Behavior* (Philadelphia, W. B. Saunders Co., 1962), p. 5.

screen. A curtain is hung between his eyes and hand so that he cannot see his performance directly. A pictorial image of performance is registered by the television camera, recorded by means of a videotape recorder, and then played back to the monitor after a short delay interval. His visual feedback of motion is subject to a constant time lag, which can be varied experimentally from a small fraction of a second to any desired interval. When the feedback from visually controlled movements is delayed in this way, the general effect on performance is disastrous. The motion pattern becomes inaccurate and disorganized, and the individual is likely to show emotional disturbances and loss of motivation.[13]

Aside from the importance of delayed sensory feedback as a means to a theoretical understanding of perceptual-motor integration, what is its immediate significance in understanding practical problems? Professor Smith notes that the disorienting and disorganizing effects of delayed sensory feedback were first noted in connection with military tracking systems developed in World War II. He also notes that currently the problem of delayed sensory feedback in human motion is of great importance in the remote control of cosmic vehicles. For example, there is an unavoidable delayed feedback due to the time required to transmit electromagnetic signals from the earth to specific places in outer space. This constitutes a new problem in human engineering.

Why is the matter of delayed sensory feedback introduced in a text on *social* psychology? To the writer the answer is simple. Social psychology is concerned with the relationships between man's behavioral environment and psychological processes. Two of the major properties of man's environment, whether behavioral or nonbehavioral, are the *spatial* and *temporal* patterns of the environment. Man lives in a world of time and space and his perceptual organization of time and space patterning are functions of the environment and his neurological systems. The social or behavioral environment of man also has space and time dimensions. The action of a human group can be conceived from the point of view of the observer of the group's behavior as a problem in behavioral tracking. Imagine what the disruptions would be to group action if the feedback system within the group is manipulated. Suppose we have a three-man group—A, B, and C. A responds to B and expects a response in return. If B does not respond or significantly delays the response, the behavioral situation is disrupted and the participants may become emotionally tense. On the other hand, B may deliberately distort his response so as to produce a desired feedback effect. The point is that sensory feedback is essential to social psychological organization as well as sensory-motor organization.

At this point in the discussion it is necessary to make an important

---

[13] *Ibid.*, p. 2.

clarification. We have just said that sensory feedback or what some have called "information feedback" is a critical factor in the behavior *organization* of the organism. Yet, previously in this chapter it is argued that "Perceptual elements become specific as well as enriched by differential reinforcement. . . ." That is to say, sensory feedback informs the individual of the results of his behavior. If his behavior achieves the goal, it is interpreted as valid, is reinforced, and will occur again under similar circumstances. If the behavior is invalid or inaccurate, it is likely not to recur. The reinforcement theory seems to roughly describe one type of behavior which appears to occur in human beings and in lower animals, particularly lower animals. A pigeon can be easily trained to always peck a given stimulus which rewards him and avoid one which does not. In other words, learning theory appears to equate sensory feedback with reinforcement, and thus would predict that learning would occur even if the feedback is delayed but that the efficiency of the learning would be reduced.

Professor Smith objects to this general interpretation by pointing out that some learning occurs under *delayed reinforcement* and that the behavior of the organism does not become disturbed. Yet, under conditions of *delayed sensory feedback* behavior is seriously disturbed. He therefore concludes that delayed reinforcement and delayed sensory feedback are two different phenomena and that the latter ". . . is a critical aspect of the intrinsic behavior organization of the organism, and delayed feedback is seriously disturbing because it interrupts this intrinsic regulation of motion." [14]

Certainly human beings acquire anticipatory responses which involve very long delayed reinforcement.[15]

I believe that Professor Smith is right in his interpretation of feedback as being a critical intrinsic aspect of behavioral organization and is therefore justified in distinguishing between delayed reinforcement and delayed feedback, particularly in regard to old stimuli. However, the experimental evidence for this distinction should clearly distinguish between delayed feedback in respect to tasks that are *new* to the subject and tasks that are *old*. It would seem that in regard to tasks which call for new responses or learning, delayed feedback and delayed reinforcement would produce similar effects.

Let us examine more in detail some effects of learning on perception.

3. THE ROLE OF LEARNING IN PERCEPTION

Among the many interesting experiments which show the importance of learning in perception is one reported in 1930 by P. H. Ewert and

[14] *Ibid.*, p. 5.
[15] Space does not permit further presentation of Smith's views. The interested student should read his book. See footnote 12 of this chapter.

it is of particular interest because of the design.[16] It is well known that the images on our retina are upside down. Knowing this, Dr. Ewert asked: What would happen to our perception of the world about us if these images were inverted so that they were now right side up? He used a system of lenses in front of the eye which inverted the retinal image. The effect was to greatly disorient the subject. Walking and moving of any kind proved very difficult. The inverting of the images also reverses the right and left positions. When the subject tries to avoid walking into a chair that to him appears to be on his left, he steps to the right and thus steps against the chair. To shake hands with someone, he would put his hand to the left when the other person's hand was on the right side. Even sounds appeared to come from the wrong direction.

The important finding in the experiment is that after the subject has worn the lenses for a period of time, his world begins to stabilize and he gradually learns to see objects in their right location and position. Although the world never comes to look completely normal to him, he does learn to adjust easier to it.

Similar results have been reported in auditory perception. So-called *pseudophones* are used to carry sounds from one side of the head to the ear of the opposite side, and vice versa. Subjects who wear these headpieces report experiences similar to the inverted lens experiment. But after a while things begin to straighten out and the subjects are able to locate sounds and to identify them with the visual objects to which they belong. This adaptation to visual and auditory inversion is perceptual relearning.

In Chapter 4 an experiment by Harlow on the formation of learning sets was cited and discussed. One of the points emphasized by Harlow was the slow and gradual process by which learning sets are developed. One could easily translate the idea of learning sets into the notion of perceptual learning. Harlow's study and the facts which we have reviewed in this section on the role of learning in perception suggest that a great deal of perceptual learning takes place in early childhood—so much, in fact, that our perceptions have become so subtle that we often no longer perceive distortions even when they are present. In other words, we learn to get used to distortion just as we learn to get used to a new noise level.

Likewise, a stimulus may on first observation appear to be very complex and confused, but after study and learning the object becomes meaningful and appears much simpler. For example, a diagram of the

[16] P. H. Ewert, "Study of Effect of Inverted Retinal Stimulation Upon Spatially Coordinated Behavior," *Genetic Psychology Monograph*, Vol. 7 (1930), pp. 177-361. Excellent general references on perception are: David C. Beardslee and Michael Wertheimer, eds., *Readings in Perception* (Princeton, N.J., D. Van Nostrand Co., Inc., 1958) and Floyd H. Allport, *Theories of Perception and the Concept of Structure* (New York, John Wiley & Sons, Inc., 1955).

human nervous system appears frightfully complex to the beginning anatomy student, but to the anatomy professor it appears much simpler and he is able to note all sorts of patterns and particular structures which seem to be invisible to the neophyte.

Everyone has had the experience of suddenly seeing something and failing to recognize it immediately. But then in a fraction of a second or so after recognition the stimulus object looked quite different from what it did just before. All this indicates that sensory stimuli become organized into meaningful patterns. The phrase meaningful patterns is actually redundant. What difference, if any, is there between the following two phrases: "they perceived the situation differently" or "the situation had different meaning for them." [17] In other words, the meaning that objects and events have acquired through our past experience with them and learning about them is an inseparable part of the way we now perceive them. To a hunter a beautiful forest has a much different meaning than it has to a lumber producer. The hunter's perception is one of a sportsman's paradise, and the lumberman sees the forest as an economic resource.

Two of the most important sources of human experience and hence important influences on perception are the behavioral and cultural environments of man.

4. BEHAVIORAL AND CULTURAL INFLUENCES IN PERCEPTION

Among the *behavioral* forces which shape perception by determining the kinds of discriminations we make among external stimuli are the behavior of our fellows, their expectations of us, the attitudes and values of our group members, and the roles we perform. Among the *cultural* forces which shape perception by determining discrimination are the basic social institutions such as the economic system, family, political system, and the institution of religion. Not among the least important institutions in influencing perception are the institutions of technology and science. These as well as the others are contributing daily to our perceptual discriminations.

[17] Some readers may object to the writer's use of the term *meaning* on the grounds that it is subjective and "mentalistic." If so, the point of the objection is appreciated; however, the writer is guided in his own thinking by the belief that unless there is a known theoretical reason or some methodological advantage in flaunting common sense, then in the early phases of the development of a concept one may find that common sense provides a fertile source for the development of scientific concepts. I am also well aware of the many pitfalls into which common-sense formulations have led science in the history of its development. However, the same can be said in regard to the development of so-called scientific concepts, for example, the "ether" theory in physics and "phlogiston" in chemistry. Finally, it is worth noting Floyd Allport's comment ". . . that phenomenological experience is still experience and as such belongs in the domain of science as legitimate content for study."

Ethnologists and anthropologists in their descriptions of "primitive" societies provide many observations of the effects of the behavioral and cultural environments on perception. For example, Hallowell describes how distance, length, and area are conceived among the Saulteaux Indians of Canada. In contrast to independent or standardized units of measure such as are found in technologically advanced societies, the Saulteaux's conceptions of distance, length, and area are in terms of "units of activity." The length of a journey was measured in terms of "sleeps" or nights on the trip.[18]

In 1944, M. Sherif studied five Turkish villages with varying degrees of isolation from centers of modern technology. He was particularly concerned with the villagers' perception of space, time, and distance in relation to their varying degrees of contact with modern technology.[19]

In Sherif's study the most isolated villagers expressed distance like the Saulteaux Indians in terms of "units of activity." Distances up to three or four kilometers were described as "within a bullet's reach," "as far as my voice can go" or "as far as it takes to smoke a cigarette." Instead of using hours to describe the divisions of the day, they described dawn as the "first rooster," "leaving of oxen" (for grazing) as sunrise, and "return of oxen" as sunset or later.

On the other hand, the least isolated village described distance in terms of days, hours, and minutes.

Levels of aspiration and self-perceptions are significantly affected by the evaluations of one's behavior and performance by others. In this sense, the behavior of others serves as a standard to compare with one's own. When individuals face a task in which they have not established their own level of achievement, but are given the achievement level of some other group that is already established as superior or inferior, then the position of this group provides a basis for setting a goal for performance of the members who have not established themselves. This was demonstrated in an interesting experiment in 1939 by Chapman and Volkmann. Their subjects (college students) did not have sufficient objective information about their own performance on a literary test for them to judge their own level of performance relative to others. The subjects were provided with statements which purported to describe the performances of other groups which occupied different vertical positions relative to the subjects' reference group. One level of performance was attributed to literary critics (that is, higher group than the subjects' college reference group) and one to WPA workers (lower than the college reference group) and one similar to the subjects' own reference group.

[18] A. Irving Hallowell, "Some Psychological Aspects of Measurement Among the Saulteaux," *American Anthropologist,* Vol. 44 (1942), pp. 66-67.

[19] Muzafer Sherif and Carolyn W. Sherif, *An Outline of Social Psychology,* rev. ed. (New York, Harper & Row, Publishers, Inc., 1956), pp. 692-698.

Four experimental groups were randomly selected and labeled A, B, C, and D. Group A was the control group which received no statements or suggestions as to the difficulty of the material or as to how others had performed on it. Group B was told that the test had been tried on a group of authors and literary critics, who made an average score of 37.2. Group C was told that the test had been tried on a group of psychology students who scored 37.2. Group D was told that the test had been tried on a group of WPA workers who made an average score of 37.2.

Group A, the uninstructed group, scored a mean aspiration-level score of 26.95. Group B, which was given the alleged experts' score, set its aspiration-level at 23.09, and Group C, which was given a performance score of a group similar to their own group, set their aspiration-level score at 31.09. Group D, which was given the performance score of the alleged inferior group, set its aspiration-level score at 33.05. All these differences except that between Group C and D are highly significant. The general conclusion is that instructions in the form of suggested achievements of other groups, when given in advance, can change the level of aspiration of the groups receiving the instruction.[20]

In a second part of the experiment by Chapman and Volkmann the subjects were allowed to previously establish standards of their own from actual performance on a task. The introduction of standards attributed to various groups produced practically no shifts in level of aspiration. In this case, aspiration goals were regulated by the subjects' personal levels of achievement.

The foregoing discussion indicates that the general setting in which a stimulus is found influences the stimulus properties. There are many experiments which demonstrate this principle. It is a basic *gestalt* principle. We will cite as one final illustration a clever piece of research by Sherif. Sherif took a general psychological phenomenon that is found in perception; namely, that our experience is organized or modified by frames of reference which participate as part of the context to any stimulus situation. He extended this principle to the social field in order to test the effect of social influence on perceptual judgment.

Sherif points out that if a reference point is lacking in the external field of stimulation, it is established internally as the temporal sequence of presentation of stimuli goes on. He then asks: What will an individual do when he is placed in an objectively unstable situation in which all basis of comparison, as far as the external field of stimulation is concerned, is absent? In other words, what will he do when the external frame of reference is eliminated? What will a *group* of people do in the same unstable situation? Will the different individuals in the group give a hodgepodge of judgments? Or will they establish a collective frame

---

[20] Theodore M. Newcomb and Eugene L. Hartley, eds., *Readings in Social Psychology* (New York, Holt, Rinehart and Winston, Inc., 1947), pp. 90-99.

of reference? Among the possible experimental conditions that could be used to test these questions he chose to use a situation suitable for producing autokinetic effects. An autokinetic effect is produced whenever a visual stimulus object lacks a spatial frame of reference. Sherif created these conditions by arranging a small stationary point of light in a completely or nearly completely darkroom. If the light is turned on and off at regular intervals, it will seem to appear at different places in the room. The apparent movement of the light is the autokinetic effect. It does not matter if the person knows that the light is stationary.

The subjects were asked to judge the perceived extent of the movement under two different conditions: (1) when alone, except for the experimenter (in order to get the reaction of the individual unaffected by other experimentally introduced social factors); and (2) when the individual is in a group situation (in order to discover modifications brought about by the responses of others).

The general results were that when the subjects were "alone," they formed, after repeated judgments, a general norm or standard estimate of the perceived movement. When they were placed in the group situation, their individual judgments converged and a group norm arose.[21] It is clear from this experiment that perceptual norms can and do arise when there are no stable *objective* external frames of reference for judging stimuli under such conditions. These perceptual norms arise out of the person's perception of the *responses of others* to these stimuli. When we apply this reasoning to help us understand the development of a person's perception of himself relative to other selves, then it becomes obvious how profoundly significant the behavioral and cultural environments of man are to the development of these perceptions which are the core to the human personality, namely, self-attitudes. This aspect of perception and social influence will be discussed in a later chapter on attitudes.

If time and space permitted, it would be possible to go on and on in a summary of the studies which show the significant effects of the behavioral environment and patterns of culture in shaping perceptual discrimination and reorganization. Certainly one of the most subtle and profound sources of perceptual influence is the effect of language on perception. The language system of a society has far-reaching and deep-seated effects on human perception.[22]

Poul Anderson, writing in *The Saturday Review*, makes a very plausible argument that the concept of relativity had to wait until the twentieth century for elucidation, instead of coming to birth in the seventeenth,

---

[21] *Ibid.*, pp. 76-90.
[22] See Benjamin L. Whorf, *Language, Thought, and Reality* (New York, John Wiley & Co., Inc., 1956).

because of the structure of the Indo-European language. Anderson points out that

> The Indo-European languages have a structure based on substantives and actions (nouns and verbs). They draw an unreal distinction between what a "thing" *is* and what it *does*, and compound this confusion by separating its qualities from the "thing" itself—as if "heaviness" had some separate existence apart from the class of heavy objects. In scientific theory, if there is reason to suppose that some action is taking place, it becomes all too natural to imagine that there must be something which acts—if you think in Indo-European terms. For instance, classical physics had cause to believe in electromagnetic undulations: or, strictly speaking, in certain phenomena describable by wave-type equations. It was therefore a linguistic (not, be it noted, a logical) necessity to postulate an "ether" which could undulate. This ether became more-or-less identified with absolute space. But the substantive concept of space or of time is due merely to the fact that in the Indo-European languages "space" and "time" are substantive nouns.
>
> Newton's contemporary Leibniz recognized the self-contradictory character of the "absolute space" concept, as shown by his correspondence with Newton's pupil and advocate, Clarke. He pointed out, for example, that the only way to detect it would be to find something which was absolutely at rest—but this particle or ether or what-have-you would, by definition of motion be moving with respect to everything else! His suggestion lay fallow to Poincaré's day, and not till Einstein did anyone base a complete physical theory on the insight. This is not a matter of Leibniz being an obscure figure like Mendel. Is it too much to suggest that his acute analysis was neglected because the structure of Western language made it difficult to understand?[23]

This discussion by Anderson of the effects of linguistic forms on thinking is a very important insight since it is taken from a page in the history of man's efforts to create and it involved no small figures in this effort. Certainly language provides a perspective for viewing nature, and every language has an inherent logical structure which in turn conditions the thinking.

Let us turn now to a consideration of a study which relates community variables to perception.

A recent study by William H. Sewell entitled *Community of Residence and College Plans* strikingly demonstrates the importance of the behavioral and cultural environment in shaping the plans of high school seniors to attend college. If we consider place of residence, particularly size of the community of residence, as a variable and control such sig-

[23] Poul Anderson, "How Social Is Science?" *The Saturday Review* (April 27, 1957), pp. 10-11.

nificant personal variables as IQ, sex, and socioeconomic status, then certain stimulus elements in the community may be viewed as frames of reference which determine one's perception of going to college as a positive goal.

Sewell conducted such a study which involved 5,317 high school seniors. The following table summarizes the results of his study.

Note that in regard to males of high intelligence and high socioeconomic status who live on farms 58 percent of this category plan to go to college. But as place of residence changes for this same category of seniors from farm to village to small urban to medium urban to large urban, the percentage who plan to go to college increases steadily to 83.1 percent. The same general trends are revealed for females. Obviously, the children in these different residential areas are being exposed to different perceptual cues and perhaps more importantly to a different frequency or intensity of exposure to positive expectations about college.

The student who reads the experimental literature on perception is likely to conclude that perception theory is concerned only with such psychophysical factors as perception of motion, form, color, brightness, distance, and space. These are important variables to which all human beings have to adapt, but perception is not limited to these phenomena. One would expect that the principles of perception which describe man's perception of these psychophysical phenomena also apply to the perception of behavioral events and other social and cultural phenomena dealt with by the sociologist and social psychologist.

As viewed in this text, perception is an adaptive process. It is the process by which the organism receives its information and organizes this information in order to make adjustments. The normal human being lives in the here-and-now, but is cognizant of the past and the future. He weighs stimuli in terms of their nearness, frequency, and intensity; more importantly, he weights them according to their *significance* and *value*, and their significance and value are largely determined by social and cultural factors. In this light let us now examine some of the properties and characteristics of perception as a process, that is, as a variable in behavior.

5. THE PERCEPTUAL PROCESS AND SOCIAL NORMS

Psychologists speak of the degree of agreement between perceptual cues and the identification of the perceptual object or relationship such that the perceiver may make correct inferences or predictions of other properties of the object of perception. This conception of veridical perception is consistent with Müller's view that we do not perceive what is "real and out there" but what our nervous system is doing. As Müller says: "Sensation consists in the sensorium receiving through the medium

TABLE 5:1

Percentage with College Plans by Place of Residence, Intelligence, and Socioeconomic Status, for Male and Female High School Seniors [24]

PLACE OF RESIDENCE	LOW INTELLIGENCE			MIDDLE INTELLIGENCE			HIGH INTELLIGENCE			TOTAL[b]
	LOW SES	MIDDLE SES[a]	HIGH SES[a]	LOW SES	MIDDLE SES[a]	HIGH SES[b]	LOW SES	MIDDLE SES[a]	HIGH SES[b]	
Males										
Farm	6.2(195)	5.5(127)	18.2(55)	15.2(125)	23.5(119)	33.3(69)	29.2(89)	47.6(84)	58.0(69)	22.0(932)
Village	5.9(171)	20.3(118)	24.0(75)	18.6(113)	30.1(113)	54.2(72)	34.3(67)	49.0(100)	73.4(109)	31.8(938)
Small urban	4.1(170)	17.1(117)	23.7(97)	19.3(135)	25.9(135)	51.1(139)	36.6(82)	53.0(125)	82.0(245)	38.4(1235)
Medium urban	7.4(136)	14.6(123)	38.1(97)	18.5(103)	36.3(113)	58.8(136)	38.4(73)	57.5(127)	81.0(185)	41.7(1093)
Large urban	6.1(66)	27.7(65)	36.8(57)	30.4(79)	40.6(96)	65.1(106)	34.0(50)	62.5(104)	83.1(183)	50.7(806)
Total rural	6.0(366)	12.7(245)	21.5(130)	16.8(238)	26.7(232)	44.0(141)	31.4(156)	48.4(184)	67.4(178)	26.9(1870)
Total urban	5.7(372)	18.4(305)	32.3(251)	21.8(317)	33.4(344)	57.7(381)	36.6(205)	57.5(346)	82.1(613)	42.7(3134)
Total	5.8(738)	15.8(550)	28.6(381)	19.6(555)	30.7(576)	54.0(522)	34.4(361)	54.3(530)	78.8(791)	36.8(5004)
Females										
Farm	5.1(196)	17.4(98)	23.4(47)	12.5(144)	22.1(122)	29.3(82)	21.1(109)	37.2(94)	61.4(57)	21.1(949)
Village	2.7(187)	17.9(106)	25.0(60)	9.2(109)	22.2(99)	47.5(101)	29.7(64)	40.7(91)	41.7(115)	23.9(932)
Small urban	2.7(187)	9.9(142)	39.0(95)	7.1(141)	24.8(137)	48.1(133)	17.6(74)	38.0(121)	72.0(189)	29.5(1219)
Medium urban	6.7(179)	11.7(120)	23.6(89)	11.0(127)	28.2(131)	51.6(128)	27.5(69)	38.9(139)	67.4(245)	32.8(1227)
Large urban	1.6(123)	17.6(108)	27.9(68)	9.5(95)	23.6(106)	55.7(140)	21.4(56)	44.1(111)	76.5(183)	35.7(990)
Total rural	3.9(383)	17.7(204)	24.3(107)	11.1(253)	22.2(221)	39.3(183)	24.3(173)	38.9(185)	48.3(172)	22.5(1881)
Total urban	3.9(489)	12.7(370)	30.6(252)	9.1(363)	25.7(374)	51.9(401)	22.1(199)	40.2(371)	71.5(617)	32.4(3436)
Total	3.9(872)	14.5(574)	28.8(359)	9.9(616)	24.4(595)	48.0(584)	23.1(372)	39.8(556)	66.4(789)	28.9(5317)

[a] Chi square significant beyond .05 level for males only.
[b] Chi square significant beyond .05 level for males and females.

[24] William H. Sewell, "Community of Residence and College Plans," *American Sociological Review*, Vol. 29 (February, 1964), pp. 24-38. Reprinted by permission of the American Sociological Association.

of the nerves, and as the result of the action of an external cause, a knowledge of certain qualities of conditions, not of external bodies, but of the nerves of sense themselves." [25] Consequently, the validity of perception is conceived not as a matter of physical representation but more as a matter of what Bruner calls "model building." [26] That is, the perceiver learns the relations between the properties of a perceptual object and some related outcome or event connected with the object. In other words, he is able to correlate or relate what goes with what. For example, an observer is able to relate a certain developing cloud formation with impending rain.

Our perceptions of physical objects are reasonably stable and definite and our perceptions of complex social relations, while often quite accurate, are generally less stable and definite than our perceptions of physical objects. One of the major reasons for this is that objects do not exhibit motivation; particularly, they are not motivated to mislead the observer. That is to say that, in the case of man, certain significant behavioral properties cannot be perceived directly and must therefore be inferred. Consequently, the actor often exhibits sham behavior to try to affect in desired ways the observer's perception. As for that matter, lower forms of animal life also exhibit sham behavior.

Physical objects, of course, also possess internal properties which can only be inferred. It is still something of a moot question as to whether man's perceptions of social stimuli are actually unstable as compared to his perceptions of objects or whether the instability derives from the complexity and sometimes deliberate and studied vagaries of human behavior. A major property of human perception is that its accuracy improves through practice and experience. With practice human perception can become very accurate. Seamstresses are well known for their skills in estimating lengths and widths of materials. Members of societies which rely heavily on hunting for subsistence are known to be able to perceive animal tracks in the sand and among leaves which nonmembers of the society cannot see even after the physical cues are pointed out to them. Certainly the *capacity* for the perception of various forms, colors, and relationships is determined by the structure of the human nervous system, but the content and meaning of a particular percept is greatly influenced by learning. Nietzsche contended that no human perception is immaculate. In other words, all observation involves some cognition. It is safe to say that at any particular perception we always know something already, and this knowledge is intimately in-

[25] Cited in Charles M. Solley and Gardner Murphy, *Development of the Perceptual World* (New York, Basic Books, Inc., Publishers, 1960), p. 227.
[26] Jerome S. Bruner, "On Perceptual Readiness," in David C. Beardslee and Michael Wertheimer, eds., *Readings in Perception* (Princeton, N.J., D. Van Nostrand Co., Inc., 1958), pp. 686-724.

PERCEIVING AND THE SOCIAL WORLD   133

volved in what we come to know next. We tend to see what we expect to see and have reason for seeing. This expectancy can make for perceptual error, but it is also responsible for perceptual accuracy. Thus, a basic assumption we are making is that all perceptual experience is *basically a process of categorization*.[27] Aspects of the process may be conscious and other aspects may be automatic or relatively unconscious. For example, the eyes perceive a car approaching and another car moving forward ahead of the viewer and the driver who perceives both the oncoming car and the ongoing one determines that he can pass the ongoing car and still have time to get into the correct lane ahead before the oncoming car approaches too close. The brain and the sense organs put together somehow a great deal of information, and the perception depends on all aspects of this information, not just part. Through experience the process becomes very accurate; however, aspects of the information may be categorized so as to produce an illusion. The following is a simple physical illustration of the preceding point. Suppose that an investigator asks a sample of observers to estimate whether the following two lines are of equal length: (1) ——————— (2) ——————— . One may be reasonably sure that a significant majority would say that they are the same, and they presumably are. However, suppose the same question is asked about these two lines?:[28] (3) >———————< (4) <———————>. Most people would say that line 3 is longer than line 4 or that it looks longer. Actually, they are the same. The principle which we wish to convey by this illustration is that *added stimuli* and *varied perceptual conditions* (distance, for example) affect the accuracy of perceptual judgments. This point has significant implications for perception of *social relationships*. Relatively accurate perception of *social* relationships, at least in the sense of shared social meanings, is a necessary condition for group coordination and efficiency.

Perceptual cues, whether of physical objects or of social behavior, are utilized adaptively as indexes to real objects and experiences. For example, assuming that one is familiar with a certain sound, then a *cue* to the perceived distance of the sound object from the hearer is the intensity or loudness of the sound. We usually judge weak sounds as being farther away than loud ones. Thus the accuracy of our perception is partially a function of the trustworthiness or validity of the cues as indexes to the environment. Inasmuch as one's environment is itself somewhat irregular and erratic, the accuracy of perception varies. If one makes an error in his perception of the degree of hardness of a ball, then, after catching it once, he will know next time to make allowances. The point is that the nature of such a physical experience as pain sets up an avoidance response by the person, and his behavior is thereby modified. But

[27] *Ibid.*, p. 686.
[28] This is the well-known Müller-Lyer illusion.

suppose that the perceptual cue is one of human skin color and the perceiver is a member of a society whose culture ranks people by skin color; then, the perceiver will perceive, say, a Negro according to the qualities which the dominant culture ascribes to the Negro. Suppose the culture teaches that Negroes and Indians are inherently "lazy"; then, irrespective of whether this is true, they will be responded to *as if* they were. This illustration suggests an important property of *social reality;* namely, that if people believe that something is real, then they act on the basis of the belief. Hence beliefs, opinions, social norms, and ideologies are *social facts* and in this sense social reality.

The point which we wish to note by contrasting the perception of "hardness" with the perception of a social cue is that the relations between individuals and inanimate objects are quite different from the relations among the individuals of a group. Certainly the same basic psychological principles apply to the interaction of individuals with inanimate objects, but there are additional conditions and processes involved in interaction in the human environment. In the first place, the objects of interaction are always persons and the persons' behavior. Therefore, the behavior of each person serves as *both* independent and dependent variables, that is, as both stimulus and response.

Sociologists have emphasized for over a century the necessity of understanding the organization and functioning of man's *behavioral environment* if one is to adequately explain how and why things and relations mean what they do to the individual. In other words, much perceptual meaning is determined by the structure and function of man's social environment. Man's dependence upon his fellows and hence the importance of other people to each of us cannot be overemphasized. How is the dependence of man upon man met? In the first place, men must be able to communicate so that the perceptions of each may be shared. In other words, cooperative human interaction presupposes shared perceptions.

What are some of the conditions under which shared perceptions develop? A very important part of the answer to this question was provided by M. Sherif in his study on the formation of group or social norms.[29] Let us first describe what is meant by the term social norm. Throughout this book this concept will be used to mean a shared evaluation or standard for behavior. The evaluation or standard may or may not be a moral evaluation. If the norms become traditional, then they constitute *cultural definitions* of a group or a society.

Social norms not only tell us *what to and what not to perceive,* but they also tell us *how to respond* to what we perceive. For example, an

---

[29] Sherif and Sherif, *op. cit.*, pp. 237-279. See also Muzafer Sherif and Carolyn W. Sherif, *Reference Groups* (New York, Harper & Row, Publishers, Inc., 1964), pp. 35-246.

umpire who referees a baseball game looks for "balls," "strikes," and "fouls," and when he observes them he knows how to respond to them. So it is with group behavior in general. The norms prescribe what to look for in a situation and often what not to see as well. They also define what to do and what not to do in given social situations. The norms which define social situations are generally the minimum necessary to insure reasonable fruitful interaction. Only when it is necessary to highly standardize some behavioral situation are the norms spelled out in great detail and precision. A military battle plan or a factory production plan would be crude examples of two social situations where the norms may be quite detailed and precise. In other words, norms are blueprints for social interaction. No two individuals performing at different times in the same social position will behave in exactly the same way even though the norms are the same. As we have said, norms are only standards; and the *actual* behavior of a role occupant must be distinguished from the standard, which is general enough to cover all occupants of a given role type. The norms for a general medical practitioner are quite general, and the public perceives some physicians as very good, some as average, and some as poor.

Norms may be said to provide frames of reference for perceiving people and people's behavior; they thus become inseparable from attitudes toward people. How are norms discerned? Some are written—such as the legal code of a society or the Bible, which provides a great storehouse of norms for human conduct in general. On the other hand, many norms are made clear by verbal statements or judgmental reactions to others' behavior. That is, someone such as a parent or a peer expresses disappointment or approval of another's behavior, and these expressions of approval or disappointment become perceptual cues to response appropriateness or inappropriateness. Thus the ongoing concepts and ideas of adults help define meanings for children. These definitions in turn become a significant part of the basis for the children's perceptions. An obvious example which comes to mind is the definitions of the behavior appropriate to the sexes in a society. For example, children in the United States have learned by the age of five or six a sizable list of behaviors appropriate for boys and another list appropriate for girls. Girls, for instance, who are observed engaging in behavior which is socially defined as more appropriate for boys are perceived as "tomboys," and boys under similar circumstances are called "sissies."

The general principle which the foregoing discussion of social norms and social roles suggests is that a *major organizing factor in determining meaning in perception is the social definitions which regulate human interaction as well as human actions toward "things" or inanimate objects.* That is to say that the meaning which derives from certain perceptions is presented to the individual by his culture. This does not mean that each individual in a community will perceive a given stimulus the same way but simply that the *general* meaning of the stimulus is determined by the web of social organization which constitutes or makes up the community. For example, the social organization of American society defines the role of women in a subordinate power relationship, and in spite of all the encouragement to the contrary, they (women) are still perceived as subordinated. This is not because the public wants or prefers to perceive women in a subordinate role, but their perception is a function of the positions actually occupied by women. This statement, as such, suggests or implies nothing about the biological differences between males and females, but instead refers to the innumerable ways in which mankind has developed social structures which define the roles of males and females, and these structures in turn provide the broader meanings upon which our perceptions of men and women depend.[30]

Let us summarize the major points of this section.

First, we have contended that the same basic processes and principles that are involved in the perception of physical or inanimate objects are also involved in the perception of social behavior, although social behavior has the added property of being both stimulus and response and the sham behavior of human beings complicates and interferes with accuracy in the perception of motives and other personal qualities.

Second, accuracy in perception is judged on the basis of the perceiver's capacity to identify perceptual cues and correctly relate these to other properties of the object of perception. Thus a basic assumption we are making is that all perceptual experience involves a basic process of categorization.

Third, concepts function to provide structure and meaning for perception and subsequently to serve as a basis for perception. For example, the social psychologist conceives of the term "attitude" as a system of positive or negative feelings toward social objects. If, then, he observes a man passing out anti-Semitic literature, he infers that the man probably possesses a negative attitude toward minority groups.

Fourth, social norms and social roles provide frames of reference for perceiving social behavior and social objects.

Perception tends to be quite stable. Sometimes it is difficult to perceive an object differently even when added cues are pointed out. This seems to be particularly true of geometric forms and ambiguous and incongruous pictures. We will return to this later. Just now we wish to note that a similar perceptual stability is involved in the perception of social objects and relationships, and this stability is hitched to or depends upon the stability and strength of social norms. The social norms may remain relatively the same over long periods of time, even though many

[30] See, for example, Margaret Mead, *Sex and Temperament in Three Primitive Societies* (New York, Mentor Books, 1950).

of the characteristics of the people for whom the norms exist may change. For example, since the Civil War the Negro in the southern United States has made remarkable progress. Yet, there remain in the South and other areas of the country many people who continue to define the Negro in a subordinate position irrespective of individual achievement. This tendency to lump an entire population of people into one general category irrespective of individual differences has been called stereotyping.[31]

On the other hand, many people strive to acquire properties which will cause them to be perceived in some stereotyped fashion which they consider desirable. That is to say, some find it desirable to manipulate stereotypes for their advantage.

Bernard de Mandeville, writing in 1714 in his famous *Fable of the Bees, or Private Vices Publick Benefits*, dramatically describes this phenomenon as follows:

> . . . the World has long since decided the Matter; handsome Apparel is a main point, fine Feathers make fine Birds, and People, *where they are not known,* are generally honour'd according to their Clothes and other Accoutrements they have about them; from the richness of them we judge of their Wealth, and by their ordering of them we guess at their Understanding. It is this which encourages every Body, who is conscious of his little Merit, if he is any ways able, to wear clothes above his Rank, especially in large and populous Cities, where obscure Men may hourly meet with fifty Strangers to one Acquaintance, and consequently have the pleasure of being esteem'd by a vast Majority, not as what they are, but they appear to be: which is a greater temptation than most people want to be in vain.[32]

Mandeville was prompted to write the foregoing from his observations on the emerging new forms of urban life of his time. These comments were made two hundred and fifty years ago, but they are nonetheless cogent today.

Man is not the only animal that is capable of exhibiting behavior to create appearances that are different from reality. Sham behavior is often exhibited by animals as a means of protecting their young offspring. All this suggests that if things are not always as they appear, then the observer must calculate and exercise judgment based on the *probable* meaning of the event or behavior observed.

Suppose one assumes that expensive clothes are an index or cue to a person's income and financial position. Nevertheless, some will underspend relative to their income and thus give cause to be misperceived, while others overspend on clothes in order to give an appearance of

---

[31] Walter Lippmann, *Public Opinion* (Baltimore, Penguin Books, Inc., 1946), pp. 59-120. First published in 1921 by The Macmillan Company.
[32] Cited by Howard Becker and Harry Elmer Barnes, *Social Thought From Lore to Science,* 2nd ed. (New York, Dover Publications, Inc., 1952), p. 407.

wealth. Therefore, it is clear that while cues may remain stable, they do not always denote the same properties. Thus the learner or perceiver has the problem of determining the most probable meaning of the cues.

The trustworthiness of cues is checked by enlarging the context of observation. Take the man whose behavior gives the appearance of wealth; the validity of the appearances may be determined by a number of different ways if the observer wishes to do so. The spy is the example *par excellence* of the taking on of characteristics for the purpose of creating a new identity. Those who have performed the role of spying only to be detected by some simple deviation in speech, manner, or custom know how accurate social perception sometimes is.

The following figure designed by the author illustrates how a shifting context of relations affects the appearance of the structure perceived.

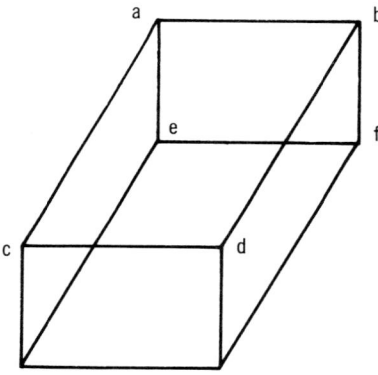

FIGURE 5:1. An Ambiguous Figure. This drawing will alternate between being perceived as a box lying on its side and as one standing on its end.

The observer's perspective for viewing Figure 5:1 shifts, if he views it for a few seconds, from one of standing on its end to one of lying down. Of course, the shift can be the other way around depending upon which perspective is seen first. For anyone who has difficulty in observing the shift, it will be helpful to focus his view on a particular set of four letters. The set *a, b, e, f* provides the perspective for perceiving the figure as standing on end and the set *a, b, c, d* provides the anchorages for viewing it as lying down.

6. SOME GENERAL PERCEPTUAL FINDINGS [33]

[33] One of the best sources for a good overview of experimental findings on perception is Robert S. Woodworth and Harold Schlosberg, *Experimental Psychology* (New York, Holt, Rinehart and Winston, Inc., 1954), Chapters 14-17.

The reader should bear in mind that perception as personal experience is not the same as perception as a variable in behavior. The reason for this distinction is quite simple. If we dealt with perception as personal experience, we would be limited to the subject's readiness or ability to report rather than his ability to perceive. Our interest is in perception as a variable in behavior—a variable to be described by the scientist rather than the subject, although the scientist may take into account the subject's reportings of his perceptual experience. However, when he does take into account such personal experience, it will be from the point of view of interpreting and explaining it rather than taking the subject's explanations.

Among the interesting facts or experimental findings on perception as a variable in behavior is that all experiences—even the simplest—are organized by the perceiver. How much of this organization is a function of experience is currently unknown. That a good deal of the organization seems to be a function of experience in interaction with neural functioning is no longer doubted. Also, apparently the building up of a perceptual set, perspective, or concept is a slow and much longer process than we are sometimes aware of. However, once the concept has been formed it can be *applied* with an instant-like insight.

Figure and Ground Factors in Experience

The perceived characteristics of any part of an object are a function of the whole to which the parts appear to belong. The figure stands out as clearly defined and in front of the ground. Hebb contends that the mechanism of figure-ground organization is innate: [34]

> In our daily lives there are constant transformations and restructurings in our perceptual fields. This process is revealed as the reader of this book reads this page. The reader sees this line of print as figure and the page as ground momentarily; but as he glances over his desk, in the next moment, he sees the same page as figure and his desk as ground. This *shift* from one component to another in the perceptual field is clearest in the phenomenon of figure and ground.[35]

The classical example of this is Rubin's Goblet figure.

Solley and Murphy summarize Rubin's conclusions on the basic features of figure-ground organizations as follows:

> 1. The figure has form whereas ground is relatively formless. The ground may have form properties but it is less definite, with weaker contour.

[34] D. O. Hebb, *The Organization of Behavior* (New York, John Wiley & Sons, Inc., 1949).
[35] Charles M. Solley and Gardner Murphy, *op. cit.*, p. 262.

FIGURE 5:2. Rubin's "Twins and Vase" Figure. (From Solley and Murphy, *Development of the Perceptual World*, New York, Basic Books, Inc., 1960, p. 264).

2. The figure has "thing-like" qualities whereas ground appears as unformed material, and once the qualities are experienced they tend to stabilize.

3. The figure appears nearer to the observer than does ground, and the ground appears to extend unbroken behind the figure.

4. The figure is more easily identified; its color is more impressive and it is more likely to be connected with meanings, feelings, and esthetic values.[36]

Solley and Murphy present a very strong argument that *what* is figure and *what* is ground can be learned, and Schafer and Murphy attempted to demonstrate this.[37]

The general conclusions which Solley and Murphy draw are that rewarded materials are more likely to be perceived as figure and punished

[36] *Ibid.*, p. 263.
[37] *Ibid.*, pp. 265-274.

materials as ground. This seemed to be particularly true of reversible figures.

Figure-ground formation is one of the basic forms of perceptual organization. Actually, the conditions and processes of segregation and grouping of stimulus elements find expression in the process of figure formation. Figure formation is facilitated when the stimulus elements are in close *proximity;* the greater the *similarity* of the elements, the greater the *contrast* between figure elements and ground elements, and the more the elements follow as regular direction or have *continuity.*

The consequences of figure-ground reversal in the real or empirical world can be serious. Such reversals, for example, sometimes occur when an aircraft pilot switches from "contact" to "instrument" flight.

> As long as the pilot can see the earth, he perceives his own aircraft to be banking, climbing, or diving with respect to the stationary earth below. However, as soon as the outside vision is excluded, the visible parts of his own aircraft, such as the instrument panel and cockpit enclosure, become the fixed background with reference to which the small moving parts of the instrument displays appear as figure. He now responds in terms of an "aircraft reference" principle. . . . When the earth was viewed through a nearby window, so that it subtended a relatively large visual angle, the aircraft was perceived to be in bank; however, when a relatively small area of the earth was seen through a distant window, the aircraft was perceived to be level and the earth tilted.[38]

Change in Perceptual Organization

Individuals tend to have a dominant form of perceptual organization in respect to a given stimulus. For example, some will first see Figure 5:1 as lying on its side, while for others the end perspective will be dominant. In any event, one mode of perceptual organization is dominant over other possibilities, and the dominance is due either to innate or learned mechanisms or both. Nevertheless, if we look long enough at a given figure, it will undergo surprising alterations. In other words, the order and stability exhibited by our perceptual processes are at best temporary. When sensory information is ambiguous, the perceptual field becomes more unstable.

This instability is well illustrated by Figure 5:3 below.

The face alternates between the face of an attractive young woman and that of an old woman. Certainly a "good" figure requires less energy and effort to maintain itself than an ambiguous one. As we indicated above, the conditions for forming a good figure are similarity, proximity,

---

[38] Paul M. Fitts, "Engineering Psychology and Equipment Design," in S. S. Stevens, ed., *Handbook of Experimental Psychology* (New York, John Wiley & Sons, Inc., 1951), p. 1308.

FIGURE 5:3. Ambiguous Face. (From Edwin G. Boring, "A New Ambiguous Figure," *American Journal of Psychology*. Vol. 42 (1930), p. 444).

contrast, and continuity. The perceptual organization can also be modified by changing the values, attitudes, and emotional states of the observer.

> Laboratory experimentation as well as research in the field of opinion and attitude change seems to demonstrate beyond a shadow of a doubt that the major condition for a change in our perception, our attitudes or opinions is a frustration experienced in carrying out our purposes effectively because we are acting on the basis of assumptions that prove "wrong." For example, Dr. Kilpatrick has demonstrated that apparently the only way in which we can "learn" to see our distorted room distorted is to become frustrated with the assumption that the room is "square" in the process of trying to carry out some action in the room. . . . It is clear that an "intellectual," "rational" or "logical" understanding of a situation is by no means sufficient to alter perception.[39]

One of the major reasons why perception changes as our attitudes, expectancies, and experiences change is that a significant portion of the content of an individual's perceptions is his own creation. That is, we give meaning and order to sensory impingements in terms of our needs and past experience; therefore, our perceptions will change as our needs and experiences change.

[39] Hadley Cantril, "Perception and Interpersonal Relations," *American Journal of Psychiatry*, Vol. 114 (August, 1957), p. 125.

Let me give an illustration by reporting an experiment which indicates that we "perceive" to a certain extent in terms of our own creation.

Hadley Cantril cites several experiments which well illustrate the point in question. An adaptation was made of the old-fashioned stereoscope by Dr. Edward Engel.

> In Engel's experiments he prepares what he calls "stereograms" consisting of photographs 2 x 2 inches, one of which is seen with the left eye, the other with the right. The photographs he used first were those of members of the Princeton football team just as they appeared in the football program. Although there were slight differences in the size and position of the heads and in the characteristics of light and shadow, still there was sufficient superimposition to get binocular fusion. And what happens? A person looks into the stereoscope and sees one face. He describes this face. And it almost invariably turns out that he is describing neither the face of the man seen with the left eye nor the face of the man seen with the right eye. He is describing a new and different face, a face that he has created out of the features of the two he is looking at. Generally the face seen in this particular case is made up of the dominant features of the two individuals. And generally the face created by the observer in this situation is more attractive and appealing than either of those seen separately.[40]

Woodworth and Schlosberg, in discussing the perception of objects, show the effects of cultural conditioning on perception. This is demonstrated by taking advantage of the visual anomaly *aniseikonia* (unequal images due to unequal lenses). If the image in one eye is larger than that in the other, this affects the disparities among images and results in incorrect and confusing depth perception. Woodworth and Schlosberg note that "The peculiar thing about this disorder is that people who have it still perceive the world normally. Houses and walls appear straight, even though they should be distorted in accordance with the optics of the situation." [41] Thus a person with unequal lenses should see a room that is square as if one corner were farther away than another. If the left eye has the smaller lens, the right corner of the room should appear to be farther away than the left-hand corner, even though both corners are equidistant.

> But he may not! That is, he may not if the wall is made of plaster or brick which is usually erected square in our culture. But if he is put in a cubicle lined with leaves, the famous *leaf room*, the corners behave as the optical laws predict they should. This makes sense if we realize that there is no reason for O (observer) to believe that the walls of the leaf room are really

[40] *Ibid.*, p. 121.
[41] Woodworth and Schlosberg, *op. cit.*, p. 487.

squared up. Hence he is free to see them according to the dictates of the unusual binocular disparity.[42]

A word of caution should be given against interpreting our earlier statement "that a significant portion of the content of an individual's perceptions is his own creation" as a voluntary and rational process. An individual may be aware of a perceptual experience, but he is not aware of how this experience develops or functions and therefore cannot himself manipulate his perceptual processes.

It is doubtful if an individual has awareness of the arousal of the primitive perceptual field, but he would have awareness of the arousal of meaning. The mediating process between the arousal of the sensory field in perception and the meaning end of the arc is not known. However, it is known that perceptual responses can and do occur below the level of visual recognition thresholds.

McCleary and Lazarus in a study called "Autonomic Discrimination Without Awareness"[43] confirmed the notion that subjects can give discriminatory galvanic skin responses to visual stimuli presented at tachistoscopic speeds too fast for correct verbal recognition. The authors called this a process of *subception*. They used ten five-letter nonsense words. The subjects were given 100 practice presentations and these were randomized for both order and exposure speeds. Following the practice period, the ten syllables were divided into two groups of five each. The two groups were equated for both the number of times the five syllables were used in the entire 100 responses, and the number of times the five syllables were correctly recognized.

After the subjects had acquired a near 100 percent recognition of the ten syllables, they were again randomly presented each of the syllables an equal number of times, but one-half of the syllables was accompanied with an electric shock. This procedure was continued until consistent conditioned responses to the five experimental syllables were established.

Following the establishment of a galvanic skin response (GSR) to the five syllables, all the syllables were shown tachistoscopically for durations ranging from extremely short to those just about long enough to recognize the words. The authors conclude that

> There is one clear conclusion that we should like to present. It is that even when a subject is unable to report a visual discrimination verbally (i.e., he reports incorrectly when forced to make a choice), he is still able to make a stimulus discrimination at some level below that required for conscious recognition.[44]

---

[42] *Ibid.*, p. 488.
[43] Robert A. McCleary and Richard S. Lazarus, "Autonomic Discrimination Without Awareness: An Interim Report," *Journal of Personality*, Vol. 18 (December, 1949), pp. 171-179.
[44] *Ibid.*, p. 178.

This conclusion was based on the fact that the subjects showed consistent discriminatory galvanic skin responses even though they were unable to verbally report the correct syllables. This is one of many studies which have shown that perceptual responses may occur at subconscious levels.

Another such study involves the perception of materials which are pleasurable and materials which are distasteful. The general findings suggest that the pupil of the eye dilates significantly when looking at pleasurable or interesting materials as compared with neutral ones, and that, conversely, it contracts when viewing distasteful materials. See Figure 5:4 below.[45]

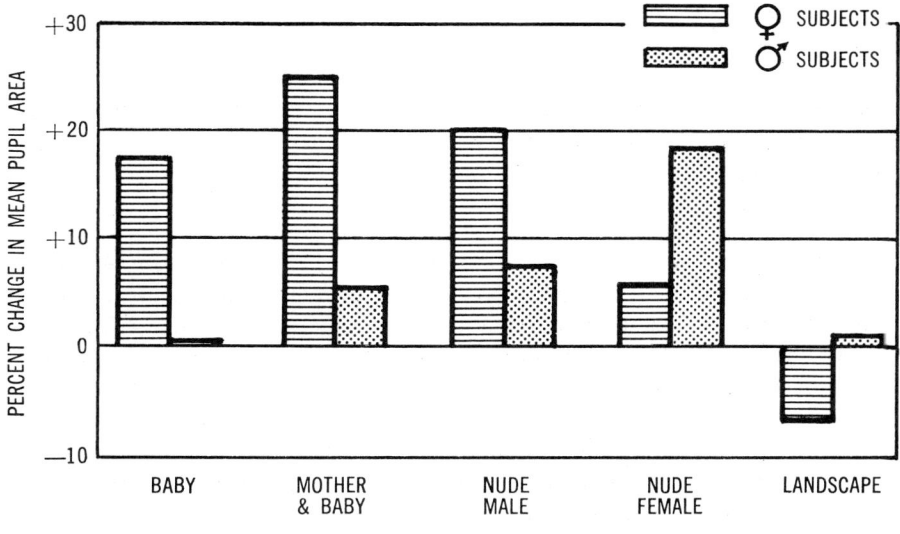

FIGURE 5:4. Changes in Mean Pupil Size, in Terms of Percentage of Decrease or Increase in Area, from Size during Viewing of Control Patterns, in Response to Various Pictures.

In discussing the findings in the above table, the authors quote the following line of Guillaume de Salluste: "Those lovely lamps, these windows of the soul." The changing size of the pupil of the eyes in relation to pleasant and unpleasant stimuli suggests that the pupils register certain activities of the nervous system.

Berelson and Steiner quote a personal communication from Hess, one of the co-authors cited above, which provides additional data on perceiving of positive and negative stimuli.

[45] Eckhard H. Hess and James M. Polt, "Pupil Size as Related to Interest Value of Visual Stimuli," *Science*, Vol. 132, No. 3423 (August 5, 1960), pp. 349-350.

... acknowledged homosexuals were discriminated from normals simply by their differential pupillary response to photographs of homosexuals versus female pin-ups: Five normal males, five normal females, and five admitted homosexual males were shown three abstract paintings, six pictures of men and six pictures of women. Scores were obtained in terms of deviation from the mean change of the pupil in response to all twelve critical pictures. No normal male showed a total negative response to the six pictures of women. No homosexual or woman showed a positive response to the six pictures of women. There is no overlap between normal male and homosexual male subjects in their responses to the two categories of pictures. While the females and the homosexuals give similar responses, the homosexuals showed a much greater rejection of pictures of women than did the female subjects.[46]

Since persons can conceal their real feelings in verbal reports, it appears that pupil reaction may be a more accurate index of subjective reaction to visual material than verbal reporting.

7. SUMMARY

We have defined perception as a process of discrimination. As such we view it as basically an adaptive process by which the organism takes into account environmental demands. The processes of taking into account environmental patterning involve both innate biological characteristics of the organism (such as capacity for depth perception and binocular vision) and the learning capacities of the organism.

It was argued that percepts are the end-products of a slow process of construction through manipulation of and experimentation with the external world. Percepts change as the effects of experience change. Therefore, learning plays an important role in the development of perceptual products. Perceptual materials become organized and form the basis for learning sets which in turn affect subsequent learning. Accordingly, from the point of view of social psychology, we may study the effects of learning on perception or the effects of perception on learning.

Riesen's studies reveal the importance of patterned stimulation to the development of perception. These studies suggest that biological potentiality depends upon the quantity and quality of environmental stimulation and support for its unfolding and manifest development.

We next considered the importance of feedback as a basis for behavioral organization. In this connection Smith's studies pointed to the importance of spatial and temporal factors as properties of man's environment which are important anchorages in perceptual orientation.

[46] Bernard Berelson and Gary A. Steiner, *Human Behavior: An Inventory of Scientific Findings* (New York, Harcourt, Brace & World, Inc., 1964), pp. 103-104.

It was noted that space and time are important dimensions of man's social environment. Some of Sherif's work was reviewed in connection with behavioral and cultural influences on perception.

Cultural and behavioral influences on perception are particularly important in regard to the perception of one's self and the formation of attitudes toward others. In this regard Chapman and Volkmann's study and Sewell's study on college plans were cited.

Next, perception was considered as a fundamental process underlying social interaction. In this connection a distinction was made between the perception of things and the perception of other persons. It was concluded that the same basic psychological processes are involved in each and that the difference was essentially one of the relative complexity of the behavior being perceived.

The major cues for social perception derive from the behavior of others and the standardized behavior or culture of groups. These latter are recognized as belief systems, social norms, and public opinion. Norms, for example, were viewed as providing a frame of reference for viewing people.

Finally, some general findings on perception were summarized. Among these were the concepts of figure and ground as organizing factors in perception. Beyond this, some general conditions which facilitate the formation of clear perceptual responses were identified. These were proximity, similarity, contrast, and continuity. In addition to stability of perception, perceptual change was also considered. In this regard, ambiguity, modified experience, and emotional factors were considered.

Further References

1. David C. Beardslee and Michael Wertheimer, Editors, *Readings in Perception* (Princeton, N.J., D. Van Nostrand Co., Inc., 1958).
2. Charles M. Solley and Gardner Murphy, *Development of the Perceptual World* (New York, Basic Books, Inc., 1960).
3. Robert S. Woodworth and Harold Schlosberg, *Experimental Psychology* (New York, Holt, Rinehart and Winston, Inc., 1954).

6
Social Judgment

•

1. *Introduction*
2. *The Relation of Attitudes and Learning to Judgment*
3. *The Function of Stereotypes and Role-Taking in Perception*
   (a) *The Meaning of Stereotypes*
   (b) *The Meaning of Role-Taking*
4. *Perceptual Judgment*
5. *Summary*

1. INTRODUCTION

WE NOTED IN Chapter 5 that a person not only perceives behavior and events, but he also forms attitudes toward these and makes judgments about such. In many instances, we are socially expected to make and express judgments about the behavior of ourselves and others. The process of social judgment is not only a necessary process in relating ourselves to others, but it is also an important means of social control. It is a means of social control insofar as the process results in responses which reflect approval or disapproval of behavior. In this sense it provides a system of rewards and punishments or positive and negative reinforcements. Parents express approval of certain behaviors of their children and disapproval of other acts. To the degree that the children identify with their parents and/or to the extent to which the parents back up their approvals and disapprovals with rewards and punishments, then this will function to motivate the children to conform to parental expectations.

From the level of presentation and point of view of this text we could just as well have labeled this chapter "The Perception of Social Behavior" instead of titling it "Social Judgment." The chapter title "Social Judgment" was chosen because of the concern in this chapter with the normative evaluation of behavior. Normative evaluation is not used here from the standpoints of the fields of ethics and religion, but simply from the sociological fact that all *social* behavior is defined either by custom, tradition, technical regulation, or law. That is to say, the underlying nature of social behavior is normative. Any act which has real or imaginary social consequences is defined. Thus American culture does not define which shoe a person should put on first, but it does define that shoes are to be worn under certain circumstances. It also defines that the driving of an automobile is always to be on the right-hand side of the street except when passing and that the driver is to follow certain safety precautions in regard to speed, passing, and other driving behavior. The driving of an automobile has potential harmful social consequences to others; hence driving behavior is defined in terms of what is appropriate and inappropriate. The foregoing examples illustrate what we mean by the statement that the underlying nature of social behavior is normative. Accordingly, if the underlying nature of social behavior is normative in that it is defined by social norms, then it follows that a given social response falls either within the boundaries of the norm or outside the boundaries. Consequently, when a person perceives a social act, it is perceived within the context of the appropriately related norms and the act is thereby judged or evaluated by the person in terms of the content of his norm or norms, however vague or implicit these may be.

It should be implicitly clear by now that the perceiver has to make at least two kinds of discriminations when perceiving social behavior. The *first* of these refers to the task of *identifying* the stimulus (an act, a sound, a statement) item. What is it and what does it mean? The *second* kind of discrimination refers to the *evaluation* of that which has been identified. Is the act or suggested act appropriate or inappropriate? Is the quality and quantity up to par in terms of the norm?

A tremendous amount of human behavior involves judgments on these two kinds of discriminations. A barely noticeable or *just noticeable difference* between two stimuli is traditionally given the shorthand label of *jnd*. In speaking of the perception of differences between stimuli by human beings, it is well to be reminded that the perception of a difference does not necessarily correspond to the actual or objective difference. Stevens cites evidence which shows "that a tonal stimulus 20 jnd's above threshold sounds far more than twice as loud as a stimulus 10 jnd's above threshold."[1] In other words, it turns out that in regard to loudness the jnd's are unequal in subjective magnitude. However, Stevens reports that for *pitch* the jnd's are subjectively equal.

The discussion of jnd's has been focused on such physical factors as loudness, pitch, weight, taste, etc., and the data indicate that in general (with the exception of pitch and perhaps others) the perceptions of differences are unequal in subjective magnitude. For example, an actual increase of a factor of two is subjectively experienced as of a different

[1] S. S. Stevens, *Handbook of Experimental Psychology* (New York, John Wiley & Sons, Inc., 1951), p. 36.

magnitude. The purpose in citing these psychophysical data is to contrast judgment of these with that of social stimuli.

In what ways do social stimuli have objective meanings which are independent of the interpretations of the perceivers? Let us look first at how the response of one person functions as a social stimulus to another. We will assume that A's response to B has an objective meaning and that B's response to A's response represents his interpretation of A's response. This exchange of responses can continue until both A and B agree that each *understands* the other. This, of course, does not mean that they necessarily agree with each other. It only means that A is convinced that B has correctly interpreted him and B agrees that A has correctly interpreted him. On the other hand, they may correctly interpret each other and also agree with each other.

The problem of objective stimulus discrimination is somewhat different when the object of discrimination is statements which describe social norms. A sample of adult citizens of the United States would probably not have any difficulty in deciding which of the following statements describes the norm for marriage in the United States:

1. It is expected that a man be married to only one woman at a time.
2. A man is permitted to be married to one or more women at a given time.

It is assumed that everyone would choose the first statement as being descriptive of the norm. This suggests that the norm of monogamy in America is a clearly established societal norm and is therefore clearly understood. However, suppose the behavioral norm or standard in question is not in regard to marriage but refers to industrial trade. What are the norms of "fair trade"? This becomes more difficult to precisely agree upon by those who are participants, let alone others. Both of these examples (the marriage norm and fair trade) have in common the fact that the difference in meaning between statements is a matter of established *social definition* rather than anything inherent or objective about the statements themselves. In other words, the discrimination involved in determining which statement describes the norm or expected behavior appropriate to a given situation depends upon a person's perception of past *patterns of other's responses* to the situation and his understanding of their *expectations* for the situation.

The "others" referred to here are not just any others, but "others" that the perceiver holds in high esteem and with whom he psychologically identifies. In other words, the discrimination between social norms assumes that the persons involved have acquired perceptual frames of reference appropriate to the particular behavioral situation or have, at least, knowledge of these.

A person may be aware of what the norms are for a given situation but not accept these as binding on him. This is often the case with delinquents and criminals. They are aware of the culture's norms on personal rights and property rights, but they reject these in regard to their problems of adaptation. In other words, they have their own frame of reference and it is derived from the delinquent or criminal groups to which they identify. Therefore, *we must distinguish between a person's perception of a social norm as he thinks the larger society defines it and his own definition of the norm.* Sometimes these are the same in reality and are perceived to be the same, and sometimes the person thinks they are the same when in fact they are not; and, finally, they are sometimes perceived as different and are in fact different. It makes an interesting study to determine the social and psychological characteristics which go with persons who possess these different sets of judgments.

In this chapter we intend to examine some of the factors and processes which provide frames of reference for making social judgments.

Let us differentiate the judgment process for purposes of conceptual and experimental specification. To this end we will follow Sherif and Hovland's scheme. They differentiate the process in terms of three lines of approach: "item discrimination, placement of items, and acceptance-rejection of items."[2]

Sherif and Hovland define these approaches as follows: "*Discrimination* refers to the task of identifying a stimulus item . . . as different from another item."[3] The previous discussion of jnd's or "just noticeable differences" is an illustration of this type of study. The distinction which Sherif and Hovland make between discrimination and placement is based on the number of discriminable items. The distinguishing between two stimuli differing on the same dimension is what they mean by *discrimination.* That kind of discrimination "which locates a given stimulus relative to *more* than two other discriminable items . . ."[4] is called *placement* or *categorization.* The reason for this distinction is that the researcher cannot be sure that there is only one dimension involved in a set of several statements or items which possess motivationally relevant content, and it is therefore simpler to categorize.

The fact that categorization is essentially an aspect of the judgmental process can be readily seen when we ask people what they think about a given issue or group of people. The respondent judges the issue in terms of his own and his groups' practices. In other words, his *preferred* practice provides the frame of reference for categorizing the issue. Likewise is the situation if the respondent is judging other people. The more

---

[2] Muzafer Sherif and Carl I. Hovland, *Social Judgment: Assimilation and Contrast Effects in Communication and Attitude Change* (New Haven, Yale University Press, 1961), p. 6.
[3] *Ibid.,* p. 6.
[4] *Ibid.,* p. 7. Italics added.

the people being judged are like the judges, the more favorable the judges rank them. In other words, a person's judgment is reflective of the strength of his attitude in regard to the item being judged. Persons who possess extreme social attitudes exhibit a high degree of displacement when evaluating motivationally relevant stimuli items.[5] That is, they are more likely to overestimate or underestimate a given item in relation to a neutral point than a person with a significantly less extreme attitude.

The third judgmental aspect and research approach which Sherif and Hovland cite is judgment carried out under *acceptance-rejection* instructions. In such a case the subjects are instructed to place or categorize items in terms of a scale of acceptance at one extreme, and of rejection at the other extreme.

2. THE RELATION OF ATTITUDES AND LEARNING TO JUDGMENT

A person's attitude on an issue may determine the way he judges it and therefore influence the way he acts irrespective of objective information available to him. People with strong attitudes are ready to pass judgment and act in terms of their attitudes and without waiting for the facts. In such cases the person's attitudes serve as the frame of reference for judgment and for the evaluation of information. It is for this reason that administrators as well as the voting public shy away from selecting officials with extreme attitudes. Former Senator Barry Goldwater is perceived by his supporters as a conservative and by the more moderate elements of the Republican Party as a reactionary.

Sherif and Hovland illustrate the same point by noting that "... Samuel Gompers ... was judged as rather radical by the conservatives of his day, but he was dubbed a conservative by left-wingers in the labor movement."[6] Thus one's attitude provides a standard for a categorization process and the act of placement or categorizing is an aspect of judgment. In other words, attitudes become points of reference for judgment.

Sherif defines an attitude as a characteristic mode of reaction to a stimulus or stimulus class. He makes it clear that attitudes are learned. In other words, the judgment of a stimulus item relevant to an individual's attitude is necessarily related to other similar items with which

---

[5] *Ibid.*, pp. 7-14. See also Harry S. Upshaw, "A Re-Examination and Re-Interpretation of the Effect of 'Own Attitude' As An Anchor on the Judgment of Neutral Items in Equal-Appearing Intervals Scaling," paper read before the 68th Annual Convention of the American Psychological Association, Chicago, Ill., September 1, 1960.

[6] Sherif and Hovland, *op. cit.*, pp. 4-5.

the person has had experience. That is to say, an individual forms attitudes as a consequence of repeated experiences with the same or similar stimuli. These experiences may be direct, indirect, or vicarious. They may be the result of one's experience with the attitudes of his associates.

Sherif and Hovland refer to the background for a particular judgment as the *reference scale* [7] of the individual. Thus the judgment of stimulus items is made relative to the person's reference scale. "The formation of reference scales by the individual whether in relation to objects, human groups, or social norms is clearly a problem of learning." [8] Suppose one enters a strange town and asks himself the question: What is the speed limit (that is, norm) in this town? How can he find out? Suppose he is an electrical engineer and he has an electronic device for measuring the speed of movement of objects. He could then stand on Main Street and clock the actual speed of a representative sample of the town's people. Following this, he could calculate the average speed and the standard deviation. But would this result necessarily give him the speed norm for this town? No, it would not. It is, of course, possible that the actual driving speeds do in fact correspond to the norms. But it is also possible that they do not. The point of the illustration is that behavior is only *reflective* of norms and is not the norm itself. Human norms are expressed as verbal statements of ideal codes of conduct—as laws, customs, and regulations of various forms. If the norms have any strength or degree of acceptance and the agencies of social control enforce the sanctions, then behavior will reflect the norms with a fairly high degree of fidelity. Unless the norms are enforced, then evasion practices will soon be substituted for the norms and in time become the new norms.

There are some norms that are societal, that is, they are uniform throughout the society; for example, the norm of monogamy in America. However, for many norms there is great variation in normative definition from region to region.

Assuming that norms or reference scales have been formed, we may next examine how they function in perception and judgment.

In this connection let us examine the processes of perceiving "masked" or hidden meanings of cues by analyzing *stereotypes* and *role-taking*.

3. THE FUNCTION OF STEREOTYPES AND ROLE-TAKING IN PERCEPTION

When individuals exhibit the same general cues, but the cues do not denote valid properties equally, then how does the perceiver determine the actual properties which they do denote? Of course, the perceiver does

[7] *Ibid.*, p. 9.
[8] *Ibid.*, p. 9.

not always determine the correct properties. Everyone is fooled many times over in this process. To be able to bluff an opponent by exhibiting cues of a strong hand of cards is a required skill of a good poker player.

Let us designate cues that actually denote a given property as *valid cues*, and cues that falsely denote a given property as *false cues*. It follows that the perceiver, having knowledge of this, must make some assessment of the probable validity of the observed cues. In doing this he may seek additional cues to help him make the assessment. Consider the case of the subject who wears clothes beyond his means. The perceiver can determine the socioeconomic status of the neighborhood or his connections with other men of known wealth.

The Meaning of Stereotypes

When a given cue is sometimes valid in regard to some people and sometimes false in regard to others, as is often the case in the social world, the perceiver effects a compromise percept based on the estimated probable validity of the cue or cues. This seems to be the basis for "stereotyping." A stereotype, in this sense, would be a generalization about a class of objects, persons, events, or relationships that is based on cues which are *perceived* as reliable. The *actual* reliability or validity of the cues is another matter. The cues may come from personal observation, reports from others, or one's readings.

It is necessary for our purposes to distinguish between stereotyping and prejudice, especially since they are often thought of as belonging together. In respect to certain circumstances stereotyping seems to be a necessary means to human interaction. There are many circumstances in which human beings have to interact with one another and with situations without adequate personal information. What does one do in the absence of more complete information or cues? On the basis of perceived similar persons or situations, of personal or vicarious past experience, our hypothetical subject acts toward a *generalized* or *stereotyped* person or situation. To be sure, he may revise the stereotype or generalization as new information from the present situation is gained. If he fails to revise his stereotype in face of repeated contrary information, then one may reasonably suspect some emotional involvement or prejudice. Thus stereotyping is a means for providing continuity or relative constancy and organization in perception. The process of perceptual organization is never perfect or complete; nor does this matter, since the ordinary needs of the person can be met with only approximately accurate percepts. However, from the point of view of biological adaptation the accuracy of cues and one's perception of them may be of great importance. For instance, when a driver of an automobile passes an ongoing car while another one is approaching from the opposite direction, then the accuracy of judging distance, speed, and time may be a matter of life or death. It should also be added that a major variable in the success of one's social and psychological adaptation is the accuracy of one's perceptions of social situations. Many individuals lose in competition primarily because someone else had a keener sense of social perceptivity.

The notion that *stereotypes serve as substitute cues for perception in the absence of known reliable cues* is of fundamental importance in understanding certain types of social psychological behavior. McCormick gives the example of the relationship:

> between host and guest, when the latter is a stranger. In many societies hospitality under such circumstances is cordial and unfailing. There has been no prior interaction between host and guest such as is necessary to create personal emotional ties, yet the host is anxious to please the guest as a person. . . . It would seem that in the host-guest relationship, emotional attitudes of a primary sort have been developed by the host toward a *generalized* guest or stranger in need of hospitality, rather than toward a particular stranger, and that the guest entertains similar attitudes toward a generalized host. These patterns have been generated in agreement with the values of the society in which each has lived, and function so long as a specific guest or host and his behavior conform reasonably well to the common notion or stereotype.[9]

On the basis of the foregoing we will define a *stereotype* as a generalization based on a set of recurring cues from behavior. *Prejudice* then is a stereotype with an emotional attachment or involvement. This, of course, includes an emotional involvement *for* as well as *against* something. From the distinction of stereotyping as a mode of perceptual adjustment, *with* or *without* emotional overtones or involvements, one might expect that stereotypes without emotional involvement would be easier modified by subsequent contrary cues than when emotional involvement is present.[10] Since this is presumably a problem in learning theory, its discussion will be delayed until the appropriate place in the next chapter. As a key to one way to conceptualize the problem, the student may equate emotional involvement with the possession of *extreme* social attitudes.

The persistence of stereotypes of social and cultural phenomena with or without the presence of prejudice is not necessarily dependent upon the objectivity or validity of the bases for the stereotypes. To quote W. I. Thomas, "If men define situations as real, they are real in their

---

[9] Thomas Carson McCormick, *Sociology: An Introduction to the Study of Social Relations* (New York, copyright, 1950, The Ronald Press Company), pp. 46-47.

[10] John T. Doby, "Some Effects of Bias on Learning," *Journal of Social Psychology*, Vol. 51 (February, 1960), pp. 199-209.

consequences."[11] But more importantly, from the point of view of Brunswik's probabilistic theory,[12] the opportunity to perceive the modal *behavior* of "significant others" is the main basis for the continuity and persistence of stereotypes. For example, if racial segregation is part of the institutional arrangement of a society and therefore exhibited by "important" people, then segregation behavior becomes a source of significant cues to the present and subsequent generations.

The example suggests that from the point of view of the effects of others' behavior upon the learner, the long-run validity of the behavior is unimportant. The important point is that people's actions are approved or disapproved, validated or nonvalidated, in terms of the *present ongoing* system of behavior of the groups of which one is directly or indirectly associated, i.e., the members of the system provide their *own* standards and definitions of validity.

Let us look next at role-taking as a factor in the social determining of perception.

The Meaning of Role-Taking

Roles are culturally defined acts which reciprocally relate the behavior of persons who occupy culturally related social positions. For example, the norms which define the appropriate general actions of a mother specify the role of a mother in *relation* to a child.

Ralph Turner has stated the traditional sociological definition of *role-taking* by saying that: "Role-taking in its most general form is a process of looking at or anticipating another's behavior by viewing it in the context of a role imputed to that other."[13] This implies that the one doing the anticipating has observed others' behavior in such positions in the past. The observations need not be direct; they may be vicarious or indirect. The point is that the *role behavior* of another in a given position constitutes an organized set of meanings which provide a basis for the organization of perception. The observer acquires an expectation of *what* a person is supposed to do in a given position and some general notion of *how* he is supposed to do it. Thus individuals come to have a perception of the role of father, doctor, professor, and so on, based on direct or indirect observations of the role behavior of such persons in relation to these respective positions. The norms which constitute a role provide both behavioral and evaluational cues to perception. By identifying a

---

[11] Cited by Robert K. Merton, *Social Theory and Social Structure*, rev. ed. (New York, The Free Press of Glencoe, 1957), p. 421.

[12] Egon Brunswik, *Perception and the Representative Design of Psychological Experiments* (Berkeley and Los Angeles, University of California Press, 1956), Chaps. 6-10.

[13] Ralph H. Turner, "Role-Taking, Role Standpoint, and Reference-Group Behavior," *American Journal of Sociology*, Vol. LXI (January, 1956), pp. 316-328.

person's position, one can infer the person's role and from this information can deduce his probable attitude toward given questions related to the role.

By now, it should be clear that role-taking is composed of perceptual and conceptual processes by which one person estimates another's perspective and this in turn provides a basis for interaction. The observer may or may not adopt this perspective as his own. However, by assuming another's role it is possible for the participants to adopt a quite similar perspective and thus define a situation similarly. Once a person perceives and adopts a given perspective as his own, it then becomes a part of his general outlook and is therefore a source of much of the consistency in human behavior over periods of time. In other words, it becomes a trait.

When one views a person from different role perspectives, he may conclude that the person's behavior is inconsistent. This is not necessarily the case from the point of view of the actor being observed and the particular groups within which he occupies multiple positions. The different groups may have conflicting ends, but the subject's roles in the separate groups may not overlap. If they do not overlap, then inconsistencies may never be perceived or noticed. If they do overlap, then inconsistencies are likely to produce anxiety and/or conflict.

In this connection Shibutani quotes William James as follows: "As a man I pity you, but as an official I must show you no mercy; as a politician I regard him as an ally, but as a moralist I loathe him." [14] In commenting on this, Shibutani says, "In playing roles in different social worlds, one imputes different expectations to others whose differences cannot always be compromised. The problem is that of selecting the perspective for defining the situation. In Mead's terminology, which generalized other's role is to be taken? It is only in situations where alternative definitions are possible that problems of loyalty arise." [15]

Let us conclude this section by calling attention to the fact that human beings largely deal with each other in terms of their *perception* of one another's *behavior* and not just in terms of *expected* behavior, although this may be inferentially taken into account. For example, someone's behavior may be harmful to another and this may have been the intent, but the person harmed may perceive the act as an unintended act and therefore make allowance for it, or he may not take into account the generally expected and may act only on the basis of the other person's behavior. On the other hand, a person may be viewed in as many different ways as there are others who have different role relationships

---

[14] Tamotsu Shibutani, "Reference Groups as Perspectives," *The American Journal of Sociology*, Vol. LX (May, 1955), p. 568.
[15] *Ibid.*

with him. For example, a man's wife holds one view of him, his children another, and his boss still another as Figure 6:1 below illustrates.

The study of role *behavior* is of great importance in understanding the social effects on perception as well as understanding the perception of social behavior. The reasons for this are that behavior is available to

FIGURE 6:1. Image Variation of Role Perception. By permission of Mr. Lloyd Lane, Amarillo, Texas.

observation as well as the conditions under which it occurs. Also, the *consequences* of behavior are observable. It is true that behavioral consequences serve as a source for confirming or denying a perceptual interpretation, but equally important is the fact that *perception of behavioral consequences* becomes an important guide to *subsequent* behavior.

The nature of social *interaction* among individuals and groups is significantly affected by the actor's perception of the intended meaning of the other's action. This raises the extremely important but difficult question of how individuals interpret and judge the actions of others. Irrespective of the question of the validity of perception or judgment, the individual actor finds that it is necessary to assign meanings to the behavior of others, particularly if the actions of the "others" have perceivable consequences to the observer.[16]

4. PERCEPTUAL JUDGMENT

All judgments are made with respect to a frame of reference. The observer is not necessarily conscious of his *actual* frame of reference, but instead may be conscious of an *idealized* version of it. Social norms, the behavior of others, one's self, or one's idealized self may serve as a frame of reference for judging a given act of one's self or of another.

To repeat a point which has been made earlier, we are assuming that judgments made about "things" and judgments made about "persons" or complex social situations obey the same general psychological laws. To be sure, persons and social situations exhibit properties which complicate the perception and judging of social behavior. For one thing, actors may assume the role of others for purposes at hand and thus exhibit qualities of behavior which are deceptive to the observer. But all that this means is that the observer must obtain additional samples of behavior of the actor in question over a wider span of circumstances and time, particularly in comparison with his past. One way of doing this is to obtain reports from others who work with the person in question in a number of different roles. Of course, the observer may not make the additional observations and efforts to validate the implications of the subject's behavior, in which case his response is different than it otherwise would be. In other words, he has been "fooled" by the actor, but then we also make errors in our judgment about "things."

Our discussion of judgmental phenomena will be limited to two kinds, and these are what Sherif and Hovland call *contrast* and *assimilation*.[17] In any act of judgment, the subject groups stimuli into categories according to some standard or *anchor* as Sherif prefers to say. *Contrast* means a shift in one's judgment *away* from some standard. *Assimilation* means a shift in one's judgment closer to an anchor or standard value.

Berkowitz illustrates the relevance of contrast and assimilation to judgmental phenomena by citing two experiments by Hovland and Sherif.

---

[16] For an interesting and stimulating discussion of meaning and related techniques for measuring it see Charles E. Osgood, *Method and Theory in Experimental Psychology* (New York, Oxford University Press, 1953), Chapter 16, pp. 680-727. Also see Charles E. Osgood, "Cognitive Dynamics in the Conduct of Human Affairs," reprinted with slight abridgment in E. P. Hollander and Raymond G. Hunt, eds., *Current Perspectives in Social Psychology* (New York, Oxford University Press, 1963), pp. 362-378. Also, for a very theoretically stimulating discussion of human interaction see Fritz Heider, *The Psychology of Interpersonal Relations* (New York, John Wiley & Sons, Inc., 1958).

[17] The interested student is encouraged to read the excellent work by Muzafer Sherif and Carl I. Hovland, *Social Judgment: Assimilation and Contrast Effects in Communication and Attitude Change* (New Haven, Yale University Press, 1961).

In the first of these (Hovland and Sherif, 1952) groups of strongly involved judges, some pro-Negro, others anti-Negro in their attitudes, were asked to sort 114 opinion statements in terms of their favorableness toward Negroes. The rather indefinite statements in the middle of the scale were displaced away from the judges' own positions (i.e., there was contrast), contrary to Thurstone's assumption that the judges' attitudes would not affect their item sorting in the "equal-appearing intervals" scaling technique. It is likely, as I will attempt to show later, that the strongly involved S perceived a clear difference between his own position, the anchorage, and the beliefs reflected in the items. In other words, the distance between these categories was relatively great. Since the items' true position was indefinite, contrast could take place readily.

The second study (Hovland, Harvey, and Sherif, 1957) demonstrates both contrast and assimilation. Three communications dealing with the then locally important issue of prohibition were delivered to Ss in Oklahoma and Texas, one communication advocating the strong "wet" position, another strongly "dry," and the third being moderately "wet." The investigators report that the Ss' evaluations of the communicator's position was a function of the distance between their own attitude and the communicator's "true" position. The Ss closest to the communicator reported his beliefs relatively accurately; those not too far from the communicator tended to judge his opinion as being more like their own than it actually was (assimilation); while those furthest from the communicator saw him as advocating a view further away from themselves than it really was (contrast).[18]

These studies have shown that assimilation and contrast effects are important aspects of the process of making social judgments. A more important consideration pertains to the question of how these processes affect judgment and how each process may be reversed.

One of the first uses we note is in connection with self-other judgments, that is, the evaluation of others on the basis of one's conception of himself. Here it is found that persons judge others in reference to themselves, and contrast results to the extent that there is a perceived significant difference between the standard, self, and the evaluated other. But if one wanted to alter the effect from one of contrast to one of assimilation, then he would have to produce a change in the person's reference standard or anchor. The question of how to achieve this end is a very important social psychological problem. Presumably it involves the necessity of altering one's self-attitudes *and* the altering of the social structure that supports and helps keep a person what he is. We will discuss this problem in more detail in Chapter 8.

If an observer perceives that another's views are similar to his own, then he is likely to conclude that they are the same as his own, and we

---

[18] Leonard Berkowitz, "The Judgmental Process in Personality Functioning," *Psychological Review*, Vol. 67 (March, 1960), pp. 131-132.

SOCIAL JUDGMENT 161

say the views are assimilated. On the other hand, if he perceives a significant gap between his own view of, say, himself and another's view of himself, then he is likely to assign a greater gap to represent the difference than actually exists.

Berkowitz conceives of the psychological mechanism of projection in paranoia as "contrast formation." "The actually generous person who perceives himself as stingy judges his fellow group members in reference to this self-anchorage, stingy, and the resulting contrast gives rise to the evaluation, generous." [19]

Perhaps a better example can be drawn from psychoanalytic theory in connection with paranoia. According to psychoanalytic theory the paranoid's basic problem is homosexuality. Berkowitz makes use of the concepts of contrast and assimilation in interpreting the projection of the homosexual as follows:

> As in analytic theory, the process commences when the individual judges himself (his "real" self) as being located towards the homosexual end of the heterosexual-homosexual continuum, while his ideals ("ideal" self) are anchored towards the extreme opposite end. The ideal self then serves as the standard by which others as well as the real self are evaluated. Several things then happen. First, the relatively great gap between the ideal and real selves upsets the individual, and in defense he (a) represses knowledge of his real self-evaluation, as well as (b) strongly insists, to himself and others, that he really is the way he would like to be. In this latter process he has not only repressed his homosexual attributes, he has exhibited reaction formation in characterizing himself as extremely non-homosexual. At the conscious level his ideals and his self-image both are strongly heterosexual, and it is from this extreme viewpoint that he judges others. The consequence, of course, is a contrast effect; other people are evaluated as more homosexual than they actually are. (But only people important to him are so evaluated because he does not bother to judge everyone he encounters.)
>
> However, this judgment of others also may be threatening. The very idea, homosexuality, may arouse anxiety, and subsequent avoidance responses, so that even the characterization of another as possessing this disapproved motive is repressed. The emotion aroused by the initial judgment remains; the person is hated for possessing the evil trait, but the basis for the hatred is kept from awareness.[20]

Irrespective of future judgment on the validity of Berkowitz's interpretation it is a good illustration of the use of the concept of contrast as an aid to understanding social judgment. Eunice Cooper and Marie Jahoda have prepared some cartoons featuring a "Mr. Biggott" which

---
[19] *Ibid.*, p. 133.
[20] *Ibid.*, p. 135.

lampoon bigotry in such a way that most readers find them funny. It is interesting that the highly prejudiced person will at first seem to recognize the similarity between himself and the idea portrayed in the cartoon, but then he extricates himself from actual identity with its message by misunderstanding the point.[21] Apparently, to recognize and admit his bigotry and thus be faced with the necessity of changing his attitudes is too threatening.

In discussing the matter of meaning and the drawing of inferences about people and people's behavior, Osgood notes the tendency of human beings to infer additional traits from observations of other traits.

> If we observe, or are told, that so-and-so is *intelligent* and *considerate*, and this is all the information we have, we are nevertheless able to generate many inferences about him—he is also likely to be *sensitive, socially adept*, alert, and so forth, we assume. The traits we infer are not haphazard: they are generated from the region of intersection of the meanings of the traits we know about. . . .[22]

We know that no matter how long a subject looks at a circle or a square, the figure is still perceived as a circle or a square. But if additional drawings are added, they may be perceived as something else. The same holds true for perception of social events and stimuli. Osgood provides an excellent illustration of this from Pudovkin's *Film Technique and Film Acting* (1954).

> Pudovkin describes a little experiment in film editing. A simple, passive close-up of the well-known Russian actor, Mosjukhin, was joined to three different strips of film. In one this close-up was followed by a shot of a bowl of soup on the table; in another it was followed by shots showing a dead woman in a coffin; in the third it was followed by shots of a little girl playing with a funny toy bear. The effects on an unsuspecting audience were terrific, according to Pudovkin. "The public raved about the acting of the artist. They pointed out the heavy pensiveness of his mood over the forgotten soup, were touched and moved by the deep sorrow with which he looked at the dead woman, and admired the light, happy smile with which he surveyed the girl at play. But we knew that in all three cases the face was exactly the same.[23]

In discussing the accuracy of the perception of behavior it is important to distinguish between two kinds of behavior, namely, *personal*

---

[21] Eunice Cooper and Marie Jahoda, "The Evasion of Propaganda: How Prejudiced People Respond to Anti-Prejudice Propaganda," *The Journal of Psychology*, Vol. 23 (1947), pp. 15-25.

[22] Charles E. Osgood, "Cognitive Dynamics in the Conduct of Human Affairs," *Public Opinion Quarterly*, Vol. 24 (1960), p. 342.

[23] *Ibid.*, p. 343.

behavior and *social behavior*. By personal behavior we mean the motives, intentions, feelings, and so on, of an individual and by social behavior we mean the interaction of two or more people in regard to a goal or some socially defined situation.

In a socially defined situation such as a game, a committee, a work group, or any social role relationship, the actions necessary to attain the social ends involved are sufficiently specified so that the behavior can be carried out independently of the motives of the individual members. A man may decide to become a scientist for any one of a great variety of motives, but his behavior, *as a scientist*, must conform to the general expectations of other scientists in his field. For example, the results of his work must be subject to verification by other members of his profession, and his motives and personal attributes are irrelevant to this process.

On the other hand, in *interpersonal* relations where the goals are not social, but personal, the perception of each other's motives, preferences, "true feelings," and so on, may become highly relevant. That is to say that interpersonal relations may be considered by the actors as *ends* in themselves, while social behavior is more generally viewed by the actors concerned as means to ends. Although it should be noted that while personal motives are irrelevant to the attainment of the social ends of the members of an organization, nevertheless these often become involved, and, when they do, the effect is generally a disruptive one.

In discussing the significance of accuracy in perceiving social and interpersonal behavior, Steiner makes a critical examination of two propositions which link accuracy in social perception with *competence* in interpersonal behavior and with *efficiency* in group behavior.

> The first of these propositions maintains that the more knowledge an individual has concerning the intentions, preferences, and beliefs of other persons, the more effectively he can participate in group activity with other persons. The proposition provides the rationale for much of the training we give to teachers, social workers, clinical psychologists, and others whose work involves continuing interaction with people. . . . The second proposition involves an extension of the first. It maintains that groups composed of individuals with accurate social perceptions will be more efficient than groups composed of members with less accurate social perception. Faith in this proposition guides much of our marriage counseling and has sometimes been a factor in the selection of work crews and play groups.[24]

Steiner notes that the evidence for the first proposition comes from the use of sociometric indexes of a person's interpersonal competence.

---

[24] Ivan D. Steiner, "Interpersonal Behavior as Influenced by Accuracy of Social Perception," *Psychological Review*, Vol. 62 (July, 1955), p. 268.

For example, Gage found that high school seniors who did the most accurate job of predicting the responses which others would make to the Kuder Preference Record also received a large percentage of their classmates' sociometric choices.[25]

Steiner cites evidence from Festinger's work for the second proposition that groups composed of members with accurate perception of social behavior will be more efficient than groups composed of members with less accurate social perception.

"Festinger and his associates . . . have frequently given group members erroneous impressions of one another and have found that such impressions can lead to restricted communication within the group, rejection of members, and a lowered group cohesiveness." [26] Thus it appears that inaccurate perception of social properties interferes with group efficiency.

On the other hand, Steiner notes that some studies contradict the foregoing. For example, Campbell failed "to obtain a positive relationship between the accuracy with which naval officers judged the attitudes of their men and the officers' popularity with the crew." [27] Steiner concludes that the existence of contradictory findings suggests that the two propositions are neither completely true nor completely false. He then attempts to ascertain or identify the conditions under which accurate social perception functions to increase interpersonal competence and group efficiency.

Steiner's conclusions which follow below justify the distinction which we made earlier between personal and social behavior in respect to accuracy of perception. He concludes:

> Accurate social perception should promote interpersonal competence and group efficiency if: (a) the group members are motivated to cooperate; (b) the accurately perceived qualities are relevant to the activities of the group; (c) members are free to alter their own behaviors in response to their perceptions of other members; and (d) the behavioral changes which are a consequence of accurate social perception are the kinds which produce a more thoroughly integrated dyadic system. Whenever any *one* or more of these conditions is not met, accurate social perception should fail to have the effect predicted by the two propositions. . . .
>
> It has been contended that much of our most highly integrated and efficient collective action must be presumed to occur within the framework provided by role systems. Whenever this is the case, individual participants are neither required nor permitted to let their perceptions of other people's intentions or preferences affect their behavior. Accuracy of social

---

[25] N. L. Gage, "Judging Interest From Expressive Behavior," *Psychological Monographs*, 1952, 66, No. 18.
[26] Steiner, *op. cit.*, p. 268.
[27] *Ibid.*, p. 269.

perception is largely irrelevant in such situations because it can have little effect upon individuals' behaviors. Indeed, if it does affect individuals' behaviors, it is likely to interfere with role enactment, and, hence, to disrupt the behavior synthesis which is provided by the role system.[28]

In general, then, we may conclude that absolute accuracy in social behavior is probably not attainable and is not necessary for efficient group performance, particularly for groups performing nontechnical activities. Greater accuracy in perception and judgment is, of course, necessary in highly technical groups. On the other hand, in regard to *interpersonal relations*, that is, interaction between individuals for personal ends, stereotypes may provide sufficient accuracy to enable efficient transactions to occur. Judgments about the transactions or exchanges are made on the basis of individual preference or value scales or what Sherif calls references scales. A reference scale is established after repeated experiences with a given type of stimulus situation. Once the scale is established, it becomes the basis or standard for comparing other stimuli of a similar sort.

One of the problems of major interest in social psychology is how standards which are external to a person become internalized. That is, how does an individual come to accept as his own the standards of others?

One of the most important problems in the area of the judgmental process is the matter of judgment in choice and decision-making. The choice of a marital mate is a complicated judgmental phenomenon. What are the values and processes by which people choose a mate? What are the values and the judgmental processes involved in deciding whom to vote for in a democratic election? How do college students choose a career? What are the social conditioning processes which affect judgment in the important areas of social life? The answers to these questions and others like them will provide us with an important foundation for understanding social judgment. These are problems of social learning and will be discussed in the next chapter.

5. SUMMARY

We began this chapter by noting that human beings not only make discriminations and thus identify objects, acts, and events, but they also evaluate these as useful-useless, right-wrong, heavy-light—and the list could be extended to a great many other categories.

In a very real sense man lives in a world that *is* and a world of *ought to be*. He lives in a world that *is* in the sense that all men have certain common adaptive problems; for example, food, shelter, thirst, sex, and

---

[28] *Ibid.*, p. 273.

many others. Solutions to these problems have important consequences for all people, and it follows that the behavior which validates the solutions is socially *defined* and therefore is normative. Accordingly, the matter of social judgment as to what the norms are for a given situation becomes a critical matter for learning and perception.

The problem of social judgment was conceptualized as involving three processes, namely, *identifying* the stimulus, *placement* of the stimulus in some category, and finally *accepting or rejecting* the stimulus on the basis of the person's preference scale.

Upon what experience does a person's discrimination of a social norm depend? It depends upon a person's perception of past *patterns of response* by others to a given situation and to his perception of others' *expectations* as to what is appropriate behavior for the situation. It was assumed that the "others" were ones with whom the perceiver identified.

Many factors affect one's judgment of social stimuli in addition to the objective properties of the stimuli. One very important factor is the intensity of the attitude of the perceiver. The more extreme the attitude, the more the attitude itself functions as the standard for judgment irrespective of information. Sherif and Hovland conceptualized the problem of judgment in regard to attitude strength as a problem in *contrast* and *assimilation*. By contrast they meant a judgment of an observer which shifted away from some objective standard with the variance being a function of the observer's own attitude toward the stimulus. By *assimilation* they meant a shift in one's judgment in the direction of some standard. Thus one's attitude functions as an internal reference scale.

There are also important *social* reference scales which are learned. We discussed the nature and function of two of these, namely, *stereotypes* and *role-taking*.

Finally, we distinguished between perception and judgment of individual behavior as contrasted with social behavior. It was noted that, in the former, personal motives became important elements in the judgmental process, but that in social behavior these were less important and the social norms became the principal anchorage for judgment.

Further References

1. Muzafer Sherif and Carl I. Hovland, *Social Judgment: Assimilation and Contrast Effects in Communication and Attitude Change* (New Haven, Yale University Press, 1961).
2. Renato Tagiuri and Luigi Petrillo, Editors, *Person Perception and Interpersonal Behavior* (New York, Basic Books, Inc., 1958).
3. Ralph H. Turner, *The Social Context of Ambition* (San Fancisco, Chandler Publishing Co., 1964).

7

Learning and the Social World

•

1. *Introduction*
2. *Some Definitions*
3. *Principles Distinguishing the Two Types of Conditioning*
4. *Reinforcement of an Operant*
   (a) *Theories of Effects of Partial Reinforcement*
   (b) *Importance of Partial Reinforcement*
   (c) *Some Conditions Affecting the Generality of Responses*
      1. Lack of Symbolic Control
      2. Generalized Threats and Promises
      3. Irregularity of Original Learning Conditions
      4. Unreproducibility of the Conditions of Learning
      5. The Complexity of the Learning Situation
5. *Reinforcement and the Concept of Feedback*
6. *Learning as Release of Potentiality*
7. *Group and Individual Performance*
8. *Summary*

1. INTRODUCTION

IN CHAPTERS 3 AND 4 we noted that learning is a fundamental process in human adaptation. Many regard learning as the basic process necessary to the understanding of behavior. Certainly, the processes which explain how behavior is acquired and changed are of fundamental importance to an understanding of human behavior. In this regard, our principal concern will be with the effects of social experience upon subsequent behavior. How do the responses of men function as rewards or punishments to other men? How are social values, habits, and attitudes formed and changed? These are fundamental questions and their answers primarily depend on an understanding of how the social environment is organized and maintained and on how this in turn affects learning.

We are going to treat motivation as a part of learning inasmuch as rewards and punishments are involved in learning, and certainly these are sources of motivation. However, from the standpoint of experimenting with learning, it is assumed that motivation is held constant. In many texts motivation is treated separately, and certainly the subject is important enough to warrant a separate treatment. But if motivation is considered as a residual part of learning, as we are so considering it, then from this point of view learning simply presupposes motivation, and motivation is a function of previous learning.

From the point of view of the release of human potentialities, learning is the principal means of release, although it should be noted that this is a two-way street; that is, one can learn attitudes and response sets which are inept and inefficient, and these would in turn interfere with subsequent learning. Certainly calculus is a more efficient means to solving problems in mathematics than algebra. In fact, algebra becomes most useful by means of its application through the use of calculus. Some children learn to achieve ends by crying and tyrannizing their parents. If these habits transfer to their relations with other adults, they produce undesirable results. Thus, while learning releases potentiality, it can also inhibit it. Nevertheless, in general, intelligence increases as thought processes are loosened and developed from their bases in perception and neurological action.

Let us next provide some general definitions of certain terms which will recur in this chapter.

2. SOME DEFINITIONS

Learning: Changes in subsequent behavior that result from previous behavior in similar situations. In other words, changes in behavior in a given situation which result from experience either direct or symbolic as opposed to changes due to physiological maturation or other biological or physical conditions.[1]

---

[1] For a detailed presentation on findings and theories of learning see Robert S. Woodworth and Harold Schlosberg, *Experimental Psychology*, rev. ed. (New York, Holt, Rinehart and Winston, Inc., 1954), chapters 18-22. Also, see James Deese, *The Psychology of Learning*, 2nd ed. (New York, McGraw-Hill Book Company, copyright ©, 1958). Quotations used by permission of McGraw-Hill Book Company, and Ernest R. Hilgard, *Theories of Learning*, 2nd ed. (New York, Appleton-Century-Crofts, 1956).

This definition applies to behavior which ranges all the way from the conditioned response to the acquisition of motor skills to the solving of complex problems. In general, we assume learning to be the correction in response to information the learner receives about his successes and failures. This suggests that behavior tends to become more efficient and more adaptive after a series of trials than it was before. This is generally true but not always true.

Response: Any act or observable output of behavior which results from a perception or the receipt of information. Responses range from the very simple act of salivation to pressing a lever, to stopping at a red light, to a gesture of surprise, to writing a word, to interpreting a statement, to solving a complex problem. Most laboratory studies of human learning have dealt with rather simple and mechanical processes by which people acquire skills, memorize items, and form concepts. However, not much of the latter has been done in terms of the acquisition of ideas and the understanding of meaning. The reasons for so much attention to simple learning are (1) the belief that complex learning may be explained by extending the principles gained from studying simple learning and (2) because of the great difficulty involved in studying complex learning.

Conditioning: We shall define conditioning in relation to learning and with sufficient generality to include both classical and instrumental conditioning. By conditioning we mean the learning of some particular response to some particular situation usually under some simple condition.

Classical Conditioning: This term is easy to describe but difficult to define by means of a single sentence or so. In brief, it is a learned response which is contingent upon the *previous* pairing of stimuli. Pavlov's dog experiment affords a good example. In this experiment a dog was placed in a soundproofed room and a tuning fork was sounded in the room a few seconds before small amounts of meat were given the dog to eat. After a few pairings of the tuning fork and the meat, the tuning fork was sounded *without* the meat. The salivation response which followed was the same as that initially produced by the meat. In other words, the fork had become associated with the meat and had therefore acquired the ability to elicit the response which was initially limited to the meat. Pavlov referred to the meat as an *unconditioned stimulus.* In other words, an unconditioned stimulus is one which has the ability to produce the response which is under study and is being paired with a stimulus that does not have this ability. This ability may result from the biological state of the organism alone, or it may be the result of previous training. In other words, the ability of an unconditioned stimulus to elicit a response may be the result of previous learning, or it may be the result of the ability of the stimulus to elicit an innate tendency. Obviously, if one intended to show that a given stimulus is able to elicit an innate tendency without benefit of prior experience, it would be necessary to carefully control the life history of the animal.

Another form of the conditioning process which is of particular importance in helping us understand how social learning occurs is called *instrumental conditioning* or what Skinner calls *operant* conditioning.[2] We will first illustrate this form of conditioning and then provide a summary definition.

An animal, usually a rat or a pigeon, is placed in a small box that is relatively soundproof. At one end of the box is a small lever or bar that extends or projects from the wall. This lever is connected to an automatic recording device and a magazine filled with small pellets of food.

If an animal that is hungry is placed in this box, it will explore the box in search of food. If it is a rat, it will sniff the air and paw and bite the walls. Eventually, in its more or less random behavior it will press the lever and this will release a food pellet. The rat may not discover the food at once, but he soon will; and when he does, he will eat it. Before long he will press the lever again and this time he will discover the food pellet almost immediately. At this point a very significant change occurs in the rat's behavior. Instead of random exploration, he will now press the lever repeatedly until he is gratified. When he is again hungry, he will proceed directly to press the lever. The sequence of events is described by Deese as follows: [3]

Response (lever-pressing) ⟶ Reinforcement (food) ⟶ Increase in Strength of Response

We may now define an *instrumental* conditioning as a response followed by a reward (reinforcement), and the response recurrence becomes fixed when the reward is associated with the response. For example, almost every father has had the experience of observing his child utter a sound like "da-da." Father takes this to be daddy and he rewards the child profusely and the child says "da-da" almost all day long. The sound soon comes to represent the *person* called daddy. Once established, this conditioned stimulus serves as reinforcement to establish similar responses to other similar stimuli. This is called *stimulus generalization*. The magnitude of response generalization decreases with the difference between the conditioned stimulus and the similar ones.

With these general definitions before us, let us now examine some of the similarities and differences between classical conditioning and instrumental conditioning.

[2] B. F. Skinner, *The Behavior of Organisms: An Experimental Analysis* (New York, Appleton-Century-Crofts, 1938).
[3] Deese, *op. cit.*, p. 11.

3. PRINCIPLES DISTINGUISHING THE TWO TYPES OF CONDITIONING

Deese asserts that

> Hilgard and Marquis [4] have most clearly distinguished between two types of learning, which they call classical and instrumental conditioning. The essential element defining classical conditioning is that reinforcement be independent of the occurrence of a conditioned response. It was because Pavlov's experiments were of this type that Hilgard and Marquis characterized it as classical conditioning. The essential condition defining instrumental conditioning is that the reinforcement be dependent upon the occurrence of the conditioned response.[5]

In the classical conditioning situation the organism already possesses the basic response, and learning or conditioning occurs through the organism's associating a new stimulus with the unconditioned stimulus. The salivary response and pupillary constriction are examples of these. For example, the dog salivated when he ate the meat or observed the meat while hungry, but he also acquired the response of salivating when the tuning fork was sounded either simultaneously with or before the appearance of the meat. We can say that this type of response is correlated with a known stimulus and that reinforcement depends upon the presence of the unconditioned stimulus.

In the second or instrumental conditioning situation the responses are not related to any known stimuli. This is why Skinner designated them as *operants,* that is, they function in an instrumental fashion. For example, a teen-ager learning to drive an automobile finds that if he wants the car to move backwards, he has to place the shift lever in a certain position. That is, we learn to make a certain response on the basis of the kind of consequence the response produces; hence it is the response that is correlated with reinforcement. For human beings, this is sometimes a trial-and-error process and sometimes a matter of observation of the behavior of others and sometimes a matter of verbal instruction or direction from someone. In any event, most human behavior is operant in character, and we shall attempt to show in the latter portion of this chapter the applicability of this concept in helping us understand the influence of the social world on individual behavior. Special application will be made of what is sometimes called *discrimination* learning or what we have referred to in previous chapters as *perceptual* learning.

---

[4] Ernest R. Hilgard and D. M. Marquis, *Conditioning and Learning* (New York, Appleton-Century-Crofts, 1940).
[5] Deese, *op. cit.,* p. 13.

If we consider classical and instrumental conditioning as two types of learning, then perceptual learning is a third type. There may be many more, and there may not be but one kind, of which these are but different aspects. This issue will have to be settled by future research. Since the interest in this text is with problems of generalization and discrimination in learning, transfer effects, and relational learning, we shall focus on instrumental (operant) and perceptual learning. Let us next examine the nature of the process of reinforcement of an operant.

4. REINFORCEMENT OF AN OPERANT

In general, a reinforcement is defined as any stimulus event that will increase or maintain the strength of a response. In the case of instrumental or operant behavior, a reinforcement is a stimulus that follows the occurrence of the response and rewards it. The consequence of the reinforcement of an operant is to increase the rate at which the operant response is emitted. Suppose the subject is a white rat and its response to an operant occurs a great number of times in a given time period; then the response is judged as a strong one. In other words, the strength of response in operant conditioning is measured by the *frequency of response emission*. Another index to the strength of the response is the resistance of the organism to efforts on the part of the experimenter to extinguish the response. This resistance to extinction of response of an operant is measured by the *total number of responses* before responding returns to its normal rate prior to conditioning.

It would be expected that the greater the number of reinforcements that occurred prior to the beginning of the extinction process, the more difficult it would be to extinguish the response. The extinction process, of course, begins when the experimenter withholds the reward. The figure below illustrates the foregoing conclusion.

Thus we see that additional reinforcements add to the persistence of responses after the reward has been withheld. As the curves level off, this means that responses have stopped. This is because of the way in which the curves were constructed. The above curves are cumulative, that is, the number of responses are successively added. Obviously, if there are no more responses to a given cumulation, then the curve would level off to the horizontal.

If an organism experiences a large number of *regular* reinforcements of a response and this strengthens the response, then what would be the effect of irregular reinforcement to a response? The latter is more likely to be the case in the social world. A child does not *always* get rewarded or punished for a given type of response. The rewards or punishments sometimes follow a given response and sometimes they do not. This is true all through life. An investor does not make a profit on every invest-

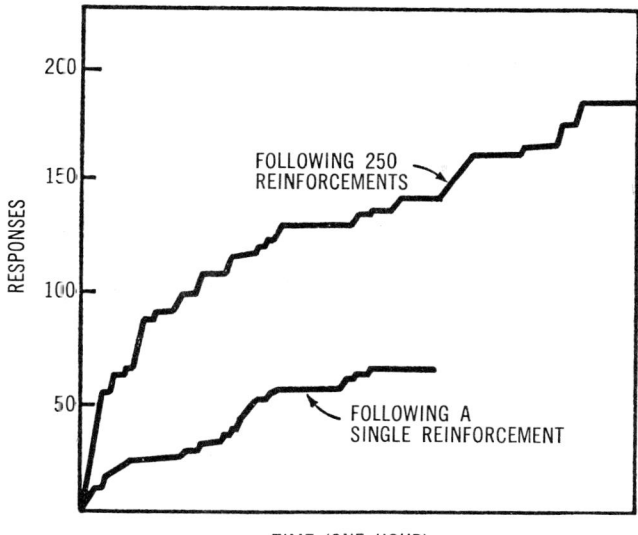

FIGURE 7:1. Extinction of Lever-pressing by Rats Following a Single Reinforcement and Following 250 Reinforcements. Although several times as many responses are emitted after 250 reinforcements as after a single reinforcement, it is evident that the total number of responses in the "reserve" does not increase in direct proportion to the number of reinforcements. Data from Skinner (1933) and F. S. Keller and A. Kerr (unpublished data, replotted from Skinner (1938), pages 87 and 91). Both curves have been moved back so that time is here shown as measured from the first response. From Ernest R. Hilgard, *Theories of Learning*, 2nd ed. (New York, Appleton-Century-Crofts, 1956), p. 87.

ment. Nor does a fisherman catch a fish every time he goes fishing, but he keeps on going fishing. This raises the question of the importance of *intermittent reinforcement* or *partial reinforcement*.

This type of reinforcement is of great importance and especially so in regard to human behavior. We must recall from our discussion of symbolic behavior in previous chapters that man has a capacity which is a function of his language ability to live in three time dimensions. That is, he can view the present in relation to the past and the future, or the future in relation to the present and the past, and so on. Thus man can calculate or estimate the probability of events occurring and then attempt to influence the estimated probability.

On the other hand, the event in question may be only in the realm of possibility and the probability of its actual occurrence may be zero, but since it is conceived as possible, then many will act as if it were highly likely. Demagogues often make use of this fact in arousing fears among voters.

Skinner has investigated extensively two types of intermittent reinforcement which have come to be called *interval reinforcement* and *ratio reinforcement*. Interval reinforcement involves the delivering of a reward for a given response at fixed intervals of, say, every three minutes or every five minutes, and so on. In ratio reinforcement, instead of delivering a reward at standard intervals of time, a reward is delivered after a standard number of *responses*. For example, a reward may be delivered after 8, 16, 32, or 64 responses. The ratios used are not always constant such as in the foregoing example. They are sometimes mixed and sometimes a variable ratio is used.

In regard to resistance to extinction it should be pointed out that extinction, to some extent, depends upon the number of reinforcements given an animal *before* the period of nonreinforced responses or extinction begins. If reinforcement has occurred only a very few times before, then few responses will be made during extinction before responding of this type ceases altogether.

As a general rule partial reinforcement will produce greater resistance to extinction than 100 percent reinforcement.[7]

The significantly greater effects of partial reinforcement on extinction may be seen in Figure 7:2.

We have remarked earlier about the great theoretical and practical importance of partial reinforcement. Particularly, we have found it helpful in understanding the effects of reinforcement in the social world. From the above figure it is clear that partial reinforcement produces a much greater resistance to extinction than does 100 percent reinforcement. Why should this be?

Theories of Effects of Partial Reinforcement

Deese has summarized the efforts to explain the effects of partial reinforcement under two general classes of theories: *stimulus theories* and *response theories*.[9]

In examining these theories, it is well to recall the distinction of levels of complexity of behavior which was made in Chapter 3. Four levels were distinguished; namely, simple reflex, conditioned reflex, sign behavior, and symbolic behavior. In this connection, we noted that man is capable of all four of these response levels but that other animals are not. Deese notes that one of the concepts offered to explain the greater

---

[7] W. O. Jenkins and J. C. Stanley, "Partial Reinforcement: A Review and Critique," *Psychological Bulletin*, Vol. 47 (1950), pp. 193-234.

[9] For a more detailed discussion of these see Deese, *op. cit.*, pp. 68-73.

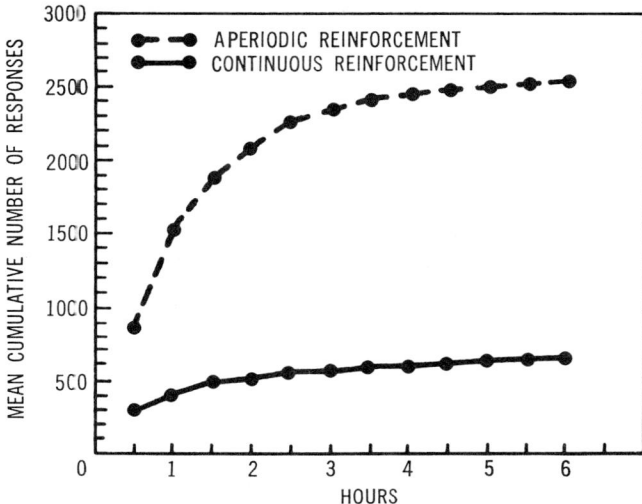

FIGURE 7:2. Cumulative Extinction Curves after Partial and Continuous Reinforcement. For the partial reinforcement condition, the animals were placed on a variable interval schedule. The animals in both groups received 200 reinforcements before extinction began. From W. O. Jenkins, H. McFann, and F. L. Clayton, "A Methodological Study of Extinction Following Aperiodic and Continuous Reinforcements," *Journal of Comparative Physiological Psychology*, Vol. 43 (1950), pp. 155-167.

persistence of partial reinforcement is the notion of *expectancy*. This notion says that animals learn to expect or predict stimulus situations associated with particular responses. Deese and others criticize this notion on two basic grounds. First, he contends that human beings are capable of learning expectancy—as a form of verbal behavior—but that it is doubtful if other animals are capable in this particular sense. Secondly, he criticizes it for its inadequacy to explain; that is, it is simply a definition and not an explanation. Therefore, we will have to look to other concepts to help us understand partial reinforcement.

Another concept which belongs to the class of stimulus theories and is offered as an explanation of the effects of partial reinforcement is the concept of *discrimination*. This idea states that under conditions of partial reinforcement, it is less easy for an animal to discriminate between conditions of reinforcement and those of extinction. This implies that the condition of partial reinforcement approximates the situation during original unreinforced training. In other words, since in the animal's natural environment the rule is partial reinforcement, then in a laboratory experimental situation it would be difficult for the animal to discriminate between actual extinction and the condition of reinforcement. This idea is not greatly different from the concept of expectancy except that it can be defined a little more clearly.

Still other ways of looking at the question of what produces the increased resistance to extinction under the condition of partial reinforcement is to examine the response situation. Deese has labeled these efforts *response theories*.

> For most purposes we define the unit of response as that which will produce a reinforcement. Thus, in the Skinner box, it is a lever push capable of operating the feeder. It does not make any difference how the lever is pressed, as long as it is pressed hard enough. By the same token, we might argue that in any partial reinforcement situation the unit response is defined by the *number* of lever presses necessary to activate the feeder. If we did this, we should consider all of the unreinforced lever pushes between reinforced ones to be part of the activity necessary for reinforcement and count them as only one response. Thus, if on a variable-ratio reinforcement schedule we reinforced 1 lever press in 10, we would count 10 lever presses as only 1 response. . . . This argument was advanced by Mowrer and Jones (1945), and they showed that when responses are counted by this scheme, actually fewer responses occur during extinction after partial reinforcement, though, of course, more single bar presses occur. The reason that fewer responses occur, argued Mowrer and Jones, is that a stronger response-induced inhibition is induced by the greater activity required under partial reinforcement.[10]

Logically, there is not any incompatibility among the expectancy, discrimination, and response theories as here presented. It is true that they are not adequate explanations; but when an adequate explanation is developed, it is likely to include probable expectancies as well as difficulties in discrimination and response-induced inhibition due to the greater effort required under partial reinforcement.

Importance of Partial Reinforcement

We have already had two occasions to refer to the importance of the concept of partial reinforcement. It is now appropriate to discuss this in more detail and particularly as it relates to human learning.

It is well known that human habits are highly resistant to extinction (disappearance of a response) and this is believed to be related to the fact that behavior in the social world, as well as man's general physical environment, is reinforced on a probable instead of a certain basis. It is highly probable that this is one of the reasons why children keep asking over and over again when they want something that has just been refused them.

Brunswik has conceived of this problem as being one in the probability

[10] *Ibid.*, p. 70.

nature of events that affect animal and human behavior. Thus, in adaptation both men and animals are constantly required to make judgments based on cues from past experience. For example, horses, dogs, and human beings seem to be able to judge whether they can jump a stream of a certain width. Sometimes they decide the stream is too wide and they decide not to jump. When they do decide to jump, they are almost always right.

Brunswik reported an experiment on a T maze in which most of the reinforcements occurred on the right side but sometimes occurred on the left. Under these conditions the rats came to distribute their choices according to the probability of reinforcement. If the right side were reinforced 80 percent of the time, and the left side only 20 percent of the time, the rats would choose to go to the right side 80 percent of the time.[11]

Deese notes that:

> Of great current interest in the theory of behavior is what determines the likelihood of an organism making a particular choice given the probability but not the certainty of a particular event happening. Most experimental research has been directed toward verbal choice in adult human beings. In a typical experimental situation, a subject is presented with a panel on which are two lights and two buttons. He is to predict by pressing a button which of the lights is going to flash on a particular trial. The experimenter has arranged a particular sequence of order for flashes on the right or left. As with Brunswik's rats in the T maze, human beings apparently choose the alternatives in proportion to the frequency of the to-be-predicted event happening. . . . This is a puzzling situation, for it is not the optimal strategy. We are not surprised, perhaps, that rats do not maximize the probability of receiving a reinforcement, but we are a little surprised that college students do not maximize the probability of being right (given a situation in which the frequency of alternative events is not even the best strategy is always to bet on the more frequently occurring event, if we have no other information).[12]

David McClelland[13] develops an interesting argument to explain resistance to extinction which this writer believes has much significance for helping us understand persistence of behavior in human beings. To help understand McClelland's argument, let us recall two findings on the relation of reinforcement to extinction. *First*, we noted that increased frequency of reinforcement increased the strength of the conditioned response; and, *secondly*, the more frequent the reward (for example, 100 percent reinforcement), the easier it is for the organism to perceive a

---

[11] Egon Brunswik, "Probability as a Determiner of Rat Behavior," *Journal of Experimental Psychology*, Vol. 25 (1939), pp. 175-197.
[12] Deese, *op. cit.*, p. 72.
[13] David C. McClelland, *Personality* (Copyright ©, 1951, by David C. McClelland). Reprinted by permisson of Holt, Rinehart and Winston, Inc., Publishers.

change in conditions when the reward is withdrawn. This was what Deese called the *discrimination of stimulus* theory. In other words, the animal will find it easier to discriminate when there are clear, distinct, and specific differences between conditions of learning and extinction. The greater the frequency of reward and the longer the history of the particular reward, the more noticeably different a series of nonreinforcing responses and the easier extinction should be.

McClelland points out that:

> The bearing of this point on the formation of motives in human beings is interesting, although somewhat conjectural at this stage. Learning psychologists who have attempted to apply their principles to child-rearing have up to now usually argued that the way to strengthen a desirable habit or attitude is to reward it consistently. Thus it might be suggested that if Johnny's father wants Johnny to strive for achievement, he ought to reward Johnny for any little efforts toward achievements that he makes. In the light of our present analysis this might strengthen the specific response of achieving for daddy's approval, but if Johnny ever found himself in a situation where approval was not forthcoming, we might expect that the response would also extinguish rather rapidly. It is on just such a basis that we could distinguish between a *habit* of achieving in response to specific situations to get a specific reward and an achievement *motive* which is based on a generalized association between *various* responses and *possible* achievement rewards.[14]

The distinction which McClelland makes between the *habit* of achieving in regard to specific reward situations and an achievement *motive* or goal which is directed toward achievement in general is a very important point. In respect to the argument and terminology used here this distinction might be labeled *response specificity* and *response generalization*. Other things being equal, 100 percent reinforcement of a response would lead to response specificity, whereas partial reinforcement would tend to produce a more generalized type of response. For example, if a mother always rewards a child for keeping his room neat but ignores other forms of neatness such as grooming, clothes, and so on, then neatness with this child may develop as a specific response rather than a general one.

The basic problem in the development of a generalized response, or motive as McClelland calls it, is one of *relational discrimination*. That is, when one discrimination has been made, how does the organism discern other different but similar stimuli? Deese cites an example from Köhler.

> Köhler once trained chickens to respond (with food as reinforcement) to the darker of two gray surfaces. The chickens were never reinforced when

---
[14] *Ibid.*, p. 450.

they responded to the lighter surface. When this discrimination was well established, the animals were presented with a new choice between the *original* reinforced gray and one *darker* still. The interesting thing was that the animals chose the darker of these two grays, even though they had always been reinforced for choosing the other one. In other words, argued Köhler, the animals had learned the relationship "darker than" rather than the association of the original stimulus with reinforcements.[15]

The foregoing illustration of Köhler's is a gestalt interpretation of relational discrimination or transposition, and this argument minimizes the role of reinforcement as an explanation. An approach which makes maximum use of reinforcement and associative learning as an explanation and relies on what we in Chapter 3 called *stimulus generalization* [16] is represented by some of Spence's work.

Spence attempts an explanation of stimulus generalization as a problem in discriminative learning.

He trained animals to discriminate between two squares, 256 square centimeters and 160 square centimeters in size. The response to 256 was reinforced and the response to 160 was extinguished. After the discrimination between stimuli 256 and 160 was established, the values of the stimuli were shifted to 256 and 409. The animals chose 409, a stimulus which had never been reinforced.[17]

In other words, the extinction generalized to the now smaller square and the conditioning to stimulus 256 generalized to the still larger square. When the original training requires the positive response to be to the larger stimulus and the experimenter subsequently selects a neighboring but still larger stimulus to be paired with the initial larger one and the response is then to the larger of the new pair, transposition is demonstrated. Spence attempts to explain the transposition effect in terms of an interaction of two phenomena—(1) the strengthening of the rewarded stimulus and (2) a simultaneous development of a relative aversion to the non-rewarded stimulus.[18]

Spence's theory is adequate to explain relative discrimination or transposition in the case of simple paired stimuli when the positive and negative stimuli are not greatly different from one another. An important

---

[15] Deese, *op. cit.*, pp. 83-84.
[16] See Chapter 3.
[17] Deese, *op. cit.*, p. 84.
[18] For a more precise statement of Spence's theory the student should read his two original articles on the matter, namely, Kenneth W. Spence, "The Differential Response in Animals to Stimuli Varying Within a Single Dimension," *Psychological Review*, Vol. 44 (1937), pp. 430-444, and K. W. Spence, "Analysis of Formation of Visual Discrimination Habits in the Chimpanzee," *Journal of Comparative Psychology*, Vol. 23 (1937), pp. 77-100. For a summary presentation of these ideas and findings see Hilgard, *op. cit.*, pp. 434-445.

question is whether his theory would account for such a phenomenon when the stimuli are not presented in pairs. Certainly in the case of human beings much relational learning occurs by means of simple logical extension. Also, the conditions of human learning are seldom restricted to a simple pairing process. More likely there are three or more similar elements which must be discriminated among. Also, the culture of a society often makes relational connections between elements which are objectively very dissimilar. This, of course, would interfere with the perceptual relating of such elements since the condition of similarity is absent.

We did not call attention to Spence's theory of associative learning or the gestalt interpretation of transposition as being explanations which are sufficient for the understanding of stimulus generalization. Instead, we have presented these interpretations to emphasize and enrich the reader's understanding of the importance of the concept of stimulus generalization in helping us understand some of the important problems of learning, particularly relational learning.

The basic problem of learning is to specify the conditions under which changes in behavior occur. In this connection, Skinner has made two useful distinctions in regard to problems of learning. These he termed the *discrimination of stimuli* and *differentiation of response*. From the point of view of operant conditioning, this means that reinforcement can be made contingent on either "(1) the properties of accompanying stimuli (when the result is a discrimination), or (2) the properties of the response (when the result is a differentiation). The rat may be taught, for example, to press the lever with a given force or to hold it down for a given duration, in order for the pellet to be delivered. The basic rule of operant conditioning applies: that the response must occur before it can be reinforced."[19]

In conclusion, reinforcement is conceived as the principal basis of instrumental conditioning; and such conditioning, under appropriate conditions, results in discriminative learning and response differentiation. In addition, we considered the very important phenomenon of generalization in regard to both stimulus generalization and response generalization. Stimulus generalization and response generalization are roughly analogous in that the generalization process in each depends on the presence of similarity among the stimuli and among the responses. We also found that partial reinforcement was a source of some of the generalization effects. Furthermore, generalized responses have a greater likelihood of reinforcement, particularly secondary reinforcement. That is, the more generalized a response, the more likely it is to be rewarded in connection with some situations even when it is unrewarded or punished in connection with others.

[19] Hilgard, *op. cit.*, p. 100.

LEARNING AND THE SOCIAL WORLD

It should be clear that response generalization (or positive transfer, as some call it) and stimulus generalization are two very important results of learning. They are important for the following reason: the more generalized a response or a stimulus, the more difficult it is to extinguish the conditioned associations; hence the more persistent the response. Therefore, it is important to consider some of the conditions which affect the generality of learned associations.

Some Conditions Affecting the Generality of Responses

Linton argues that the formation of generalized responses, particularly affective associations, is related to the conditions of early childhood learning. He says, "generalized responses of the value-attitude type seem to be easy to establish in childhood but exceedingly difficult to establish in adult life." [20]

Furthermore, in a more general way, Linton approaches the explanation of how generalized responses are learned by noting the irregularity of the natural environment and hence the probable nature of cues

> The process of developing and integrating new responses and extinguishing old ones goes on throughout the lifetime of the individual. Without such flexibility it would be impossible for him to survive in a world in which not only the external environment but also his own potentialities are in a constant state of flux. However, there seems to be a fairly close correlation between the ease with which a particular response can be extinguished and its position in the scale of specificity. In general, the more specific a response the easier it is to extinguish it. The reason for this is fairly obvious. Laboratory experiments have shown that habits are extinguished either when they fail to achieve the desired ends or when they expose the individual to too much punishment. Owing to environmental or other changes, a response which is linked with a single situation or with a very small number of situations, can easily become subject to the conditions which will lead to extinction. More generalized responses, on the other hand, are likely to be rewarded in connection with some situations even when they are unrewarded or punished in connection with others. It is a common experience that while specific patterns of overt behavior are fairly easy to extinguish, value-attitude systems are extremely hard to extinguish. Such systems tend to survive even when their overt expressions have been inhibited in many situations and to reassert themselves with almost undiminished vigor when new situations involving the particular value factor arise.[21]

---

[20] Ralph Linton, *The Cultural Background of Personality* (New York, Appleton-Century-Crofts, 1945), p. 116.
[21] *Ibid.*, p. 115.

McClelland later formulated the same general thesis and stated it as follows:

> Affective associations laid down in childhood are often so exceedingly general because of the child's undeveloped powers of discrimination that they persist because it is difficult to produce the conditions that would make it possible to extinguish them. This argument assumes that associations do not decay simply through disuse, which seems a safe assumption in view of the fairly overwhelming evidence that it is what happens *in time* rather than time itself that causes forgetting.[22]

McClelland postulates the following specific conditions as being some of the conditions that promote generality in initial learning.

(1) *Lack of Symbolic Control.*[23] As was indicated in Chapter 3, language provides an advantage in adaptation which can hardly be overemphasized. The use of symbols enables man to describe his environment and make discriminations with a precision which would otherwise be impossible. He can classify and group together a large number of complex experiences, often separated by sizable time spans, and discriminate and generalize from these experiences. The young child does not have this advantage. He cannot define and categorize or establish the boundaries of classes of things or acts. Symbolic control through language enables a person to create his own internal order from his observations and classification of externals. If the child is too young to have such skills, then the conditions of learning are vague and the boundaries unclear. Therefore, any associations which the infant would make between a situation and a response would be vague and general until symbolic control has been developed. Finally, McClelland notes:

> If we accept the principle of mass action or the greater overall responsiveness of the infant to stimulation, it would be logical to assume that many more of the infant's associations would have an affective component. Since pleasure and pain (or affective arousal) are easier to produce in an organism which has not yet developed its discriminatory or symbolic capacities, it should follow that many more situations in infancy would get associated with affective states than would be true later on.[24]

In summary, we see that the relative lack of symbolic control in the periods of infancy and early childhood tends to produce generalized responses and generalized responses with an affective component. The affective component reinforces even more the already considerable resistance of a generalized response to extinction. Hence responses learned

[22] McClelland, *op. cit.*, p. 452.
[23] *Ibid.*, p. 452.
[24] *Ibid.*, p. 443.

LEARNING AND THE SOCIAL WORLD

in early childhood are primary and have great persistency and therefore form a base for interacting with subsequent learning. Because of the strong generalized and affective nature of early childhood responses, they are exceedingly difficult to modify through subsequent experience. However, as the child matures and symbolic control develops, it becomes possible to attach specific symbolic meaning to certain general cues or responses and thus render them more specific and thereby enable some unlearning and relearning to occur. This may be more difficult in connection with affective or emotional states since these seem to be less under the influence of cortical control. In this connection, McClelland suggests that "One of the benefits of psychotherapy may be that affective states are sufficiently reinstated to become associated with symbolic cues, which can then be attached to new responses which will take the place of the old, maladaptive, affective ones." [25]

(2) *Generalized Threats and Promises*.[26] McClelland musters evidence and a good argument to show that prohibitions established on the basis of vague threats and promises are much harder to unlearn than those established by direct punishment. It is well known that fear responses or avoidance responses are difficult to extinguish

> because it leads to a response which does not permit the person to discover that the situation is changed. . . . It suggests a type of learning situation which may prevent unlearning because the responses are instrumental to goals which are so high, vague, or indeterminate that *it is impossible for the person to evaluate how well he is doing*. At one extreme, a child may be punished regularly for stealing candy. He knows he will be spanked if he takes it and may learn to inhibit this response. Later on he may try taking it again and if he goes unspanked will soon extinguish the inhibitory response. At the other extreme, a child may be told if he steals candy that "something bad" will happen to him, his conscience will hurt him, God will disapprove, etc. This too will in time inhibit his response but now if he breaks through this inhibition at any time he has no way of knowing accurately whether he is being punished or not. "Something bad" may not happen immediately, but it may later; sins may be stored up in heaven, etc. In short, prohibitions established on the basis of vague threats are much harder to unlearn than those established by direct punishment. . . .[27]

In the human social world much learning in regard to prohibitions and prescriptions or punishment and reward situations is under conditions such as those just described. Learning under these conditions would help explain the persistency of generalized moral values.

[25] *Ibid.*, p. 447.
[26] *Ibid.*, p. 452.
[27] *Ibid.*, p. 453.

(3) *Irregularity of Original Learning Conditions.*[28] It is well known that partial reinforcement delays extinction. We explained this effect earlier on the basis of interference with the subject's opportunity to discriminate between reward conditions and extinction conditions. The more that reward conditions and extinction conditions become similar, the more difficult it is for the learner to discriminate between the two and learn to stop responding.

McClelland states the general principle as follows: "Any method of increasing the similarity between acquisition and extinction will delay extinction."[29] He cites an experiment by himself and McGown as evidence for the above proposition.[30] In this experiment

> the reinforcement factor was held constant at 100 percent but the relevant cues and responses to receiving food were varied. They trained two groups of white rats to associate a goal box with food, one in the standard specific way and the other in an irregular, "general" way. The goal box consisted of a circular alley. In the specific alley-trained group a barrier was inserted in the alley and food reward on the training days was *always* placed just in front of this barrier. Consequently the rats in this group learned to enter the circular alley, turn left, and run a certain fixed distance to find a food pellet. They learned to associate a particular left-turning response, a particular location in the alley, and a particular time delay with food reward. The group of rats which received generalized reinforcement training were treated quite differently. They too were always fed in the circular alley but there was no barrier in it and the reinforcement was given in such a way as to prevent the animal from associating any particular response, or portion of the alley, or time delay, with food reward. This was done by leaving the food rewards in different sections of the circular alley and by sometimes feeding the animal only when he *stopped* in a certain section of the alley. In other words, the occurrence of the food reward in the goal alley was so irregular with respect to time and place and so inconsistent with respect to the response reinforced that the rats must have formed only a very general association between the circular alley and food reward. After both groups of rats had received 100 percent reinforcement in the goal alley on three successive days in this fashion, the crucial test was made of determining which group would continue to run into the alley longer when the food reward was withdrawn. Both groups showed evidence of the fact that the goal alley, by being associated with food, had attained some secondary reinforcing power. That is, both groups ran into the goal alley more often and faster on the test day than did control groups which had not received reinforcement in it. The group which had been rewarded for a specific response during training extinguished rather rapidly as in all other experiments of this sort. But the general group be-

---

[28] *Ibid.*, pp. 453-456.
[29] *Ibid.*, p. 454.
[30] *Ibid.*, pp. 454-455.

haved quite differently. In the first place, the rats in this group ran into the goal alley significantly faster than the specific animals did, showing that the generalized training had developed a more powerful secondary reward. In the second place, they showed little evidence of extinction in the twenty-five extinction trials given them. On the contrary, they showed slight evidence of a tendency to run faster at the time when the specific animals had definitely begun to extinguish.[31]

On the basis of the foregoing experiment we would conclude that generalized learning is stronger and will persist longer than specific learning. In this experiment three factors associated with reward were controlled in the specific group and varied in the general group. These were the response, the time delay, and the place where the food was.

Suppose as McClelland suggests that both reward and punishment are made irregular and that they occasionally occur together. That is, suppose the rats had been shocked occasionally while they were eating. What would have happened then? Would this have delayed extinction still more? McClelland cites evidence to show that it would. Such mixed associations are often presumed to be the basis for mixed or ambivalent attitudes. Many experiences which an infant has are such that he is incapable of separating the conditions which produce pain and pleasure. "The breast which does not supply the milk may be regarded as 'bad' or frustrating one moment and as 'good' the next, when the milk flows and satisfies hunger." [32]

Certainly, the child as well as the adult has many such mixed experiences throughout life. In other words, much human learning takes place under conditions of motive and value conflict.

(4) *Unreproducibility of the Conditions of Learning*.[33] Item (4) as a factor involved in early childhood learning that contributes to generality of response is related to reasons (1) and (3) above. Many scientific observers have pointed to the fact that in early childhood or infancy the child is unable to distinguish between self and not-self or between inner and outer sensations. In other words, a child is unable to distinguish the source of many of the pleasurable and painful things which he experiences. In such a case learning would be highly general. Later, as the child develops symbolic skills, he is then able to distinguish between inner and outer cues. But suppose we have the task of now extinguishing a cue which was acquired before he was able to distinguish between inner and outer cues. How could the cue situation which was present when the association was first learned be re-established? The point is that it cannot be re-established in its entirety. In such a case, if one

[31] *Ibid.*, pp. 454-455.
[32] *Ibid.*, p. 456.
[33] *Ibid.*, pp. 456-457.

wanted to extinguish the old association, he would strengthen the visible cues which he wishes to replace the old ones (whatever they were); and by this process of increased stimulus attraction the new cues would gradually become dominant over the old ones.

To summarize: Any learning situation in which the original conditions of learning are difficult to reproduce will interfere with the extinction of associations learned under these conditions.

We have emphasized that early childhood learning, largely because symbolic skills have not sufficiently developed, is conducive to the formation of generalized responses. Perhaps it should be emphasized that generalized responses learned in early childhood are more resistant to change than those learned after full powers of symbolic discrimination have been developed. In other words, strong generalized associations are formed throughout the lifetime of a person and are not, of course, peculiar to childhood learning. What does seem to be peculiar to childhood learning are the many more conditions of learning which interfere with the process of discrimination; and, as has been shown, this interferes with efforts to change responses which have been learned under such conditions.

In concluding this section on factors affecting the generality of responses, we wish to note one other condition which contributes to generalized responses and this one is more peculiar to adults than to children.

(5) *The Complexity of the Learning Situation.* It is probably safe to say that in all or almost all human learning situations, for every given stimulus there are several potential or latent responses that are aroused, and that some responses have a greater probability of being activated than others. And, of course, some social stimulus situations would arouse more potential responses than others. It seems reasonable to hypothesize that the larger the number of potential responses aroused, the greater the difficulty in response choice or resolution. To the extent that the responses are similar, the subject could generalize and formulate a new and more general response which would in his opinion, at least, resolve the differences. This is apparently a major aspect of the psychoanalytic process of rationalization. It, of course, is also an aspect of deductive and inductive reasoning.

Some social situations are very complex and involve a large number of potential responses, some of which are similar, some mutually exclusive or in conflict, and some competitive. For example, take the matter of taxes for public education. In terms of short-range economic responses the subject may be motivated to want a tax cut or to at least hold the line, but from a long-range economic view he knows that education is a major economic resource and a necessary means to both personal and social progress. The potential increase in taxes may also arouse political responses, and these may be in conflict with or in competition with the economic responses.

To summarize: The more competing responses and concepts involved in a social learning situation, the more the situation is conducive to the formation of generalized responses.

5. REINFORCEMENT AND THE CONCEPT OF FEEDBACK

Since we in this book are primarily interested in instrumental conditioning, we shall restrict our concern with the concept of reinforcement to instrumental conditioning. As was stated in an earlier section, a reinforcement in the case of instrumental or operant behavior is a stimulus that follows the occurrence of a response and rewards it. For an animal to learn, there must be something or some pattern to learn. For a rat to learn to run one channel in a maze rather than another, he must discover that the channel in question has some adaptive significance or meaning. For example, it may provide a source of food, it may delay anxiety, or it may provide a source of protection. On the other hand, the rat may associate a particular stimulus with a previously learned cue. For example, Saltzman [34] trained rats to run down a straight runway to a goal box which contained food. The goal box was either black or white. In one condition, the goal box always contained food when it was black but did not when it was white. After this training the rats were taught a simple maze in which they had to choose between two pathways, one leading to a black goal box and the other to a white one. The rats learned to go to the black goal box, even though it *never contained food*. The black goal box was itself reinforcing because it had been paired with a primary reinforcement, food, in another situation. The black goal box was a *secondary reinforcement*.

A secondary reinforcement is anything that acquires reinforcing power because it is paired with a previously learned reinforcer.

It is clear that a stimulus that reinforces an instrumental response will strengthen the response. In other words, reinforcement clearly modifies behavior. Everyone will admit that reinforcement affects what an animal will do, but some will argue that it has nothing to do with what the animal learns.[35] We are not concerned with this issue, since by our definition of learning as "any modification or change in the behavior of an organism which results from the experience of the organism rather than maturation or physiological change in the organism," then changes in performance presuppose learning. Presumably, sheer practice results

[34] I. J. Saltzman, "Maze Learning in the Absence of Primary Reinforcement: A Study of Secondary Reinforcement," *J. Comp. Physiol. Psychol.*, Vol. 42 (1949), pp. 161-173.

[35] Deese, *op. cit.*, pp. 34-35.

in the elimination of errors by learning and hence the strengthening of a response.

More important than efforts to distinguish between learning and performance is the distinction between *reinforcement* and *feedback*.

In terms of operant or instrumental conditioning, reinforcement depends upon the organism's perceiving an association between some cue and a reward. In other words, reinforcement necessarily has a sensory and a perceptual basis. We can show that either primary or secondary reinforcement is necessary to the modification of behavior. But having shown that reinforcement affects behavior, we have not explained *how* it affects behavior. In other words, reinforcement seems to be a necessary condition for learning to occur, but it is not an adequate explanation of how it occurs.

Most psychologists have interpreted sensory feedback as being equivalent to reinforcement, or knowledge of results. However, we cited evidence in Chapter 5 from Smith which indicated that reinforcement and feedback are not the same.[36] The studies of partial reinforcement have shown that a feedback delay interval of the magnitude of those used in most experiments has only an initial minor disruption effect on learning, whereas all studies of delayed sensory feedback have shown that all delay intervals are seriously disturbing to behavior organization. This causes Smith to

> believe that sensory feedback processes are an aspect of neurophysiological control of behavior more fundamental than the temporal relationships involved in learning discrete reactions, that the feedback regulatory mechanisms are built-in components of the behaving system, as necessary to organized behavior as the receptors and effectors. Feedback delay interrupts the regulatory pattern and consequently disturbs the intrinsic organization of motion.[37]

Smith presents the foregoing conclusion in more detail as follows:

> In recent years, psychological theory has been dominated by concepts drawn from the study of learning. Theoretical constructs derived from investigations of one aspect of behavior organization have been applied almost across the board to many diverse kinds of human activity and performance. Thus, the theories of conditioning, reward reinforcement, stimulus reinforcement, and information reinforcement have been accepted almost without question as general models of behavior integration. The processes of conditioning or reinforcement are assumed to be the primary mechanisms by means of which discrete responses are linked or molded into organized

---

[36] Karl U. Smith, *Delayed Sensory Feedback and Behavior* (Philadelphia, W. B. Saunders Co., 1962), pp. 1-15.
[37] *Ibid.*, p. 97.

behavior patterns. According to this general view, all human perceptual-motor skills are specifically learned, i.e., built up from the human repertoire of discrete reflexes or responses by means of conditioning or reinforcement effects. The basic organization is sequential; unit responses are linked in series to form complex patterns.

From the point of view of learning theory, the process of sensory feedback is conceptualized most naturally as a form of reinforcement, or "information feedback" to the individual of the results of his behavior. He moves, and his sensory organs inform him of what he has done. If the movement achieves its goal—if it is accurate—it is reinforced, and consequently more likely to occur another time. If the movement is inaccurate, it is more likely to be eliminated.

The fallacy in this reasoning becomes apparent when we compare the phenomena of delayed sensory feedback with certain other "delay" phenomena studied in relation to learning behavior. A delayed conditioned response is produced by prolonging the interval between the conditioned stimulus (CS) and unconditioned stimulus (UCS). In the normal process of conditioning, as in conditioning a dog to salivate in response to a sound, the optimal interval between the CS (sound) and the UCS (food) is about 0.5 second. If, after the conditioned salivary response to sound is formed, the time interval between CS and UCS is increased, the dog learns to delay its conditioned response to the sound beyond the original latency. A comparable situation in the instrumental learning experiment is known as delayed reinforcement, when the time interval between some adaptive or operant pattern of behavior and the reinforcing reward or punishment is extended. For example, when a rat is trained to press a bar in order to get a food reward, and the interval between response and reinforcement is increased, in the condition of delayed reinforcement, the animal learns more slowly and shows a lower rate of sustained reaction in the situation.

The temporal relationships just described are accepted generally in learning psychology. When the optimal interval between a conditioned and unconditioned stimulus is increased, or when the reinforcement following an instrumental response is delayed, learning still occurs, but somewhat less efficiently. Thus, if we were to equate sensory feedback with reinforcement, we would have to predict that delayed feedback might decrease the efficiency of learning, but that it would not be seriously detrimental to organized behavior.

Actually, the most obvious effect of delayed sensory feedback, even with very short delays of a fraction of a second, is a serious disturbance of behavior. There is nothing in conventional learning theory to account for this disturbance. The temporal relationships and delay phenomena emphasized by learning experiments have involved the modification or control of organized behavior patterns by means of *temporal manipulation of extrinsic stimulus factors*. Sensory feedback is a critical aspect of the intrinsic behavior organization of the organism, and delayed feedback is seriously disturbing because it interrupts this intrinsic regulation of motion.[38]

[38] *Ibid.*, pp. 4-5. Italics added.

Professor Smith is concerned with a much larger problem than the matter of the differences between reinforcement and sensory feedback. In fact, his theory is an elaborate attack on the inadequacy of reinforcement theory to account for human learning, and he proposes a new approach which is based on the contention that behavior is integrated according to spatial and temporal patterns and that the spatial factor is primary.[39]

Smith's distinction between delayed reinforcement and delayed sensory feedback is based on the recognition that reinforcement theory controls behavior by the temporal manipulation of *external* stimulus conditions and that sensory feedback is a critical aspect of the *internal* organization of behavior. It would seem that for this distinction to hold we must assume that the stimulus pattern that is being interrupted must be a familiar one. For example, it is doubtful if a delay in the auditory receipt of nonsense syllables would be disorganizing or seriously disruptive to behavior.

Anyway, we accept the general distinction or emphasis which Professor Smith makes between external stimulus factors and the internal organizing behavior of the central neural processes and his recognition of the importance of feedback as a necessary condition for stable neural functioning. But until something better than reinforcement theory is available, we must rely on current usage.

Let us next consider learning as a means of releasing potentialities.

6. LEARNING AS RELEASE OF POTENTIALITY

In one sense learning is behavior development, and behavior development is the manifestation of potentialities. Consequently, efficient organization and control of the learning situation becomes an important source for controlling development.

If a child is exposed to a dull and inefficient series of learning experiences, the result is to slow and impede development. The role of education in releasing potentialities is too well known to mention.

The following is a quotation from an editorial in *Life* magazine dated January 26, 1962:

> The public school once provided a path for European immigrants to move from the slums into the huge American middle class. It is a logical route for Negroes, Puerto Ricans and other underprivileged pupils to do likewise. But they face some tremendous obstacles even in fully integrated schools. . . .
>
> In New York, as in other cities, Negro slum schools are the most over-

---

[39] *Ibid.*, pp. 5-15.

crowded, have the least experienced teachers and the highest ratio of students to teachers.

Learning seems to the children to have nothing to do with their slum lives, which leave them so distressed, so distracted, so frustrated that many never learn to read properly. Because of this, they fall behind in other subjects, even manual skills which usually require them to read instructions. Three out of five Negro youngsters drop out of slum schools before completion—uneducated, seemingly uneducable, virtually unemployable. Such were the gloomy findings of Educator James B. Conant in his recent, widely read *Slums and Suburbs* study.

It doesn't have to be that way. Children with seemingly hopeless IQs, given the right stimulation, encouragement at home and belief in themselves, can achieve fantastic progress. Two pioneering movements have proved this:

When St. Louis' bold-visioned Negro principal, Dr. Samuel Shepard, began his program in 1958 in 22 elementary schools of that city's worst slum, only 7% of his eighth grade graduates were able to qualify for the "top track" in high school; now 20% qualify. In 1958, half were in the third, or bottom track; now only 20% have to go there. Three years ago his eighth-graders were a full year behind the U.S. reading norm; now they are actually ahead. He has changed the Negro community's attitude toward the school by a steady fire of field trips, pep talks, contests. He shows the parents by slides, charts and film strips exactly how poorly their children are doing. And he proves they can have a better life by pointing to specific jobs now open in St. Louis for which no qualified Negroes can be found. Above all he emphasizes reading as the crucial key to such jobs, and to everything else.

In New York, in 1956, Dan Schreiber, then principal of Junior High School 43, and others began the "Higher Horizons" program, which has since been extended to 65 integrated elementary and junior high schools. Children's sights were raised by their being taken to engineering schools and hospitals where they saw Negroes and Puerto Ricans getting a higher education; to plays, operas and symphonies where performers received them backstage; on "dream college" trips to Yale and Princeton. One boy who began with a 75 IQ, another with 97, have since been awarded college scholarships. The latter went off the top of the Pinter IQ scale at 139.[40]

What this means is that not only are one's innate resources conditioned and released through activity and experience, but also one's opinions of himself and his aspirations. In regard to the latter, a point of particular significance is a person's perception of the abilities and opportunities available to members of his class or race. That is, if one perceives all others *of his kind* as possessing certain characteristics, then he will also perceive himself as having these characteristics and evaluate himself in terms of these.

[40] Quotation from *Life* magazine, January 26, 1962, p. 4.

One of the fundamental problems of behavioral science is this: how can experience be designed and deliberately aimed at developing individual potential and fostering the individual's capacity and readiness for creative thinking and problem solving? How can one's range of problem-solving ideas be enlarged? How can one be encouraged to reflect and to experiment with the construction of new ways of thinking? The answers to these questions will enable us to understand more clearly the relationships between learning and the release of potentialities.

Not all learning is conducive to efficient subsequent learning. For example, prejudice against racial, religious, and minority groups is learned and it is well known that prejudice interferes with interaction and one's capacity to objectively assess the objects of prejudice. Incorrect information and incorrect learning of any kind are interfering factors in subsequent learning. Consequently, for learning to efficiently release potentialities, the content of the learning must be valid.

For example,

> Nissen, Machover, and Kinder . . . have shown how the visual learning of childhood may be selective in its later effects. West African natives made low scores on form boards, in an intelligence test. In this sort of test the subject is asked to fit a series of wooden blocks with simple geometrical shapes into holes with the same shapes, as fast as he can. In conversation, Dr. Nissen has made the point that the low scores were not due to slowness of movement, but to a slowness in identifying shapes—a slowness of perception. At the same time, he found himself just as inferior in seeing things in the bush that seemed completely obvious to the natives. Suppose now that a native and a city-dwelling scientist were shown the trail of a *new* animal in the same habitat: though it is strange to both, which would remember it better, and be able to recognize it on a second occasion? What a native could learn from a text on geometry, or what one of us could learn about following a trail, must be far more a function of pre-existent learning than of the inherited properties of our respective brains.[41]

Thus the quality and validity of what we learn is very important to the quality of performance and subsequent problem-solving efficiency.

Different groups have different subcultures and hence different systems for doing the same things, and some are more efficient than others. Consequently, it follows that the children who are members of the different groups will acquire different problem-solving techniques. Thus one set of factors which determine the efficiency of the release of potentialities consists of the external forces in the group life of people and their culture. These external factors greatly condition the internal forces of the organism.

[41] D. O. Hebb, *The Organization of Behavior* (New York, John Wiley & Sons, Inc., 1949), pp. 119-120.

LEARNING AND THE SOCIAL WORLD 193

In a very real sense creativity is a release of new potentiality within a person. Of course, the results of creativity also affect the potentialities of a social system. But creativity is often blocked by the subject's inability to break out of the prison of his own culture. Karl Duncker is cited in *Life* magazine as follows:

> "Make four equal-sided triangles using six matches," he would tell his subjects as he laid the matches on the table before them. Most of the subjects only shuffled and reshuffled the matches on the surface of the table, gradually becoming convinced that the problem was insoluble. Finally, though, a few of them realized that Duncker had never said the matches must be in the same plane. These few immediately put the matches together in a tetrahedron, the three-dimensional figure that looks like a pyramid with three sides. The others remained frustrated. Having first visualized matches in a plane, they were unable to get beyond that preconception.[42]

In the Duncker study a major difficulty which most of the subjects had was escaping or breaking through the bonds of preconception. The reader should recall that in discussing creativity in Chapter 4 we noted the research finding which seems to always accompany children who are creative. This was the social and psychological security of the parents and children in the family. If the parents were secure with one another and with their peers, then the children were secure; and with a strong feeling of security there are no fears of failing. Even if they experiment and fail, this is no stigma. In other words, the supportive and non-evaluating environment is enormously freeing of internal resources and hence a means of releasing potentialities.

Berelson and Steiner summarize some of the findings on the psychological characteristics which more or less describe creative individuals. The first group described is composed of a more or less creative group of industrial chemists. The second group is composed of forty of the most creative architects in the country.

    1. The more and less creative men do not differ significantly from each other in a test of verbal intelligence.
    2. The more creative men are less anxious than the less creative men.
    3. The more creative men are more autonomous, more dynamic, and more integrative than their less creative colleagues.
    4. The more creative men see their own attitudes as being more different from others.
    5. The less creative man has more authoritarian attitudes than does his more creative colleague.
    6. The more creative men place higher value on practical matters and utility; more emphasis on harmony and form and less emphasis on mystical

[42] Quotation from *Life* magazine, May 16, 1955, p. 187.

values and the acceptance of the church as an institution in comparison to their less creative colleagues.

7. In describing themselves the two groups differ in that while the more creative men are more oriented to achievement and acceptance of their own inner impulses, the less creative men are more oriented to avoiding situations in which they might be blamed for their activities or in which they might feel inferior.

8. The more creative men give more evidence of psychological well-being than do the less creative men.

9. The less creative man appears to take risks where they are less warranted, more than is true of his more creative colleague.

10. In a problem-solving situation, the more creative man works slowly and cautiously while he is analyzing his problem and gathering his data. Once he obtains the basic data and approaches the point of synthesis, he works rapidly. The less creative man spends less time in analyzing the problem but more time in attempting to synthesize his material.[43]

Now here is a summary of the distinguishing characteristics of the creative architects for contrast and comparison:

> If I were to summarize what is most generally characteristic of the creative architect as we have seen him, it is his high level of effective intelligence, his openness to experience, his freedom from petty restraints and impoverishing inhibitions, his aesthetic sensitivity, his cognitive flexibility, his independence in thought and action, his high level of energy, his unquestioning commitment to creative endeavor, and his unceasing striving for creative solutions to the ever more difficult architectural problems which he constantly sets for himself.[44]

It is clear that above-average intelligence is involved in creativity, but so are social and psychological factors which involve one's attitudes toward himself and toward independent thought.

Let us next examine some of the group-related factors that have been shown to affect performance.

7. GROUP AND INDIVIDUAL PERFORMANCE

Does social interaction facilitate performance, make no difference, or reduce performance efficiency? To some extent the answer depends upon the performance task. Of course, it is assumed that the tasks involved

---

[43] Morris I. Stein, "Social and Psychological Factors Affecting Creativity of Industrial Research Chemists," unpublished ms., quoted in Bernard Berelson and Gary A. Steiner, *Human Behavior: An Inventory of Scientific Findings* (New York, Harcourt, Brace & World, Inc., 1964), p. 227.

[44] Donald W. McKinnon, "Creativity in Architects," quoted in Berelson and Steiner, *op. cit.*, p. 227.

are capable of performance by individuals. Certainly an individual could not carry a heavy log as well—if at all—as could a number of people in collective action.

In attempting to answer this question, Collins and Guetzkow formulate the following proposition from their summary of related research. "Group members may collectively achieve more than the most superior members are capable of achieving alone." [45]

> Barnlund has demonstrated that the group can surpass its most capable member. . . . On the first day of a college course in group discussion, Barnlund administered the "Recognition of Valid Conclusions" test to the freshmen students. The problem is to select the conclusion which follows logically from the premises. According to Barnlund, "The arguments cover a wide range of subjects and are phrased deliberately to complicate the decision for the reader; that is, statements involve atheists, Communists, Republicans, college professors, and other terms likely to prejudice judgment."
>
> Eight or nine weeks later, the students were formed into groups of approximately equal ability on the first test score. Experimental groups were then given an alternate form of the same test and told to reach a group decision on each of the 30 problems. Control students took the test individually as before. The interacting groups performed significantly better than their superior members had performed on the previous form of the test (p. < .01).[46]

If valid task performance is improved under group conditions as compared to individual conditions, then what explains this result? Collins and Guetzkow summarize Barnlund's reasons for group superiority in terms of the four following propositions: [47]

> 1. Membership in the experimental groups produced a higher level of interest in the successful completion of the task. The sharing of the division of labor tends to stimulate mutual expectations of performance and this in turn would heighten individual interest.
> 2. Membership in the experimental groups had an inhibiting as well as facilitating effect. Knowledge that one's opinions were to be shared publicly made group members more cautious and deliberate in their own thinking. This point is the opposite to our proposition in Section 6 above regarding the effect of a nonevaluative environment on creativity. The fact that others will severely judge one's ideas and suggestions may tend to make the participants more conservative in their thinking. In Section 6 we had shown that freedom from personal evaluation by others released one's sense of security and this in turn stimulated his imagination.

---

[45] Barry E. Collins and Harold Guetzkow, *A Social Psychology of Group Processes for Decision-Making* (New York, John Wiley & Sons, Inc., 1964), p. 45.
[46] *Ibid.*, p. 46.
[47] *Ibid.*, p. 47.

3. Groups had greater critical resources than did individuals working alone. This does not mean that groups as groups create and make decisions. It means that each person whose action relates to others is stimulated and behaviorally complemented by the others. The collective feedback response of the members of the group to each other's responses provides a multitude of perspectives for the assessment of ideas. This increases the probability of formulating new and novel combinations of ideas.

4. A more objective view of the problem resulted from competition between the private prejudices of group members.

If we think of a group as a behavioral or action *system* through which the behaviors of the individuals are coordinated and integrated toward an end or ends, then it should be clear that groups are adaptive, facilitative, and instrumental. Groups do not take the place of individuals or of individual behavior. Instead, they allow for the combining of whatever qualities the individuals have into a new and larger, more powerful and more efficient system. In other words, a group is a form of social system which regulates the action and energies of a number of people. In commenting on the study of social behavior, Professor George Homans said that "Groups are not what we study but where we study it." [48]

In other words, groups provide varying types of social environments for studying human behavior.

The reader should not be trapped by the common clichés about the red tape of bureaucracy and the stifling of action by committees. When and if such is actually observed, the observer should try to find out if the apparent inefficiency is due to the inadequacies of the system or to a perversion of the system by some for personal motives or ends. In other words, we must distinguish between the relative efficiency and validity of various *systems of behavior* and the motivation and skills of the participants in executing the behavioral requirements of the system. One may design the most efficient behavioral system for a given end that has ever been conceived and find that in a given situation it fails because the participants do not want it to succeed or at least they do not want it to succeed so well.[49] Many a system of organization or administration has failed not because of intrinsic defects in the system but because of perverted use of the system by individual members.

Perhaps from a certain point of view it might be said that if the system were more efficient it would have built-in checks against the possibility of perversion. This kind of argument is spurious because systems of deviancy and avoidance can be devised as counterparts to any system. The point that should be kept in mind is that social systems are adaptive systems and they emerge to meet the needs of certain people,

---

[48] George C. Homans, *Social Behavior: Its Elementary Forms* (New York, Harcourt, Brace and World, Inc., 1961), p. 7.

[49] F. J. Roethlisberger and William J. Dickson, *Management and the Worker* (Cambridge, Mass., Harvard University Press, 1939).

but not *all* of the people who are involved in the action system see the system from the same set of personal needs, values, motives, or goals. Consequently, in assessing the outputs of a system, the motives, loyalties, and goals of the individual members must be taken into account as well as their role skills. For example, a county may have evolved an excellent law enforcement system, but if the sheriff decides that it is more profitable to him not to enforce the law than to enforce it, then law enforcement in that county may appear to be weak and confused. Systems of action, like systems of knowledge, may be directed toward ends which are not generally approved as well as toward ends that are approved.

The principle that is suggested by the foregoing discussion is that the system of rewards and punishments should take into account the individuals as individuals as well as the group as a whole. That is, individual contributions as well as failures and misuses should be ascertainable and responded to appropriately.

It should be getting obvious by now that man's social organization is not only a source of personal and social need satisfaction, but it is also a source of motivation, goal definition, and the means by which the species is maintained and perpetuated.

The social system contains within it a system of rewards and punishments. Thus it provides reinforcement for and against various forms of action. In this sense a given social system elicits certain kinds of responses from its members. Thus a social system conditions the perception, motivation, learning, and thinking of its members. Let us see in the next chapter how individuals in learning to meet their own needs also learn simultaneously to meet the needs of the society. In other words, let us see how individual and social needs are but different aspects of the same coin.

8. SUMMARY

Learning was broadly defined as changes in behavior in regard to a given situation which result from experience as opposed to changes due to physiological maturation or other physical states.

From the point of view of the social psychologist we viewed learning both as a means for social and psychological *adaptation* and as a means for *releasing biological potentialities.*

Theories of classical and instrumental conditioning were briefly summarized. Instrumental or operant conditioning was emphasized as being a useful concept in helping to understand the results of human learning —particularly in regard to social behavior—since when a person acts in a certain way he is rewarded or punished by the behavior of another person.

Partial reinforcement or variable reinforcement was found to be highly effective in producing resistance to efforts to extinguish the response in question. Certainly there are many instances of human behavior which conform to this outcome. Gambling, of course, is a classical example. There is a great amount of energy and effort expended on the hope or expectation that eventually a great reward will result. Of course, human society affords many examples of fixed or constant reinforcement. This is the case of a fixed payment per hour of work by a person. Such a procedure has the merit of maintaining a constant and predictable work flow over fixed time periods.

The importance of symbolic learning in human behavior and the persistence of early childhood learning were tentatively explained by using an argument drawn from the work of David McClelland.

McClelland distinguished between the *habit* of responding to a specific reward and the *motive* to respond a certain way in general. The former is easily extinguished and the latter is very difficult to extinguish. He explains the greater persistency of the latter in terms of four conditions of learning which he argues are conducive to the formation of highly generalized responses. These were: (1) lack of symbolic control; (2) generalized threats and promises; (3) irregularity of the original learning conditions; and (4) the unreproducibility of the conditions of learning.

A distinction was made between the concepts of reinforcement and feedback because of the different effects on behavior which were produced by delay in each case.

Finally, learning was discussed as a means for releasing biological potentialities, and group organization was noted as one of the most efficient conditions for improving performance.

Further References

1. Clark L. Hull, *Principles of Behavior* (New York, Appleton-Century-Crofts, 1943).
2. Gregory Razran, "Extinction Re-examined and Re-analyzed," *Psychological Review*, Vol. 63, No. 1, 1956.
3. B. F. Skinner, *The Behavior of Organisms: An Experimental Analysis* (New York, Appleton-Century-Crofts, 1938).
4. S. S. Stevens, Editor, *Handbook of Experimental Psychology* (New York, John Wiley & Sons, Inc., 1951).

8
Some Effects of Social Learning on Behavior

•

1. *Introduction*
2. *Socialization and Resocialization*
   (a) *Learning and the Family*
   (b) *Drive and Motive*
   (c) *Societal and Local Structures: Universal and Particular Conditions*
   (d) *Some Effects of Early Experience on Behavior*
3. *The Social Context of Behavior Development*
   (a) *Sex Role Identity*
4. *Summary*

1. INTRODUCTION

THERE ARE at least two broad sets of constants which affect human learning and hence affect behavior. These are, *first*, such biophysiological factors as sex, hunger, genetic quality, and the capacity for certain emotional abilities for fear, anger, and pleasure; and, *secondly*, the great dependence of the human offspring on the societal system into which he is born.

Sexual differences which relate to physical size, strength, and fighting ability are reflected in the general human pattern of male dominance. In other words, the physical superiority of the male has had considerable effect on the development of social institutions. While women assist in many wartime activities, the business of war is still the responsibility of men.

Linton argues that:

> It is questionable whether there is any society in existence which is actually dominated by women. Nevertheless, it is possible to imagine a situation

in which this might come to be the case. Economic considerations are of great importance in the organization of all social systems. We all recognize that even in our own society the ultimate control of the family is vested in the partner who makes the greatest contribution to its support. The poor man who marries a rich wife is under his wife's thumb no matter what the theoretical relation of husband and wife may be in that particular society. When any group becomes mainly dependent for its subsistence on an occupation or series of occupations carried on exclusively by women, the social importance of women will be increased and their actual if not their theoretical position in the society correspondingly raised. If the inheritance of property necessary to the particular industry is involved, the position of women will be still further strengthened.[1]

Among the second set of universals, that is, the individual's dependence on others, are the infant and adult need for the company, care, and security of others; the desire for emotional support; and the need for the response and recognition of others.

These foregoing two sets of factors are so universal that they appear to be innate properties. Certainly, the capacity to respond with anger, fear, or pleasure and the need or dependence of the child for the care and emotional security which the responses of others provide for the child are general biological predispositions. But the stimuli which evoke these emotions and responses in later life are dependent upon experience.

In summary, we can say that the human offspring possesses a set of biological potentialities or raw materials which are functions of the genotypes and that human behavior derives from the interaction of these biological capacities with environmental stimulation and conditioning. It is our purpose in this chapter to organize and present some of the findings on the effects of social experience upon the development of behavior.

2. SOCIALIZATION AND RESOCIALIZATION

In Chapter 4 (The Release of Human Potentialities) it was pointed out that men can increase their problem-solving power and adaptive capacity by coordinating and integrating the correlated efforts of several people toward particular goals. This means that with man's inventive capacity it is possible to change his adaptive capacity at any point in time through the process of cultural invention.

If a society is to survive, its systems of knowledge, techniques, beliefs, and methods of social organization provided by its culture must become established as patterns of habitual response on the part of its members. The process by which the culture patterns of a society become the

[1] Ralph Linton, *The Study of Man* (New York, Appleton-Century-Crofts, 1936), p. 138.

habitual response patterns of the members is the process of *socialization*. In other words, socialization is the complex process by which patterns of behavior are socially transmitted from one generation to the next.

It is not enough simply to say that socialization is learning. Certainly symbolic communication, parental example, and parental love are means which facilitate the learning of culture patterns, but in addition to these the human offspring is dependent upon the social system to meet all his needs. Consequently, the ongoing systems of behavior as reflected by the major social structures such as the church, the school, the family, and the community are fundamental sources which guide and direct *what* the new members of the society are expected to learn.

Linton notes that

> The individual's incentive for assuming these patterns lies in the satisfaction which they afford to his personal needs, especially his need for favorable response from others. However, from the point of view of his society such satisfactions are important mainly as bait. He learns the patterns as wholes, and these wholes subtend the necessities of social living quite as much as they subtend his own needs. He takes the bait of immediate personal satisfaction and is caught upon the hook of socialization. He would learn to eat in response to his own hunger drive, but his elders teach him to "eat like a gentleman." Thus, in later years, his hunger drive elicits a response which will not only satisfy it but do so in a way acceptable to his society and compatible with its other culture patterns.[2]

It should be clear by now that the processes of socialization function to transform the biological offspring into a *person,* that is, an individual who has acquired the values and roles appropriate to his age and sex and in keeping with the characteristics of his society. If human society is an adaptive system which functions to meet the needs of the human organism and thus maintain the species, then it (the societal system) must also be maintained. The processes of socialization are obviously one of the major ways in which a society maintains itself.

Each generation receives a set of values, traditions, concepts of honor, and notions of justice from the preceding generations. This means that men of the past decided on what they thought was right and established it as a pattern. For example, our Constitution and Bill of Rights represented hammered-out decisions about freedom and justice, and we would not have these today if these decisions had not been made. The point is that generations of the future will not possess these values unless the members of the current generations renew these decisions. This means that the decisions on the great issues of human interaction must be made

---

[2] Ralph Linton, *The Cultural Background of Personality* (New York, Appleton-Century-Crofts, 1945), pp. 24-25.

again and again and renewed in each generation or patterns of evasion arise and the important values are eroded away. We are not talking about values which are deleterious to the society; they will, of course, be transformed in time through evolution. Instead, we are referring to those values which represent the wisdom of the ages and are expressed in the great books of mankind. In spite of the wisdom contained in a given value, the value is not self-maintaining. Human behavior is not always rational, and values—like any other human product—must be supported and maintained by human effort.

Let us examine some of the specific social groupings which function to socialize the human offspring.

LEARNING AND THE FAMILY

Sociologists and anthropologists distinguish several organizational aspects of the family and these involve patterns of child rearing, courtship patterns, kinship patterns, and a system of division of labor. In other words, the family constitutes a social system. The nature of the system of social organization which characterizes the family in a given society is closely correlated with the level of technology and economic organization of the society.[3]

The basic form of family organization is the *nuclear family*. It consists of a married couple and their children and is the typical form in Western society.

> Two other family forms are built on the nuclear family and are found in many other societies. The first consists of the *polygamous family*, which affiliates two or more nuclear families by means of plural marriages. The second is the *extended family*, which unites nuclear families through the extension of the parent-child, rather than the husband-wife relationship, as in the polygamous family. The typical extended family includes three generations who live in a single dwelling or closely adjacent households.[4]

How does a system of family relationships influence the formation and development of behavior of the child? In the first place, the parents are, at least during the early period of infancy, the sole source of gratification, relief from discomfort, protection from danger, and source of reward and recognition. Thus the child's first glimpse of the world and the nature of adults is provided by the behavior of his parents and other members of the family who may be present. If we want to know what kind of person a newborn will grow up to become, we will need to know

---

[3] See Margaret Mead, *Cultural Patterns and Technical Change* (New York, Mentor Books, 1955).
[4] Harry C. Bredemeier and Richard M. Stephenson, *The Analysis of Social Systems* (New York, Holt, Rinehart and Winston, Inc., 1962), p. 194.

the kind of world in which he will live. What are the rules or norms of everyday life which define how the game of life is to be played? These help define the newborn's responses and solutions to problems of living and the demands of others.

What contributions to the processes of behavioral development derive from the physical and biological characteristics of the individual? A review of Chapter 4 will indicate that this is an inaccurate question. The biological and physical raw materials for behavior are necessary, but not sufficient for its development. In addition to the raw materials is the necessity for experience as a condition for learning. In other words, behavior is a function of the *interaction* of the properties of the person with the properties of some environmental system at a given time period.

DRIVE AND MOTIVE

We shall define *drive* as the mustering or focusing of energy as an impetus to behavior. The action tendency is initiated by shifts in physiological balance and is accompanied by heightened sensitivity to particular stimuli.

Motive and drive are often used synonymously as terms which refer to the acts of an organism that are determined largely, but not necessarily wholly, by its own nature or internal structure. We shall distinguish between these two concepts in terms of the origin of motive and drive. We have defined drive as originating from a change in some physiological balance such as hunger and the related sensitization to certain stimuli such as food in the case of hunger.

By *motivation* we mean purposive or goal-directed behavior which is acquired through experience by learning. Both physiological drive and motivation involve changes in activity level, sensitivity, physical and emotional tension, and perception. But, for the moment, the point of distinction between the two terms which we wish to make is in regard to the differences in sources of origin which bring on the internal change, the source of origin for drive being *internal* to the person and the source of origin for motive being both internal and external—internal in the sense that physiological processes are involved and external in the sense that the *goal directedness* of the behavior is learned in relation to the demands of the external world, particularly the social world; also, external in the sense that actual change or desired change in the person's social relationships affects his motivation. For example, if two children are close playmates in a neighborhood and a new family moves in with a child of the same age and sex of these two and one of the two becomes friendly to the new resident, then the other child becomes disturbed over his relationship with his old playmate. Emotional tension mounts between the two and the one who perceives himself as threatened will be motivated to restore his former position. This may take many forms. He may seek to alienate his old friend from the new one or he may seek to bring in a fourth member to the group.

It should be clear by now why we have defined motive as purposive or goal-directed behavior resulting from changes or desired changes in one's behavioral environment. In case it is not clear, let me point out that an internal change or physiological imbalance is not logically or empirically adequate to account for a businessman's anxiety and motive behavior in regard to a competitor or the anxiety and political pressure by a local American Medical Association officer on a candidate for Congress in regard to Medicare legislation. Obviously, these motives are formed through perception and learning and are aroused through disturbances in one's sociocultural world. The origin and even the nature of the motive are often determined by the structure of the social system. For example, the motivation of a scientist may be the pursuit of knowledge for its own sake. He may or may not be concerned with whether there are any immediate practical advantages to his findings. Why should one be motivated to do research if there are no tangible or practical rewards? The answer is found in the nature of the institution and organization of the field of science in which the participant is a member. The membership of scientific societies and associations recognizes and rewards their fellows on the basis of creative work. Those who receive the highest rewards and who have the highest prestige in the scientific community are the ones who have pushed the frontiers of knowledge the farthest. In other words, those who receive the highest rewards and recognition are the ones who *exhibit superior role performance* in their field.

What does this mean from the standpoint of motivation? It means that when one becomes a participant in a social system, his behavior is evaluated by the other participants in terms of a set of rules and goals set up for the organization. Thus one's behavior is defined on a subjective scale of quality in terms of the rules and goals of the organization. Therefore, one's performance is good, average, or poor in terms of one's contribution to the goals of the system. The evaluations which one's peers in an organization place upon one's performance are an important source of one's self-image. Those who are actually creative and receive the esteem of their colleagues reflect this acceptance in their self-attitudes. There are some who are less than average performers and who refuse to accept the judgment of their peers. The assumption here is that the subject is *actually* a poor performer. The motivation which results from the negative evaluation by the peers and the person's refusal to accept their judgment leads to his engaging in defensive action by often making charges of cliques, favoritism, persecution, and efforts to counterorganize within the organization.

EFFECTS OF SOCIAL LEARNING ON BEHAVIOR

The foregoing illustration clearly shows that the rules and norms for problem-solving and decision-making by the members of an organization function to partially determine the motivation of the individual. In addition, the ability and skill limitations of the members also function to effect motivation. If their ability and skill are below par as reflected by the group norms, then this may generate defensive motives and contribute to lowered self-esteem. We may conclude that a person's behavior in a social situation is a function of the requirements of the rules and norms of the group or organization and the person's abilities and skills to perform in respect to these. The rules and norms of the group or organization set the goals for behavior and the boundaries for right and wrong action; they also define the rewards and recognitions for performance. The individual brings into the social structure his own attitudes, abilities, motives, and skills. Of course, these help determine to some extent his perception of the judgments of others and the properties of the social structure.

Thus we have assigned causal status to the rules and norms of a social structure, and we have assigned causal status to the psychological and physiological properties of the person. In addition, we have indicated that these are interrelated sets of properties. This means that if a researcher manipulates the social environment of an actor, this will affect his perception of the situation and hence his response. It also means that his perception of the situation is affected by his personal values and attitudes.

Societal and Local Structures: Universal and Particular Conditions

In Chapter 3 (Evolution) we stressed the concept of evolving cultural and social systems as systems of adaptation that are peculiar to the biological capacities of man as a species. This form of evolution is largely an unconscious process and its discernment requires a time span of at least several decades and perhaps longer. This would refer to such major changes in human culture as the change from water power to steam power as sources of energy for industrial and commercial organization or changes in agricultural practices from scratching the soil with small instruments to moldboard plowing or again from a system of feudal social organization to one utilizing the concept of the nation-state. Of course, these major alterations were preceded by many small changes which accumulated and made possible the larger changes. In other words, these types of change refer more to changes which are related to the survival of the human species or at least to human societies as wholes.

There is another type of change which is more a result of deliberate human design to attain specific ends. Thus a man builds and establishes a department store on Main Street as a way of making a monetary profit. The engineering department of an industrial firm develops through research a new means for processing the company's product and at the same time maintaining or improving its quality but reducing the cost of production, and the firm orders the old process discontinued and adopts the new. This form of social organization is the deliberate action on the part of men to increase their power for the attainment of specific ends. Hence social organization is a form of human energy the power of which can be assessed in terms of relative rates of output as compared to other systems of organization.

We now see that some forms of social organization and some patterns of culture are societal in nature—that is, they apply to all members of the society—while on the other hand other forms of social organization are specific in that they apply only to particular groups. All people in American society are affected by our culture pattern of monogamy, but only certain people are affected by the Druid Hills Bird Watchers' Club.

The distinction between social systems and cultural systems that are societal in scope and those that are local in scope of influence is important in regard to several factors, but we wish to note its importance in regard to motivation. It can be argued that in general the motivation conditioned by societal systems is more likely to be subconscious while that conditioned by specialized local systems is more at the conscious level. For example, the economic motives which derive from the American consumer market (for instance, status emulation) are largely subconscious in their effects. On the other hand, the motivation which is related to one's role performance in the local plant or office is likely to be quite conscious. We are here interested in the effects of both of these systems.

Some Effects of Early Experience on Behavior

Harlow and Zimmermann report research on the relationship between affectional responses in the infant monkey to the infant's mothering experiences.[5] Because of the importance of the experimental design to the understanding of the findings of this research we are reproducing the entire article below:

Investigators from diverse behavioral fields have long recognized the strong attachment of the neonatal and infantile animal to its mother. Although this affectional behavior has been commonly observed, there is, outside the field of ethnology, scant experimental evidence permitting identification of the factors

---

[5] Harry F. Harlow and Robert R. Zimmermann, "Affectional Responses in the Infant Monkey, *Science*, Vol. 130, No. 3373 (August, 1959), pp. 421-431.

critical to the formation of this bond. Lorenz (1) and others have stressed the importance of innate visual and auditory mechanisms which, through the process of imprinting, give rise to persisting following responses in the infant bird and fish. Imprinting behavior has been demonstrated successfully in a variety of avian species under controlled laboratory conditions, and this phenomenon has been investigated systematically in order to identify those variables which contribute to its development and maintenance [see, for example, Hinde, Thorpe, and Vince (2), Fabricius (3), Hess (4), Jaynes (5), and Moltz and Rosenblum (6)]. These studies represent the largest body of existent experimental evidence measuring the tie between infant and mother. At the mammalian level there is little or no systematic experimental evidence of this nature.

Observations on monkeys by Carpenter (7), Nolte (8), and Zuckermann (9) and on chimpanzees by Kohler (10) and by Yerkes and Tomilin (11) show that monkey and chimpanzee infants develop strong ties to their mothers and that these affectional attachments may persist for years. It is, of course, common knowledge that human infants form strong and persistent ties to their mothers.

Although students from diverse scientific fields recognize this abiding attachment, there is considerable disagreement about the nature of its development and its fundamental underlying mechanisms. A common theory among psychologists, sociologists, and anthropologists is that of learning based on drive reduction. This theory proposes that the infant's attachment to the mother results from the association of the mother's face and form with the alleviation of certain primary drive states, particularly hunger and thirst. Thus, through learning, affection becomes a self-supporting, derived drive (12). Psychoanalysts, on the other hand, have stressed the importance of various innate needs, such as a need to suck and orally possess the breast (2), or needs relating to contact, movement, temperature (13), and clinging to the mother (14).

The paucity of experimental evidence concerning the development of affectional responses has led these theorists to derive their basic hypotheses from deductions and intuitions based on observation and analysis of adult verbal reports. As a result, the available observational evidence is often forced into a preconceived theoretical framework. An exception to the above generalization is seen in the recent attempt by Bowlby (14) to analyze and integrate the available observational and experimental evidence derived from both human and subhuman infants. Bowlby has concluded that a theory of component instinctual responses, species specific, can best account for the infant's tie to the mother. He suggests that the species-specific responses for human beings (some of these responses are not strictly limited to human beings) include contact, clinging, sucking, crying, smiling, and following. He further emphasizes that these responses are manifested independently of primary drive reduction in human and subhuman infants.

The absence of experimental data which would allow a critical evaluation of any theory of affectional development can be attributed to several causes. The use of human infants as subjects has serious limitations, since it is not feasible to employ all the experimental controls which would permit a completely adequate analysis of the proposed variables. In addition, the limited response repertoire of the human neonate severely restricts the number of discrete or precise response categories that can be measured until a considerable age has been attained. Thus, critical variables go unmeasured and become lost or confounded among the complex physiological, psychological, and cultural factors which influence the developing human infant.

Moreover, the use of common laboratory animals also has serious limitations, for most of these animals have behavioral repertoires very different from those of the human being, and in many species these systems mature so rapidly that it is difficult to measure and assess their orderly development. On the other hand, subhuman primates, including the macaque monkey, are born at a state of maturity which makes it possible to begin precise measurements within the first few days of life. Furthermore, their postnatal maturational rate is slow enough to permit precise assessment of affectional variables and development.

Over a 3-year period prior to the beginning of the research program reported here (15), some 60 infant macaque monkeys were separated from their mothers 6 to 12 hours after birth and raised at the primate laboratory of the University of Wisconsin. The success of the procedures developed to care for these neonates was demonstrated by the low mortality and by a gain in weight which was approximately 25 percent greater than that of infants raised by their own mothers. All credit for the success of this program belongs to van Wagenen (16), who had described the essential procedures in detail.

These first 3 years were spent in devising measures to assess the multiple capabilities of the neonatal and infantile monkey. The studies which resulted have revealed that the development of perception, learning, manipulation, exploration, frustration, and timidity in the macaque monkey follows a course and sequence which is very similar to that in the human infant. The basic differences between the two species appear to be the advanced postnatal maturational status and the subsequent more rapid growth of the infant macaque. Probably the most important similarities between the two, in relation to the problem of affectional development, are characteristic responses that have been associated with, and are considered basic to, affection; these include nursing, clinging, and visual and auditory exploration.

In the course of raising these infants we observed that they all showed a strong attachment to the cheesecloth blankets which were used to cover the wire floors of their cages. Removal of these cloth blankets resulted in violent emotional behavior. These responses were not short-lived; indeed, the emotional disturbance lasted several days, as was indicated by the infant's refusal to work on the standard learning tests that were being conducted at the time. Similar observations had already been made by Foley (17) and by van Wagenen (16), who stressed the importance of adequate contact responses to the very survival of the neonatal macaque. Such observations suggested to us that contact was a true affectional variable and that it should be possible to trace and measure the development and importance of these responses. Indeed there seemed to be every reason to believe that one could manipulate

EFFECTS OF SOCIAL LEARNING ON BEHAVIOR

all variables which have been considered critical to the development of the infant's attachment to a mother, or mother surrogate.

To attain control over maternal variables, we took the calculated risk of constructing and using inanimate mother surrogates rather than real mothers. The cloth mother that we used was a cylinder of wood covered with a sheath of terry cloth (18), and the wire mother was a hardware-cloth cylinder. Initially, sponge rubber was placed underneath the terry cloth sheath of the cloth mother surrogate, and a light bulb behind each mother surrogate provided radiant heat. For reasons of sanitation and safety these two factors were eliminated in construction of the standard mothers, with no observable effect on the behavior of the infants. The two mothers were attached at a 45-degree angle to aluminum bases and were given different faces to assure uniqueness in the various test situations (Fig. 8:1). Bottle holders were installed in the upper middle part of the bodies to permit nursing. The mother was designed on the basis of previous experience with infant monkeys which suggested that nursing in an upright or inclined position with something for the infant to clasp facilitated successful nursing and resulted in healthier infants (see 16). Thus, both mothers provided the basic known requirements for adequate nursing, but the cloth mother provided an additional variable of contact comfort. That both of these surrogate mothers provided adequate nursing support is shown by the fact that the total ingestion of formula and the weight gain was normal for all infants fed on the surrogate mothers. The only consistent difference between the groups lay in the softer stools of the infants fed on the wire mother.

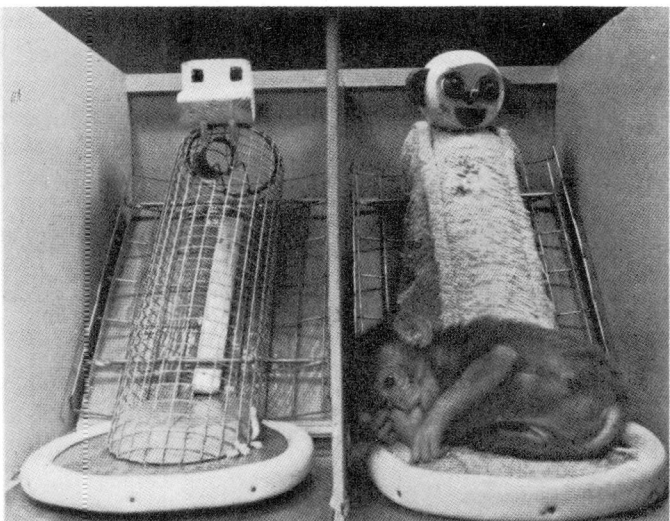

FIGURE 8:1. Wire Mother and Cloth-Covered Mother Surrogates.

Development of Affectional Responses

The initial experiments on the development of affectional responses have already been reported (19) but will be briefly reviewed here since subsequent experiments were derived from them. In the initial experiments, designed to evaluate the role of nursing on the development of affection, a cloth mother and a wire mother were placed in different cubicles attached to the infant's living cage. Eight newborn monkeys were placed in individual cages with the surrogates; for four infant monkeys the cloth mother lactated and the wire mother did not, and for the other four this condition was reversed.

The infants lived with their mother surrogates for a minimum of 165 days, and during this time they were tested in a variety of situations designed to measure the development of affectional responsiveness. Differential affectional responsiveness was initially measured in terms of mean hours per day spent on the cloth and on the wire mothers under two conditions of feeding, as shown in Fig. 8:2. Infants fed on the cloth mother and on the wire mother have highly similar scores after a short adaptation period (Fig. 8:3), and over a 165-day period both groups show a distinct preference for the cloth mother. The persistence of the differential responsiveness to the mothers for both groups of infants is evident, and the overall differences between the groups fall short of statistical significance.

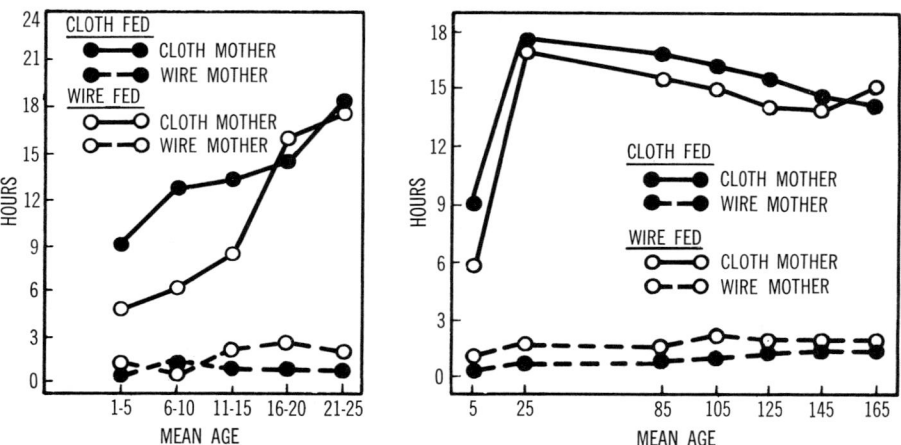

Time Spent on Cloth and Wire Mother Surrogates. FIGURE 8:2 (*left*), Short Term. **FIGURE 8:3** (*right*), Long Term.

These data make it obvious that contact comfort is a variable of critical importance in the development of affectional responsiveness to the surrogate mother, and that nursing appears to play a negligible role. With increasing age and opportunity to learn, an infant fed from a lactating wire mother does not become more responsive to her, as would be predicted from a derived-drive theory, but instead becomes increasingly more responsive to its nonlactating cloth mother. These findings are at complete variance with a drive-reduction theory of affectional development.

The amount of time spent on the mother does not necessarily indicate an affectional attachment. It could merely reflect the fact that the cloth mother is a more comfortable sleeping platform or a more adequate source of warmth for the infant. However, three of the four infants nursed by the cloth mother and one of the four nursed by the wire mother left a gauze-covered heating pad that was on the floor of their cages during the first 14 days of life to spend up to 18 hours a day on the cloth mother. This suggests that differential heating or warmth is not a critical variable within the controlled temperature range of the laboratory.

Other tests demonstrate that the cloth mother is more than a convenient nest; indeed, they show that a bond develops between infant and cloth-mother surrogate that is almost unbelievably similar to the bond established between human mother and child. One highly definitive test measured the selective maternal responsiveness of the monkey infants under conditions of distress or fear.

Various fear-producing stimuli, such as the moving toy bear illustrated in Fig. 8:4, were presented to the infants in their home cages. The data on differential responses under both feeding conditions are given in Fig. 8:5. It is apparent that the cloth mother was highly preferred to the wire mother, and it is a fact that these differences were unrelated to feeding conditions—that is, nursing on the cloth or on the wire mother. Above and beyond these objective data are observations on the form of the infants' responses in this situation. In spite of their abject terror, the infant monkeys, after reaching the cloth mother and rubbing their bodies about hers, rapidly come to lose their fear of the frightening stimuli. Indeed, within a minute or two most of the babies were visually exploring the very thing which so shortly before had seemed an object of evil. The bravest of the babies would actually leave the mother and approach the fearful monsters, under, of course, the protective gaze of their mothers.

These data are highly similar, in terms of differential responsiveness, to the time scores previously mentioned and indicate the overwhelming importance of contact comfort. The results are so striking as to suggest that the primary function of nursing may be that of insuring frequent and intimate contact between mother and infant, thus facilitating the localization of the source of contact comfort. This interpretation finds some support in the test discussed above. In both situations the infants nursed by the cloth mother developed consistent responsiveness to the soft mother earlier in testing than did the infants nursed by the wire mother, and during this transient period the latter group was slightly more responsive to the wire mother than the former group. However, these early differences shortly disappeared.

Additional data have been obtained from two groups of four monkeys each which were raised with a single mother placed in a cubicle attached to the living-cage. Four of the infants were presented with a lactating wire mother and the other four were presented with a nonlactating cloth mother. The latter group was hand-fed from small nursing bottles for the first 30 days of life

FIGURE 8:4. A Typical Response of an Infant Monkey to a Fear-Producing Stimulus in the Presence of a Cloth Mother Surrogate.

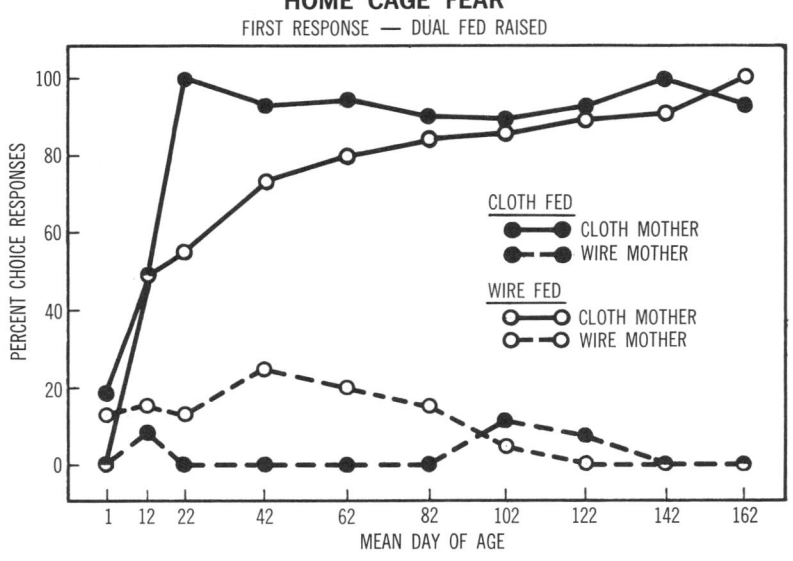

FIGURE 8:5. Differential Responsiveness in Fear Tests.

and then weaned to a cup. The development of responsiveness to the mothers was studied for 165 days; after this the individual mothers were removed from the cages and testing was continued to determine the strength and persistence of the affectional responses.

Figure 8:6 presents the mean time per day spent on the respective mothers over the 165-day test period, and Fig. 8:7 shows the percentage of responses to the mothers when a fear-producing stimulus was introduced into the home cage. These tests indicate that both groups of infants developed responsiveness to their mother surrogates. However, these measures did not reveal the

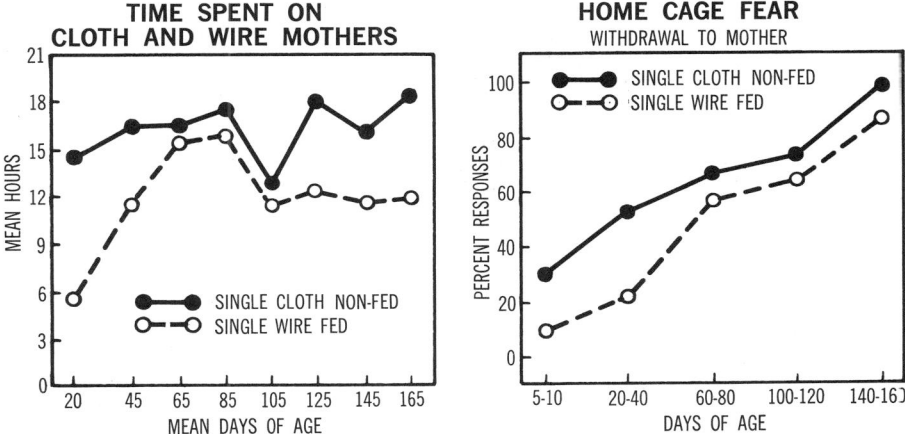

FIGURE 8:6 (*left*), Time Spent on Single Mother Surrogates. FIGURE 8:7 (*right*), Responsiveness to Single Surrogate Mothers in Fear Tests.

differences in behavior that were displayed in the reactions to the mothers when the fear stimuli were presented. The infants raised on the cloth mother would rush to the mother and cling tightly to her. Following this initial response these infants would relax and either begin to manipulate the mother or turn to gaze at the feared object without the slightest sign of apprehension. The infants raised on the wire mother, on the other hand, rushed away from the feared object toward their mother but did not cling to or embrace her. Instead, they would either clutch themselves and rock and vocalize for the remainder of the test or rub against the side of the cubicle. Contact with the cubicle or the mother did not reduce the emotionality produced by the introduction of the stimulus. These differences are revealed in emotionality scores, for behavior such as vocalization, crouching, rocking, and sucking, recorded during the test. Figure 8:8 shows the mean emotionality index for test sessions for the two experimental groups, the dual-mother groups, and a comparable control group raised under standard laboratory conditions. As can be seen, the infants raised with the single wire mother have the highest emotionality scores of all the groups, and the infants raised with the single cloth mother or with a cloth and wire mother have the lowest scores. It appears that the responses made by infants raised only with a wire mother were more

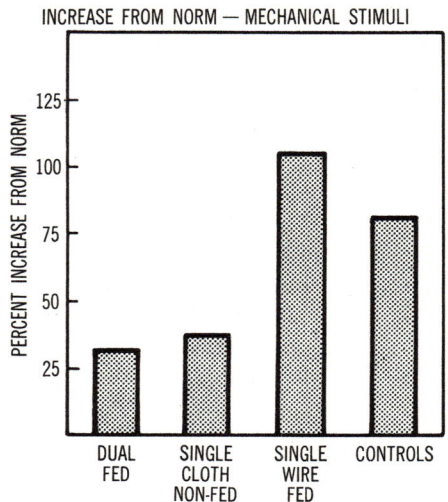

FIGURE 8:8. Change in Emotionality Index in Fear Tests.

in the nature of simple flight responses to the fear stimulus and that the presence of the mother surrogate had little effect in alleviating the fear.

During our initial experiments with the dual-mother conditions, responsiveness to the lactating wire mother in the fear tests decreased with age and opportunity to learn, while responsiveness to the nonlactating cloth mother increased. However, there was some indication of a slight increase in frequency of response to the wire mother for the first 30 to 60 days (see Fig. 8:5). These data suggest the possible hypothesis that nursing facilitated the contact of infant and mother during the early developmental periods.

The interpretation of all fear testing is complicated by the fact that all or most "fear" stimuli evoke many positive exploratory responses early in life and do not consistently evoke flight responses until the monkey is 40 to 50 days of age. Similar delayed maturation of visually induced fear responses has been reported for birds (3), chimpanzees (20), and human infants (21).

Because of apparent interactions between fearful and affectional developmental variables, a test was designed to trace the development of approach and avoidance responses in these infants. This test, described as the straight-alley test, was conducted in a wooden alley 8 feet long and 2 feet wide. One end of the alley contained a movable tray upon which appropriate stimuli were placed. The other end of the alley contained a box for hiding. Each test began with the monkey in a start box 1 foot in front of the hiding box; thus, the animal could maintain his original position, approach the stimulus tray as it moved toward him, or flee into the hiding box. The infants were presented with five stimuli in the course of five successive days. The stimuli included a standard cloth mother, a standard wire mother, a yellow cloth mother with the head removed, a blank tray, and a large black fear stimulus. The infants were tested at 5, 10, and 20 days of age, respectively, and then at 20-day intervals up to 160 days. Figure 8:9 shows the mean number of 15-second time periods spent in contact with the appropriate mother during the 90-second tests

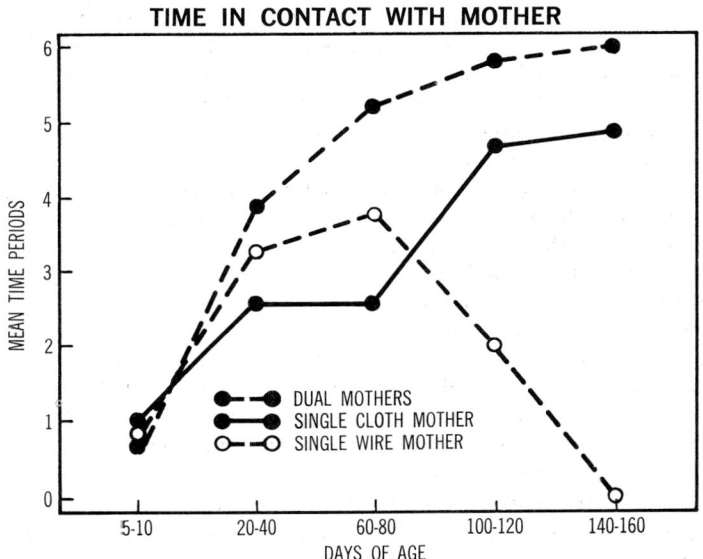

FIGURE 8:9. Responsiveness to Mother Surrogates in Straight-Alley Tests.

for the two single-mother groups, and the responses to the cloth mother by four infants from the dual-mother group.

During the first 80 days of testing, all the groups showed an increase in response to the respective mother surrogates. The infants fed on the single wire mother, however, reached peak responsiveness at this age and then showed a consistent decline, followed by an actual avoidance of the wire mother. During test sessions 140 to 160, only one contact was made with the wire mother, and three of the four infants ran into the hiding box almost immediately and remained there for the entire test session. On the other hand, all of the infants raised with a cloth mother, whether or not they were nursed by her, showed a progressive increase in time spent in contact with their cloth mothers until approaches and contacts during the test sessions approached maximum scores.

The development of the response of flight from the wire mother by the group fed on the single wire mother is, of course, completely contrary to a derived-drive theory of affectional development. A comparison of this group with the group raised with a cloth mother gives some support to the hypothesis that feeding or nursing facilitates the early development of responses to the mother but that without the factor of contact comfort, these positive responses are not maintained.

The differential responsiveness to the cloth mother of infants raised with both mothers, the reduced emotionality of both the groups raised with cloth mothers in the home-cage fear tests, and the development of approach responses in the straight-alley test indicate that the cloth mother provides a haven of safety and security for the frightened infant. The affectional response patterns found in the infant monkey are unlike tropistic or even complex reflex responses; they resemble instead the diverse and pervasive patterns of response to his mother exhibited by the human child in the complexity of situations involving child-mother relationships.

The role of the mother as a source of safety and security has been demonstrated experimentally for human infants by Arsenian (22). She placed children 11 to 30 months of age in a strange room containing toys and other play objects. Half of the children were accompanied into the room by a mother or a substitute mother (a familiar nursery attendant), while the other half entered the situation alone. The children in the first group (mother present) were much less emotional and participated much more fully in the play activity than those in the second group (mother absent). With repeated testing, the security score, a composite score of emotionality and play behavior, improved for the children who entered alone, but it still fell far below that for the children who were accompanied by their mothers. In subsequent tests, the children from the mother-present group were placed in the test room alone, and there was a drastic drop in the security scores. Contrariwise, the introduction of the mother raised the security scores of children in the other group.

We have performed a similar series of open-field experiments, comparing monkeys raised on mother surrogates with control monkeys raised in a wire cage containing a cheesecloth blanket from days 1 to 14 and no cloth blanket subsequently. The infants were introduced into the strange environment of the open field, which was a room measuring 6 by 6 by 6 feet, containing multiple stimuli known to elicit curiosity-manipulatory responses in baby monkeys. The infants raised with single mother surrogates were placed in this situation twice a week for 8 weeks, no mother surrogate being present during one of the weekly sessions and the appropriate mother surrogate (the kind which the experimental infant had always known) being present during the other sessions. Four infants raised with dual mother surrogates and four control infants were subjected to similar experimental sequences, the cloth mother being present on half of the occasions. The remaining four "dual-mother" infants were given repetitive tests to obtain information on the development of responsiveness to each of the dual mothers in this situation. A cloth blanket was always available as one of the stimuli throughout the sessions. It should be emphasized that the blanket could readily compete with the cloth mother as a contact stimulus, for it was standard laboratory procedure to wrap the

EFFECTS OF SOCIAL LEARNING ON BEHAVIOR

infants in soft cloth whenever they were removed from their cages for testing, weighing, and other required laboratory activities.

As soon as they were placed in the test room, the infants raised with cloth mothers rushed to their mother surrogate when she was present and clutched her tenaciously, a response so strong that it can only be adequately depicted by motion pictures. Then, as had been observed in the fear tests in the home cage, they rapidly relaxed, showed no sign of apprehension, and began to demonstrate unequivocal positive responses of manipulating and climbing on the mother. After several sessions, the infants began to use the mother surrogate as a base of operations, leaving her to explore and handle a stimulus and then returning to her before going to a new plaything. Some of the infants even brought the stimuli to the mother. The behavior of these infants changed radically in the absence of the mother. Emotional indices such as vocalization, crouching, rocking, and sucking increased sharply. Typical re-

FIGURE 8:10. A Typical Fear Response of an Infant Monkey in a Strange Environment.

sponse patterns were either freezing in a crouched position, as illustrated in Fig. 8:10 above, or running around the room on the hind feet, clutching themselves with their arms. Though no quantitative evidence is available, contact and manipulation of objects was frantic and of short duration, as opposed to the playful type of manipulation observed when the mother was present.

In the presence of the mother, the behavior of the infants raised with single wire mothers was both quantitatively and qualitatively different from that of the infants raised with cloth mothers. Not only did these infants spend little or no time contacting their mother surrogates but the presence of the mother did not reduce their emotionality. These differences are evident in the mean number of time periods spent in contact with the respective mothers, as shown in Fig. 8:11, and the composite emotional index for the two stimulus conditions depicted in Fig. 8:12. Although the infants raised with dual mothers spent considerably more time in contact with the cloth mother than did the infants raised with single cloth mothers, their emotional reactions to the presence and absence of the mother were highly similar, the composite emotional index being reduced by almost half when the mother was in the test situation. The infants raised with wire mothers were highly emotional under both conditions and actually showed a slight, though nonsignificant, increase in emotionality when the mother was present. Although some of the infants reared by a wire mother did contact her, their behavior was similar to that observed in the home-cage fear tests. They did not clutch and cling to their mother as did the infants with cloth mothers; instead, they sat on her lap and clutched

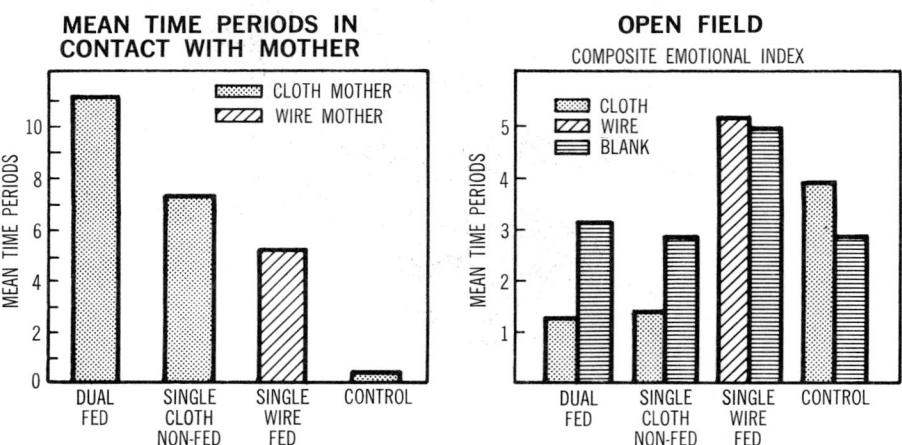

FIGURE 8:11 (*left*), Responsiveness to Mother Surrogates in the Open-field Test. FIGURE 8:12 (*right*), Emotionality Index in Testing with and without the Mother Surrogates.

themselves, or held their heads and bodies in their arms and engaged in convulsive jerking and rocking movements similar to the autistic behavior of deprived and institutionalized human children. The lack of exploratory and manipulatory behavior on the part of the infants reared with wire mothers, both in the presence and absence of the wire mother, was similar to that observed in the mother-absent condition for the infants raised with the cloth mothers, and such contact with objects as was made was of short duration and of an erratic and frantic nature. None of the infants raised with single

EFFECTS OF SOCIAL LEARNING ON BEHAVIOR

wire mothers displayed the persistent and aggressive play behavior that was typical of many of the infants that were raised with cloth mothers.

The four control infants, raised without a mother surrogate, had approximately the same emotionality scores when the mother was absent that the other infants had in the same condition, but the control subjects' emotionality scores were significantly higher in the presence of the mother surrogate than in her absence. This result is not surprising, since recent evidence indicates that the cloth mother with the highly ornamental face is an effective fear stimulus for monkeys that have not been raised with her.

Further illustration of differential responsiveness to the two mother surrogates is found in the results of a series of developmental tests in the open-field situation, given to the remaining four "dual-mother" infants. These infants were placed in the test room with the cloth mother, the wire mother, and no mother present on successive occasions at various age levels. Figure 8:13 shows the mean number of time periods spent in contact with the respective mothers for two trials at each age level, and Fig. 8:14 reveals the composite emotion scores for the three stimulus conditions during these same tests. The differential responsiveness to the cloth and wire mothers, as measured by contact time, is evident by 20 days of age, and this systematic difference con-

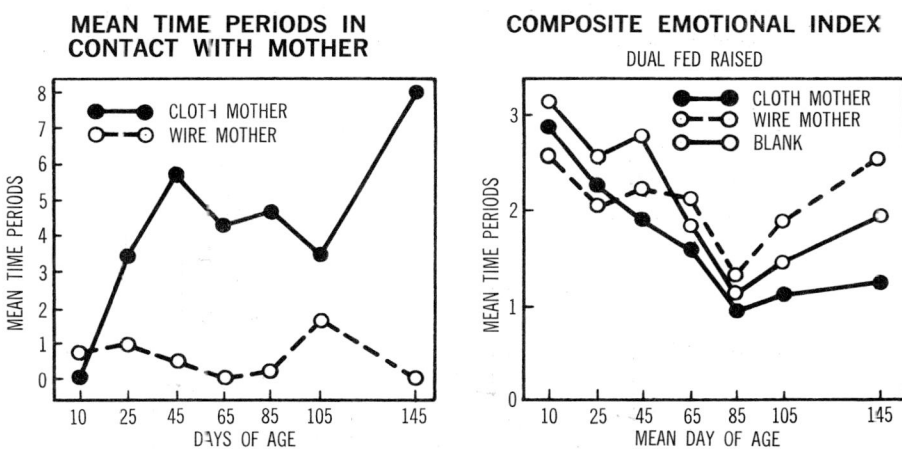

FIGURE 8:13 (*left*), Differential Responsiveness in the Open-Field Test. FIGURE 8:14 (*right*), Emotionality Index under Three Conditions in the Open-field Test.

tinues throughout 140 days of age. Only small differences in emotionality under the various conditions are evident during the first 85 days of age, although the presence of the cloth mother does result in slightly lower scores from the 45th day onward. However, at 105 and 145 days of age there is a considerable difference for the three conditions, the emotionality scores for the wire-mother and blank conditions showing a sharp increase. The heightened emotionality found under the wire-mother condition was mainly contributed by the two infants fed on the wire mother. The behavior of these two infants in the presence of the wire mother was similar to the behavior of the animals raised with a single wire mother. On the few occasions when contact with the wire mother was made, the infants did not attempt to cling to her; instead they would sit on her lap, clasp their heads and bodies, and rock back and forth.

In 1953 Butler (23) demonstrated that mature monkeys enclosed in a dimly lighted box would open and reopen a door for hours on end with no other motivation than that of looking outside the box. He also demonstrated that rhesus monkeys showed selectivity in rate and frequency of door-opening in response to stimuli of different degrees of attractiveness (24). We have utilized this characteristic of response selectivity on the part of the monkey to measure the strength of affectional responsiveness of the babies raised with mother surrogates in an infant version of the Butler box. The test sequence involves four repetitions of a test battery in which the four stimuli of cloth mother, wire mother, infant monkey, and empty box are presented for a 30-minute period on successive days. The first four subjects raised with the dual mother surrogates and the eight infants raised with single mother surrogates were given a test sequence at 40 to 50 days of age, depending upon the availability of the apparatus. The data obtained from the three experimental groups and a comparable control group are presented in Fig. 8:15. Both groups of in-

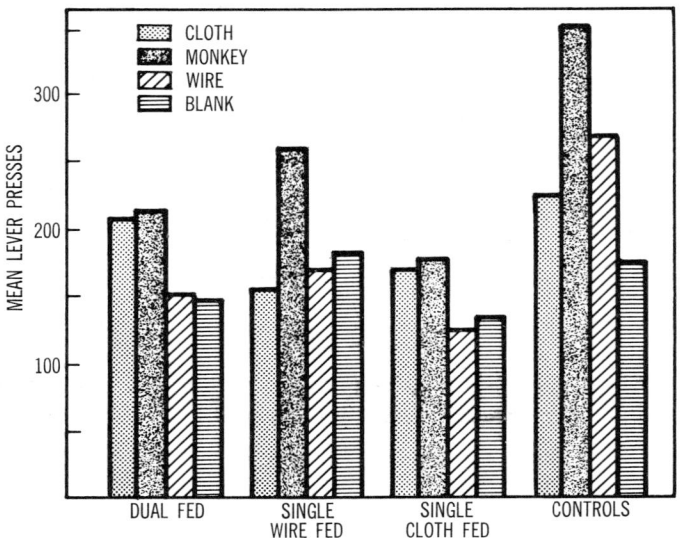

FIGURE 8:15. Differential Responses to Visual Exploration.

fants raised with cloth mothers showed approximately equal responsiveness to the cloth mother and to another infant monkey, and no greater responsiveness to the wire mother than to an empty box. Again, the results are independent of the kind of mother that lactated, cloth or wire. The infants raised with only a wire mother and those in the control group were more highly responsive to the monkey than to either of the mother surrogates. Furthermore, the former group showed a higher frequency of response to the empty box than to the wire mother.

In summary, the experimental analysis of the development of the infant monkey's attachment to an inanimate mother surrogate demonstrates the overwhelming importance of the variable of soft body contact that characterized the cloth mother, and this held true for the appearance, development, and maintenance of the infant-surrogate-mother tie. The results also indicate that, without the factor of contact comfort, only a weak attachment, if any, is formed. Finally, probably the most surprising finding is that nursing or feeding played either no role or a subordinate role in the development of affection as measured by contact time, responsiveness to fear, responsiveness to strangeness, and motivation to seek and see. No evidence was found indicating that nursing mediated the development of any of these responses, although there is evidence indicating that feeding probably facilitated the early appearance and increased the early strength of affectional responsiveness. Certainly feeding, in contrast to contact comfort, is neither a necessary nor a sufficient condition for affectional development.

Retention of Affectional Responses

One of the outstanding characteristics of the infant's attachment to its mother is the persistence of the relationship over a period of years, even though the frequency of contact between infant and mother is reduced with increasing age. In order to test the persistence of the responsiveness of our "mother-surrogate" infants, the first four infant monkeys raised with dual mothers and all of the monkeys raised with single mothers were separated from their surrogates at 165 to 170 days of age. They were tested for affectional retention during the following 9 days, then at 30-day intervals during the following year. The results are of necessity incomplete, inasmuch as the entire mother-surrogate program was initiated less than 2 years ago, but enough evidence is available to indicate that the attachment formed to the cloth mother during the first 6 months of life is enduring and not easily forgotten.

Affectional retention as measured by the modified Butler box for the first 15 months of testing for four of the infants raised with two mothers is given in Fig. 8:16 above. Although there is considerable variability in the total response frequency from session to session, there is a consistent difference in the number of responses to the cloth mother as contrasted with responses to either the wire mother or the empty box, and there is no consistent difference between responses to the wire mother and to the empty box. The effects of contact comfort versus feeding are dramatically demonstrated in this test by the monkeys raised with either single cloth or wire mothers. Figure 8:17 shows the frequency of response to the appropriate mother surrogate and to the blank box during the preseparation period and the first 90 days of retention testing. Removal of the mother resulted in a doubling of the frequency of response to the cloth mother and more than tripled the difference between the responses to the cloth mother and those to the empty box for the infants that had lived with a single nonlactating cloth mother surrogate. The infants raised with a single lactating wire mother, on the other hand, not only failed to show any consistent preference for the wire mother but also showed a highly significant reduction in general level of responding. Although incomplete, the data from further retention testing indicate that the difference between these two groups persists for at least 5 months.

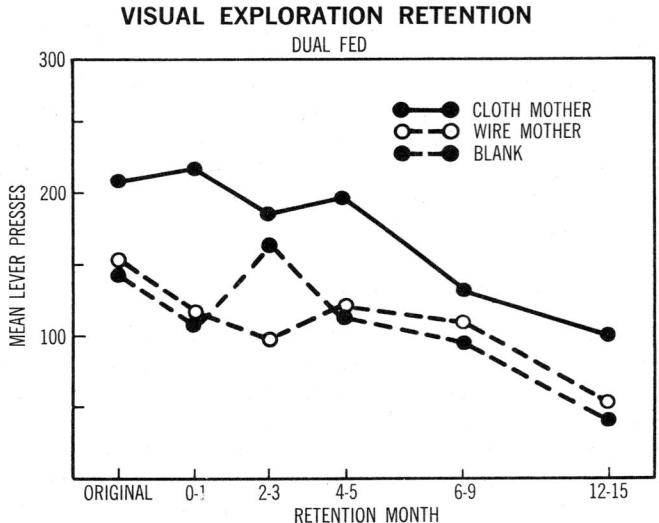

FIGURE 8:16. Retention of Differential Visual-exploration Responses.

Affectional retention was also tested in the open field during the first 9 days after separation and then at 30-day intervals. Each test condition was run twice in each retention period. In the initial retention tests the behavior of the infants that had lived with cloth mothers differed slightly from that observed during the period preceding separation. These infants tended to spend more time in contact with the mother and less time exploring and manipulating the objects in the room. The behavior of the infants raised with single wire mothers, on the other hand, changed radically during the first retention sessions, and responses to the mother surrogate dropped almost to zero. Objective evidence for these differences are given in Fig. 8:18, which reveals the

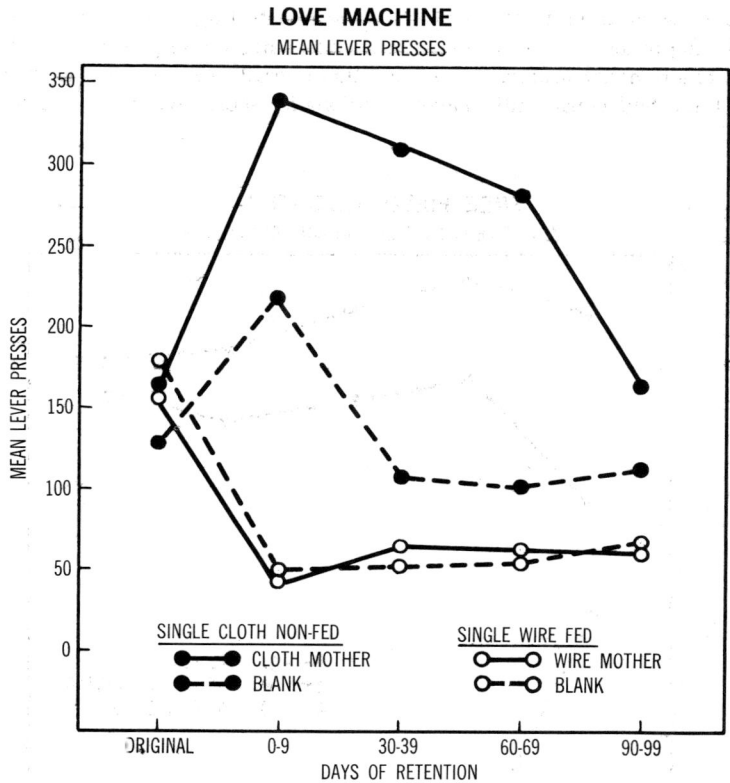

FIGURE 8:17. Retention of Differential Visual-exploration Responses by Single-surrogate Infants.

mean number of time periods spent in contact with the respective mothers. During the first retention test session, the infants raised with a single wire mother showed almost no responses to the mother surrogate they had always known. Since the infants raised with both mothers were already approaching the maximum score in this measure, there was little room for improvement. The infants raised with a single nonlactating cloth mother, however, showed a consistent and significant increase in this measure during the first 90 days of retention. Evidence for the persistence of this responsiveness is given by the fact that after 15 months' separation from their mothers, the infants that had lived with cloth mothers spent an average of 8.75 out of 12 possible time periods in contact with the cloth mother during the test. The incomplete data for retention testing of the infants raised with only a lactating wire mother or a nonlactating cloth mother indicates that there is little or no change in the initial differences found between these two groups in this test over a period of 5 months. In the absence of the mother, the behavior of the infants raised with cloth mothers was similar in the initial retention tests to that during the preseparation tests, but with repeated testing they tended to show gradual adaptation to the open-field situation and, consequently, a reduction in their emotionality scores. Even with this overall reduction in emotionality, these infants had consistently lower emotionality scores when the mother was present.

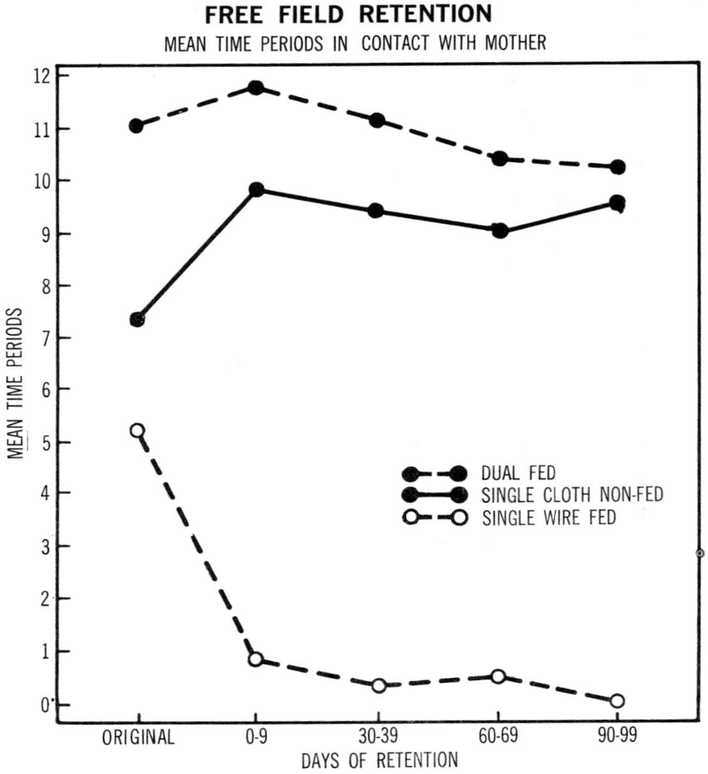

FIGURE 8:18. Retention of Responsiveness to Mother Surrogates in the Open-field Tests.

At the time of initiating the retention tests, an additional condition was introduced into the open-field test: the surrogate mother was placed in the center of the room and covered with a clear Plexiglas box. The animals raised with cloth mothers were initially disturbed and frustrated when their efforts to secure and contact the mother were blocked by the box. However, after several violent crashes into the plastic, the animals adapted to the situation and soon used the box as a place of orientation for exploratory and play behavior. In fact, several infants were much more active under these conditions than they were when the mother was available for direct contact. A comparison of the composite emotionality index of the babies raised with a single cloth or wire mother under the three conditions of no mother, surrogate mother, and surrogate-mother-box is presented in Fig. 8:19. The infants

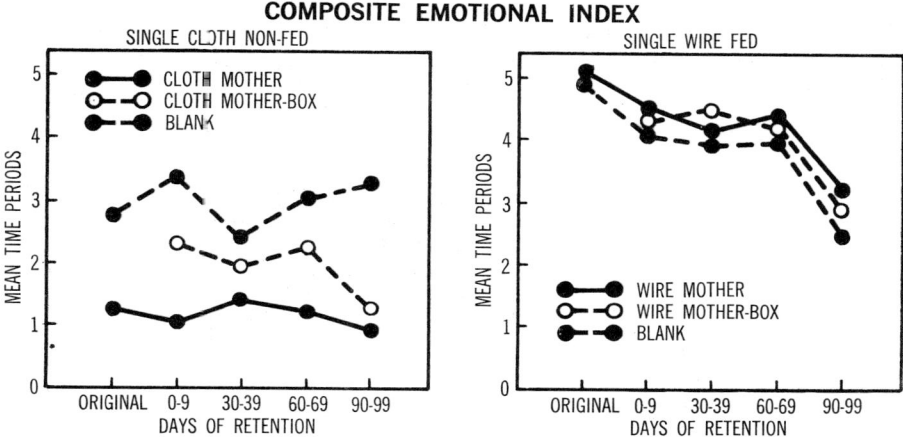

FIGURE 8:19. Emotionality Index under Three Conditions in the Open-field Retention Tests.

raised with a single cloth mother were consistently less emotional when they could contact the mother but also showed the effects of her visual presence, as their emotionality scores in the plastic box condition were definitely lower than their scores when the mother was absent. It appears that the infants gained considerable emotional security from the presence of the mother even though contact was denied.

In contrast, the animals raised with only lactating wire mothers did not show any significant or consistent trends during these retention sessions other than a general overall reduction of emotionality, which may be attributed to a general adaptation, the result of repeated testing.

Affectional retention has also been measured in the straight-alley test mentioned earlier. During the preseparation tests it was found that the infants that had only wire mothers developed a general avoidance response to all of the stimuli in this test when they were about 100 days of age and made few, if any, responses to the wire mother during the final test sessions. In contrast, all the infants raised with a cloth mother responded positively to her. Maternal separation did not significantly change the behavior of any of the groups. The babies raised with just wire mothers continued to flee into the hiding booth in the presence of the wire mother, while all of the infants raised with cloth mothers continued to respond positively to the cloth mother at approximately the same level as in the preseparation tests. The mean number of time periods spent in contact with the appropriate mother surrogates for the first 3 months of retention testing are given in Fig. 8:20. There is little, if any, waning of responsiveness to the cloth mother during these 3 months. There appeared to be some loss of responsiveness to the mother in this situation after 5 to 6 months of separation, but the test was discontinued at that time as the infants had outgrown the apparatus.

The retention data from these multiple tests demonstrate clearly the importance of body contact for the future maintenance of affectional responses. Whereas several of the measures in the preseparation period suggested that the infants raised with only a wire mother might have developed a weak attachment to her, all responsiveness disappeared in the first few days after

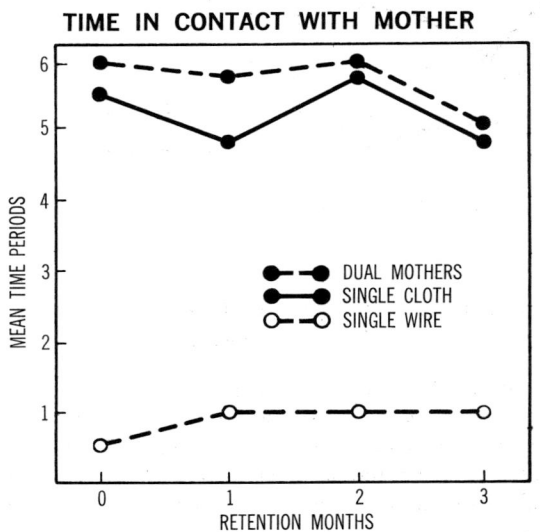

FIGURE 8:20. Retention of Responsiveness to Mother Surrogates in the Straight-alley Test.

the mother was withdrawn from the living-cage. Infants that had had the opportunity of living with a cloth mother showed the opposite effect and either became more responsive to the cloth mother or continued to respond to her at the same level.

These data indicate that once an affectional bond is formed it is maintained for a very considerable length of time with little reinforcement of the contact-comfort variable. The limited data available for infants that have been separated from their mother surrogates for a year suggest that these affectional responses show resistance to extinction similar to the resistance previously demonstrated for learned fears and learned pain. Such data are in keeping with common observation of human behavior.

It is true, however, that the infants raised with cloth mothers exhibit some absolute decrease in responsiveness with time in all of our major test situations. Such results would be obtained even if there were no true decrease in the strength of the affectional bond, because of familiarization and adaptation resulting from repeated testing. Therefore, at the end of 1 year of retention testing, new tests were introduced into the experimental program.

Our first new test was a modification of the open-field situation, in which basic principles of the home-cage fear test were incorporated. This particular choice was made partly because the latter test had to be discontinued when the mother surrogates were removed from the home cages.

For the new experiment a Masonite floor marked off in 6- by 12-inch rectangles was placed in the open-field chamber. Both mother surrogates were placed in the test room opposite a plastic start-box. Three fear stimuli, selected to produce differing degrees of emotionality, were placed in the center of the room directly in front of the start-box in successive test sessions. Eight trials were run under each stimulus condition, and in half of the trials the most direct path to the cloth mother was blocked by a large Plexiglas screen. Thus, in these trials the infants were forced to approach and bypass the fear stimulus or the wire mother, or both, in order to reach the cloth mother. Following these 24 trials with the mothers present, one trial of each condition with both mothers absent was run, and this in turn was followed by two trials run under the most emotion-provoking condition: with a mechanical toy present and the direct path to the mother blocked.

We now have complete data for the first four infants raised with both a cloth and a wire mother. Even with this scanty information, the results are obvious. As would be predicted from our other measures, the emotionality scores for the three stimuli were significantly different and these same scores were increased greatly when the direct path to the mother was blocked. A highly significant preference was shown for the cloth mother under both conditions (direct and blocked path), although the presence of the block did increase the number of first responses to the wire mother from 3 to 10 percent. In all cases this was a transient response and the infants subsequently ran on to the cloth mother and clung tightly to her. Objective evidence for this overwhelming preference is indicated in Fig. 8:21, which shows the mean number of time periods spent in contact with the two mothers. After a number of trials, the infants would go first to the cloth mother and then, and only then, would go out to explore, manipulate, and even attack and destroy the fear stimuli. It was as if they believed that their mother would protect them, even at the cost of her life—little enough to ask in view of her condition.

The removal of the mother surrogates from the situation produced the predictable effect of doubling the emotionality index. In the absence of the mothers, the infants would often run to the Plexiglas partition which formerly had blocked their path to the mother, or they would crouch in the corner behind the block where the mother normally would have been. The return of the mothers in the final two trials of the test in which the most emotion-evoking situation was presented resulted in behavior near the normal level, as measured by the emotionality index and contacts with the cloth mother.

Our second test of this series was designed to replace the straight-alley test described above and provide more quantifiable data on responsiveness to fear stimuli. The test was conducted in an alley 8 feet long and 2 feet wide. At one end of the alley and directly behind the monkeys' restraining chamber was a small stimulus chamber which contained a fear object. Each trial was initiated by raising an opaque sliding door which exposed the fear stimulus. Beginning at a point 18 inches from the restraining chamber, the alley was

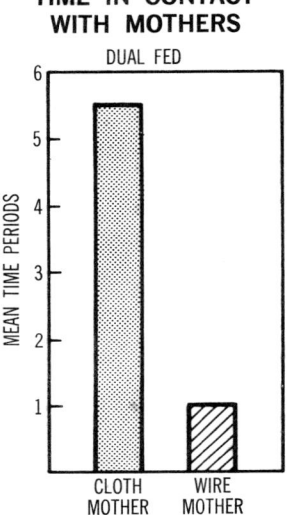

FIGURE 8:21. Differential Responsiveness in the Modified Open-field Test.

divided lengthwise by a partition; this provided the infant with the choice of entering one of two alleys.

The effects of all mother combinations were measured; these combinations included no mothers, two cloth mothers, two wire mothers, and a cloth and a wire mother. All mother conditions were counterbalanced by two distance conditions—distances of 24 and 78 inches, respectively, from the restraining chamber. This made it possible, for example, to provide the infant with the alternative of running to the cloth mother which was in close proximity to the fear stimulus or to the wire mother (or no mother) at a greater distance from the fear stimulus. Thus, it was possible to distinguish between running to the mother surrogate as an object of security, and generalized flight in response to a fear stimulus.

Again, the data available at this time are from the first four infants raised with cloth and wire mothers. Nevertheless, the evidence is quite conclusive. A highly significant preference is shown for the cloth mother as compared to the wire mother or to no mother, and this preference appears to be independent of the proximity of the mother to the fear stimulus. In the condition in which two cloth mothers are present, one 24 inches from the fear stimulus and the other 78 inches from it, there was a preference for the nearest mother, but the differences were not statistically significant. In two conditions in which no cloth mother was present and the infant had to choose between a wire mother and no mother, or between two empty chambers, the emotionality scores were almost twice those under the cloth-mother-present condition.

No differences were found in either of these tests that were related to previous conditions of feeding—that is, to whether the monkey had nursed on the cloth or on the wire mother.

The results of these two new tests, introduced after a full year's separation of mother surrogate and infant, are comparable to the results obtained during the preseparation period and the early retention testing. Preferential responses still favored the cloth as compared to the wire mother by as much as 85 to 90 percent, and the emotionality scores showed the typical 2:1 differential ratio with respect to mother-absent and mother-present conditions.

The researches presented here on the analysis of two affectional variables through the use of objective and observational techniques suggest a broad new field for the study of emotional development of infant animals. The analogous situations and results found in observations and study of human infants and of subprimates demonstrate the apparent face validity of our tests. The reliability of our observational techniques is indicated, for example, by the correlation coefficients computed for the composite emotional index in the open-field test. Four product-moment correlation coefficients, computed from four samples of 100 observations by five different pairs of independent observers over a period of more than a year, ranged from .87 to .89.

Additional Variables

Although the overwhelming importance of the contact variable has been clearly demonstrated in these experiments, there is reason to believe that other facts may contribute to the development of the affectional response pattern. We are currently conducting a series of new experiments to test some of these postulated variables.

For example, Bowlby (14) has suggested that one of the basic affectional variables in the primate order is not just contact but *clinging* contact. To test this hypothesis, four infant monkeys are being raised with the standard cloth mother and a flat inclined plane, tightly covered with the same type of cloth. Thus, both objects contain the variable of contact with the soft cloth, but the shape of the mother tends to maximize the clinging variable, while the broad flat shape of the plane tends to minimize it. The preliminary results for differences in responsiveness to the cloth mother and responsiveness to the inclined plane under conditions that produce stress or fear or visual exploration suggest that clinging as well as contact is an affectional variable of considerable importance.

Experiments now in progress on the role of rocking motion in the development of attachment indicate that this may be a variable of measurable importance. One group of infants is being raised on rocking and stationary mothers and a second group, on rocking and stationary inclined planes. Both groups of infants show a small but consistent preference for the rocking object, as measured in average hours spent on the two objects.

Preliminary results for these three groups in the open-field test give additional evidence concerning the variable of clinging comfort. These data revealed that the infants raised with the standard cloth mother were more responsive to their mothers than the infants raised with inclined planes were to the planes.

The discovery of three variables of measurable importance to the formation and retention of affection is not surprising, and it is reasonable to assume that others will be demonstrated. The data so far obtained experimentally are in excellent concordance with the affectional variables named by Bowlby (14). We are now planning a series of studies to assess the effects of consistency and inconsistency with respect to the mother surrogates in relation to the clinical concept of rejection. The effects of early, intermediate, and late maternal deprivation and the generalization of the infant-surrogate attachment in social development are also being investigated. Indeed, the strength and stability of the monkeys' affectional responses to a mother surrogate are such that it should be practical to determine the neurological and biochemical variables that underlie love.

References and Notes

1. K. Lorenz, *Auk* 54, 245 (1937).
2. R. A. Hinde, W. H. Thorpe, M. A. Vince, *Behavior* 9, 214 (1956).
3. E. Fabricius, *Acta Zool.* Fennica 68, 1 (1951).
4. E. H. Hess, *J. Comp. Physiol. Psychol.*, Vol. 52 (1959), pp. 515-518.
5. J. Jaynes, *ibid.*, 51 (1958), pp. 234-242.
6. H. Moltz and L. Rosenblum, *ibid.* 51, 658 (1958).
7. C. R. Carpenter, *Comp. Psychol. Monograph No. 10* (1934), p. 1.
8. A. Nolte, *Z. Tierpsychol.* 12, 77 (1955).
9. S. Zuckerman, *Functional Affinities of Man, Monkeys and Apes* (Harcourt Brace, London, 1933).
10. W. Kohler, *The Mentality of Apes* (Humanities Press, New York, 1951).
11. R. M. Yerkes and M. I. Tomilin, *J. Comp. Psychol.* 20, 321 (1935).
12. J. Dollard and N. E. Miller, *Personality and Psychotherapy* (McGraw-Hill, New York, 1950), p. 133; P. H. Mussen and J. J. Conger, *Child Development and Personality* (Harper, New York, 1956), pp. 137, 138.
13. M. A. Ribble, *The Rights of Infants* (Columbia Univ. Press, New York, 1943); D. W. Winnicott, *Brit. J. Med. Psychol.* 21, 229 (1948).
14. J. Bowlby, *Intern. J. Psycho-Analysis* 39, part 5 (1958).
15. Support for the research presented in this article was provided through funds from the graduate school of the University of Wisconsin; from grant M-772, National Institutes of Health; and from a Ford Foundation grant.
16. G. van Wagenen, in *The Care and Breeding of Laboratory Animals*, E. J. Farris, Ed. (Wiley, New York, 1950), p. 1.
17. J. P. Foley, Jr., *J. Genet. Psychol.* 45, 39 (1934).
18. We no longer make the cloth mother out of a block of wood. The cloth mother's body is simply that of the wire mother, covered by a terry-cloth sheath.
19. H. F. Harlow, *Am. Psychologist* 13, 673 (1958); ———— and R. R. Zimmermann, *Proc. Am. Phil. Soc.* 102, 501 (1958).
20. D. O. Hebb, *The Organization of Behavior* (Wiley, New York, 1949), p. 241 ff.
21. A. T. Jersild and F. B. Holmes, *Child Develop. Monograph No. 20* (1935), p. 356.
22. J. M. Arsenian, *J. Abnormal Social Psychol.* 38, 225 (1943).

23. R. A. Butler, *J. Comp. Physiol. Psychol.* 46, 95 (1953).
24. R. A. Butler, *J. Exptl. Psychol.* 48, 19, (1954).

Harlow's data make it obvious that contact comfort is an important factor in the development of affectional responses. If one follows the drive reduction theory of learning, he would predict that the infant monkeys fed by a lactating wire mother and those fed by a lactating cloth mother would be equally affectionate toward their surrogate mothers since the mothers were equally efficient in reducing the hunger drive. Harlow's data show that this is not the case.

> With increasing age and opportunity to learn, an infant fed from a lactating wire mother does not become more responsive to her, as would be predicted from a derived-drive theory, but instead becomes increasingly more responsive to its nonlactating cloth mother. These findings are at complete variance with a drive-reduction theory of affectional development.[6]

It seems clear that learning plays an important part in the monkeys' development of attachments and their seeking the protection of the surrogate. However, as Bowlby points out in the material cited by Harlow, these affectional responses are independent of drive reduction and the possibility exists that they are related to an instinctual base. As we have pointed out in earlier chapters, it is hazardous to generalize from the data on a variable from one species to another. This is particularly true in the case of human beings and lower animals. However, there are experimental and clinical observations on human infants which show a relationship between the human infant's sense of safety and security and the presence or absence of the mother. When the mother is present, the young child is much less emotionally disturbed than when she is absent.

Love as an emotion and an affectional response can be expressed in so many more ways by human beings both by contact and by means of abstract language that the role of learning in its development is much greater than in any other species. It is highly probable that a child who has never been loved would not be able to express feelings of love. In other words, this assumes that the expression of love is a function of having the experience of being loved, particularly during childhood.

Clinical psychology and psychiatry report many cases of the damaging effects of repeated maternal separation on young children. The findings are not clear enough to enable the pinpointing of any specific age as being most vulnerable. However, Bowlby notes that

> in practically all these cases, the separation which appears to have been pathogenic occurred after the age of six months, and in a majority after

[6] *Ibid.*, p. 425.

twelve months. This suggests that there is a lower age limit, before which separations, whilst perhaps having undesirable effects, do not produce the particular results we are concerned with here—the affectionless and delinquent character.[7]

Apparently the deleterious effect of maternal separation depends less on the absence of the biological mother than upon the quality of the surrogate mothering while the biological mother is absent and the quality of the mothering prior to separation. Yarrow cites the following as evidence for this:

> In the anthropological accounts of multiple mothering in different contexts (DuBois, 1944; Eggan, 1945; Mead, 1935; Roscoe, 1953) there are variations in the number of people who share mothering functions as well as variations in the role of the natural mother. In cultures in which the extended family is the traditional pattern, the mothering functions may be shared by the mother, grandmother, aunts, and other female relatives of the child; in some groups, male relatives may take over some maternal functions. The biological mother may be clearly identified as the central, most significant person in some cultures; in others she may be assigned a very secondary role.
>
> In Western cultures, grandmothers frequently assume some of the mothering functions, and in some social groups, child nurses play an important role. . . . In none of these situations are disturbances in infant functioning associated with multiple mothering practices, nor are later personality characteristics or deviations attributed to this aspect of early maternal care.[8]

We know from the data presented in Chapter 4 that sensory deprivation in chimpanzees is seriously impairing and delayed sensory feedback in human beings is seriously disruptive of behavior. Also, studies of the effects of solitary confinement in prisons show that isolation leads to serious mental disturbances. Social and cultural deprivation are probably damaging in a similar way—similar in the sense that subsequent development is likely to be impaired.

Let us be as precise as we can in specifying what we mean by social and cultural deprivation. By *social deprivation* we mean (1) that the rate of social interaction of the child with parents and others is significantly below the average rate for his group and for his society; and (2) the quality of the interaction has been lacking in affectional stimulation and emotional and affectional support. By *cultural deprivation* we

---

[7] J. Bowlby, "Forty-four Juvenile Thieves," *Int. J. Psychs. Anal.*, Vol. 25 (1944), p. 41. For a good summary and interpretation of the literature on maternal deprivation see: Leon J. Yarrow, "Maternal Deprivation: Toward an Empirical and Conceptual Re-Evaluation," *Psychol. Bull.* Vol. 58, 1961, pp. 459-490.

[8] Leon J. Yarrow, "Maternal Deprivation: Toward an Empirical and Conceptual Re-Evaluation," *Psychological Bulletin*, Vol. 58 (1961), p. 477.

mean that the child's exposure to knowledge, techniques of problem-solving, and social values is significantly below that of children of his age in the population at large. Thus a child may be adequately stimulated socially but be culturally deprived. On the other hand, one may be physically exposed to the highest levels and sources of knowledge and other cultural forms but suffer social and affectional deprivation.

Two major consequences of social deprivation are formulated as hypotheses. *First*, social deprivation would be expected to produce social apathy, inadequacy in managing one's social relations with others, and character disorders insofar as the child has experienced prolonged affectional deprivation. *Secondly*, it is predicted that social deprivation retards a child's intellectual development.

Assuming that the child's culture is not disorganized, then cultural deprivation is not necessarily *disruptive* of behavior development. What it means is that the child is functionally inadequate to adjust in the larger cultural milieu of the society. However, if he tries to break out of the shackles of his local culture without acquiring the skills of the larger culture, he will be faced with severe adjustment problems which can and do lead to deviant behavior of various kinds and to personality disorders.[9] Of course, in a modern industrial society such as ours with its system of mass communication the members of culturally deprived groups are intensely stimulated by the "outside world." Consequently, there is a *desire* to escape their poverty but without the means to do so. The deprivation of the parents becomes the deprivation of their children and the process is continued. It seems that the only preventive measure is for the larger community to intervene early, probably not later than age three, and start building a foundation of symbolic skills for facilitating later school experience.

An interesting way to ascertain some of the effects of social experience and social organization on behavior is to consider attempts to restructure or resocialize the personality.

Lambert and Lambert report the effort of the Chinese Communists to *de*socialize American prisoners of war, that is, to wipe out the effects of their previous socialization. The Lamberts draw their materials from Edgar Schein, a social psychologist who studied many of the released prisoners.

> The Chinese attempted not only to wipe out the socialization of the American soldiers but also to *re*-socialize them, make the Americans similar to themselves, particularly in political beliefs and values. But the Chinese failed in their basic aim. They did succeed in peripheral ways, and these

---

[9] For a recent review of research on child development see Martin L. Hoffman and Lois W. Hoffman, eds., *Review of Child Development Research*, Vol. 1 (New York, Russell Sage Foundation, 1964).

frail successes give us insight into the juggernaut power of the usual massive socialization through which all human beings continually pass.

To desocialize a man to the point where he can be fundamentally changed requires a control of the great social structures that help keep him what he is. The United States Army, like all military bodies, is set up to turn a man into a courageous soldier (a socialization process in itself). The Chinese took officers away from their men, and with the officers went the constant rehearsal of learned roles that helps maintain army structure. They separated out the noncoms lest army structure and cohesion be reinvigorated at a lower level. They broke up companies and squads, to leave each man even more alone. They put minority-group members together so that lurking feelings of injustice could not be tempered by close companionships that might develop among captives of different backgrounds.

This policy left only the less tangible structures of informal social organization—the friendships that intertwine and overlap in a group and provide much of the social cement for day-to-day behavior. But the captors were highly inventive in breaking friend from friend and preventing acquaintance-ships from forming so that men might find peace with one another. Weak men were lured by special treatment into informing on their comrades; their special treatment became clear enough to the other prisoners to be demoralizing. Yet they could never be certain whether other men were also hidden informers. To know and like another person, of course, requires trust—and the principal aim of the Chinese was to destroy trust. For without it, the main social controls on everyday behavior would disappear. At least, so went the theory.

The men, now isolated and alone, were then lured or forced to listen to constant and clever propaganda devised to teach them the bad side of what they had come from and the good aspect of what they would join if they would recant and take on the beliefs of their captors. But listening was not enough. The captives had to be induced to participate actively in their own retraining. Not all at once, however. Let them first develop the habit of confessing trivial wrongdoings, such as minor infractions of prison rules. Such confession, if rewarded, would possibly lead to a habit of public apology that might spread to other actions, to deeper beliefs.

To become like persons in control may depend on envying their power and privileges. And envy was easy for the Chinese captors to arrange. But they also had sense enough to know that they must themselves seem potentially likeable. Added to threats, then, were the lures that patience and kindness could provide, the rewards that accrued from collaboration.

In all, then, the men were made to feel alone, to be afraid; their minds were filled with constant propaganda, with both living proofs of the changes in fortune that a change in beliefs could bring about and with the terror that lay in resistance. We called it "brainwashing" and for a time saw in it something mysterious and frighteningly powerful. Now we know that we were seeing an everyday technique, but from a perspective that could give us insight into the technique's potential for taking away from human beings some of their hard-won identity.

But by and large the Chinese failed. They were dealing with mature men and these men were set against them. Some did break, but usually because of some insufficiencies in their background training. Some were bent, but straightened out when they returned to their usual world. Some rebelled and either died or endured great trouble. Most, though, used their wits, played it cool, and survived with a deepened insight into themselves and others. We do not know exactly why the Chinese failed, but their failure highlights the effectiveness and strength of the processes that had made these men into "Americans" and later into "American soldiers." [10]

The Chinese manipulated rewards, punishment, fear, and the process of identification in their efforts to re-socialize the captured American soldiers.

Since Section 2 is so long, it is desirable that we stop and summarize its major ideas.

We defined socialization as the process by which the culture patterns of a society become the habitual response patterns of the members. This process was analyzed from two points of view: *First,* from the phylogenetic point of view in which the emphasis is upon the maintenance and perpetuation of the social system as a means of species adaptation and survival. Here the emphasis is upon the transmission of skills, values, and ideologies necessary to the maintenance of the institutions of a society. Among these are the family, religion, the economic order, the political order, and the formal educational organizations such as the schools. *Secondly,* the emphasis was on the great dependence of the human offspring on the care, physical protection, and the emotional support of adults. This means that if we are to effectively understand the processes of social influence on behavior development and change we must describe and analyze the person's relationships with the social structures that support him.

In regard to the latter we examined some of the influence from the family.

We particularly considered effects of early experience on learning. To this end we first distinguished between drive and motive and went on to emphasize the dependence of motive formation upon learning, particularly learning in regard to goal achievement.

Let us turn now to a more detailed examination of the social influences that affect the development of behavior.

3. THE SOCIAL CONTEXT OF BEHAVIOR DEVELOPMENT

It is very easy to demonstrate the influence of social experience and conditions on the development of behavior. However, it is not so easy

[10] William W. Lambert and Wallace E. Lambert, *Social Psychology* (Englewood Cliffs, N.J., Prentice-Hall, Inc., 1964) taken from E. H. Schein, *Psychiatry,* 1956, 19, pp. 149-172.

to explain why and how the social effects operate as they do. The general assumption which we offer is that social responses are contingent upon the responses of others who control the avenues to goal attainment of the respondent. In the case of children, and presumably also in adults, emotional attachments develop with those whom one perceives as sources of need satisfaction or as means to goal attainments. Lifetime friendships may develop from such early relationships. However, in the case of adults, equally lasting friendships may develop from discovering someone who has similar attitudes and ideas as oneself. Reinforcement is here derived from having one's own thinking and feelings confirmed.

Research indicates that operant conditioning of social responsiveness as measured by frequency of vocalization occurs with very young infants. By three months of age the infant gives a well-defined social response to the appearance and gestures of adults. He looks at them with interest, becomes active, and vocalizes. The principles of operant conditioning suggest that adult responses function as reinforcers. Rheingold, Gewirtz, and Ross have found a positive relationship between verbal stimulation and language development in a study of three-months-old infants.[11] In other words, can the frequency of vocalizing be increased if the adult makes a social response contingent upon it? The results of the Rheingold *et al.* study indicate that it can. Thus it appears that operant conditioning is one of the processes by which social responses are formed.

We wish to note two important social conditions under which the operant conditioning of social behavior functions. The *first* condition is well illustrated by the Rheingold study just cited. In other words, a person develops a given response to another on whom he is dependent or to whom he psychologically identifies because he soon learns that a desired response from the other person is contingent upon a particular type of response from him. Let us label this social situation which involves operant conditioning as *interpersonal response* conditioning. In this condition the attitudes of the participants toward each other are very important. This is true irrespective of whether they love or hate each other. If they love each other, then the response contingencies of each are likely to be mutually rewarding. If one loves the other, but the other does not love him, then the relationship is likely to be exploitative. That is, the one who does not love the other finds it easy to exploit the one who loves him. If they dislike each other and are nevertheless dependent one upon the other, then the tendency is to develop a response accommodation based upon their mutual interests. However, this is an uneasy accommodation since each is motivated to distrust the other.

To briefly summarize: We have here emphasized the social situation

[11] H. L. Rheingold, J. Gewirtz, and H. Ross, "Social Conditioning of Vocalizations in the Infant," *Journal of Comparative Physiological Psychology*, 1959, 52, pp. 58-73.

where goal attainment is dependent upon one's eliciting a given type of response from another or others by making the fulfillment of a goal of the other contingent upon his giving a desired response. Thus a mother may make her baby's receipt of the bottle for feeding contingent upon a smile by the baby. A great part of one's repertory of social responses is determined by one's personal dependence upon others and the expectation of these others in respect to this dependence. Dependence here is not restricted to power and economic dependence. If someone loves or admires another, then this attitude is dependent for its maintenance upon certain types of response from the person in question.

In the *second* type of social condition the personal relations and attitudes of the participants toward each other are not relevant to the action situation. In this case, the action is geared toward the achievement of ends that are largely material and impersonal; for example, the production of goods in a factory, the building of a house, or the organizing and directing of a political campaign. In such a situation the object is to achieve or produce something which one would not be able to do alone or at least not nearly so efficiently.

It should not be imagined that such organization of correlated multiple human efforts is restricted to such activities as labor or assembly-line activities. It is true that a large enough number of men could move a very heavy object, but such an object may be moved by one man with the right type of machine. But it took men to conceive, design, and produce the machine.

The history of the development of technology and of the development of new forms of social organization reveals that their earlier forms as well as those of the modern industrial age were primarily concerned with extending man's muscle power. These activities were largely directed toward controlling the physical and geographic environment of man.

The forms of institutional discipline that developed to integrate and coordinate these activities were control patterns aimed at regulating *human motor activities* since manual tasks were the principal activities demanded by the technological system of that time. It was this type of coordinated activity in ancient Egypt that enabled the Egyptians to build the pyramids. In a sense, the same is true of the nineteenth- and early twentieth-century factory assembly line. Different groups of people assemble or produce different parts of a structure such as a motor or an automobile.

More recently, modern man in his efforts to increase the efficiency and improve the economy of productivity has tended to substitute machines to carry out the tasks that formerly called for manpower and motor activity. This means that the man-made environment has evolved in complexity in that a greater demand exists on the population at large for a greater use of mental activity as compared to motor activity. Human societies have from the dawn of civilization onward emphasized mental discipline and training in a few of its members, namely, those chosen for positions of leadership. In more recent times, however, the demand is for trained brainpower with less need for trained muscle power. This means that the adaptive processes of modern society are more dependent on processes of creativity than on problems of manual labor. It should not be concluded from this that there are no more tasks to be performed by manual labor. There are many such tasks. What it does mean is that the proportion of people involved in manual labor is decreasing at a very rapid rate. For example, refrigerators, electric motors, and so on, were once solely designed by men and put together in the manufacturing process by men while today they are, in some cases, designed by machines and put together by machines. But, of course, it is men who design the machines that design the other machines. Thus it is clear that as the man-made environment has evolved in technological complexity the socialization of new members into the system has become more and more dependent on the quantity and quality of the formal education of these members.

The social organization of a society is largely made possible by a system of division of labor, a system of knowledge and skills, and a system of values and related attitudes which help define the expected behavior of the participants. This means that those who are responsible for operating and maintaining a system will have expectations or standards which they will enforce on the members of the system. Likewise, those who expect to participate in the system will find it desirable to identify with the leaders of the system if they expect to receive their affection and rewards. This is largely a problem in the learning of role standards. It may be illustrated by a consideration of how a child acquires a sex role identity.

Sex Role Identity

The learning of role standards presupposes some identity with the role and the role models. For example, if a boy wants to become an airplane pilot, a professor, a policeman or whatever, then he must first have observed either directly or at least vicariously the behavior of the actual occupants of such roles. That is, some perception of the behavior of the role occupants is assumed on the part of the would-be occupant if identity is to have an opportunity to develop.

Following Kagan,[12] we will distinguish between sex *role identity* and sex *role standards or norms*. The degree to which a person regards him-

---

[12] Jerome Kagan, "Acquisition and Significance of Sex Typing and Sex Role Identity" in Martin L. Hoffman and Lois Wladis Hoffman, eds., *Review of Child Development Research*, Vol. 1 (New York, Russell Sage Foundation, 1964), pp. 144-146.

self as masculine or feminine will be called his sex identity. In other words, one's sex identity is one aspect of one's cluster of self-attitudes. Sex role standards refer to those attributes and behavior patterns that the members of a culture label as masculine or feminine. In other words, sex identity refers to a person's conceptions of himself in regard to the sex role and sex role standards refer to the norms which define the culturally appropriate attitudes and behavior of the sexes in regard to particular situations.

The degree of similarity or dissimilarity between one's sex identity and the sex role standards may be viewed as a measure of one's role adjustment in this area. Sex identity and sex norms were chosen for analysis of the interrelations among the self and social norms because everyone must have some sex identity. That is to say that sex norms are universal in that they apply to everyone in a society. An occupation or profession is important for most people, but a few may not have to identify with such either because they have inherited great wealth or because they have elected to be a "bum." Accordingly, if we know how one comes to identify with his expected sex role, this should be useful in enabling the formulation of generalizations about the relationships between social norms and role identity in general.

Since all societies ascribe some behavior on the basis of sex, it is assumed that all children have or develop a need to acquire a self-image that is congruent with their biological sex. This is true irrespective of the fact that some individuals have difficulty in adopting their culturally prescribed sex roles. This simply means that they are in conflict with their prescribed role. Some societies have recognized such conflicts and provided institutionalized roles for people who for whatever reasons are unable to make the usually prescribed or expected sexual identity. The institution of the *berdache* among certain North American Indians provides an illustration of such a special status alternative. Although homosexuality was not positively sanctioned as a status for males, men who were unable to assume the usual masculine status roles were permitted to take on certain roles usually reserved for women. They could assume the attire and occupation of women and sometimes married other males. They were granted the right to self-respect and social position on their own terms. This institution provided shelter for both male inverts and those who simply found the requirements of the male status too demanding.[13]

Let us now consider some of the factors and conditions related to the acquisition of sex role identity and sex role standards or norms. We will look first at the matter of role identity.

---

[13] Cited in H. C. Bredemeier and Richard M. Stephenson, *The Analysis of Social Systems* (New York, Holt, Rinehart and Winston, Inc., 1962), p. 164 and taken from Ruth Benedict, *Patterns of Culture* (New York, Mentor Books, 1950), pp. 242-245.

Kagan defines *identification* as a belief that some of the attributes of a model (parents, siblings, relatives, peers, and so on) belong to one's self.[14]

But what motivates a child to develop an identification with a model? Kagan specifies three conditions which he contends are necessary for identification to occur. These are:

> (1) the model must be perceived as nurturant to the child; (2) the model must be perceived as being in command of desired goals, especially power, love from others, and task competence in areas the child regards as important; and (3) the child must perceive—before the identification belief begins its growth—some objective bases of similarity in external attributes or psychological properties between himself and the model.[15]

In effect, then, the child seems to assume that if he acquires or exhibits the perceivable characteristics of his model he will also come to possess the power, competence, and achievements of the model. Accordingly, he exhibits the behavior of his model by consciously or unconsciously imitating him. Thus the male child imitates his father by wearing his father's shoes and the little girl by wearing her mother's shoes and by playing with dolls. Thus a strong identification by a child with the same-sexed parent facilitates the future establishment of an appropriate sex role identity.

The success of the child's identification with the parent of the same sex depends upon the degree of confirmation of his masculine behavior by the "other boys," that is, his peers. In other words, if the child's father's standard of masculinity correlates closely with the expectations of the larger community, then the child's identification is positively reinforced. If a discrepancy exists, then the child is in conflict because his behavior does not match that of the male peer group. As a result his sex identity may be weakened.

In other words, successful adjustment to the sex role occurs when the child's *parental identification* is reinforced by the sex *role standards or norms* of the peer group and larger society.

> The clinical literature, despite its methodological deficiencies, is in general accord in indicating that boys who have a stronger identification with mother than with father (owing to maternal dominance of the family, a perception of greater maternal than paternal competence, and paternal rejection with maternal acceptance) tend to be dependent and more prone to anxiety in threatening situations. . . . Moreover, the occurrence

---

[14] Kagan, *op. cit.*, p. 146.
[15] *Ibid.*, p. 147.

EFFECTS OF SOCIAL LEARNING ON BEHAVIOR 241

of maternal dominance over a passive father, together with maternal rejection of the child, is frequent in the histories of schizophrenic males.[16]

This assumes that the child is a member of a culture where the sex standards call for male dominance. Since rehearsal and practice by the child of the model's behavior is necessary before the child can adequately learn his sex role, then it would be expected that the male child would have difficulty in establishing an adequate sex identification and role standards when the father is frequently absent from home.

In this regard, Kagan notes

> In a study of Norwegian children with father absent or present, boys with father absent had greater difficulty establishing peer relations than boys from intact families. Failure to develop the masculine skills valued by the peer culture often leads to peer rejection. Thus the relation between father-absence and poor peer relations could result from retardation in the acquisition of masculine interests as a consequent of a weak identification with the father.[17]

Other studies summarized by Kagan suggest

> the importance of a nurturant relation between father and son in the formation of an identification . . . junior and senior high school boys and their parents filled out the California Psychological Inventory. The 20 boys with the highest father identification scores, defined in terms of similarity of father-son answers on the Inventory, were compared with 20 low father-identified boys. The 40 boys were then given an incomplete-stories test to assess perception of the father-son relation. The boys with a strong identification with father produced more frequent evidence of warm father-son relations and a perception of the father as nurturant, than did the low-identified subjects. Moreover, the boys who were identified with the father possessed more sex-typed masculine behavior and attitudes than did the boys with minimal identification with their fathers.[18]

Sex role identity is largely related to the child's desire to identify with a model of the same sex. Sex role behaviors are also related to parental identity but they are perhaps more related to the desire for acceptance from significant others. This is particularly true of girls.

> It is almost impossible for a girl to assess whether she is attractive, socially poised, or passive with others without continued interaction and feedback from the social environment. The girl is forced to be dependent upon peo-

---
[16] *Ibid.*, p. 148.
[17] *Ibid.*, p. 149.
[18] *Ibid.*, p. 149-150.

ple and to court their acceptance in order to obtain those experiences that help to establish sex-typed behaviors. The critical significance of adult and peer acceptance for girls probably contributes to the greater degree of conformity and concern with socially desirable behaviors typically found among females.[19]

In a society where male aggressiveness is defined as a behavioral index to masculinity and the male parent is the chief disciplinarian, then there is a tendency toward aggressiveness by the male child. This implies that the male child continuously carries a level of latent aggression. Consequently, any stimulus which triggers this latent attitude will produce aggressive behavior. For example, Berkowitz reports that there is more hostility in children's play after viewing a film which portrays aggressiveness than when viewing a nonaggressive cartoon. He explains this similarity to the interpretation just given. He postulates that

> the filmed aggression had set previously learned aggressiveness habits into operation. The depicted aggression was a cue, stimulating hostile tendencies within the children, and as a result, they were readily instigated to overt aggression in a subsequent situation. This approach suggests a number of mediating factors governing the probability that hostile actions will occur in these later situations: (1) the *strength* of the aggressiveness habits; (2) the *intensity* of the hostile tendencies evoked by the media violence; (3) the degree of association between the fantasy situation and (a) the situations in which the hostile habits were learned, and (b) the post fantasy setting; and (4) the intensity of the guilt and/or aggression anxiety also aroused by the fantasy violence.[20]

Again we see the interaction between the results of past learning by the individual and the pressures and characteristics of the social situation which provide the context for behavior. This suggests the importance of analyzing in some detail the nature of the social environment, particularly group behavior. This will be the subject of the next chapter.

4. SUMMARY

This chapter was concerned with the interdependence of personal and social needs. It was emphasized that the child is born into an ongoing system of social relationships that are managed and maintained by adults. Hence the child has the problem of acquiring role identities and role standards in order to become a functioning member of society. To do so he must perceive roles as providing a means for goal or need satisfaction.

---

[19] *Ibid.*, pp. 151-152.
[20] Leonard Berkowitz, *Aggression: A Social Psychological Analysis* (New York, McGraw-Hill Book Co., 1962), p. 238.

At the same time the culture of a society provides the standards for role behavior, thus enabling the individual to meet his own needs, but at the same time to help meet some of the needs of the larger community.

Following this, we discussed the process of socialization. Socialization was defined as the processes of social control and social conditioning which result in the transmission of the culture patterns from one generation to the next. Studies show that social and emotional deprivation hinder the development of a child's potentialities. Prolonged and serious deprivation probably results in permanent damage. However, if the child's environment is corrected so that his emotional and social needs are met, then it is possible to upgrade the quality of a child's responses to a very significant degree.

The family as a social system provides the principal raw materials in the form of behavior examples, ideals, and values for the formation of the child's character and the outline of his ideology.

Harlow reported experimental data which showed a relationship between early experience and affectional responses. Harlow's data show that contact comfort is an important variable in the development of affectional responses.

Following this, the effects of maternal and paternal separation on child development were considered. It is generally agreed that the research data in this area are not sufficient for adequate generalizations to be made. This is especially true in regard to the effects of day-care centers and nursery schools. However, in regard to institutional programs where there are no clear opportunities for the children to form emotional relations with parental surrogates, there is evidence to indicate that such experiences are damaging to the child. The child's learning ability and its capacity to effectively relate to others are significantly reduced.

In conclusion, we tried to show the interrelations between psychological processes and social processes by examining how role identity and role norms are acquired. To do this we analyzed how a child acquires his sex role and sex identity.

Further References

1. Edward C. Banfield, *The Moral Basis of a Backward Society* (New York, The Free Press of Glencoe, 1958).
2. Yehudi A. Cohen, *The Transition From Childhood to Adolescence* (Chicago, Aldine Publishing Co., 1964).
3. Douglas H. Lawrence and Leon Festinger, *Deterrents and Reinforcement* (Stanford, Calif., Stanford University Press, 1962).
4. Martha T. Mednick and Sarnoff A. Mednick, Editors, *Research in Personality* (New York, Holt, Rinehart & Winston, Inc., 1963).

5. Daniel Miller and Guy Swanson, *The Changing American Parent* (New York, John Wiley & Sons, Inc., 1958).
6. Robert Sears and E. Macoby, Editors, *Patterns of Child Rearing* (Harper & Row, Publishers, Inc., 1957).
7. Tamotsu Shibutani, *Society and Personality* (Englewood Cliffs, N.J., Prentice-Hall, Inc., 1961).
8. Beatrice B. Whiting, Editor, *Six Cultures: Studies of Child Rearing* (New York, John Wiley & Sons, Inc., 1963).

Part IV
SOCIAL INTERACTION: GROUPS AND ORGANIZATIONS IN CONTINUITY AND CHANGE

9

Social Interaction: Groups and Organizations

•

1. Introduction
2. Conditions Underlying Group Formation
3. Norms and Social Behavior
   (a) Introduction
   (b) Cicourel's Working Model for Norms
4. Social Behavior and Meaning
   (a) Exchange Theory
   (b) Meaning and Social Organization
      1. General and Specific Social Organization
5. Interaction and the Formation of Small Groups
   (a) Some Findings
   (b) Influence of Small Groups on the Individual
      1. Cohesiveness and Problem-Solving
      2. Status and Power Influences
      3. Some Forms of Power
6. Sherif's Experiment on In-Group Formation and Intergroup Relations—The Red Devils and Bull Dogs
   (a) Results of the Experiment
7. Summary

1. INTRODUCTION

FROM THE PRECEDING CHAPTER it should be clear that the effects of the social world on the nervous system are no less real than the effects of the physical world of climate and climatic exposure on the body. Thus it should be just as natural for us to expect psychophysical changes from social experience as we should physiochemical changes from physical experience.

Human society is an ongoing system which has evolved over a very long period of time. Its evolution has accelerated greatly in the last century. It has been estimated that man has quantitatively evolved as much knowledge in the last decade as in all the previous decades. Knowledge is the mainstay of society and its development depends upon the opportunity for untrammeled research, dissemination of the results of research, and the rewarding of the man of knowledge. The development and application of human knowledge reveal perhaps more clearly than anything else the *interdependence* of men. This interdependence is concretely reflected in two important forms of social life: *social groups* and *social organizations*. A brief definition and characterization of these two types of social structures will enable a clearer statement of the problem of this chapter.

A *social group* is defined as two or more persons in interaction under the following conditions: (1) the relations among the members are *interdependent*, that is, each member's behavior involves some role relationship with the others; and (2) the members or participants share a common set of norms or standards which regulate their mutual or reciprocal behavior. The *set* of norms or beliefs is sometimes referred to as an *ideology*. The shared norms or ideology evolve out of the members' interaction in regard to common tasks or endeavors. There are many kinds of such groups. Perhaps a play group, such as a baseball team or football team, best typifies what we mean by a social group. But there are many others which meet the criteria of the definition. For example, families, peer groups, friendship groups, clubs, neighborhood groups, and work groups are social groups.

When social groups are functionally related to other similar groups and the relationships are designed to attain ends or goals which could not be attained or at least attained as well by individual groups separately, then the interrelated set of groups constitutes an *organization*. In other words, an organization is a hierarchically arranged set of groups with their related norms, beliefs, and rules formed to accomplish stated purposes or objectives. The Democratic Party, a factory, a labor union, a community chest, an infantry company, a battalion, or the United Nations are examples of what is meant by the foregoing definition of a social organization. If we refer to a concrete set of interrelated groups, then the term *social organization* denotes an entity or structure—this is what we meant by the above definition. However, the term *social organization* may be used to refer to the process or processes of organizing the collective and interdependent acts of a number of groups toward some end. In this case, the reference is to types of prescribed social behavior rather than to types of social structures. The discerning student will immediately recognize that the concepts of structure and process are but different aspects of a whole. Different types of social organiza-

GROUPS AND ORGANIZATIONS

tions condition and produce different response patterns among the group members. Also, different forms of social organization vary in efficiency and adequacy for task attainment. Football coaches, factory managers, and office managers are constantly experimenting with new ways of organizing the collective efforts of the participants. The form of organization affects not only the efficiency of a group to solve a problem or achieve a goal, but it also affects the feelings, motivation, and morale of the members.

Thinkers have tried for many centuries to explain the presence and development of human social organization. Rousseau contended that the "social contract" was the basis for human social organization and Hobbes saw social control as a necessary but negative means for controlling human greed and passion.[1] These and other after-the-fact "explanations" assumed a rationality on the part of man which was not justified by the facts.

Let us turn now to an examination of conditions which we assume are necessary for the formation of human groups and organizations.

2. CONDITIONS UNDERLYING GROUP FORMATION

Two of the more obvious and yet fundamental properties of man which relate to his tendency to group behavior are: (1) his long period of biological helplessness during infancy and the long period of socialization during childhood and adolescence; and (2) the great dependence of the individual on the cumulated results of past learning of previous generations for adjustment and adaptation. In other words, the child is conditioned to social interaction during infancy by parental care and feeding and later by play with other children and by training in church, school, and neighborhood activities.

Inasmuch as the human offspring is born into an ongoing system of group life and his very survival and the maintenance of his needs—even the definition of many of his needs—depend upon the system, then it follows that his tendencies to group behavior have a strong biological *and* experiential base. Given this basis for group life in the biological nature of man and in the conditioning of his social organization, then it is to be expected that man would seek interaction with his fellows. However, it is assumed that when specific cases of interaction occur the interaction is motivated whether the motivation is conscious or subconscious. In regard to conscious motivation for interaction it is assumed that individuals will not seek group solutions to problems which they perceive can be solved more efficiently by individual action. In other

---

[1] See Talcott Parsons *et al., Theories of Society* (New York, The Free Press of Glencoe, Inc., 1961), Vol. 1, pp. 85-139.

words, it is assumed that groups and organizations form to attain ends that could not be attained or at least as well attained by individual effort as by collective or group effort. For example, one person may carry an ordinary bucket of water more easily than a group, but in the case of a dangerous fire a bucket brigade is more efficient.

In describing group behavior it is well to note what is sometimes called the "is-ought" problem. Certainly the *behavior* of the members of a group constitutes the *observable "is"* aspect of the problem. We see the members of a football squad perform a play in a certain way. But why should they perform it in this particular manner? Why even should they perform this particular play rather than some other play? Clearly there appears to be an "ought" side to the problem of explaining group behavior. What is the "ought" side of the problem? This is the question of the imperativeness of *given patterns* of behavior. Why should a set of individuals find it necessary to perform an act a certain way? We might say that the behavior is instinctive and that the performance is therefore patterned because of biological mechanisms. But this would assume a consistency in response throughout the lifetime of the individuals, and we know this is not true since the rules of the game may be different next year and different plays may then come into vogue. We must therefore look elsewhere for the patterning of human social behavior. We must look for the existence of *social norms.* Let us take a closer look at social norms by asking ourselves the question: Why do social norms exist?

To answer this question, let us re-emphasize certain characteristics of human social or group behavior. *First,* it involves an *interdependent* or reciprocal act. That is, the response of one individual is contingent upon the response of another individual or individuals. A mother-child relationship or a pitcher-catcher relationship on a baseball team are examples. *Secondly,* it follows that if the relationship is interdependent the acting out of the relationship assumes some integration of action. Integration and coordination of action presuppose that agreed-upon action patterns exist. These agreed-upon action patterns become the standards or norms by which social behavior is made *predictable.* In other words, norms become the guides or rules by which the behavior of the members of a group becomes predictable to each other; and if the reciprocal behavior of the members were not predictable, then group and organizational behavior would be impossible.

We have just shown that social norms function to make patterned group behavior possible. At this point in our analysis the explanation of the existence of social norms sounds terribly teleological. Teleological or not, we certainly do not intend to imply that men one day discovered that problems which involved social interaction could not be solved without the invention of norms to regulate the interaction. Obviously, such a proposition assumes knowledge prior to experience and Hume laid that argument to rest many years ago.

The foregoing argument which related the predictability of social behavior to the presence of social norms was a description of a major function of social norms assuming that the group members are motivated to conform to the normative definitions. This, of course, is not always the case. Therefore, let us look closer at the biological characteristics of man and see if there is a logical basis for assuming the existence of social norms to be indirectly related to biological attributes of man. This, at first, may sound like a violation of the warnings about the hazards of mixing levels of abstraction, but I do not think it is such a violation.

The following argument is based on materials in Part II of the text.

First, man is a biosocial animal and his sociability is regulated by learning rather than by instincts. *Secondly,* the social, psychological, and biological needs of man may be satisfied in a variety of ways. In other words, problems of adaptation have *more* than one solution and different individuals may perceive different solutions. This is attested to by the observation of the great variety of human behavior that is exhibited in response to any particular need. *Thirdly,* if problems have more than one possible solution and some individuals perceive two or more solutions to a given problem and the problem requires social action for its solution and regulating, then only one of the solutions can be adopted at a given point or period of time and hence norms would give a sense of "ought" or feeling of obligation to a given solution. The patterned solutions that are evolved in regard to problems of social interaction within a society constitute elements of the society's culture. That is, problems of social interaction which arise out of the biosocial interdependence of man upon man require him to evolve a particular action pattern to a given problem at a given time or else integration and coordination of social behavior is not possible. In other words, *social norms arise out of the problems of an experience with social interaction. Fourthly,* once norms have arisen and the members have learned them, they then become a part of the self or ego and psychologically function to produce a sense of right and obligation to conform to the established modes of behavior. In other words, norms emerge as means for regulating the ever-present potentiality for human *conflict.*

Let us now summarize the main argument contained in the four statements above:

1. Man is biologically interdependent or social, but he is not equipped with biologically built-in behavior patterns.
2. Being biologically social, his survival depends upon his interaction with those who can help him meet his needs.
3. His interaction skills depend in turn upon the processes of percep-

tion and learning and the quality of the cultural materials available for learning and problem-solving.

4. Norms develop out of efforts to solve problems through social interaction. We would hypothesize that the particular norm or norms that evolve would be the ones which the more powerful participants perceived as best insuring their goal aspirations or definitions.

Thus it is clear that norms function to regularize and integrate group behavior. Norms also serve as guides or standards for judgments about behavior. It is a truism that it is extremely difficult to evaluate something without the benefit of clear standards or norms. Yet, individuals almost daily find themselves in such ambiguous situations. We will borrow an illustration from Professor Peter M. Blau of how individuals deal with such ambiguous situations:

> How valuable a woman is as a love object to a man depends to a considerable extent on her apparent popularity with other men. It is difficult to evaluate anything in the absence of clear standards for doing so, and individuals who find themselves in such an ambiguous situation tend to be strongly influenced by any indication of a social norm for making judgments. Evaluating the intrinsic desirability of a woman is an ambiguous case of this kind, in which any particular man is strongly influenced by her general popularity among men that socially validates her value as a love object. Of course, a girl can only become generally popular by being attractive to many particular boys, but her attractiveness to any one depends in part on evidence that others find her attractive too. Good looks constitute such evidence, and so does her behavior on dates.
>
> A woman whose love is in great demand among men is not likely to make firm commitments quickly, because she has so many attractive alternatives to weigh before she does. The one who is not popular is more dependent on a man who takes her out and has more reason to become committed to him. A woman who readily gives proof of her affection to a man, therefore, provides presumptive evidence of her lack of popularity and thus tends to depreciate the value of her affection for him. Her resistance to his attempts to conquer her, in contrast, implies that she is in great demand and has many alternatives to choose from, which is likely to enhance her desirability in his eyes. Her reluctance to become committed helps to establish the value of her affection, partly because he takes it as an indication of her general desirability, notably in the absence of any direct knowledge of how desirable she appears to other men.[2]

The point which we wish to emphasize by the quotation from Blau is that people frequently find it necessary to make judgments about social

---

[2] Peter M. Blau, *Exchange and Power in Social Life* (New York, John Wiley & Sons, Inc., 1964), pp. 81-82.

behavior without the benefit of clear-cut norms to provide a basis for judgment. Does this mean that people will not or cannot make judgments under such conditions? The answer is, of course, they can and do. But the next question is how? Again we will refer to the Blau quotation. Note that in the absence of explicit norms or standards to judge a girl's attractiveness men look for *indirect* evidence; for example, the girl's general popularity with other men. This suggests that in the absence of direct standards for judgment people look for elements which they believe are *correlated* with the qualities in question. These qualities represent aspects of social reality which the individuals concerned have gleaned from previous social interaction. In this regard Durkheim states that

> the elementary qualities of which the social fact consists are present in germ in individual minds. But the social fact emerges from them only when they have been transformed by association since it is only then that it appears. Association itself is also an active factor productive of special effects. In itself it is therefore something new. When the consciousness of individuals, instead of remaining isolated, becomes grouped and combined, something in the world has been altered.[3]

In a very real sense the human mind is a product of social forces. It is in social relations that men establish interests and values, and it is through social relations that these find expression and are realized.

Since social relations give rise to social norms, let us further analyze norms and their relation to behavior.

3. NORMS AND SOCIAL BEHAVIOR

INTRODUCTION

In Chapter 6 (Social Judgment) it was indicated that normative standards that restrict the range of permissible conduct are essential for social life. This does not mean that all restraints on social behavior derive from *shared* norms. Many norms exist that are not shared by all the members of a group or organization. The recent contract agreements that were arrived at by the automotive industry and the CIO contained elements which were not altogether to the liking of all parties. There were power elements which neither side could offset; hence some compromise was necessary. In addition, there were outside interests (the nation's economy) which were being watched over by the federal government and these were reflected in the bargaining discussions.

[3] Émile Durkheim, *Suicide* (New York, The Free Press of Glencoe, 1951), p. 310.

In complex social structures where conflicting interests are involved and many interdependent groups are interacting, the norms that arise generally reflect the power balances and bargaining skills of the groups. To a lesser degree the same is true of small groups. Since power and skills sometimes combine to produce competitive advantages, the *trust* required for social exchange could not be maintained without social norms prohibiting force and fraud. It is obvious that the power gained by superior resources makes it possible to exploit others, hence the need for norms to define the limits to behavior. "The most dramatic manifestation of the need for social norms is found in social situations where the interests of *all* parties, not only those of most, require protection by social norms because the pursuit of self-interests without normative restraints defeats the self-interests of all parties concerned." [4]

Blau suggests that some forms of exploitation, such as economic exploitation, are difficult to discern because they are not in violation of basic cultural taboos in our society. This is evidenced in Western society by the phrase *caveat emptor* or let the buyer beware. Thus while social norms legitimate social practices, the absence or ambiguity of norms may permit *de facto* legitimation. Let us make a closer examination of the nature and function of norms.

Cicourel's Working Model for Norms

Cicourel's working model for norms is an amplification and application of the notion of a game.[5] We have already referred to the game many times as a way of calling the student's attention to the meaning and function of norms. Thus the norms or basic rules of a game indicate what is considered as "normal" behavior by those who seek to abide by the rules. Cicourel borrows from Garfinkel a definition of basic rules. Garfinkel defines basic rules as constituting the behavioral expectancies of the participating members of a game. These rules are defined by three properties which he collectively calls "constitutive expectancies."

> (1) The "constitutive expectancies" provide a set of boundary conditions within which each player must make decision choices regardless of personal likes and dislikes, plans and consequences for himself or others. The choices are independent of the number of players, patterns of moves or territory of play. (2) Each player assumes a norm of reciprocity with respect to the alternatives which are binding on each other. (3) The players assume

[4] Blau, *op. cit.*, p. 255.
[5] Reprinted with permission of The Free Press of Glencoe, a division of The Macmillan Company, from *Method and Measurement in Sociology*, by Aaron V. Cicourel. Copyright © 1964, by The Free Press of Glencoe, a division of The Macmillan Company.

that whatever they expect of each other is perceived and interpreted in the same way.[6]

The rules of a game—whether the game is a formal game such as football or an informal "game" involving a salesman and a customer or any other social situation—are constituted by the mutual expectancies of the actors. If there are no *mutual* expectancies, then there are in effect no rules and the interaction will be unstable or disorganized. On the other hand, when basic rules do exist and are perceived by the actors, there are at least two other types of rules which are critical in understanding the behavior of the actors.

> Garfinkel calls these "rules of preferred play" and "game furnished conditions." "Rules of preferred play" are distinguished from basic rules by the discretion provided the player with respect to compliance on his part. The player defines "correct procedure" within the limits of the basic rules, but the "preference rules" tend to operate independently of the basic rules. The independence stems from various kinds of traditional play, "efficiency" procedures, aesthetic preference, and the like, which are open to the player. *Game-furnished conditions* help to fill out how the game tends to be played and correspond to each set of basic rules. The players' decisions are always constrained by them and they are independent of whether the player wins or loses. They describe the general characteristics of the game but are invariant to any particular state of the game because they always enter into each decision. Garfinkel finds a good example of the game-furnished conditions in chess where the basic rules provide a situation of perfect information at all times. A different game with different basic rules may not provide for such conditions. Thus in poker the situation is quite different and the game-furnished conditions are such that every decision contains a varying amount of uncertainty.[7]

Everyday social behavior is more like the game of poker; that is, the decisions regarding it generally contain varying amounts of uncertainty. The participants may know what the basic rules are that define what is normal or expected. What each may not know is just how the other intends to "play" his part, or what his *preferred* rules of play are. Nevertheless, as Garfinkel and Cicourel note, the basic rules do define the events and acts that are perceived as normal. Given the existence of norms and the acceptance of their meaning by the participants, the foundation exists for predictable social interaction. The basis for this predictability is what Garfinkel calls "trust."

[6] *Ibid.*, p. 204. Cicourel credits Harold Garfinkel with this conception and it is taken from a paper by Garfinkel on "A Conception of and Experiments with 'Trust' as a Condition of Stable Concerted Action." Paper read at the annual meetings of the American Sociological Association, Washington, D.C., 1957.

[7] *Ibid.*, pp. 204–205; Garfinkel's ideas as discussed by Cicourel.

However, the stability and *compliance of persons to norms in everyday social behavior* is quite different from that in a game. As Cicourel and Garfinkel point out, the game is only a single social episode and is relatively uninfluenced by external change and events. In other words, the outcomes of games are not dependent on the development of conditions outside the game (although in regard to *some* neighborhood little-league baseball teams one might argue the contrary). Instead, the outcomes depend upon the skill of the plays in their application of the rules and strategies of the game.

On the other hand, the norms or rules of everyday social life are not so clearly or precisely formed; hence there is great ambiguity and differences in interpretation of what the norms are and the consequences of their violation. The ambiguity of social norms and their sanctions are two of the reasons why the notion of "trust" is important in understanding social behavior. Given the condition of an actor having to interact with others in the face of uncertainty, then how does he perceive and interpret his environment?

If we recall the results of the autokinetic effects experiments of Sherif and the discussion of stereotypes in Chapter 6, these suggest the hypothesis that the actor draws cues from the pool of present stimuli and interprets these in terms of past experience and upon the basis of his interpretation forms a judgment. The judgment is always made in the face of incomplete and often conflicting information; hence an element of "trust" is necessary or else a decision could not be made at all.

Sherif and Hovland offer two generalizations which pertain to individual judgments under conditions of ambiguous stimuli or judgment standards. These are:

> (1) an individual confronted with a series of stimuli tends to form a psychological scale of judgment, even when the stimulus series is not well graded and when explicit standards are lacking. Henceforth, judgment of a related stimulus is made in terms of the categories of this reference scale . . . (2) to the extent that a stimulus series lacks explicit standards, the judgment scale is less stable and placement is less accurate. . . .[8]

In other words, if one has to make judgments in the absence of an external frame of reference, a subjective frame of reference is evolved, but it is modifiable once an external frame of reference develops.

As Cicourel says, "The notion of 'trust' implies that the actor must 'accept' and rely upon definitions of the situation which are potentially

---

[8] Muzafer Sherif and C. I. Hovland, *Social Judgment: Assimilation and Contrast Effects in Communication and Attitude Change* (New Haven, Yale University Press, 1961), p. 179.

problematic and for which explicit rules do not exist."[9] Since the norms are ambiguous, the actor must make some judgment of his own as to what to expect from others involved and as to his own course of action. This raises the question as to what are the elements which determine how the actor makes "sense" of his environment. Cicourel derives five sets of elements which he believes provide an approach to answering this question. These are:

> (1) the *typicality* of everyday events and their *likelihood* of occurrence, (2) the ways in which they *compare* with events in the past and suggests how future events might be evaluated, (3) the actor's assignment of *causal significance* to events, (4) the ways events fit into an actor's or society's *means-ends* relationships, and (5) the ways events are deemed necessary to an actor's or society's *natural* or *moral order*.[10]

In summary we note that Cicourel employs the notion of game rules with their invariant properties to call attention to the unbounded and variant characteristics of norms and rules of everyday social behavior. In a game, if the rules are broken they permit unambiguous decisions. In everyday social behavior when rules or laws are broken we find that very elaborate procedures are sometimes necessary to even determine whether a violation has occurred.

> This is true of our determination of violations of rules of law; the police, witnesses, the jury, the judge, the defense and prosecuting attorneys, the victim, and the accused may all very seriously entertain judgments which taken together are at once contradictory, overlapping and vague. The situation is compounded when we are confronted with judgments on unclear nonlegal matters: evaluations of another's character, of affect, of physical attractiveness, of art objects, of marriage partner and the like. I would like to view the "rules" of everyday life as essentially "noncalculable" in the sense of conventional measurement because of the discrepancy between their ideal description and their practiced and enforced character. The "noncalculability" is not to be found merely in the actor's judgments, but also in the observer's model of the actor. This is not to say that a precise model of the actor's judgment is impossible, but that conventional measures which are, for example, found in two-valued logic, ordinal scales, and mathematical game theory do not adequately depict everyday decision.[11]

As the discussion in Chapter 7 of McClelland's theory of the persistency of the effects of early experience showed, one of the sources of strength of a norm is its vagueness. One's concept of perfection is never

---

[9] Cicourel, *op. cit.*, pp. 206-207.
[10] *Ibid.*; Cicourel's discussion of Garfinkel's unpublished paper.
[11] *Ibid.*, p. 209.

precisely clear; therefore he keeps striving for improvement because he believes that his performance is not as good as it could be. Thus in regard to certain kinds of behavior it may be that the strength of some norms to induce conformity lies in their ambiguity or vagueness. It appears that this may be true in respect to moral and religious behavior or other kinds of behavior where there is a long delay between one's act and any subsequent punishment or reward.

By what standards and processes of judgment does an actor assign *meaning* to the signs and symbols which he perceives?

4. SOCIAL BEHAVIOR AND MEANING

What are the conditions which make possible shared meanings in social behavior? Whatever these conditions and standards are for a group, they will be somewhat different for individuals as individuals in the context of their personal needs and values.

Mills, in referring to a group, asks,

> What . . . *are* the conditions which, if fulfilled, permit identification, confirmation, and verification of a definition? There can be no identification, confirmation, or verification without established cognitive standards that not only operate for a single person over various time periods, but also are shared simultaneously by a number of persons. For example, the minimum conditions for the verification of the statement and corresponding definition of "the house is green" include cognitive standards covering what a "house" is, what "green" is, and what "is" is. Without such standards the statement is "meaningless." [12, 13]

In other words, before any meaning can be signified there must exist some cognitive standard for identifying and determining it. We indicated in Chapter 3 that signs and symbols are conveyers of meaning for those who have learned them. A *sign* may be thought of as an external cue to an object, event, or fact whose recognition presupposes a subjective cognitive standard. We reserve the word *symbol* to refer to the world of arbitrary meaning as represented by language. The language technique used may be that of the artist who speaks through music or paintings, the mathematician's formulae, or the ordinary written or spoken word.

We are not here concerned with how these standards evolve or with the specific goals of the members of a group. In other words, we *assume*

---

[12] Theodore M. Mills, *Group Transformation: An Analysis of a Learning Group* (Englewood Cliffs, N.J., Prentice-Hall, Inc., 1964), p. 40. Mills presents a method of sign process analysis (SPA).

[13] For a theory of signs and behavior the student is invited to read Charles Morris, *Signs, Language and Behavior* (Englewood Cliffs, N.J., Prentice-Hall, Inc., 1946). See also Charles E. Osgood, George J. Suci, and Percy H. Tannenbaum, *The Measurement of Meaning* (Urbana, University of Illinois Press, 1957).

GROUPS AND ORGANIZATIONS

the existence of cultural standards and concern ourselves with the question of how social behavior affects the meaning of one's perception of others and of himself, that is, person-perception and self-perception.

Jones has recently written an excellent volume on *Ingratiation* in which he describes a series of experiments which succeed in showing how a person's behavior is significantly shaped by the importance of "winning favor" from another.[14] Jones argues that the social interaction process can be partially conceived as a process of *self-presentation* and *other-enhancement*. By self-presentation he means that the person makes tactical presentations to others of his personal qualities in manners congruent to his motivational needs of the moment. By other-enhancement he means that a person publicly responds to another's personal qualities or achievements in ways that enhance or flatter the other's self-image. In other words, the presentation of personal qualities that are attractive to another and the responding in ways which enhance another's self-image combine to produce a sense of ingratiation in the other.[15]

Exchange Theory

Thus, meaning in social behavior is partially determined by the outcome of an *exchange* process between or among the actors. In the experiments summarized by Jones the exchange process consists of a set of responses which lead to mutual attraction. It must be kept in mind that we are, at this point, referring to a particular exchange process, namely one which leads to ingratiation. Obviously, not all social exchanges lead to mutual attraction. The social and psychological conditions which lead to responses of mutual attraction or to mutual rejection are quite different.

Exchange theories conceive social attraction as a function of the degree to which persons achieve satisfactory rewards at low costs in their interaction with others.[16] Any activity on the part of one person that contributes to the satisfaction or gratification of the needs of another is considered a reward. Costs on the other hand are punishments incurred, embarrassments and anxieties produced because of the interaction. In

---

[14] Edward E. Jones, *Ingratiation: A Social Psychological Analysis* (New York: Appleton-Century-Crofts, 1964).

[15] Two interesting aspects of this process which Jones discusses, but space here will not allow, are self-deception and status differences. The interested student should read this.

[16] For a detailed analysis of exchange theory see George Homans, *Social Behavior: Its Elementary Forms* (New York, Harcourt, Brace and World, Inc., 1961); also, John W. Thibaut and H. H. Kelley, *The Social Psychology of Groups* (New York, John Wiley & Sons, Inc., 1959) and H. H. Kelley, J. W. Thibaut, R. Radloff, and D. Mundy, "The Development of Cooperation in the 'Minimal Social Situation,'" *Psychological Monograph*, Vol. 76, No. 19, 1962.

the broadest sense rewards may be considered from the point of view of Chapter 7 as positive reinforcements and costs as negative reinforcements.

In regard to specific exchange or interaction situations, the participants have developed judgments from past experience as to what reward-cost outcome to expect as fair. That is, they have developed subjective standards as to some minimum level of reward relative to cost in regard to specific relations. These experiences need not be and indeed are not always restricted to one's own experience. The standard may be based on one's perceptions of what others like him have been obtaining in comparable situations. Thibaut and Kelley call these standards *comparison levels*. They distinguish two kinds of standards or comparison levels. The first is called the *comparison level*, which is the standard against which a person evaluates the "attractiveness" of an anticipated or actual relationship. The second is called the *comparison level for alternatives*, and it is the standard the participant uses in deciding whether to enter, remain, or leave a relationship.[17] In other words, the comparison level is a standard by which a person evaluates the rewards and costs of a given relationship in terms of what he feels is fair or what he thinks he deserves. And the comparison level for alternatives is the minimum level of outcomes a person will accept in the light of his available alternative opportunities. If the outcome of rewards to costs drops below this level, then the relationship becomes negative and the person will withdraw.

Exchange theory may be related to the distribution of sociometric choices among members of a group. Patterns of sociometric choice refer to the distribution of choices for association, rejection, or indifference among the members of a group. It is well known that individuals regularly choose certain persons for association and ignore others. Assuming that the group members are of equal social status or social power, then the choices are generally determined by the members' degrees of personal attractiveness. If there are status differences, then this adds another dimension to the sociometric structure. We shall label the regularities of interpersonal association as the sociometric structure of an interaction network.

Exchange theory provides an explanation of why some persons receive a high number of choices and others receive few choices. Some members provide high rewards at low costs to those with whom they interact, and others low rewards at high costs.

Recall Jones' analysis of ingratiation and we shall see that exchange theory also offers an explanation of why similarity between persons leads to mutual attraction. Similarity in values, occupation, personality

---

[17] Thibaut and Kelley, *op. cit.*, p. 21.

traits, and in ability provides high rewards at low costs to both members. The reason is clear. People who are alike or similar in these respects are less likely to arouse anxiety or embarrassment in each other. We recognize, of course, that in some instances different or complementary traits form the basis for a high-reward, low-cost outcome in interaction.[18] It might be argued that a person who has difficulties making decisions would find attractive someone who loves decision-making.

It could be argued that, in general, people are attracted to one another on the basis of their perception of qualities in the other that enhance or are congruent with their self-image.[19]

Exchange theory has implications for leadership behavior. First, a leader may influence the interaction outcomes for others. That is, he can help make the rewards exceed the cost. Jennings, in referring to the person who receives a large number of sociometric choices (the overchosen person), notes:

> Each leader "improves" from the point of view of the membership, through one method or another, the social milieu. Each widens the social field for participation of others (and indirectly her own social space) by ingratiating them into activities, introducing new activities, and by fostering tolerance on the part of one member towards another. Each leader shows a feeling for when to censure and when to praise and apparently is intellectually and emotionally "uncomfortable" when others are "unhappy" or "left-out." [20]

To summarize: The exchange process in social interaction is a major determinant of meaning in that it provides an important basis for the person's judgment of the personal desirability or nondesirability of a social relationship. In this regard it is interesting to observe individuals when they first meet. The initial conversation centers around "small talk" which functions to allow the participants to get an estimate of one another without exposing themselves. Each person explores through a sequence of events, and at varying degrees of costs to himself, the potential rewards available among those around him. This does not mean that each person is consciously calculating a potential net reward over costs in relation to those present. It simply means that people are attracted or repelled in their relationships on the basis of the capacity of these relationships to satisfy or not to satisfy the person's perceived needs.

---

[18] Robert F. Winch, *Mate-selection: A Study of Complementary Needs* (New York, Harper & Row, Publishers, Inc., 1958).

[19] Prescott Lecky, *Self-Consistency: A Theory of Personality* (New York, Island Press, 1945).

[20] Helen H. Jennings, *Leadership and Isolation*, 2nd ed. (New York, copyright, 1950, by David McKay Co., Inc.), p. 203.

The personal qualities exhibited by the actors in the exchange processes just described are only one source of meaning in a social situation that are exhibited through interaction. We might label the source just described as the *personality system* of the members. That is, each member of a group has needs, motives, abilities, and traits that are perceived by others as rewarding, complementary, or threatening, and in this sense these perceived cues provide meaning for a social situation. However, for these cues to provide meaning to a participant the participant must have some cognitive standard or image of himself so that he can assess the significance of the other person's traits for his needs and motives.

A person's perception of the meaning and significance of another's action for himself will vary with the perceived context of the action. For example, it is well known that if a set of subjects are told that they are being given an intelligence test, this produces tension as compared to being told that it is not an intelligence test. In other words, if an interaction situation reveals signs that are perceived by a member as indicating that other members are evaluating him, then this may produce anxiety. To carry the reasoning a little further, we can speak of meaning within a context of identification and definition and/or in respect to evaluation. When the social stimulus situation involves evaluation in addition to cognitive standards, this arouses emotion since the participant's self-image may be threatened.

Atkinson and Litwin have found that people who have high motivation for achievement and are low in test anxiety tend to select tasks that are challenging and difficult. Those with low achievement motivation and high test anxiety tend to choose tasks in a test situation that are less difficult and where failure is less likely to occur.[21]

In the foregoing analysis of exchange theory as a means of understanding interpersonal relationships, we did not explicitly take into account the social system as a source of meaning. Let us suppose the interaction situation involves an organizational context, that is, a social system, composed of statuses and the related mutual expectations of interaction patterns or roles. In what ways do these factors contribute to the actors' perceptions of meaning and definitions?

Meaning and Social Organization

Perhaps the major difference between the context of interpersonal relations and the context of an organization is the difference in the sense of constraint or compliance felt and expected. The participants in an

---

[21] John W. Atkinson and George H. Litwin, "Achievement Motive and Test Anxiety Conceived as Motive to Approach Success and Motive to Avoid Failure," *Journal of Abnormal Social Psychology,* Vol. 60 (1960), pp. 52-63.

interpersonal situation can move in and out of such relationships more or less at will. The maintenance of an interpersonal relationship is principally determined by the participants' personal attraction to one another. On the other hand, interaction within a formal social system is more determined by organizational goals and policy and the formal skills of the participants who occupy specific roles in the system.

(1) *General and Specific Social Organization.* By *general social organization* is meant those forms of social interaction and related values peculiar to a society or an entire community, such as a political system or a marriage and family system. Such general forms also include the ultimate values of a society, such as religious and ethical systems. These forms of general or societal social organization function to provide some elements of common focus for public opinion and for societal goals. Consensus on general values may aid in gaining consensus on specific goals for particular organizations, but such general value consensus is not a necessary condition for consensus on specific organizational goals or means.[22]

An organization, say a health department or a factory, is composed of a set of interrelated groups whose members provide the skills and manpower for the division of labor necessary to attain the goals. The organization leaders cannot assume that the members will always express actions and values in harmony with the ends of the organization. Therefore, the organization will utilize either formal or informal socialization procedures to train members ideologically as well as technically. For example, large corporations have their own executive-training programs. The amount of socialization required by organizations depends on the degree to which organizational behavior differs from the behavior the members have learned elsewhere and before becoming a member of the organization. The discipline and behavioral requirements of an army provide a good example. Recruits need a great deal of intensive socialization before they can become efficient troops. Individuals with different degrees of experience with traditional authoritarian social life would require different degrees of army training and indoctrination. This fact was demonstrated by Stouffer in his World War II studies of the American soldiers.[23] For example, army life appears to resemble the traditional authoritarian social life of rural people more than it does the life of the urban middle class.

Once a person becomes a member of an organization, he occupies a position within the organization and his perception of himself relative

[22] Amitai Etzioni, *A Comparative Analysis of Complex Organizations* (New York, The Free Press of Glencoe, Inc., 1961), p. 129.
[23] Samuel A. Stouffer et al., *The American Soldier*, Vol. 1 (Princeton, N.J., Princeton University Press, 1949), pp. 105-150.

to others in the organization and other people's perception of him is largely determined by the position he occupies. In other words, meaning is here more determined by one's position in the social organization than by one's personal qualities. One generally holds memberships and therefore occupies positions in several organizations. Often these have conflicting values and ideologies, and one's rank may vary from organization to organization. When this is the case, the participants often suffer a great deal of psychological strain in attempting to adapt to the demands of conflicting roles and hence conflicting social expectations by others.

Mirra Komarovsky in a study of cultural contradictions and sex roles well illustrates one form of such conflict. The following excerpts illustrate the conflicts faced by some of Komarovsky's students:

> How am I to pursue any course singlemindedly when some way along the line a person I respect is sure to say, "You are on the wrong track and are wasting your time"? Uncle John telephones every Sunday morning. His first question is: "Did you go out last night?" He would think me a "grind" if I were to stay home Saturday night to finish a term paper. My father expects me to get an A in every subject and is disappointed by a B. He says I have plenty of time for social life. Mother says, "That A in philosophy is nice, dear. But please don't become so deep that no man will be good enough for you." And, finally, Aunt Mary's life is careers for women. "Prepare yourself for some profession. This is the only way to insure yourself independence and an interesting life. You have plenty of time to marry."
>
> A senior writes: I get a letter from my mother at least three times a week. One week her letters will say, "Remember that this is your last year at college. Subordinate everything to your studies. You must have a good record to secure a job." The next week her letters are full of wedding news. This friend of mine got married; that one is engaged; my young cousin's wedding is only a week off. When, my mother wonders, will I make up my mind? Surely I wouldn't want to be the only unmarried one in my group. It is high time, she feels, that I give some thought to it.
>
> A student reminisces: All through high school my family urged me to work hard because they wished me to enter a first-rate college. At the same time they were always raving about a girl schoolmate who lived next door to us. How pretty and how sweet she was, how popular, and what taste in clothes! Couldn't I also pay more attention to my appearance and to social life? They were overlooking the fact that this carefree friend of mine had little time left for school work and had failed several subjects. It seemed that my family had expected me to become Eve Curie and Hedy Lamar wrapped up in one.
>
> Another comments: My mother thinks that it is very nice to be smart in college but only if it doesn't take too much effort. She always tells me not to be too intellectual on dates, to be clever in a light sort of way. My father, on the other hand, wants me to study law. He thinks that if I applied my-

self I could make an excellent lawyer and keeps telling me that I am better fitted for this profession than my brother.[24]

If one views the foregoing conflicting demands over a sufficiently long span of time, then they are not necessarily conflicting. For example, one can be a good student while in college and plan to get married afterwards. It is when the demands occur concurrently or over short time spans that the conflicts appear more sharply, especially if the person involved is unable or finds it difficult to delay anticipated gratification.

Social meaning has many dimensions when multiple roles become involved in a specific situation and this can produce strain in those so involved. This is sometimes the source of much humor as well as tragedy. W. S. Gilbert's dialogue between Ko-Ko and Pooh-Bah in *The Mikado* has often been cited as illustrative of such a dilemma in politics:

Ko-Ko. Pooh-Bah, it seems that the festivities in connection with my approaching marriage must last a week. I should like to do it handsomely, and I want to consult you as to the amount I ought to spend upon them.

Pooh-Bah. Certainly. In which of my capacities? As First Lord of the Treasury, Lord Chamberlain, Attorney-General, Chancellor of the Exchequer, Privy Purse, or Private Secretary?

Ko-Ko. Suppose we say as Private Secretary.

Pooh-Bah. Speaking as your Private Secretary, I should say that, as the city will have to pay for it, don't stint yourself, do it well.

Ko-Ko. Exactly—as the city will have to pay for it. That is your advice.

Pooh-Bah. As Private Secretary. Of course, you will understand that, as Chancellor of the Exchequer, I am bound to see that due economy is observed.

Ko-Ko. Oh! But you said just now "Don't stint yourself, do it well."

Pooh-Bah. As Private Secretary.

Ko-Ko. And now you say that due economy must be observed.

Pooh-Bah. As Chancellor of the Exchequer.

Ko-Ko. I see. Come over here, where the Chancellor can't hear us. (*They cross the stage*) Now, as my Solicitor, how do you advise me to deal with this difficulty?

Pooh-Bah. Oh, as your Solicitor, I should have no hesitation in saying, "Chance it."

Ko-Ko. Thank you. (*Shaking his hand*) I will.

Pooh-Bah. If it were not that, as Lord Chief Justice, I am bound to see that the law isn't violated.

Ko-Ko. I see. Come over here where the Chief Justice can't hear us. (*They cross the stage*) Now, then, as First Lord of the Treasury?

Pooh-Bah. Of course, as First Lord of the Treasury, I could propose a spe-

[24] Mirra Komarovsky, "Cultural Contradictions and Sex Roles," *American Journal of Sociology*, Vol. 52 (1946), pp. 184-189. Reprinted by permission of the University of Chicago Press.

cial vote that would cover all expenses, if it were not that, as Leader of the Opposition, it would be my duty to resist it, tooth and nail. Or, as Paymaster-General, I could so cook the accounts that, as Lord High Auditor, I should never discover the fraud. But then, as Archbishop of Titipu, it would be my duty to denounce my dishonesty and give myself into my own custody as First Commissioner of Police.

Ko-Ko. That's extremely awkward.[25]

The foregoing well illustrates a fact of social life, namely, that the social meaning of a situation varies with one's status and role and that multiple role relationships can and sometimes do produce extremely awkward situations.[26]

Another aspect of meaning and social organization concerns such matters as initiative, motivation, and creativity. As any plant executive or foreman well knows, the organization of the division of labor within the plant can vary from chaotic to very efficient and this, of course, affects group output.[27] In a very important sense the study of social organization is a study in the development and use of social power for the attainment of ends.

In summary, we have seen how one's perception of the qualities of others affects his interpretations of their meaning to him; also, we have shown that group structure and social organization contribute to the definition of social situations and hence to meaning.

The reader should not conclude that all meaning is determined by social interaction. It can, of course, be argued that all shared meanings are socially conditioned. What is contended specifically is that all elements of human experience that are perceived as having consequences for persons or the system that sustains them will be assigned meaning in terms of the perceived consequences. In other words, the meaning of a stimulus situation or an experience lies in its implications. As William James put it, a difference which makes no difference is no difference.

It is true that people affiliate and form group structures for utilitarian ends such as profits, power, and to solve the numerous problems of living in human society. However, it is also true that groups emerge out of less rational considerations, often having to do with pleasure and recreation. Let us examine next some of the findings on interaction and the *formation* of small groups. *Interaction* is here defined as the exchange of meaning between people.

[25] W. S. Gilbert, *Original Plays, Third Series* (London, Chatto and Windus, 1903), pp. 182-183.
[26] S. A. Stouffer, "An Analysis of Conflicting Social Norms," *American Sociological Review*, Vol. 14 (1949), pp. 707-717.
[27] Charles D. Orth et al., *Administering Research and Development* (Homewood, Ill., Richard D. Irwin, Inc., and The Dorsey Press, 1964).

5. INTERACTION AND THE FORMATION OF SMALL GROUPS

The formation of small informal groups rests on the interaction of people under the conditions of shared values, attitudes, and beliefs. Informal groups may be voluntary, that is, free-formed, or they may be involuntary. Friendship groups are an example of free-forming groups and the family and work groups are examples of involuntary or institutionalized associations.

Traditionally, the concept of the small group has been less than precise. The sociologist is more concerned with the nature and properties of the social relationships that constitute the interaction system than with the number of people as such. Although it is difficult to describe either with precision, the number of people is generally assumed to vary from two to twenty. If the total is much larger than twenty, there is a tendency to break up into smaller subgroups.

What are the properties of the social relationships that constitute a small group? *First*, the interaction and activity spring from inner feelings rather than from external pressures. That is, the relations are personal and face-to-face. *Secondly*, the members value the relationships as ends in themselves.

Obviously, there may be many kinds of such small groups. Berelson and Steiner in their survey of findings on human behavior identify four varieties of small groups. These are

> (1) the autonomous group, e.g., a circle of close friends built on free choice and voluntary association; (2) the institutionalized small group, e.g., the family; (3) the small group within a large organization, often called a mediating group because of its linking position between the individual and the organization, e.g., the work group in a factory or office, a group of soldiers (buddies) in the army; and (4) the problem-solving group, e.g., a committee with a task to perform.
>
> Taken as a whole, these categories come down to two broad types—those small groups with specific tasks to do and those, like the family, with more diffuse purposes. Another way to look at them is to think of those groups mainly oriented to the task (such as a work group), those mainly oriented to social and emotional satisfactions (such as a bridge club), and those oriented to achieving roughly equivalent amounts of each objective (such as some voluntary associations involved in charitable activity).[28]

---

[28] Bernard Berelson and Gary A. Steiner, *Human Behavior: An Inventory of Scientific Findings* (New York, Harcourt, Brace & World, Inc., 1964), p. 326.

Some Findings

Many studies have shown that the sharing of personal beliefs, particularly beliefs which are relevant to group ends, facilitates friendships among the members. Also, close personal interaction produces a similarity of relevant attitudes.

Homans postulates that

> Interaction between persons leads to sentiments of liking, which express themselves in new activities, and these in turn mean further interaction. . . . The more frequently persons interact with one another, the stronger their sentiments of friendship for one another are apt to be. . . . The more frequently persons interact with one another, the more alike in some respects both their activities and sentiments tend to become.[29]

The would-be wit will, of course, remonstrate that if Homans' second statement is true then all husbands and wives should become more and more attached through time. However, Homans' generalization is not intended to cover interaction under any or all conditions. It is more in respect to free-forming groups and groups of relatively short, not lifetime, durations. Homans' generalization is, in most cases, true. The more interaction there is within a group, the more positive are the feelings of the members toward the group.

Since physical distance between people would affect their opportunity for interaction, then, other things being equal, it would be expected that people would tend to choose others as friends on the basis of the physical distance between them. For example, a study of housing projects shows

> a strong relationship between sociometric choice and physical distance. In both projects the greatest number of choices were made to people living closest to the persons choosing and the choices decreased continuously as distance from the home of the chooser increased. The actual measured distances involved were quite small, in no case being larger than 180 feet. Yet the effect of even these small distances is . . . marked. . . . This same relationship holds for choices outside of the court or building. The greater the physical separation between any two points in these communities, the fewer the friendships.[30]

The net effect of distance on social interaction can be assessed only by holding constant the other factors which affect mutual attraction. For example, like or similar occupations significantly affect choice of

---

[29] George C. Homans, *The Human Group* (New York, Harcourt, Brace & World, Inc., 1950), pp. 119, 120, 133.

[30] Leon Festinger, Stanley Schachter, and Kurt Back, *Social Pressures in Informal Groups* (New York, Harper & Row, Publishers, Inc., 1950), pp. 431-444.

friends, but one's choice of friends within his occupation is affected by physical distance.

The general conclusion cited from Festinger et al. is illustrated by the following set of data:

TABLE 9:1

The Relationship Between Sociometric Choice and Physical Distance on One Floor of a Westgate West Building [31]

1 UNITS OF APPROXIMATE PHYSICAL DISTANCE	2 TOTAL NUMBER OF CHOICES GIVEN	3 TOTAL NUMBER OF POSSIBLE CHOICES	4 CHOICES GIVEN (2) (DIVIDED BY) POSSIBLE CHOICES (3)
1	112	8 × 34	.412
2	46	6 × 34	.225
3	22	4 × 34	.162
4	7	2 × 34	.103

If a group relationship is not satisfying in a psychological sense, then the participants who are not being satisfied will work to modify the relationship or to find membership in a new group. Berelson and Steiner generalize as follows:

> There is a tendency for people to gravitate into groups or subgroups with the effect of maximizing their shared values.
> We say "with the effect of" rather than "in order to" because the gravitation is not always rational and deliberate. But if the group is insufficiently comfortable, in a psychological sense, the individual will be on the lookout for a more congenial set of associates, either within or outside of the group —for congeniality he must find in order to feel assured of the correctness of his own behavior.[32]

The failure to have one's beliefs and opinions validated is one of the reasons why some people with unusual personality traits or characteristics have difficulty adjusting in small towns or villages, but can adjust reasonably well in large cities. In this regard Newcomb notes that: "The one way in which it is possible for a population to satisfy both the individual-autistic demands and the demands of social reality is to sort itself into subgroups which are in fact characterized by this kind of

[31] Ibid., p. 38.
[32] Berelson and Steiner, op. cit., p. 328.

consensus." [33] Newcomb is referring to a consensus of values among the group members.

Homans generalized that there is a mutual dependence of activity and interaction, that is, interaction generates engagement in activities and activities strengthen bonds for interaction. A study by Deutsch and Collins indicates that in situations where prejudice is not very high the introduction of personal contact between the members of different ethnic groups tends to lessen the prejudice.

TABLE 9:2

Percentages of Housewives in the Project Reporting Favorable Change, No Change, or Unfavorable Change in Their Attitudes Toward Negroes [34]

PRESENT ATTITUDE	INTEGRATED INTERRACIAL PROJECTS		SEGREGATED BIRACIAL PROJECTS	
	Knoaltown	*Sacktown*	*Bakerville*	*Frankville*
Favorable change	59%	62%	27%	18%
No change	38	31	66	69
Unfavorable change	3	7	7	13
Total number of cases	(99)	(89)	(99)	(100)

Stouffer also found that white troops in World War II who had experience with Negro troops or who were in units related to other units that had Negro troops expressed attitudes favorable to serving in a company containing Negro and white platoons. For example, 7 percent of a sample of infantrymen in a company that had a Negro platoon stated that they would very much dislike serving in an integrated company, whereas 62 percent of a sample that had not had such experience stated that they would very much dislike such a set-up.[35]

It seems reasonable to argue, as Berelson and Steiner do, that a situation even more favorable to the lessening of prejudice is when ethnic groups meet on personal terms, or on common tasks where the interests cut across ethnic lines.[36] The combining of personal motivation and the external pressure arising from common tasks increases the conditions favorable to attitude change.

The interracial housing and combat situations contain elements of

[33] Theodore M. Newcomb, "The Study of Consensus," in Robert K. Merton et al., eds., *Sociology Today: Problems and Prospects* (New York, Basic Books, Inc., Publishers, 1959), pp. 277-292.

[34] Morton Deutsch and Mary E. Collins, *Interracial Housing: A Psychological Evaluation of a Social Experiment* (Minneapolis, University of Minnesota Press, 1951), p. 97.

[35] Samuel A. Stouffer, *op. cit.*, p. 594.

[36] Berelson and Steiner, *op. cit.*, p. 513.

cross-pressures. That is, the members simultaneously feel pressures to conform and not to conform. The demands and pressures of the immediate situation call for conforming while at the same time leaders from certain other groups of which some participants are also members may be calling for nonconformity. This is well illustrated by efforts to racially integrate schools in certain communities of both the northern and southern areas of the United States. For example, there are those who place the norm of maintaining stability and order in the schools above the norm of school segregation, while on the other hand there are those who would rather see the schools disrupted than see them integrated. How are such cross-pressures resolved?

There are at least one general principle and two corollary ones which will explain the outcome of such cross-pressures. *The individual caught in cross-pressures between the norms of different groups of which he is simultaneously a member will resolve the conflict in the direction of the most strongly felt norm.* But what determines the weight of a norm to a participant? The answer, in general, is two kinds of sanctions—*rewards* and *punishments*. Are the rewards greater and the punishments less on one side than the other? We can now state the two corollary principles as: (1) The strength of the norm is determined by the size and importance of the reward to the person and the group for conforming, and (2) the seriousness and certainty of punishment for violating the norm. For example, taking the illustration on school integration, the principal reward for conforming is the continuing of public schools. Given the federal law which states that segregation of public schools is "inherently unequal" and hence illegal, then what are the consequences of violation? The consequence seems to be quite clear that most people, white and Negro, would not get an education. Hence the punishment would be two-fold. That is, it would have severe consequences to the children of individual families, and obviously a breakdown in the education of the citizenry of an industrial society would have grave consequences for the social system itself. Accordingly, it is easy to see why resistance to efforts to integrate public schools waned sharply once it was clear that the federal government had the will and the right to enforce it.

Space will not permit us to summarize even the majority of the literature on conditions and factors involved in the formation of groups. Unquestionably the principal element underlying the formation of groups is an evolutionary one. That is, man is biologically a social animal in that human needs and human society are maintained and perpetuated through a process of division of labor, sometimes called social organization. In other words, group life is a *form of social organization* and one which has been so successful as to suggest almost boundless possibilities.

Perhaps we should elaborate on the idea of the group as a form of social organization. Is a number of people who appear by chance at a given time to ride an elevator a group? They may interact silently or verbally as they ride the elevator. That is, they may accommodate to each other by automatically taking into account perceived needs, such as pushing the button for another or moving over to make room, and so on. Obviously, interaction is present, but is interaction alone all that is meant by the term group? Of course, the answer lies in our identifying the aspects of social reality referred to by the use of the concept of group. There are two major aspects which we have emphasized. The first is the element of mutual attraction to mutual activities, and the second is the sharing of beliefs and values and an explicit or implicit division of labor or responsibilities in regard to the shared activities.

Influence of Small Groups on the Individual

If the small group is a human resource for obtaining recognition, validation of one's ideas, affection, esteem, and a means of social power, then group influences on individual behavior should be expected to be strong. It is also expected that group processes influence the development of behavior as well as affect one's response at a particular time.

The small group greatly influences the behavior of its members by exhibiting and enforcing norms for expected or proper behavior by its members not only for the activities of the group itself but for many situations in which the group is not directly involved.

The learning of group norms is like learning a language. In the learning of a language one does not just memorize sentences. One learns words and how to combine words into phrases and how to combine phrases into sentences. The problem of how to combine these elements is solved by implicitly and explicitly learning the rules of syntax for a language. I say "implicitly" because many rules of language are learned and correctly practiced without the person being able to verbalize the exact rule involved. Group norms have a logical structure in the sense of the group's given means-ends schema. Given the means-ends schema, the norms are perceived in terms of their implications for the individual per se and in terms of their implications for the goals of the group. This, of course, assumes that the members value the group; otherwise, it is assumed that the group would break up.

The small group is where a great deal of efficient as well as inefficient behaviors are learned. Children who grow up in the isolation produced by poverty and who are surrounded by a sea of plenty acquire a self-image that is self-defeating. Their aspirations are reduced and their self-confidence for moving into the larger society is severely weakened. It would be easier to resocialize an able child from an underdeveloped country such as one of the new nations of Africa than to resocialize an equally able American child born into a fourth generation family of poverty. The child from the primitive culture has not been repeatedly "told" that he cannot achieve this or that. This dramatic example is intended to call attention to the fact that the group life of a society in which a child is reared exhibits a ready-made answer for the child to the question, "Who am I?" The answer is different in different social and cultural contexts and relationships, and the child soon discovers in a variety of ways the answer appropriate to his immediate situation.

Human socialization is not just the process of learning specific skills for using machines, language, and problem-solving behavior, but also the learning of the cultural prescriptions and proscriptions of a particular society. These include attitudes toward different ethnic, religious, and racial groups; toward authority; toward right and wrong; toward one's responsibility to fellows and the larger community.

Most of these are not explicitly taught but are implicitly illustrated by those in positions of authority and by those with whom we identify. The following quotation from an unpublished manuscript on "The Transmission of Racial Attitudes Among White Southerners" well illustrates the process in respect to the use of the term "lady" in the reminiscing of a college student.

> Once when I was a little girl a Negro woman came to the door. I told my aunt a lady wanted to see her. She went to the door, and when she came back she told me that I should have said a colored woman was there to see her. I wondered about it a little, but I think I didn't question it.
>
> Once when we were in the car, I said, "Oh, Mother, look! That colored lady has on a dress just like yours." Well, Mother was a little upset about the dress, but she didn't say so. She said, "Agnes, call them colored women. There are no colored ladies."
>
> I remember when I learned that lesson. I told Mother the wash-lady was here. She said to say "woman," and I asked why. Mother explained that you never say Negro lady. She said "lady" was a term of respect applied to a few white ladies and to no Negroes at all.
>
> About five years ago we were riding through Memphis one day, and I saw a Negro standing on the street corner. She was all dressed up, and she looked very pretty. I said to Mother, "Isn't that a pretty Negro lady?" Mother called me down for it. She told me to say woman. I wanted to know why, and she didn't answer me. I said, "I don't believe there is any reason. I think you just don't like them . . . like Grandmother." Golly, was I sorry I'd said that! Mother lectured me about respect for my elders.[37]

It is interesting to note that instruction was given after the child had "erred" in racial behavior. In other words, the norms of a group usually

[37] From page 4 of an unpublished and undated paper on "The Transmission of Racial Attitudes Among White Southerners," by Olive Westbrooke Quinn. Paper read before the Southern Sociological Society, date not given.

convey, but not always clearly, what is meant by misbehavior as well as expected behavior. Models for behavior are concepts of what behavior should be. The model does not and is not intended to describe actual behavior. The difference between the model and actual behavior may or may not result in self-examination and evaluation. The likelihood of its doing so depends upon how closely the subject identifies with the model.

The group influences we have discussed so far are general influences of the sort one expects in group socialization. Let us turn now to more specific influences by first examining some effects of the property of group cohesiveness on problem-solving.

Cohesiveness and Problem-Solving. By cohesiveness we mean a high degree of mutual acceptance and mutual attraction among the members of a group. How does this affect problem-solving or decision-making? The answer is, as always, that the effects vary with other conditions of the group. What other conditions? First, do the members have equal ability or are they significantly unequal?

If the abilities are unequal and the group is highly cohesive, then the pressures are strong toward agreement, so strong that there is a tendency to avoid resistance in favor of keeping the peace.[38] Because of the mutual acceptance of everyone's ideas, this may result in the loss of the more highly creative ideas of the more able members of the group. Thus a high degree of group cohesiveness where the members' abilities and skills are heterogeneous leads to a great degree of "getting along well together" but at the expense of quality. On the other hand, a high degree of cohesiveness or liking is likely to facilitate communication.

Status and Power Influences. Every group develops norms necessary to regulate behavior toward the attainment of the ends of the group leaders. This suggests that power is unequally distributed within groups. This is especially true among the members of work groups, institutional groups and problem-solving groups. In these types of groups the power differences are arranged by the status structure of the group. There is also an unequal distribution of power with a peer group or friendship group, but the basis for the power difference is individual differences in abilities and skills rather than status differences.

But how do status differences within a group influence behavior? First, there is a tendency for the higher status members, that is, the more powerful ones, to define the rules and specify the attitudes and behaviors desired and expected. The reasons for this are not hard to find. The high status members of the group are also the members with the greatest responsibility and resources for goal attainment. The social power of a person depends directly upon the quantity and quality of

---

[38] Kurt W. Back, "Influence Through Social Communication," *Journal of Abnormal Social Psychology,* Vol. 46 (1951), pp. 9-23.

his resources to attain the ends of the group and/or organization and to reward or satisfy those who depend upon him. Thus a person with great economic resources is very powerful because he possesses the means on which a great many others are dependent. One's social power also varies with what Thibaut and Kelley have called the number and quality of alternatives available to the dependents. If they have no alternatives, then the power is very great. If they have other alternatives or better alternatives, then the power of the group's high status members relative to the other members is less.

Parents have great power over children, and family norms develop in the direction of parental interests rather than the children's. However, as the children become older and become members of other groups, their position in the family changes and likewise their power and influence. In other words, their status alternatives have increased.

Max Weber [39] and Robert MacIver, to name only two, have differentiated several kinds of power. More recently, French and Raven [40] have made similar distinctions and discussed these in terms of their social psychological effects. We will briefly note five types or bases of power as delineated by French and Raven and note some of the effects of each.

Some Forms of Power. Reward power is based on one person's perception of another's ability to mediate or influence rewards for him. A parent has power over a child because so many of the child's wants are dependent upon the parent's approval and procurement. In regard to adults, a supervisor or an employer has power over an employee because he holds the key to promotions and salary increases. Many new "friendships" are formed when someone learns that an acquaintance of his or hers is a close friend to someone who holds potential rewards for the former.

Just as one has power to reward, he also has power to coerce and thus a second type of power is *coercive power*. The withholding of rewards is a form of punishment or coercion. The strength of these power sources and hence their degree of influence depends upon (1) the magnitude of the rewards or punishments involved and (2) the perceived likelihood of their occurrence should one elect a given course of action.

Another type of power derives from the fact that a person may come to like so well the one who significantly rewards him that he psy-

[39] Max Weber, *The Theory of Social and Economic Organization*, translated by A. M. Henderson and Talcott Parsons (New York, Oxford University Press, 1947). See especially Part III. See also Part II on power in *From Max Weber: Essays in Sociology*, translated and edited by H. H. Gerth and C. Wright Mills (New York, Oxford University Press, 1946).

[40] J. R. P. French, Jr., and B. H. Raven, "The Bases of Social Power," in Dorwin Cartwright, ed., *Studies in Social Power* (Ann Arbor, The University of Michigan Press, 1959), pp. 118-149.

chologically *identifies* with the rewarder. This type of power is called *referent power*. Thus reward power may acquire the added property of referent power, but of course coercive power would not. Referent power means that the person is so attracted to his referent that he models his behavior after the referent, presumably because he wants to become like him. To the extent that one person perceives another as his ego ideal, then the latter has witting or unwitting power over the former. Referent power has the advantage of being obeyed even in the absence of the referent, whereas reward power and coercive power do not.

The other two forms which French and Raven mention are *expert power* and legitimate power. The latter is sometimes called *authority*. Expert power is derived from someone holding scarce knowledge that is highly prized. The scientist who possesses special knowledge which enables him to solve important problems for society and make important discoveries or the physician who can cure or prevent dreaded diseases each possesses power to influence those in need of such knowledge or skill.

Legitimate power derives from the norms and rights of an office and the acceptance of these norms by those dependent upon or related to the office. Thus a police officer has the power under certain conditions to make arrests, and corporation and organizational officials have the power to hire and dismiss an employee.

Legitimate power is restricted to the office or position and may be broad or narrow in scope. The President of the United States has great power as President, but when his term of office expires he loses this power.

The problem of how power is transformed into legitimate power (or the processes of power legitimation) constitutes a sociological problem of great importance. It provides the basis for the stability of governments and it underlies the basis of consent or the acceptance by the governed of the right of governments to govern. In other words, it is the source of the people's definition of the validity of the uses of power and one's belief in the justice of power decisions. The explanation to the question of what makes for a mutual feeling of justice and fairness in social exchange is far from satisfactory. Certainly, one of the conditions necessary for a mutual feeling of fairness in exchange, whether the exchange is service in return for money or whatever form of exchange, is mutual acceptance by the participants of the norms or standards for exchange and their mutual compliance with these. In other words, submission to authority or legitimate power is willing compliance. But this is reinforced by the social constraints of the group or organization.

Referring back to the Thibaut-Kelley and Homans' *exchange theory* of behavior, we can see that the above forms of power may be translated into notions of rewards and costs. Hence the probability of one's significantly influencing another depends upon his ability to present the other with a clear possibility of rewarding him if he refuses to comply. If the student will observe carefully, he will note that the above formulation on rewards and costs will help explain much everyday behavior. For example, since man is a biosocial animal he necessarily depends upon his fellows for need satisfaction. Since he is *dependent* upon others, then, he is subject to the power of others and so are the "others" dependent upon a different set of others and so on *ad infinitum*.

Man's interdependency is reflected in his social organization. In the introductory part of this chapter we defined a concrete or particular organization as a set of interrelated groups. A person who receives a satisfactory reward for associating with another is motivated to continue the association. The same holds for groups that are dependent upon other groups.

Sherif conducted an experiment on in-group formation and intergroup relations which will help clarify some of the discussion in Section 5 on group formation.

6. SHERIF'S EXPERIMENT ON IN-GROUP FORMATION AND INTERGROUP RELATIONS—THE RED DEVILS AND BULL DOGS

The principal purpose of this experiment was to experimentally produce friction and negative stereotypes between two groups and, following this, to ascertain means and conditions for re-establishing harmony and cooperation between the groups.

Sherif formulated the following hypotheses:

> 1. When individuals having no established relationships are brought together in a group situation to interact in group activities with common goals, they produce a group structure with hierarchical positions and roles within it. This group structure implies positive in-group identifications and common attitudes, and tends in time to generate by-products or *norms* peculiar to the group. . . .
> 2. If two in-groups thus formed are brought into functional relationship under conditions of competition and group frustration, attitudes and appropriate hostile actions in relation to the out-group and its members will arise. . . .[41]

What conditions must be arranged in order to test these hypotheses? In the first place, the conditions must be arranged so as to preclude the

---

[41] *Groups in Harmony and Tension*, by Muzafer Sherif and Carolyn W. Sherif. (Copyright, 1953, by Harper & Bros.) Reprinted by permission of Harper & Row, Publishers, Inc., pp. 236-237.

formation of the groups and the development of positive or negative relations between them on the basis of factors other than those to be introduced experimentally. Some of the major factors that were controlled were previous experience, ethnic and class differences, religion, education, age, and sex.

Sherif selected twenty-four boys who were homogeneous in background. They were all close to twelve years of age. All were Protestant, lower middle-class. Nineteen came from the same denomination and the remaining five from highly similar denominations. The educational opportunities and backgrounds of the boys were similar.

The experiment was planned in three stages.

> *Stage I* was planned as the period of informal groupings on the basis of personal inclinations and interests. All activities were camp-wide, offering maximum freedom for choice and "mixing up" of boys in various games and camp duties. Thus it became possible to single out budding friendship groups and, more or less, to equate the weights of such personal factors in the two experimental groups of Stage II.
>
> *Stage II* was planned as the stage of formation of in-groups as similar as possible in number and composition of members. Each experimental group would participate separately in activities involving all the members of the group. Activities were chosen on the basis of their appeal value to the boys and their involvement of the whole group. Different activities afforded varied situations in which all members of a group could find opportunities to participate and "shine." All rewards given in this period were made on a group-unit basis, not to particular individuals.
>
> *Stage III* was planned to study *intergroup relations* between the two experimental in-groups thus produced when these groups were brought into contact (1) in a series of competitive activities and situations and (2) in mildly frustrating situations so arranged that the actions of one group were frustrating to the other.[42]

The frustrating experiences were so arranged that all the members of a group saw the frustrations as their own because they interfered with *their group*, and great care was taken to insure that the frustrating situations were not blamed on the adults in the situation, but on the other group of boys. Sherif reports that this effort was successful. Let us turn now to an examination of the results of the experiment.

RESULTS OF THE EXPERIMENT

Let us recall that the data obtained related to in-group formation, differentiation of group structure, and the development and subsequent reduction of intergroup tensions.

---

[42] *Ibid.*, p. 239.

In Stage I the boys were allowed to interact freely so that budding friendship clusters could be developed and ascertained.

Recall that if the hypotheses are to be tested certain conditions must be experimentally created. First, if we are to argue about group behavior, then we must be able to show that groups have been created and not just an aggregate of personalities. Sherif was able to demonstrate this by sociograms which revealed the existence of clusters of boys who restricted their interaction to the cluster members. It was also revealed by such observations as the following: "When one of us doesn't do something, then none of us do it."[43] This remark of one set of boys was a fairly typical index of the group-oriented behavior that arose among the participants in Stage I.

Now if we are to argue that in-groups arise out of interaction in response to common goals, then we need to have subjects who are not already related to one another as in-group members. Inasmuch as the experience in Stage I has revealed who the members of the in-group or friendship clusters are, then with this information we are able to split up the friendship groups and make two experimental groups composed of a minimum number of preference or friendship choices.

The two experimental groups were formed by taking boys who showed preference for one another and putting them into separate groups. If more than one friendship choice was made, the experimenters put the boy in the group holding the *fewest* of *his* friendship choices. The two resulting experimental groups came to be known as the Red Devils and the Bull Dogs and with these two groups Stage II was started.

Stage II was the period of experimental in-group formation, which lasted five days. Activities were designed to create a feeling of group membership and identity of the group as such. Rewards were made on a group basis rather than to individuals. In this period, leadership patterns emerged and the data clearly indicated that a group structure with a high degree of solidarity arose despite the splitting of the initial friendship clusters.

The experimenter tested to see if the friendship choices that arose during Stage I persisted through Stage II. He did this by asking the boys to list those boys they liked best *in the whole camp*, that is, from the other group as well as their own. It is interesting to note that the reversals were almost total. The table below summarizes the friendship choices at end of Stage I and again at the end of Stage II.

It is clear from the above table that friendship choices, at first, were predominantly for individuals who were placed in the experimental outgroups; however, by the end of Stage II the choices shifted and were definitely in the direction of the developing in-groups.

[43] *Ibid.*, p. 245.

TABLE 9:3

Total Choices of Friends at the End of Stage I
and End of Stage II (Note the Reversals) [44]

	CHOICES MADE BY:	CHOICES RECEIVED BY:	
		Eventual In-Group	Eventual Out-Group
End of Stage I	Eventual Red Devils	35.1%	64.9%
	Eventual Bull Dogs	35.0%	65.0%
		In-Group	Out-Group
End of Stage II	Red Devils	95.0%	5.0%
	Bull Dogs	87.7%	12.3%

The foregoing table affords clear evidence which affirms hypothesis 1. In other words, it was found that when experimentally formed groups were placed in situations and engaged in activities calling for group cooperation toward common goals, in-group structures developed with hierarchical positions and roles.

Stage III was the stage of *intergroup relations* and it formally lasted nearly five days. In Stage III open competition was fostered between the groups. Certain frustrating experiences were carefully manipulated by the experimenters so that one group's failure or unfortunate experience would appear to be caused by the other group. Daily ball games and tugs of war were participated in with the winner receiving so many points and a prize. A poster with two thermometers was placed on the bulletin board and reflected the rising score of each group.

As the competition became keener, the two groups began making posters which were caricatures of the other.

Near the end of the experiment a big party was held for both groups. Half of the food was slightly damaged by the experimenters, and the Red Devils were allowed to eat first so they took the undamaged food. When the Bull Dogs entered, they saw the damaged goods and attributed it to the Red Devils. Some wanted to fight immediately but they decided to eat what they could. Following this, they retired to a corner and began to hurl insults at the Red Devils. When the Red Devils started to leave, one Bull Dog was seen putting an empty ice cream carton on the Red Devils' table. This led to physical contact and one Bull Dog opened a knife and had to be restrained.

This later led to a series of raids and fights between the two groups which had to be stopped. In other words, Stage III ended with the production of great tensions and open hostilities. At this point the experi-

[44] *Ibid.*, p. 268.

GROUPS AND ORGANIZATIONS

menters decided to concentrate on breaking down the in-groups. To a considerable extent they were successful. The principal means used was to initiate programs in which all boys would participate on a camp-wide basis. This tended to break down the in-group structures.

This study clearly shows that by careful designing of social situations it is possible to form or create social groups. It is also possible to instill beliefs in the minds of group members that are antagonistic to the out-group irrespective of what the out-group itself does.

Another striking result from this experiment showed that, despite the fact that these boys did not have a history of any "behavior problems" or had not previously engaged in fighting, by manipulating certain variables dealing with frustration and competition it was possible to generate such problems. This has many very important implications for crime and delinquency as well as for emotional disorders. For example, the Red Devils and Bull Dogs blamed each other more sharply when one thought that the other was violating the rules or cheating. In other words, unequal application of the rules to people who expect equal application will generate hostility and, if continued, then eventually aggression. In this regard, Cloward and Ohlin have developed an important theory of delinquency. In general, they argue that when a segment of a society is denied the legitimate means to attain legitimate goals there is a tendency for the members to employ illegitimate means of goal attainment.[45]

7. SUMMARY

In this chapter we have analyzed social behavior from two different perspectives. First, we examined it from the perspective of societal and group functioning; and secondly, we examined it from the standpoint of the effects of group-structured environments on individual behavior.

Let us review first from the perspective of societal and group functioning. In this regard, we started with the observation that man is biologically a social animal and as such he is greatly dependent one upon another. This interdependence is reflected in two important forms of social life: social groups and social organizations. Though men are biologically and socially interdependent, they meet their needs and the needs of their system of social organization by developing a division of labor which *roughly* distributes and assigns the members to positions in the population in terms of ability, training, and skills. There are, of course, generally more people of high ability and training than there are top positions in a society, but this allows, potentially at least, for increased competition and circulation of men of ability.

[45] Richard A. Cloward and Lloyd E. Ohlin, *Delinquency and Opportunity: A Theory of Delinquent Gangs* (New York, The Free Press of Glencoe, Inc., 1960).

Man has concerned himself for centuries with the problem of explaining the presence and development of human social organization. We have not concerned ourselves with trying to explain this, but instead we have assumed that given the biological nature of man, then man's social organization is an evolving system of human adaptation. The essential ingredient of the system is man's accumulated stock of information and ideas. However, data and ideas are by themselves inert. To activate them for the service of man, some form of organization is necessary. *The smaller the stock of information and ideas, the less elaborate the social organization that is needed to implement these.* The student who is familiar with ethnographic data may cite the Arunta or Aranda as an exception to this statement. The Arunta have a very simple material culture but a very involved social organization.

A careful analysis will show that they do not constitute an exception but instead a good example of the statement. Kinship has become extremely important to the Arunta and as a consequence a great deal of information and classification of kin exists. Their kinship system becomes, in fact, the core or heart of their very extensive social organization.

The converse of the above proposition on social organization is also assumed to be true; that is, the larger the stock of information and ideas possessed by a society, the more elaborate the social organization needed to utilize the information. Evidence for this proposition is easily noted by simply comparing the social organization of a small business firm to that of a large corporation.

Man's social organization, unlike the social organization of the ant, is transmitted from generation to generation through social communication and learning. Given a biological species like man whose sociability is directly a function of culture and learning, then it is reasonable to assume that human social organization and group behavior are necessary concomitants to these species' characteristics.

One of the important characteristics of human social organization is that the individual members are not biologically compelled to conform to the organization patterns as are, for example, ants and bees. Nevertheless, conformity is in fact the rule, so an important sociological problem is "Why?" And, of course, related to this is the question of how is this conformity and stability achieved? These two questions were given a tentative answer by making certain basic assumptions about social behavior.

These assumptions are: (1) Man individually is dependent upon other men for the meeting of his sociological, psychological, and biological needs and these dependencies extend from conception until the end of life. (2) Each and all of man's needs may be satisfied in one of several ways. (3) However, since the actual meeting of particular needs requires the cooperation and coordination of the efforts of others, then only one particular pattern of solution may be practiced at a given time. (4) To enable the coordination and integration of efforts to occur, norms arise out of the interactions involved. (5) These norms are reinforced by rewards and punishments.

Social norms were discussed in relation to social behavior. Norms were conceived as the basic rules for interaction in regard to specific situations. However, it was recognized that many social norms do not provide clear prescriptions and proscriptions for behavior and even when they do individuals are not equally committed to them. Nevertheless, people often have to interact under such "fuzzy" normative conditions and they do interact with reasonable skill and predictability. Thus it is clear that we need some additional concepts to account for the regularity in social behavior.

These additional concepts we borrowed from Cicourel reporting on some of Garfinkel's work. Garfinkel noted that in addition to the basic norms of a group or organization there are what he called "rules of preferred play" and "game-furnished conditions." "Rules of preferred play" were distinguished from basic rules by noting that the players or actors have some discretion in respect to compliance and in interpretation of the basic rules. This preference stems from tradition, skill, and efficiency of the actor. By "game-furnished conditions" Garfinkel means that some game situations like chess are completely defined and other games are less completely defined. Therefore, some game conditions contain more uncertainty than others. Everyday social behavior, for example, requires many decisions on the part of everyone and these decisions contain varying amounts of uncertainty. Hence a goodly amount of social interaction is based on "trust" and estimation.

Since the external environment contains a considerable amount of uncertainty, the person over time develops probabilistic estimations from which he makes modal judgments. In other words, the person over time develops an internal psychological stability and reacts to the external irregularities in terms of his internal model.

Following this, social behavior and meaning were discussed. It was argued that from the perspective of social psychology there were two major sources of meaning: *first*, the implications of the actions of others for one's own gratification or frustration; and *secondly*, the implications of the changes in a system of action or an organization for one's own position in the system. These sources of meaning were discussed in terms of *exchange theory* as per Homans, and Thibaut and Kelley. For example, it was recognized that social interaction provides a basis for a person's judgment as to the desirability or nondesirability of an actual or potential social relationship.

Finally, interaction and the formation of small groups were discussed. Four basic types of small groups were distinguished. These were (1) the autonomous group (example: close friends); (2) the institutionalized small group (example: the family); (3) the mediating group (example: the small group within a large organization); (4) the problem-solving group (example: the committee).

Group behavior was analyzed in terms of its rewards and punishments and as a system of power relationships. Four kinds of power were identified and the significance of each for behavior was discussed. These were (1) coercive power; (2) expert power; (3) referent power; and (4) legitimate power.

As an illustration of some of the findings on group behavior, Sherif's experiment on in-group formation and intergroup relations was presented and discussed in detail.

Further References

1. Peter M. Blau, *Exchange and Power in Social Life* (New York, John Wiley & Sons, Inc., 1964).
2. Dorwin Cartwright, Editor, *Studies in Social Power* (Ann Arbor, The University of Michigan Press, 1959).
3. Robert L. Kahn et al., *Organizational Stress: Studies in Role Conflict and Ambiguity* (New York, John Wiley & Sons, Inc., 1964).
4. James G. March and H. A. Simon, *Organizations* (New York, John Wiley & Sons, Inc., 1958).
5. Clovis R. Shepherd, *Small Groups: Some Sociological Perspectives* (San Francisco, Chandler Publishing Co., 1964).
6. Muzafer Sherif and Carolyn W. Sherif, *Reference Groups—Exploration into Conformity and Deviation of Adolescents* (New York, Harper and Row, Publishers, Inc., 1964).
7. John W. Thibaut and Harold H. Kelley, *The Social Psychology of Groups* (New York, John Wiley & Sons, Inc., 1959).

10
Behavior and Social Change

•

1. *Introduction*
2. *Aspects of Social Change That Tend to Evoke Anxiety*
3. *Social Organization, Social Values, and Related Psychological Attitudes*
   (a) *Institutions*
   (b) *Social Values and Social Change*
4. *Theories of Attitude Change and Organization*
   (a) *Introduction*
   (b) *The Nature and Meaning of Attitudes*
   (c) *Selected Theories of Attitude Structure and Change*
      1. Rosenberg's Affective-Cognitive Consistency Theory
      2. Festinger's Theory of Cognitive Dissonance
      3. Kelman's Three-Process Theory of Attitude Change
5. *Some Conclusions on Attitude Change*
6. *Social Influence, Social Change, and Social Attitudes*
7. *Summary*

1. INTRODUCTION

IN CHAPTER 9 it was shown that the individual develops an internal psychological stability in reaction to significant external uncertainties and irregularities and that he responds to these in terms of this internal model. This, of course, does not mean that he creates patterns from aspects of his environment that are totally irregular or random. It simply means that most, if not all, environmental factors and conditions show properties of variation as well as stability. This is particularly true in regard to man's institutions and his behavioral environment. In such circumstances the individual still has to respond to these variations and uncertainties and he does so on the basis of his estimation of what he conceives to be *typical.* This suggests that one's internal or psychological organization is correlated with one's perception of the externally typical. The fundamental question which we wish to consider in this chapter is this: How does the individual react and respond when fundamental change occurs in the typical structure of his environment? That is to say, given the individual's developed psychological stability which is based on one type of typicality, then what happens when change occurs in the external conditions on which the psychological stability is based?

We shall make the following assumptions about change—whether internal or behavioral, or external or environmental.

First, it is assumed that change in environmental properties and behavioral properties is continuous. We are not here concerned with giving a mathematical meaning to the term continuous, although such meaning is implied. It is sufficient to say it occurs in the behavior of a person throughout his lifetime although there are plateaus of stability and peaks and troughs of change. It is assumed that, within the life span of an individual, attitude change is least in the years of aging and greatest during the early years of experience and early manhood. Change in man's sociocultural environment is assumed also to be continuous, and the rate of change is probably in the form of a geometric progression. It is further assumed that the rate of social change increases with the increased complexity of the culture. The more elaborate the division of labor and the more extensive and rapid the systems of transportation and communication, then the higher the rate of social change. In other words, the more people change places of residence, and the more frequently more people contact other people, the greater the influence of the forces of change and hence the increasing rate of environmental change.

Secondly, it is assumed that change is a normal and natural property of all life and matter. Since our concern in this chapter is with changes in the human social system, we shall restrict our remarks about change to this system.

Change is both a source of human social problems and a means to their amelioration and control. The change from an agricultural mode of economic organization in the Western world to a commercial and industrial form made possible the urbanization of Western society. This in turn aggravated many existing social problems such as crime, disease, sanitation, and intergroup relations. In addition, it produced some new problems peculiar to the urban system. Some of these are an increased interdependence of the groups in the urban area, and the urban area itself with surrounding areas and other urban centers. The increased concentration of the population has created problems of air, water, and soil pollution, and traffic congestion. Urban change is also related to an increased rate of conflict in interests among the many local, state, regional, and federal governmental and administrative agencies and organizations both public and private. This in turn leads to the necessity for more centralized control in order to regulate and reduce the conflicts in interest and this, in a democratic society, produces a strain on traditional democratic values.

The foregoing discussion is intended to convey the notion that as the web of social life extends and as it generates more connecting strands and threads it becomes more and more difficult to maintain integration between the forces of changes and the forces of continuity. To somewhat oversimplify, we can say that in general the fewer the parts in interaction, the easier it is to maintain stability; and the greater the number of parts and systems in interaction, the more difficult it is to maintain a relative state of integration of parts.

Thus far we have emphasized the problems which accompany change, but this in reality appears to be the smaller part of the picture in social change. Let us look on the positive side for a moment. When we focus on the positive side, we see the great concentration of almost limitless power for solving problems irrespective of whether the problems are man-generated or derive from some other aspect of nature. Out of the social organization of urban life have come the many great contributions to knowledge that have reduced communicable diseases to manageable proportions and provided housing, employment security, health security, educational opportunities, and leisure for whole populations. While change will never open the gate to Utopia, it does yield in the long run an increase in human attainment of human ideals. It is a process of continuous becoming. Even this *faith* in the human capacity for improvement and betterment seems absolutely essential. If the majority of the members of a society assumed any other mental perspective toward change than that of faith in man's powers in the long run to become better situated, then that society's stability and perpetuation would indeed be in mortal danger. The reason for this is simple. Change is constantly with us. It is a part of life. Consequently, it is rational to expect man in the future to learn to explain and control change in his social environment just as he has learned to control aspects of his physical environment; and by so doing he would be gaining the means to regulate his future states and thus reduce the uncertainties and anxieties associated with social change.

Let us look now at some of the reasons for anxiety as well as hope in man's attitude toward change.

2. ASPECTS OF SOCIAL CHANGE THAT TEND TO EVOKE ANXIETY

It is necessary that we recall or review the portions of Chapter 9 which pertain to social norms. In this chapter we spoke of two types of social organization. These were groups and organizations. A social group was defined as two or more people in interaction for the purpose of some common interest. We defined an organization as a collection of groups whose activities are coordinated toward some goal or set of goals. These two forms of social organization (groups and organizations) are, in effect, external systems of adaptation.

The rules or norms which regulate interaction among individuals within groups as well as between individuals and groups or between groups in an organization constitute a *cognitive system*. A cognitive system is composed of any set of knowledge, beliefs, or opinions about any object of reference. Thus we have systems of ideology about political and economic organization. We have systems of technology for industrial organization and systems of mores and folkways for family and religious organization in a given society. In other words, a cognitive system is viewed as a part of the larger cultural system of a society and it functions to provide meaning for experience, whether individual or social.

In our discussion of group behavior in Chapter 9 a distinction was made between the norms or basic rules for behavior within a group or an organization and the preferred rules of action by the individual members. This distinction is necessary in order to take into account the variation of the participants' actual behavior from the normative standards. The participants may know equally well the norms but their perception of what is the best strategy for them to follow will vary with the person's personality, his position in the social structure, and his past experience with similar situations.

The foregoing will allow us to define what we mean by social change. Keeping in mind that we have derived two types of social organization, namely, groups and organizations, we now define *social change* as any modification in the social organization of a collection of people. Change in the American family system from its structure of monogamy to, say, polygyny or polyandry would be an example. The recent Civil Rights Bill which made segregation of the American Negro illegal is another example. These two examples are societal in scope and it should not be construed that all social change is of this range. It may be restricted to a community or a group. For example, a community may change from a community of local land and business ownership to one of largely absentee ownership.

Now that we have a clearer view of what we mean by social change, it should be easier to follow the discussion on reasons for anxiety about social change.

Since change implies a difference in the state of a system at different points in time, it is important to ask what difference would a change of a given sort make to the participants or those involved? As William James put it, a difference which makes no difference is no difference. A given change may be perceived by some as not making any difference to their situation; hence they would be expected to have a neutral attitude toward the change in question. Others may perceive the change as having negative consequences for their positions; hence they would have negative attitudes toward it. And for others the change may be perceived as contributing positively to their situations; therefore they would be expected to reveal a positive attitude.

While new knowledge properly applied brings forth progress, it also brings forth sorrow. Bredemeier and Stephenson, in discussing the reasons for man's resistance to the acceptance of scientific knowledge, suggest three major factors. These factors apply equally well in our effort to understand man's anxiety toward social change. They explain the resistance of the nonscientists to new knowledge by noting that new knowledge is threatening because it makes traditional ways of doing things obsolete. They note three kinds of obsolescence that are of especial importance in helping us understand the anxiety associated with social change.[1] These three kinds of obsolescence are the obsolescence of *ideas*, the obsolescence of *status*, and the obsolescence of *irresponsibility*.

Those who are familiar with the history of ideas will know the anxiety shown by the Church in the Western world over Darwin's concept of evolution. Also, those who are familiar with the history of physics will know of the great effort which physicist Max Planck exerted in trying to prevent the acceptance among physicists of the new theories of Albert Einstein. Men's self-images are threatened when they perceive that their ideas are about to become obsolescent.[2]

The development and application of new knowledge in automation is making it necessary for many people to develop new careers within their lifetime or else they become obsolescent. Hence, change in the processes of industrial organization renders obsolete many occupational careers. This is a form of status obsolescence and it threatens a man's sense of worth and his means to adapt. Of course, important new positions are

---

[1] Harry C. Bredemeier and Richard M. Stephenson, *The Analysis of Social Systems* (New York, Holt, Rinehart and Winston, Inc., 1962), pp. 269-271.
[2] Robert K. Merton, "Priorities in Scientific Discovery," *American Sociological Review*, Vol. 22 (December, 1957), pp. 635-659.

ushered in with change, but this is not much satisfaction or comfort to those who are displaced or ushered out at the moment.

> Perhaps the most disorganizing of all the effects of new knowledge is one that is not as immediately apparent as the obsolescence of ideas and of statuses and, therefore, is not so likely to be a *conscious* source of resistance. This is the fact that new knowledge often makes necessary deliberate decisions that men formerly did not have to make. The most vivid illustration of this in the contemporary world is the case of population control. Throughout most of man's history the struggle against death and disease has been so unequal that cultural values leading to high birth rates were functional for survival. Scientific discoveries leading to the control of death and disease were therefore eagerly welcomed and put to use. Now, however, so effective are the scientific methods of death control that a leading physician can say that if men succeed in winning the struggle against heart disease and cancer, it may be nothing short of a disaster, so overcrowded is the planet even now becoming. But the use of scientific methods to control birth rates continues to be resisted on both religious and nonreligious traditional grounds. The result is an extraordinary growth in the world's population, which in the long run simply cannot be maintained; and even in the short run can be maintained only at the cost of lowered living standards for everyone.
>
> This means that whereas in the past the question of what size population to have was not a question men had to decide (it was decided for them by events beyond their control), now it is a question that must be decided deliberately. That is to say, once the power to control population size has been given to men by science, the decision must be made to use that power in one way or another. There is simply no escaping the fact that either there will be a decision to allow people to multiply to the point at which the pressure on living standards will generate widespread dissatisfaction, or there will be a decision to control births and deaths so as to maintain population at a level considered desirable. In either case, the important point is that there now must be a decision—and one affecting the heretofore highly private activity of reproduction.[3]

Knowledge gives the possibility of control, and the possession of control often makes necessary the making of decisions which without the control it would not be necessary or possible to make.

Change in a social system would be a much simpler matter if it affected everyone involved in the same way and degree. This, of course, is not the way the effects are distributed; consequently, some people will desire given changes and others will resist them. But as Justice Holmes said, "We do not measure things by our fears," so let us turn now to a consideration of some psychological correlates to social organization.

[3] Bredemeier and Stephenson, *op. cit.*, pp. 270-271.

3. SOCIAL ORGANIZATION, SOCIAL VALUES, AND RELATED PSYCHOLOGICAL ATTITUDES

INSTITUTIONS

If human beings could not standardize the results of successful experience, then each generation would have to start from the beginning and man would be no better equipped to deal with problems of adaptation than an intelligent ape. Apes, dogs, and cats learn rapidly by observing and playing with others of their kind, particularly the older ones. However, each generation of these has to solve all over again the same set of problems.

Man differs from other animals in being able by means of language to formulate the results of experience into verbal and/or written statements, that is, symbolic statements which describe the meaning or results of experience. These statements are revised in light of new experience and consequently their validity and accuracy improve cumulatively. In this way human experience is *cumulative* and each generation can acquire the knowledge of all the generations of the past by simply learning the generalizations and problem-solving skills acquired in the past.

Human behavior is principally composed of learned habits. The fact that past experience is committed to habit frees man to deal creatively with new problems. In this regard the most significant characteristic of man is his capacity to construct symbolic formulations of experience and subsequently to learn *from* experience rather than just *by* experience.

It is doubtful if the reader ever asked himself or herself how it is that the essential accumulated knowledge gets transmitted from generation to generation. One might think that the process would break down from sheer increase in quantity, but it does not. In fact, each generation receives a more efficient set of knowledge than the preceding generation. This is accomplished by refining the state of knowledge through the development of higher levels of generalization and more efficient means of transmission.

One of the most efficient means of transmitting knowledge (and at the same time productive of little conscious awareness of transmission, as such) is the transmission of behavior patterns by learning to meet one's needs by institutional means. In order to handle in an habitual manner the *common* problems of everyday living, man has evolved a set of social institutions. Some of these are the institutions of marriage and family, religious institutions, economic institutions, political institutions, and educational institutions. These institutions are socially standardized ways of meeting common human needs. In other words, a great deal of child-rearing and child-care information, some good and some not so good, is transmitted from parent to child simply by the child's observing what the parents did for him as a child in the family. When the child grows up and becomes a parent, he almost automatically repeats many of the things he observed or learned from his parents.

Sex behavior is to a very significant extent automatically regulated by the institution of marriage, and the social functions of production and consumption are regulated by the economic institutions. If the systems which regulate the satisfying of basic social and biological needs of human beings do not have stability from generation to generation, the new generations have to start anew and failure may be great. In a very real sense this was the case with primitive man. His institutional structure was so simple and rudimentary that much effort was spent simply learning how to keep alive by avoiding dangerous animals, by obtaining food, by trying to keep dry and warm, and by learning to protect himself from his human enemies.

The solutions to these basic problems which have been worked out and evolved through the ages have become institutionalized. This does not mean that they do not change at all. It means that they evolve with relatively slow modification through the ages. But children and adults learn these patterns by simply being participants in a society and to that extent this is societal transmission.

In one sense these institutions are complex systems of rewards and punishments. The rewarding and punishing agents are, of course, the adults who occupy controlling positions of power and authority within the institutional structures. These controlling adults learned as children to meet their needs in the institutional systems of their time and, upon becoming adults, acquired positions of responsibility and strong positive attitudes of identification with the institutions. For example, parents often take a certain pride in claiming that systems and ways were "harder" but "better for you" when they grew up. This is a form of justification to make the neophytes feel and believe that the "hardships" they are now experiencing are good for them.

In general, people in the United States eat three meals per day at roughly the same hours; children go to school five days per week; and the people obey the laws or, if caught and convicted, they have to go to jail. In all these instances and many many more, people are behaving in ways influenced by or regulated by institutions set up for the purpose. In other words, *institutions* are complex networks of culture patterns composed of folkways, norms, customs, and laws which regulate the ways in which people interact in order to meet biological, psychological, and sociological needs. In a sense, institutions function for the whole of a society as norms function for a group.

One sometimes hears the remark that "this practice should be institutionalized." What is meant by such a remark? It means that the speaker would like to see the practice made the standard or required practice which in turn means that sanctions and an organizational structure would be established as means for enforcing reasonable conformity to the institutionalized patterns. The passage in 1964 of the Civil Rights Bill was an act of institutionalizing the rights of certain minorities— rights which members of the majority already had.

It should be clear by now that institutions are forms of social organization which regulate social interaction in the meeting of individual *and* societal needs. Once the institution is established, then it provides an orderly means to regulating need satisfaction. Take, for example, the matter of Social Security for people over 65 years of age. Many people at retirement age do not have the personal economic resources to maintain themselves even at a minimum standard of living. The Social Security system was devised as a system of forced collective savings to insure a certain minimum of social security for all in old age. The participants automatically begin receiving their checks upon reaching the age of sixty-five. This is an institutionalized means to protect the aged against economic destitution. But a situation must have existed which motivated people to *want* to do something. In other words, institutions do not emerge without causes. Let us look at some of the changes in modern Western society which were associated with the development of the Social Security law.

In the first place, the great Depression of the early 1930's alerted the nation to the danger of the existence of large numbers of people without resources to meet the basic needs of life. Hence steps were taken to prevent such from recurring. The Unemployment Compensation Act was passed to assist those who are temporarily unemployed and the Social Security Act was passed to cover those in industry and agriculture who have reached retirement age.

Secondly, the number of people who reach retirement age is increasing at a faster rate. Therefore, if the retired are not insured for income after retirement, then society would soon have a very great problem on hand.

Thirdly, technological change was revolutionizing industry and agriculture. This in turn greatly affected the structure of the Western family. The rapid industrialization of the United States was to a significant extent accomplished by attracting young people from the farms to the city for higher wages. Thus many farm parents were left without young sons and daughters to help them in their old age. Furthermore, the children who moved to the urban areas found the cost of living too high to support both their own family and their parents. There were other factors as well; for example, the great mobility that is required in an industrial society. We do not intend to be exhaustive or necessarily precise in this analysis. What we wish to show is that major change in one sector of a society often produces strains in adjustment which require for solution that existing institutions be modified and sometimes new institutional structures be developed. Furthermore, we wish to point out that if a *sense of respect and concern* for the welfare of the aged had not existed in our society these institutionalized means would not have been proposed, much less created. In other words, institutions arise to maintain human values and interests and to provide standard and predictable ways for attaining these. This indicates that the underlying or basic elements which support given forms of social organization are social values and public opinion. What happens when the social values that underlie one institutional practice are in conflict with the interests and functioning of the values underlying another institution?

Social Values and Social Change

In answering the foregoing question, we must distinguish whether the value and interest interference between the two institutional systems involves the *same* or *different* people. If it involves the same people, then the problem is a matter of internal or in-group readjustment. If it involves different groups of people, then it is a problem of intergroup adjustment. What difference does it make whether the conflict in institutional values involves groups who subscribe to both sets of values or groups who subscribe to one set but not the other?

If the conflict in values involves groups that subscribe to both sets of values, then the following possibilities exist: (1) The conflicting values may be so compartmentalized in the minds and thinking of the members that they are unaware of the existence of any conflict or contradiction. (2) They may be aware of the conflict, but rationalize its existence by invoking some higher order value or belief. For example, people may rationalize their continued cigarette smoking and its hazard to their health by an appeal to the value of pleasure and relaxation. (3) They may recognize the conflict, analyze its meaning and consequences, and decide in favor of the value with the least perceived deleterious effects. Thus the dominant value wins.

If the conflict in values involves different groups of people, that is, some who strongly identify with one set of the values and others who identify with the other set, then these possibilities exist: (1) The leaders of each will perceive the other as a threat to their cherished values. (2) If one group possesses power over the other either economically, politically, or both, then the advantaged group will apply this power in efforts to make the *behavior* of the other group comply with their wishes. (3) The disadvantaged group will solicit support from other groups by appealing to values common to themselves and the other groups. A sympathy strike by one labor union for another is an example. (4) If societal interests or the general welfare of either the nation or a community becomes involved, then the appropriate level of government will intervene and arbitrate the conflict. For example, suppose the conflict endangers public safety or health, then the ultimate authority of the state through its regulative agencies or its courts will make a decision for the contending parties, and as a consequence of the superior power of the state they comply. (5) If the general welfare does not become involved and the parties are nearly equal in power, then the parties to the conflict may achieve a temporary accommodation based on mutual interests. Or, (6) if they are unequal in power, then the more powerful is likely to force a decision to their own liking.

The point should be clear by now that if value conflict is *within* a group it may produce a great deal of strife, but the likelihood is great that the conflict will be worked out without involving other groups.[4] However, if the institutional conflicts involve different groups, then we have *de facto* between-group conflict, which automatically tends to involve the use of power in all of its forms.

Social and personal values develop from the perceived *consequences* of people's experiences in regard to their personal and the public's well-being. For example, the trade of money-lending or banking did not rate high as a social value until commerce and trade began among different cities and principalities. Banking then became an important value because it was a necessary bookkeeping procedure for long-distance trading. Thus we see that out of *conditions* of experience and action, consequences and circumstances arise that have perceived advantages or disadvantages for the goals of men at points and spans of time. If the perceived consequences or effects are positive, then they are valued, that is, they become *values*, and men create institutions or organizational structures to implement and regulate the pursuit of the values. For example, if the value is gold and men are searching for gold, then institutionalized procedures are established to determine claims rights. If industrial and political leaders of a society discover that the maintenance and growth of their economic structure depend upon a well-educated labor force, then public education is perceived as a value. Historically, it is well to recall Thomas Jefferson's definition of the value of public education as the foundation for democratic government. It was his belief that democratic government presupposed an enlightened and informed electorate and to this end public education was essential.

---

[4] The reader should keep in mind that we are talking about genuine institutional conflicts, not personal conflicts between persons seeking personal gain. Institutional conflict can generate personal conflicts also, but it tends to remain more on the impersonal level.

Therefore, Jefferson set out to institutionalize the value of higher public education, founding the University of Virginia as the organizational structure to attain the value.

The foregoing discussion and examples regarding values should be sufficient to allow the statement of certain generalizations in which we are interested. Values refer to the subjective realm of human preference and in this sense are determinants of meaning in the world of events. They arise out of human experience with specific conditions of life and become embodied in the institutional structures of man. The worship of things as values themselves is *not* the use of the term that is of interest here. I have used the term "value" to refer to the *standards or principles* of worth which men employ which in turn make something have value. If the object or relationship were not relevant to the standard or principle involved, then it would not have value.

Now, if it is true that men formulate values from their experiences with conditions of life and these values are standards for defining men's relationships to these conditions, then if the conditions change, the values may become obsolete. For example, high tariffs as a value made sense in the early days of the development of American industry, but in this day of international interdependence this value is less meaningful than before.

We have now arrived at a very crucial point in the unfolding of this chapter. Until now we have spoken only of the values or standards which underlie the organizational basis for an institution. In other words, we have looked at the institutional structure as an *external* system which regulates social interaction in regard to the social values involved. Inasmuch as the institutional system is a source of need satisfaction and reward for the individual participants, then they develop *attitudes* toward the values embodied in the institutional system. In fact, the individuals may even, in time, confuse the values or standards with "things," and thus develop inflexible and often irrational attitudes toward the values. This is similar to the Biblical case of the two women who claimed the same child and Solomon in his wisdom suggested that they cut the child in half and one take one half and the other the remaining half. Solomon assumed that the real mother would at this point agree to give her child to the other woman and he could, on the basis of this assumption, then make his decision as to which was the real mother. Sometimes, however, individuals assume such inflexible attitudes toward a given value that they will allow the value to be destroyed before modifying their attitude. This is what is generally meant when we say that certain behavior is irrational.

To summarize and restate the point about attitudes in regard to institutions, we can say that when given conditions give rise to a certain value, the people involved develop, at the same time or subsequently,

BEHAVIOR AND SOCIAL CHANGE

psychological attitudes that are congruent to the values of the institutional system. As long as the conditions which gave rise to the value remain stable, then the value base of the institution and the attitudinal counterpart of the individuals are in balance. However, if the conditions which gave rise to the value have so changed as to make the value disfunctional to the system or some related system, then the members' attitudes and the value are both disfunctional to the system. It is clear that such a joint set of sociological and psychological conditions poses a problem in attitudinal and institutional reorganization.

It should now be clear that optimum psychological adaptation to social change requires that one's attitudes be congruent with the value implications of the institution and that one's behavior be in accord with the institutional role demands appropriate to one's position in the institution.

Let us next examine what happens when such a psychosocial balance is disturbed by social change.

4. THEORIES OF ATTITUDE CHANGE AND ORGANIZATION

INTRODUCTION

The following discussion of selected theories of attitude change and organization will be confined to theories that are principally concerned with attitude change as a function of related environmental change. We will not be concerned with therapeutic or psychiatric notions of attitude organization and reorganization.

We have already shown that social values arise out of human encounters with living conditions, efforts to adjust, and efforts to meet one's needs and aspirations. The implementation of the values is accomplished through the creation of institutions for this purpose. Institutional participation on the part of individuals leads to the development of personal attitudes toward the institutional values. The strength of the attitude is principally dependent upon the place of the value in the person's hierarchy of needs and personal values. If the value is central in the life activities of the person, then it would be expected that he would possess a strong positive attitude toward the value in question.

Suppose there are individuals who perceive the value in question to be important to their livelihood, but they are denied institutional participation, then what attitude would they be expected to have? This would not necessarily cause them to have a negative attitude toward the value, but it would produce negative attitudes toward those whom they perceive to be obstructing their participation and hence their need satisfaction. Such is the case with the American Negro in regard to school segregation and segregation of public accommodations in certain geographic areas of the United States. This is a complicated and complex area of behavior and the degree of felt deprivation under such conditions is probably to some extent a function of the quality and quantity of leadership available to the deprived. The point in introducing the idea of the socially deprived is to call attention to the fact that they through their leaders will be and would be expected to agitate for *change* of those institutional elements that obstruct their participation and hence need satisfaction. This is a case where two or more groups share the same value, but one is denied by other means, often institutional, what he believes are his full rights of participation. In such a case the target of conflict would be over the means by which the one group denies participation to the other.

A society is composed of a population that shares a common culture. The content of a culture is expressed through the actions of a population which shares a network of common institutions. These institutions are, in varying degrees, intercorrelated with each other. This means that change in one institution will in time produce strains in the operation of other institutions, and thus, through frustration, the participants are motivated to make corrective changes in these related institutional structures. For example, the innovation of the automobile as a form of private transportation has through the frustrations of the drivers led to a tremendous number of institutional changes. To name a few, I shall mention the development of our massive public highway system, changes in urban family residential patterns, compulsory automobile liability insurance, highway patrol, and the current agitation for control of exhaust fumes.

It is clear that inasmuch as social institutions are interrelated and each regulates the implementation of different social functions and hence serves different values, then change in one is likely to produce strain or conflict in others and this motivates the participants to make alterations in the related structures.

If institutional values become obsolete or disruptive as a consequence of change, then the institutional structure which represents the values will disintegrate. However, it must be made clear that if the "obsolete" value is not obsolete for some, then they will fight to preserve it. For example, the institution of racial segregation is disruptive to the economic and political life of the United States, and the Civil Rights Bill was passed to eliminate this disruption. But many people who practice segregation and believe in it as a value did not see it as disruptive to themselves or the community. In this case, it was public opinion on a nationwide basis which brought about the change.

The point in the foregoing discussion is to call attention to the fact that social change is environmental change—and environmental change toward which people have psychologically related attitudes. It should be clear, then, that we are arguing that attitudes develop as a function of experience and that they change as experience changes. Let us now state more clearly what we mean by the term *attitude*.

The Nature and Meaning of Attitudes

Attitudes refer to consistencies or regularities of an individual's *thoughts, feelings,* and *predispositions* to act toward values or objects. The thought part of the attitude is commonly referred to as the *cognitive* element. The feelings are referred to as the *affective* element and the predispositions to act as the *behavioral* elements. Thus Katz and Stotland say an attitude is an individual's tendency or predisposition to evaluate an object or the symbol of that object in a certain way. They note that the evaluation is essentially a process of assigning qualities along a dimension of "desirability-undesirability," that is, to value either positively or negatively, and in terms of "goodness"-"badness." [5]

Attitudes may pertain to anything in one's environment. They may involve nearby objects or abstract ideas such as religion, or they may be personal such as one's attitudes toward his own behavior or self. As indicated by the definition, they involve three elements—thoughts, feelings, and tendencies to act a certain way which reflects the thoughts and feelings.

An attitude is not directly observable but is inferred from verbal expressions or overt behavior. If a person expresses a dislike for another's behavior, the assumption is that the person expressing the dislike will actually have a negative evaluation of the person. Likewise, if a person gives a verbal evaluation of another that is positive, it is assumed that he will have a definite evaluation of the person in question. However, from Chapter 6 (Social Judgment) you will recall that more than one attitude may be involved in any given situation of evaluation. Consequently, the action situation may be blurred, thus making it difficult to infer the attitude involved. For example, suppose a person has a very negative attitude toward his boss, but at the same time he knows that his advancement depends to a significant extent upon his superior's attitude toward him. Therefore, he behaves in ways that are calculated to create a favorable impression of himself in the mind of his boss. In this case it appears that one's behavior is incongruent with one's attitude, but this is not quite correct. It would be more correct to say that his behavior is congruent with the *dominant* attitude of the moment. In other words, he views his own personal and economic progress as more important than his personal feelings or evaluations of his boss. How-

---

[5] Daniel Katz and Ezra Stotland, "A Preliminary Statement to a Theory of Attitude Structure and Change," in Sigmund Koch, ed., *Psychology: A Study of a Science*, Vol. 3 (New York, McGraw-Hill Book Company, Inc., 1959), pp. 423-475.

ever, if these feelings were to become intolerable, then they would gain the ascendancy and he would elect to leave his present job and accept another, provided there is an acceptable alternative available to him.

The point in the foregoing example is that we cannot successfully conceptualize behavior in terms of simple relations between stimuli and isolated processes. Human behavior is always more or less fluid. That is, one attitude may be involved at one moment because at that moment only one value is involved; but at the next moment, if an additional value becomes involved, then another attitude is added to the dynamics of the background to action. In such a situation, and this is almost always the case, the individual must make a judgment on the basis of his assessment of the alternatives in relation to his preference scale.

The last sentence in the above paragraph should make it clear that attitudes necessarily have cognitive elements. This is true since one's feeling or affective evaluation depends upon one's recognition of the values and objects involved and his interpretation of the meaning of the situation to him. Following the interpretation or the perceived consequences, an affective evaluation is made and this is what we mean by attitude.

The behavioral elements of an attitude refer to the action tendencies associated with the attitude. If the object of the idea is the value of honesty and the person's attitude toward honesty is positive, then his behavior will correspond to his cognitive definitions of honesty. Recall the earlier example of the person's sham behavior toward his boss, that is, he really held a negative attitude toward his boss, but acted as if he held a positive attitude. This is perfectly consistent when we take into account the value he was protecting, namely, himself. In other words, his sham behavior was an expression of his positive attitude toward his own *position in relation to his boss.*

To summarize: We have conceived attitude as a construct which links a person's feeling states via his cognitive functions to a value. The cognitive element may be very detailed and in the forefront of consciousness or it may be minimal. It becomes minimal and virtually subconscious when the behavioral part of the attitude has been made habitual.

We will close this section of the chapter with the customary distinction between attitude and *opinion or belief.* An opinion differs from an attitude by lacking the affective element that is common to an attitude. In other words, an opinion or belief is almost wholly cognitive or factual and without emotional attachment. If a person develops an attitude that is congruent to the value base of an institution, but in the meantime environmental conditions change and set into motion pressures that make necessary the alteration of the institutional structure and a redefinition of its values, then the person's attitude is inconsistent with the new value demands. Under such circumstances how does attitude reorganization occur?

Several people have formulated theories of attitude organization and change.[6] We will consider three of these since they are more in harmony with the point of view formulated up to now in this chapter.

Selected Theories of Attitude Structure and Change

Three approaches will be considered in this section. They are Rosenberg's theory of *Affective-Cognitive Consistency,* Festinger's *Cognitive Dissonance* theory, and Kelman's *Three-Process Theory of Attitude Change.*

Rosenberg's Affective-Cognitive Consistency Theory. Rosenberg is principally concerned with specifying what happens within a person when attitudes change. He is particularly concerned with investigating the correspondence in change between the affective and cognitive components of attitudes.

Rosenberg defines the affective element of an attitude in the usual way as the positive or negative feelings that an individual has toward the object of the attitude. In the cognitive component he concerns himself with the person's *beliefs about the potentialities of the object of attitude for the realization or blocking of valued states.* In other words, he conceives the cognitive component in terms of beliefs about the relations between the attitude object and other values of the person. Suppose a person has a positive feeling toward democracy. He also has certain beliefs about democracy in relation to other values such as religion and economic opportunity. He might argue that democracy values the right and dignity of the individual and so does his religion. Then if democracy values individual freedom, it is positively related to his religious and economic values. Hence a threat to one of these values would be perceived as a threat to the other.

Rosenberg's principal hypothesis is that the nature and strength of the feeling toward an attitude object are correlated with the beliefs associated with the attitude object. He states it as follows:

> Strong and stable positive affect toward a given object should be associated with beliefs that it leads to the attainment of a number of important values, while strong negative affect should be associated with beliefs that the ob-

---

[6] Some other formulations that are similar to the three presented in this chapter are Fritz Heider using a theory of balance in his *The Psychology of Interpersonal Relations* (New York, John Wiley & Sons, Inc., 1958); Daniel Katz and Ezra Stotland, "A Preliminary Statement to a Theory of Attitude Structure and Change," in S. Koch, ed., *Psychology: A Study of a Science* (Vol. 3) *Formulations of the Person and the Social Context* (New York, McGraw-Hill Book Company, 1959), pp. 423–475; and Charles E. Osgood and P. H. Tannenbaum, "The Principle of Congruity in the Prediction of Attitude Change," *Psychological Review,* Vol. 62 (1955), pp. 42-55.

ject tends to block the attainment of important values. Similarly, moderate positive or negative affects should be associated with beliefs that relate the attitude object either to less important values or, if to important values, then with less confidence about the relationships between these values and the attitude object.[7]

The principal notion in Rosenberg's theory is contained in the concept of affective-cognitive consistency. When a state of consistency exists between the affective and cognitive components in regard to an object of value, then the subject can be said to have an attitude toward that value. Rosenberg formulates the following basic proposition derived from this concept:

> When the affective and cognitive components of an attitude are mutually consistent the attitude is in a stable state; when the affective and cognitive components are mutually inconsistent (to a degree that exceeds the individual's present tolerance for such inconsistency) the attitude is in an unstable state and will undergo spontaneous reorganizing activity until such activity eventuates in either (1) the attainment of affective-cognitive consistency or (2) the placing of an "irreconcilable" inconsistency beyond the range of active awareness.[8]

Rosenberg argues that if one's affect or feeling toward an object is based upon the rank or relative position of the value in the personal value system, then the strength of the affect will vary with the "perceived instrumentality" of the attitude object for attaining the value. To give an example, suppose that a young Negro leader has as one of his major values the goal of achieving equality of civil rights and that a number of ways have been suggested for attaining this value. Imagine further that one of the perceived "ways" is the idea of "peaceful demonstration" and that the leader believes this procedure has the greatest possibility among the list of procedures for success in attaining the value; then the leader's emotional feeling or *strength of affect* toward the attitude objects will vary with his perception of their instrumentality for value attainment. In this particular case, his strongest feeling would be toward the attitude object "peaceful demonstration." On the other hand, if this particular Negro leader happened to be Malcolm X, then the perceived instrumental value of "peaceful demonstrations" would be zero. This follows because he did not believe that this procedure has any utility for attaining the value of equal civil rights.

---

[7] M. J. Rosenberg, "An Analysis of Affective-Cognitive Consistency," in M. J. Rosenberg, Carl I. Hovland *et al.*, *Attitude Organization and Change* (New Haven, Yale University Press, 1960), p. 18.

[8] *Ibid.*, p. 22.

To test propositions about the relationship between the cognitive component of an attitude and the affect component, Rosenberg constructed a scale to index *cognitive structure*. This was constructed out of two separate rating scales that we shall now briefly describe.

The first is an index to *value importance* and the second an index to *perceived instrumentality*. By value importance he means the relative rank of the value in one's preference or value system, and by perceived instrumentality he means the perceived capacity of the attitude object for attaining the value in question.

To ascertain value importance, Rosenberg uses a set of thirty-five value statements, such as "all human beings have equal rights," and "members of the Communist Party should be allowed to address the public." The subject rates each statement or item in terms of its *value importance* to him. To do this a subject is asked to place each item on a twenty-one category scale to indicate how much satisfaction he gets from the value described. The categories range from "gives me maximum satisfaction" (category +10) through "gives me neither satisfaction nor dissatisfaction" (category −10).

Second, the subject is asked to rate some suggested procedure for attaining the value described in the value statement. This index gives the measure of "perceived instrumentality." The attitude objects or suggested procedures for value attainment are rated on an eleven-category scale. Category +5 represents what the subjects believed would yield "complete attainment" of the value. Category 0 represents neither attainment nor blocking and category −5 represents "complete blocking." [9] For example, suppose the value statement concerned maintenance of democracy and the instrumental statement concerned "allow anyone or any organization to address the public." If the subject thought this would insure the attainment of the value he would check +5; if he thought it would interfere, then he would check some negative number between −1 and −5 inclusive.

From the ratings of value importance and perceived instrumentality, Rosenberg constructed a *cognitive index* for the attitude object "allow anyone or any organization to address the public." This index represents the subject's belief pattern about the extent to which freedom to speak will enable the attainment of democracy. This index is obtained by algebraically summing the importance-instrumentality products for each of the value statements or items. For example, if "maintaining democracy" is ranked 15 in importance, and freedom of speech receives an instrumental rating of 3, the product of these is 45. This procedure is continued for the other thirty-four value statements in relation to freedom of speech and are then summed to obtain a cognitive index for the atti-

[9] M. J. Rosenberg, "Cognitive Structure and Attitudinal Affect," *Journal of Abnormal and Social Psychology*, Vol. 53 (1956), pp. 367-372.

tude object "freedom of speech." The procedure is repeated for other attitude objects. The sum of all the products for any one attitude object in relation to a given value represents the total import of the subject's pattern of beliefs about the instrumentality (or lack of such) of this attitude object for the value.

The foregoing should be sufficient to make clear Rosenberg's procedure. Let us now return to his basic proposition about attitude organization and change. Recall that his basic proposition asserts that when the affective and cognitive components of an attitude are mutually consistent, the attitude is in a stable state. From this it follows that if changes in external factors bring about a change in either the affective or cognitive components of an existing attitude, pressure arises from this imbalance to change the other component until consistency is restored.

Rosenberg conducted a series of experiments to test this proposition and found dramatic confirmation. We will briefly describe one of these. In order to test the cognitive consequences of change in the affectual component, he tried to produce as "pure" an affect change as possible, that is, one which was unmixed with cognitive elements. The procedure that seemed most effective for this purpose was hypnotic suggestion.

Eleven deeply hypnotized subjects were drawn from Yale's professional and graduate schools and assigned to an experimental group in which each subject was given posthypnotic suggestions of affect change toward certain objects.

Eleven other subjects were assigned to a control group which was to undergo all the testing procedures used with the experimental group except the posthypnotic suggestions of affect change.

In the first phase of the experiment each subject was given an attitude questionnaire designed to measure his affective responses toward certain social issues and also requiring him to rate these issues from most to least interesting. Coombs'[10] scaling procedure was used, which generates sixteen-scale positions running from extreme positive affect to extreme negative affect. Seven issues were used. Some of these were labor's right to strike, Federal medical insurance, and Negroes moving into white neighborhoods.

A week or so later the experimental subjects were run through a final session. At this time the cognitive index for each subject was determined for one of his two high-interest attitude areas. He was tested twice on his cognitive structure, once just before being hypnotized and once after an interval of a half-hour after the hypnotic suggestion had been induced. The control subjects were tested similarly in an identical physical setting after being instructed to "try to fall asleep."

[10] C. H. Coombs, "A Theory of Psychological Scaling," *Engineering Research Bulletin* No. 34 (1952), Ann Arbor, The University of Michigan Press.

For six of the experimental subjects the affective manipulation was from negative to positive; and for the remaining five, from positive to negative.

We will confine our discussion of the experimental results to the major proposition that when *affects* are altered, beliefs about the objects of those affects will be changed in a congruent direction. To test this proposition, it was necessary to have two measures of each subject's cognitive structure, one before the experimental treatment and one after. The difference between these two measures was computed for each experimental subject and compared to those of the control subjects. On this comparison the experimental subjects showed significantly more cognitive change than the control subjects. Thus the major prediction that cognitive reorganization follows an induced change in affective state was confirmed.

Rosenberg looked beyond the matter of the fact of cognitive reorganization to the question of whether the change comes about through modifications of perceived instrumentality, of value importance, or of both. If a person's affect is changed from positive to negative on the issue, say, of federal aid to education, will he then see federal aid to education as blocking the same values he formerly thought it advanced, or will he renounce the values that led him originally to favor the policy? This question was investigated by computing for each subject an index of *mean change in value importance* and an index of *mean change in perceived instrumentality*.

When the experimental and control groups were compared on these indices, it was found that they differed significantly, the experimental subjects having the higher change scores. The changes were consistent and in the expected direction.

Rosenberg's study of attitude change differs from most other studies by emphasizing that change in *affect* will produce cognitive changes instead of emphasizing change in cognitive components as a cause of shifts in affective components.

The effects observed in this experiment persisted in most subjects for an entire week; at the end of this period the experimenter removed the affect change and explained the entire experiment to the subjects.

We have reported this experiment in some detail since it has much in common with the formulations about social change and social values in Parts 2 and 3 of this chapter. Rosenberg has linked cognitions about an attitude object with the person's values. Strong positive feeling toward an object of attitude should be associated with beliefs that it leads to the achievement of important values, and negative affect toward an object or idea with beliefs that it blocks or interferes with the maintenance or attainment of these values. Rosenberg's studies have demonstrated that such linkages exist.

Festinger's Theory of Cognitive Dissonance. Let us begin by specifying the meaning which Festinger assigns to the basic terms in the theory.[11] By cognition Festinger means "any knowledge, opinion, or belief about the environment, about oneself, or about one's behavior."[12] A person has many beliefs, many facts and opinions, and these viewed as separate items in respect to a given object may be thought of as cognitive elements. Cognitions are thoughts, verbal statements, or symbols which describe aspects of experience and reality. As Festinger says, these elements of cognition are responsive to "reality" and by and large they map reality. The truth of this is noticeable when someone's behavior shows that he is "out of touch with reality." This suggests that there is a common consensus about aspects of reality even though it is a changing one. If a person has a cognitive element that is objectively at marked variance with reality, then the relative aspects of reality which impinge on a person will exert pressures toward reducing the variance between the cognitive element and the meaning of reality. This is brought about by a cognitive reorganization, or the learning of new meaning, which is more in correspondence with reality.

The terms "dissonance" and "consonance" refer to relations which exist between pairs of elements. If two elements are unrelated or are perceived to be unrelated, then one element implies nothing for the other.

Two elements are dissonant if, for any reason, they do not fit together. Festinger formally defines dissonance thus: "two elements are in a dissonant relation if, considering these two alone, the obverse of one element would follow from the other,"[13] for example, a person with heart disease who knows that smoking is deleterious to his system but goes on smoking. His knowledge of his heart condition and the effects of smoking upon it are dissonant with one another. The dissonance may exist because of what one has learned, because of the demands of one's culture, or because of the expectations of one's friends or peers.

Festinger lists four principal sources for the origin of dissonance:[14]

1. Dissonance can arise from logical inconsistency. However, to psychologically experience it, one would have to become or be made aware of the inconsistency.

2. Dissonance may arise because of cultural mores. For example, if someone sitting at your side in church tries to talk to you during the sermon, the knowledge of what he is doing is dissonant with your knowledge of what he is expected to do. The dissonance exists because the culture defines what is consonant and what is not.

---

[11] Leon Festinger, *A Theory of Cognitive Dissonance* (New York, Harper & Row, Publishers, Inc., 1957).
[12] *Ibid.,* p. 3.
[13] *Ibid.,* p. 13.
[14] *Ibid.,* p. 14.

3. Dissonance may arise because one specific opinion is subsumed under a more general opinion and the two are not consistent in their behavioral implications. An example is a southern Democrat who votes Republican. "Being a Democrat" includes, as part of its meaning, favoring Democratic candidates.

4. Dissonance may arise because of past experience. If a person who can sense pain pricks himself with a pin and does not sense anything, then these two cognitions are dissonant since he knows from experience that pain is supposed to follow a pin prick or cut.

In any of these situations, as Festinger points out, there might exist many other elements of cognition that are consonant with either of the two elements under consideration. For example, if the pin prick follows a local anesthetic, then one would not expect to feel pain. The consideration in which we are interested involves the relation between two elements when other elements are for the moment disregarded or not relevant.

From the foregoing discussion of dissonance we can infer the meaning assigned to consonance. If, in the case of two elements, either follows from the other, then the relation between them is consonant.

Obviously, as Festinger notes, the definitions of dissonance and consonance present serious problems of measurement. One must be able to identify dissonance and consonance and thereby be able to show that a subject does in fact experience one or the other.[15]

If one argues as Festinger does that there is a tendency toward consistency between one's cognitions and one's behavior, then the theory of cognitive dissonance has the great advantage of connecting or linking attitudes to overt behavior. This allows the researcher to get around the problem of assuming that a person behaves in terms of his verbally expressed attitudes. It is well known that in many cases one does not. The theory of cognitive dissonance takes this into account by specifying the conditions under which attitudes and behavior do correspond. For example, if a person believes in democracy, then he will not believe in communism or fascism and his behavior will reflect a consistency with these beliefs. If his behavior is inconsistent with his stated beliefs, then his verbal statements are intended to deceive or his behavior and cognitions are *actually* dissonant.

What happens when the cognitions of a person are discrepant? Festinger assumes that variant or discrepant cognitions create tension which the individual strives to reduce by making his cognitions more consistent. This tension is called cognitive dissonance; and the motivation toward consistency, dissonance reduction. "When two or more cognitive ele-

---

[15] Space will not permit us to deal with this operational problem as we did with Rosenberg's theory. The student is invited to read Festinger's own work in this regard, particularly pages 48-137.

ments are psychologically inconsistent, dissonance is created. Dissonance is defined as psychological tension having drive characteristics."[16]

Festinger states several propositions which provide a theoretical answer to the foregoing question of what happens when the cognitions of a person are discrepant. Some of these propositions are:

>1. The existence of dissonance, being psychologically uncomfortable, will motivate the person to try to reduce the dissonance and achieve consonance.
>2. When dissonance is present, in addition to trying to reduce it, the person will actively avoid situations and information which would likely increase the dissonance.[17]

The *magnitude* of dissonance would be expected to be an important variable in determining the pressure to reduce dissonance, and Festinger formulates certain propositions in this regard. Two of these are:

>1. The magnitude of the dissonance (or consonance) increases as the importance or value of the elements increases. . . .
>2. The strength of the pressures to reduce the dissonance is a function of the magnitude of the dissonance.[18]

If dissonance exists between two elements, it can be eliminated by changing one element so it is consistent with the other. Festinger suggests a number of ways in which this can be accomplished, depending upon the type of cognitive element involved and upon the total cognitive context. Three ways of reducing dissonance are:[19]

>1. *Changing a Behavioral Cognitive Element.* When a person learns that something he is *doing* is dissonant with some environmental element, the dissonance can be removed by changing the behavioral cognitive element in such a way that it is consonant with the environmental demand. If a person who is a racial segregationist learns that he will not be allowed to operate his business on a segregated basis and it is a goal of his to continue operating the business, then he can make his behavior comply with the law. If a person drinks and later thinks that it is bad for his health, he may stop drinking. On the other hand, he may not. The difficulty of changing may be too great. The eliminating of one dissonance may produce a whole set of new ones.
>2. *Changing an Environmental Cognitive Element.* This procedure is essentially the reverse of number one. Just as it is possible to change a be-

---

[16] P. G. Zimbardo, "Involvement and Communication Discrepancy as Determinants of Opinion Conformity," *Journal of Abnormal and Social Psychology,* Vol. 60 (1960), pp. 86-94.
[17] Festinger, *op. cit.,* p. 3.
[18] *Ibid.,* p. 18.
[19] *Ibid.,* pp. 19-24.

havioral element of a person, it is often possible to change the *environmental cognitive* element. This seems particularly appropriate in respect to the social environment. If one's neighborhood environment is dissonant with one's behavioral or cognitive tastes, then one can seek out a more consonant neighborhood.

If one has a particular belief about some particular person, this belief can be changed by one's learning that others whom he respects hold views toward this person that contradict his. Likewise, one's views toward another can change because others' views of him have changed.

3. *Adding New Cognitive Elements.* Suppose it is not possible to change either the behavioral cognitive element or the environmental element. If it is impossible to eliminate the dissonance by changing one of the elements involved, then it may be possible to reduce it by adding a new cognitive element.

The smoker who is worried about lung cancer can tell himself that a pipe or a filter cigarette will not harm him. In such a case the person may still have to deal with reality. That is, he may find that neither the filter nor the pipe works. In such a case he will have to add another element or suffer a rise in dissonance. He could contend that smoking is less harmful to him than not smoking.

Some Implications of Festinger's Theory: One of the most significant implications of dissonance theory in relation to attitude change is the notion that dissonance is at a maximum when two opposing cognitive elements are equal in value importance and involve equal perceived instrumentality. In other words, if the amount of attitude change is a function of the amount of dissonance, then dissonance is greatest when the opposing cognitive elements are equal; hence the greatest attitude change would occur under this condition.

On the other hand, a man may have such pressure brought to bear against him that he is forced to make a decision on the side of the greater pressure, but under the condition of forced compliance the behavior will change but the attitude will not necessarily change. Festinger refers to this as the factor of excessive rewards or punishments. Suppose someone has a positive attitude toward smoking or drinking and that he in fact smokes or drinks. Festinger, then, raises a hypothetical situation as follows: Let us assume that someone approaches the smoker and tells him that he will give him a million dollars if he will publicly denounce smoking and quit smoking. No doubt the person would publicly denounce and stop smoking, pocket the million dollars, be happier than ever, and still retain his favorable attitude toward smoking. Why? The reason is simple according to Festinger, namely, that the reward was so out of proportion that it reduced the dissonance to a negligible amount. There may be some slight dissonance derived from the effects of the old habit and the fact that the public denouncement does not really represent his belief, but this is small compared to the consonance produced from having the million dollars. In other words, the greater the reward beyond the minimum necessary to elicit the change, the *less* the attitude will change. The principal point is that if the reward or punishment goes significantly beyond the minimum necessary, then other motives and attitudes become involved rather than the initial two under consideration, and the additional ones become dominant; hence the initial two are really no longer relevant.[20]

Kelman's Three-Process Theory of Attitude Change.[21] Kelman's three-process theory of attitude change is particularly useful in that it suggests the conditions which lead to attitude change and also identifies which conditions lead to simple compliance and which lead to real or internal acceptance and change. It is also useful in that it logically ties in with our discussion on group behavior in Chapter 9, particularly the discussion on forms of power.

Kelman focuses on the relationship between the processes of social influence and behavior change. This is a very useful approach, since behavior may change without concomitant attitude change; but if one's behavior is induced to change so that it is in line with the expectations of the community and this condition remains or is perceived to be permanent, then the pressure is great for one's feelings and cognitions to change in accord with his behavior. Also, different forms of social influence have qualitatively different effects on the behavior of those subject to the influence. For example, some forms of influence produce mere public conformity, that is, superficial verbal and overt compliance; in other situations they may produce personal acceptance and more lasting change.

These considerations led Kelman to distinguish three processes of social influence, each characterized by a specific set of antecedent conditions and each leading to a different outcome. He called these three processes *compliance, identification,* and *internalization.*

Compliance: Compliance is conformity to the expectations of another person, a group, or the authority of the occupant of an office in order to gain expected rewards or avoid anticipated punishment. Thus one may privately disagree with the "others" involved but publicly comply because the consequences of not complying are judged worse than compliance. This is a familiar type of behavior and a familiar form of social influence. Many are the times that one observes individuals giving the

---

[20] For a critique of dissonance theory see Natalia P. Chapanis and Alphonse Chapanis, "Cognitive Dissonance: Five Years Later," *Psychological Bulletin,* Vol. 61, No. 1, January, 1964.

[21] The materials in this section are taken from H. C. Kelman, "Compliance, Identification, and Internalization: Three Processes of Attitude Change," *Conflict Resolution,* Vol. 2 (1958), pp. 51-60, and H. C. Kelman, "Processes of Opinion Change," *Public Opinion Quarterly,* Vol. 25 (1961), pp. 57-78.

expected response in order to gain admission to some club or social set. Expressions of this sort are only given when they can be observed by the rewarding or influencing agent. Thus one's behavior will be different when the influencing agent is not around. For example, we frequently note that automobile driving behavior suddenly becomes different when the drivers discover a policeman or a patrolman to be nearby.

Identification: "Identification can be said to occur when an individual adopts behavior derived from another person or a group because this behavior is associated with a satisfying self-defining relationship to this person or group." [22]

This means that a person adopts the behavior of another or others because it is satisfying to his self-image. Thus a medical student adopts what he thinks are the attitudes and behavioral expectations of his favorite medical professor. It is perhaps most clearly observable in young children who pattern their attitudes and behavior after their parents. In other words, the acceptance of influence through identification may occur as a function of one's role relationship with another. One may be a professor and the other a student and the student identifies with the professor because he aspires to become a professor himself. This form of identification may be reciprocal. That is, the role participants may have mutually shared expectations of one another's behavior.

On the other hand, identification may be one-way in that one identifies with a membership group or a desired or would-be membership group. That is, one may identify with the Democratic party.

> Identification is similar to compliance in that the individual does not adopt the induced behavior because its content per se is intrinsically satisfying. Identification differs from compliance, however, in that the individual actually believes in the opinions and actions that he adopts. The behavior is accepted both publicly and privately, and its manifestation does not depend on observability by the influencing agent. It does depend, however, on the role that an individual takes at any given moment in time.[23]

Attitudes or opinions adopted through compliance or identification are dependent upon social support.

Internalization: Internalization occurs when an individual accepts influence because the expected behavior is consistent with his own value system. In this case, it is the content or meaning of the induced behavior that is itself rewarding. The individual adopts it because he perceives it as satisfying and useful in his efforts to achieve his values. Thus a

---

[22] Herbert C. Kelman, "Processes of Opinion Change," *Public Opinion Quarterly*, Vol. 25 (1961), p. 63.
[23] *Ibid.*, pp. 64-65.

person who believes in the importance of public education and public health would likely support government programs for education and medicare.

Kelman points out that whichever one of these processes actually occurs depends principally on the *source of the influencing agent's power* and the *manner* in which he employs this power. What kind of motivational system is appealed to by the influencing agent? What is it about the influence situation that makes it important?

Kelman summarizes the differences between the three processes thus:

(a) To the extent that the individual is concerned—for whatever reason—with the *social effect* of his behavior, influence will tend to take the form of compliance. (b) To the extent that he is concerned with the *social anchorage* of his behavior, influence will tend to take the form of identification. (3) To the extent that he is concerned with the *value congruence* of his behavior (rational or otherwise), influence will tend to take the form of internalization.[24]

The foregoing difference in influence is based on the kind of motivational system aroused in the subject who is being influenced. The type of motivational system aroused is somewhat dependent upon the subject's perception of the influencing agent's source of power. Kelman hypothesizes three sources of the influencing agent's power: (1) If the agent's power is based on his control of *means*, then the influence will tend to take the form of compliance. (2) If the agent's power is based on his personal *attractiveness* or appeal to the subject, influence will tend to take the form of identification. Attractiveness is here used to refer to the possessing of qualities which make the *continuation of a relationship* desirable. (3) If the agent's source of power is based on his *credibility*, influence will tend to take the form of internalization. An agent possesses credibility if his statements are considered truthful and valid. This is based on expertness and trustworthiness.

In summary, we note that compliance occurs when a person accepts influence from another because he expects a reward or favorable reaction from the other. Identification occurs when a person adopts certain attitudes or behavior because this provides a self- or ego-satisfying relation with another person or a group. Internalization occurs when a person is influenced by another because the induced behavior change is congruent with his existing values.

We have now briefly surveyed three theories of attitude organization and change, namely, Rosenberg's, Festinger's, and Kelman's. Let us now look at what these have in common.

[24] *Ibid.*, pp. 67-68.

5. SOME CONCLUSIONS ON ATTITUDE CHANGE

Rosenberg's theory views attitudes as being composed of two components—an affective and a cognitive component. He succeeds in showing that attitudes are instrumentally related to social and personal values. His argument is similar to Festinger's in that he emphasizes consistency, but it is unlike Festinger's in that he restricts consistency to "internal consistency," that is, consistency between the affective and cognitive components.

The principal advantage of Festinger's dissonance theory is that it links attitudes with behavior. Thus dissonance may arise as a function of a discrepancy between belief and behavior, between two beliefs, or between one's feelings and beliefs. The difficulty in this approach lies in measuring dissonance.

Kelman also recognizes the importance of consistency in attitude change. However, he makes a sharper distinction between private attitude and one's public expression of it.

These theories as well as others [25] not reported have many ideas in common with the general view of this book. The reader should keep in mind the three theories we have just presented and try to apply them in connection with change in a person's sociocultural environment. For the most part, human motives, values, and attitudes arise out of the reward and punishment results which individuals experience in their respective social environments. All through this book we have conceived the social and cultural systems as systems of adaptation. If the system is principally one of hunting and berry-gathering as a means of subsistence, then one set of motives and values would be expected to develop. On the other hand, if the system is an industrial system of economic organization, then one would expect a different value system to predominate. In other words, there exists a system of values which guide and regulate the system of social organization in effect at any given time in a society. Since the system of social organization is a *means-ends* system for the population, one would expect personal attitudes and values to develop that are reasonably consistent with the expectations of the leaders in the system of social organization. This particularly applies to economic leaders, political leaders, religious leaders, and educational leaders.

Let us provide a hypothetical illustration of the implications of the foregoing. We know, for example, that social change is largely a function of the development of new knowledge and the application of this knowledge in the form of new technology by the leaders of a society.

---

[25] Katz and Stotland, *op. cit.*

We also know that any given form of social organization, to some extent, takes the form it does as a function of the prevailing value system of the society in question. For example, the American system of legal justice is to a major degree traceable to the concepts of freedom, compassion, and the dignity of man as these are reflected in the religious heritage and judicial history of our people.

Consider our present attitude toward the individual and personal right to have children through marriage—that is, to have as many as we want or can. What would happen to our attitude toward this value if the expanding technology continues to expand, allowing our population to increase to a point of virtual standing room only? The point in asking this question is to indicate the great dependence and connection of attitude formation and change to the adaptive demands of the social organization of one's society.

How much crowding can a population stand and still remain physically and mentally healthy? What difference does it make in the formation of one's attitudes, values, and motives if he lives in families of, say, four or five members to the family and on not less than five-acre lots, or, on the other hand, if everyone lives wall to wall or back to back with someone else? We know that change is unceasing; therefore, it is and has always been with us. It has occurred in more or less random and evolutionary ways. Man has reached the point in his development of knowledge that he now possesses the *means* to conceive the type of future environment in which he desires to live and the *means* to bring about the desired future states.

This is probably extremely fortunate, considering the current fantastic rate of change and the possibly dangerous consequences of unplanned change under such conditions of rapidity and interdependence. In other words, we need to peer into the future with all the intelligence we can muster with an eye for ascertaining future consequences of existing trends. Given the results of such careful investigating and assessing of probable future states, then desired courses of action could be formulated and brought into being and undesired future states avoided.

We know that there is a correlation between psychological attitudes and motives on the one hand with the values and behavioral demands of the social organization in practice within a given society. Therefore, it follows that if one wishes to maintain certain values, then he must plan to create the kinds of social environments which will nourish those values. This itself may involve the members of a society in a conflict over values. For example, one may have a positive attitude toward change when the change is a result of his own motivation, but have a negative attitude toward change when it involves the needs and motives of others or even the general welfare of the community.

In the United States we are accustomed to planning change in our individual enterprises often without much consideration for the consequences of such change to others, the argument being that since the property involved is our own, our management of it is our own affair. However, conditions change and as we become more and more interdependent, then change in one system may have great consequences for another. When this occurs, then the "others" involved seek adjustments by appealing to the proper state or federal authorities. This suggests that as change becomes more significant in its consequences and in its scope and rate of occurrence, it then becomes necessary to plan and coordinate it. Metropolitan administration in large cities which involve overlapping county units is an example. However, there is in our society a negative attitude toward central planning when the planning involves or is done by the government. Such an attitude involves a contradiction since any group that is capable of planning for an entire society would *de facto* be the government. If planned and coordinated change have become essential, then it follows that in a democratic society this could best be carried out by involving government, industry, labor, and professional bodies working together toward goals for the general welfare. In fact, a negative attitude toward long-range societal planning could be lethal to a society. If such an attitude prevailed, it would mean that problems could so accumulate as a result of accelerated change that the society would not be able to successfully compete with other societies. For example, suppose that adequate planning did not occur in respect to future education and health needs, then a breakdown in these two areas alone could be disastrous. This raises the difficult question of the relationship between change and attitudes toward change.

6. SOCIAL INFLUENCE, SOCIAL CHANGE, AND SOCIAL ATTITUDES

It is true that social change occurs through time irrespective of a society's attitude toward it. Ancient man and his subsequent offspring for a long time believed that social change was in no way related to human action or purpose. Early notions about social change were in the form of theories and beliefs about "progress." Theories of progress which involved ideas that man can plan for his future are only about three hundred years old, and just recently has it become possible to implement and direct such thinking in concrete action programs. This suggests that the recency of the idea and the very recent possibility of doing anything about long-range planning can help us understand the lag in the public's thinking and attitudes toward planned social change.

In other words, prior learning can interfere with the learning of new material. The psychologist calls this *proactive inhibition*. The reverse of this is the theory of interference with retention of the content of *past* learning by *new* learning and this form of interference is called *retroactive inhibition*.

The general explanation that is offered for the interference of retroactive inhibition is that when something new is being learned, something old is being unlearned. In other words, if one has some new information that contradicts some old ideas, the new learning produces some unlearning of the old ideas. However, we saw in Section 2 of this chapter that change produces fears of becoming obsolescent on the part of some, and not anyone wants to become obsolete. Therefore, anticipated change involves the interests and often the fortunes and status positions of many people and thus old ideas may block the acceptance of new ones. The point is that change *occurs unceasingly, and it affects some negatively whether it is planned or unplanned.*

Just now some writers are referring to the "triple revolution" in change, namely, the revolution in *automation, weaponry,* and *human rights.* These areas of change have great significance—and on a worldwide basis rather than just a national basis. They involve many interrelated consequences and their significance will grow as knowledge and technology expand. The advent of the computer has revolutionized the development of knowledge. Its great advantage is that it speeds up data processing and it can simultaneously consider many, many more variables than the most intelligent of all men. It can be programmed so that it can take into account all of the relevant information in connection with a problem analysis; man seldom does and generally cannot.

One of the most elaborate efforts to simulate human problem-solving has been developed by Newell, Shaw, and Simon through the development of what they call a "General Problem Solver." [26] They took the definitions, axioms, and rules used by Whitehead and Russell in their famous *Principia Mathematica* (1925) and developed a program for theorems in symbolic logic. After the computer was programmed with the symbolic logic program, it was put to work to see if it could derive the 52 theorems of the second chapter of Whitehead and Russell's work. It succeeded in deriving 38 of the theorems using the programmed method of searching for answers. At least one of the proofs was considered more elegant than that which Whitehead and Russell had been able to develop.

The most complex of all of man's undertakings is the one of understanding the environment of man's own creation. It is this environment

[26] A. J. Newell, J. C. Shaw, and H. A. Simon, "Elements of a Theory of Human Problem Solving," *Psychological Review,* Vol. 65 (1958), pp. 151-166.

which produces his problems and provides him with the means for solving them. However, man may have the means in the form of knowledge and technology, but these are inert until someone becomes *concerned and begins to develop the cooperation necessary to apply the knowledge and technology to human needs and problems.* When man fails, it is generally failure at the level of not being concerned or the inability to obtain the necessary cooperation to activate a plan of action. Thus, behind all human achievement is human interest, purpose, energy, and cooperation. How to harness these so that modern man can give rational and planned direction to the tides of change is his most pressing modern problem How is the necessary cooperation achieved? The question is relevant at this point, but to attempt to give an answer would take us far from our main theme. I will point to where I think the answer lies. It lies in learning and accepting the general principle that the best decision for each and all in the long run is the one that gives the greatest good to the greatest number. For example, if we followed this principle in connection with underdeveloped countries, we would facilitate their progress toward modernization and this would by its very nature reduce the differences in values, motives, and national purpose between them and us and hence facilitate communication and cooperation.

When we consider the increasing rate of change in man's environment in relation to the related but slower rate of change in man's attitudes, this implies the possibility of an increasing gap between the social and psychological demands of the new environment and the psychological structure of the participants. In other words, man may be entering, with the development of the computer, a social and technical world which assumes, perhaps requires, values and attitudes that are increasingly at variance with the values and attitudes which he has acquired through ages past. This type of situation is what Gardner Murphy calls "Man's Invention of an Environment for Which He Is Unfitted." [27]

Primitive man was more controlled by his physical environment than modern man. However, modern man has evolved such a complex social and cultural environment that this external system has a certain degree of autonomy over the human participants. This appears to be the result of inertia within the system and the dependence of man upon the *ongoing* functions of the system. If man is to have some manageable control over his own created systems, then he must plan with this in mind.

Modern man can give rational direction to planned change and as an incorrigible optimist I believe that he will—in fact, he must. From the point of view of adaptation and survival there is no other attitude which we can assume.

[27] This is the subject title of a lecture given by Dr. Murphy at Emory University on April 2, 1962.

7. SUMMARY

This chapter was concerned with the very difficult problem of the interrelationships between psychological attitudes and the social values expressed in human social organization. It was shown that the individual develops an internal psychological stability in reaction to significant external uncertainties and that he responds to these in terms of his subjective models. These models represent his perception and conception of the many happenings and events about him and are greatly dependent upon the meaning of these events for his well-being.

We assumed that change in environmental and behavioral properties is continuous. We then focused on the effects of environmental change on individual attitudes and behavior.

It was emphasized that change is both a source of human social problems and a means to their subsequent control. In this regard we took note of the increasing interdependency of a social system as it increases in complexity of organization and harnessing of energy and in its division of labor. This, however, does not result in a concomitant psychological feeling of increased interdependency. In fact, it seems to have just the reverse effect.

In Part 2 of the chapter, aspects of social change which produce anxiety were considered. These were analyzed in terms of three forms of obsolescence, namely, obsolescence of *ideas*, of *status*, and of *irresponsibility*. The first two were fairly self-explanatory, but the third form needed some explanation. It refers to the situation where men have to make decisions which were formerly made for them by factors beyond their control. For example, the high infant mortality rate of the past made a high birth rate functionally desirable; but if the present birth rate continues indefinitely, men will be forced to make a decision regarding desired fertility. To fail to do so would be dangerous. It is clear that social change produces effects that are perceived by some as negative to their interests and by others as positive for theirs.

In Section 3 of the chapter we learned that human knowledge is put into operation and standardized through the creation of human social organizations or institutions. As new knowledge is developed and worked into the ongoing systems of organization, it becomes cumulative. Human behavior is principally composed of learned habits, and these habits are largely acquired out of interaction with other men. The fact that past experience is committed to habit frees man to deal creatively with new problems. In this regard the most significant characteristic of man is his capacity to construct symbolic formulations of experience and subsequently to learn *from* experience rather than just *by* experience.

Institutions or social organizations arise to standardize man's interaction in his efforts to meet his needs and to achieve his purposes or values. Consequently, man develops attitudes toward these institutional patterns since they involve means to rewards or punishments. During time, change occurs within these social systems and this necessitates some psychological reorganization on the part of participants who possess attitudes congruent to the old system. This was discussed at length from the point of view of both the conditions of social change and the conditions of psychological change.

The theories of attitude change which were considered were those of Rosenberg, Festinger, and Kelman. Following the presentation of these, an effort was made to relate the formation and change of human motives and attitudes to changes in the systems of adaptation which meet the needs of man.

Finally, the chapter was concluded with a discussion of the inevitability of social change and the rapidly accumulating significance of such change. It was pointed out that while planned change is feared by some, the alternative is worse because the consequences of unplanned change today have far greater significance than ever before and man's survival may depend upon his capacity and willingness to rationally plan the direction of change. It was shown that, to accomplish this, it will be necessary for men to achieve a new understanding of the nature and potentialities of change for man.

Finally, it was hypothesized that change in man's social and technical environments is occurring at a faster rate than man's emotional and attitudinal make-up is changing. In other words, as Gardner Murphy has said, man appears to have invented an environment for which he is unfitted. The significance of this situation was discussed. It was suggested that if man is to have some manageable control over his own created systems, then he must plan the future states of these systems with this in mind.

Further References

1. H. G. Barnett, *Innovation—The Basis of Cultural Change* (New York, McGraw-Hill Book Company, 1953).
2. Howard Becker and Alvin Boskoff, *Modern Sociological Theory in Continuity and Change* (New York, Holt, Rinehart and Winston, Inc., 1957), especially Chapter 9 on Social Change by Boskoff.
3. Amitai Etzioni and Eva Etzioni, *Social Change* (New York, Basic Books, Inc., 1964).
4. Carl I. Hovland and Irving L. Janis, *Personality and Persuasibility* (New Haven, Yale University Press, 1959).

5. Carl I. Hovland, Irving L. Janis and H. H. Kelley, *Communication and Persuasion* (New Haven, Yale University Press, 1953).
6. Carl I. Hovland, A. A. Lumsdaine and F. D. Sheffield, *Experiments on Mass Communication* (Princeton, N.J., Princeton University Press, 1949).
7. Carl I. Hovland and W. Weiss, "The Influence of Source Credibility on Communication Effectiveness," *Public Opinion Quarterly*, XV (1951), pp. 635-650.
8. Douglas H. Lawrence and Leon Festinger, *Deterrents and Reinforcements* (Stanford, Calif., Stanford University Press, 1962).
9. Wilbert E. Moore, *Social Change* (Englewood Cliffs, N.J., Prentice-Hall, Inc., 1963).
10. M. J. Rosenberg, Carl I. Hovland et al., *Attitude Organization and Change* (New Haven, Yale University Press, 1960).

Part V
SOME METHODS OF ANALYSIS

11

A Perspective for Analyzing Human Behavior

●

1. *Purpose of Chapter*
2. *Introduction*
3. *Science as a Method of Understanding Nature*
4. *The Metaphysics of Science: The Concept of Reality*
5. *The Characteristics of Science*
    (a) *An Illustration: The Physical Problem*
    (b) *Some Characteristics of Science*
        1. Science is propositional
        2. Science is empirical
        3. Science is logical
        4. Science is operational
        5. Science is public
        6. Science is problem-solving
        7. Science is systematic and tends toward a system
        8. Science is open-ended or on-going
6. *The Role of Prediction in Science*
7. *Summary*

1. PURPOSE OF CHAPTER

SINCE THE CONTENTS of this chapter and the next deal with subject matter that is methodological in nature, it is necessary to explain this digression in subject matter.

One might think that by virtue of being a human being it would be easier for a person to understand man's behavior than other aspects of nature. However, this is far from the case. Just as man has found it necessary to invent systems of logic and methods of research to prevent himself from fooling himself in his search to understand the physical world, he has found the riddle of man no less a task and probably the most complex of his scientific ventures. One of the more subtle reasons for man's difficulties in understanding human nature is that he is so attuned to certain aspects of the world about him that he is unaware of its exerting any influence. L. K. Frank, in referring to the lateness of man's discovery of culture as a source of influence on human behavior, suggests that this is due to the great dependence of man on culture. He illustrated this idea by asking: What would be the last source of influence on the behavior of fish that a fish would probably think to study if he were endowed with the capacity to study? He answered by saying that it would probably be the water about him. And so it has been with man: the last part of his environment that he has thought to study is the most intimate part, namely, culture. I suppose Frank's hypothetical fish might be made painfully aware of his dependence upon water if he were to find himself removed from it. But since man internalizes culture from the moment of birth, and is affected by it even before, it is impossible for him to "step outside culture." Nevertheless, if we are to comprehend human nature in any scientific way, we must develop procedures for objectively assessing the *effects* of culture.

To do this, we must first be aware of the fact that the common-sense understanding of human behavior that every human being has by virtue of being a human being is inadequate for a scientific understanding. In fact, it may even interfere with students' efforts to appreciate the *constructive* efforts of the scientist in his work toward understanding man. The same is true in physics. The man in the street can get along very well by conceptualizing *work* as labor and *force* as coercion, but these are hardly adequate for the purposes of the physicist, and so it is with the social psychologist.

Since the social psychologist cannot literally remove the effects of culture in his study of man, if he is clever enough he may contrive conditions of study and methods of control which will enable him to assess the separate effects of factors and their combined effects. But such an undertaking will require the student to make an effort to break out of the crust and shackles of traditional ways of viewing human behavior and to develop new and bold ways for viewing and studying behavior.

There are many ways for viewing man, or anything else for that matter, since the perspective depends to some extent upon the purpose of the investigator. Man may be viewed aesthetically, philosophically, morally, or scientifically. Since it is our purpose to view man from a scientific perspective, it is essential for the reader to have this perspective in mind. Unfortunately, it cannot be assumed that the scientific perspective which the student has already learned in other disciplines will automatically transfer to a behavioral science discipline. It is for this reason that we are providing in this chapter a brief overview of the scientific perspective in the hope that this will enable transfer to occur more efficiently. With this purpose in mind let us now consider some of the basic assumptions of science in general.

2. INTRODUCTION

Science, says James B. Conant, is ". . . a process of fabricating a web of interconnected concepts and conceptual schemes arising from experiments and observations and fruitful of further experiments and observations." [1]

Definitions are always relevant to one's purposes and seldom meet the logician's requirements for adequacy. Certainly the institution of science is so elaborate and many-faceted that any definition of it will only encompass selected aspects for emphasis, and so it is with Conant's definition. He chooses to emphasize the *method* by which we arrive at verified knowledge, but he also suggests or implies the *logical* priority of theory to data, at least within the *research* context.

Science constitutes one kind of knowledge, but it is not the only kind of knowledge. ". . . we are willing to admit that there are several different kinds of knowledge. Or, in particular, we do not wish to suppose that science is synonymous with knowledge. In our definition, science is known, but not all that is known is science." [2]

3. SCIENCE AS A METHOD OF UNDERSTANDING NATURE

The word *science* as used here will be taken to include all the natural sciences (physical and biological) and the social sciences (anthropology, economics, psychology, sociology, and political science insofar as the latter, that is, political science, is concerned with empirical subject matter). It will exclude philosophy, logic, history, and mathematics. If the reasons for these exclusions are not clear to the student from what he already knows, then the matter should clear up when he reads Section 3 below.

An examination of the achievements of scientists will indicate that the function of a science is to establish general principles covering the

---

[1] James B. Conant, *Modern Science and Modern Man* (Garden City, N.Y., Doubleday & Co., Inc., 1953), pp. 106-107.
[2] Roy G. Francis, *The Rhetoric of Science* (Minneapolis, University of Minnesota Press, 1961), p. 5.

behavior of empirical regularities or events with which the science in question is concerned, and to order these into a system which will adequately represent existing scientific data.

The preceding paragraph referred to *empirical regularities* as being the scientist's object of explanation. A basic assumption of all fields of science is that there exists a "knowable" real world and that this world is made up of events and processes which recur with a remarkable regularity through time. These recurring patterns or uniformities are what we mean by empirical regularities. If there were no such regularities, then there could be no science. The fact that human behavior exhibits a stability and uniformity over time is what makes it amenable to scientific understanding and of interest to science. Anyone who has read carefully the Old Testament of the Bible will quickly recognize that these ancient writers were describing human problems and traits that are as much a part of modern man as they were of man then.

The facts of a science are composed from the data of experience. These data describe empirical regularities. For example, water freezes at 32° Fahrenheit at sea level. This is a statement which describes an empirical regularity. The problem of explanation begins when the scientist attempts to show what processes and conditions cause H_2O to freeze. The data of empirical experience are either directly or indirectly observable by the researcher. Many would argue that observation is always indirect. This is, of course, true in the sense that the observer is always apart from the behavior being observed. Furthermore, he observes only some aspect of the behavior and not the underlying dynamics and conditions which are producing the behavior he is observing. If an observer sees a man beating his dog, he only sees him beating the dog, that is, he does not see the factors which explain the beating behavior. These are inferred and the inferences can be checked, but the process of checking is sometimes a very extended and complex series of steps.

It was earlier asserted that the fundamental aim of science is the establishment of laws or principles. These principles are developed to provide explanations of the empirical facts investigated. How do we know whether a certain theory is true? The answer is that by logical deduction one can derive the expected consequences from the theory and check these deductions by appropriately controlled observation or experimentation. It is to these logically deduced "consequences" that we are referring when we speak of the data of experience. If the logically deduced consequences of the theory are actually confirmed by properly controlled observation, then we accept the theory as true.

It should be evident by now that science as a method of explaining relationships in nature involves two broad but inseparable aspects of human knowledge. These are *experience* and *reason*. Logical thinking alone can give us no knowledge of the world of experience. Conclusions based solely upon purely rational processes are empty so far as "reality" is concerned. The history of science credits Galileo with first clearly recognizing this, and it is for this reason that he is generally recognized as the father of modern science.

If reason is empty insofar as knowing reality is concerned, then what role is it assigned in science? Reason and logic give structure and guidance to the system of concepts and theories which compose the explanatory body of a science.

Research is solidly linked with scientific theory. Theory provides the framework within which any research design must be formulated. New formulations must logically connect with existing theory. This does not mean that all new formulations must agree with existing ones. It simply means that they are related in a logical sense and that they are capable of being falsified or affirmed. Thus reason, abstraction, generalization, and the formulation of descriptive variables are all construction aspects of the daily work of the scientist. These constructions must point to a sufficiently clear set of observable referents to permit decisive scientific tests to be carried out. Hence the *creative* aspects of scientific work involve reasoning or, as I have called them, the construction efforts of the scientist. But we must always remember that these creative efforts refer back to sense experience and must be formulated in a manner which permits the theory to be either falsified or affirmed by experience. One should not assume that once a theory has been affirmed, its status is then fixed forever and a day. Scientific knowledge constitutes an open system in that it is never complete but is constantly on-going and public. This implies the finiteness of man's ability in his eternal quest for knowledge. But science is a social institution, which means that its advances are the result of the communication and interaction of many men present and past. Consequently, scientific achievements are cumulative. This, of course, allows each generation to accomplish things which were not possible for previous generations to achieve.

A basic assumption of scientific thought is that all events are determined or caused and that the ultimate function of science is to discover what determines what. There are, of course, previous stages such as the ascertaining or the discovery of the existence of something. The phrase "what determines what" is the meaning given to the term *reality*, which has been referred to several times before.

Scientific theories are validated or tested by harmonizing the theoretical and empirical parts in the structure of a science. This is a rather difficult and complex operation and its importance can hardly be overemphasized. The procedures are too involved to be discussed with a few brief sentences. Yet, some additional discussion of what the scientist means when he speaks of "reality" should be helpful toward this end.

4. THE METAPHYSICS OF SCIENCE: THE CONCEPT OF REALITY

The student may wonder why metaphysics is discussed in connection with a field of science. The reason is that science is related to metaphysics. Its relation to logic is perhaps obvious to the reader, but its relation to metaphysics may not be so obvious. It is related to metaphysics through the assumptions which a science makes about reality. Three broad assumptions are often made.

> The *first* is, that we live in a knowable real world. The *second* is, that this world is not changed by our knowledge of it. The *third* is that our relation to the world may be changed by that knowledge. An example, however trivial: if we observe a "stove," it may be hot or cold. Knowing that it is, say, hot, does not change the stove, although our behavior towards it would be different than if it were cold.[3]

It should be noted that some scholars object to the second assumption as stated by Francis. For example, Heisenberg contends that when measuring subatomic behavior, there are uncontrollable disturbances produced by the observer; but when measuring large-scale objects, these effects are negligible and can be ignored. In other words, Heisenberg contends that certain aspects of reality are affected by our application of knowledge. He states that

> the interaction between observer and object causes uncontrollable and large changes in the system being observed, because of the discontinuous character of atomic processes. The immediate consequence of this circumstance is that in general every experiment performed to determine some numerical quantity renders the knowledge of others illusory, since the uncontrollable perturbations of the observed system alters the values of previously determined quantities.[4]

Does a publishing of the results of a public opinion poll subsequently affect voter behavior? These are currently unanswered questions. In fact, many good authorities do not accept Heisenberg's "uncertainty principle" which was alluded to by the quotation above.[5]

The point is that one should be aware of the assumptions that he is

---

[3] R. G. Francis in John T. Doby, ed., *An Introduction to Social Research* (Harrisburg, Pa., Stackpole Books, 1954), p. 5.

[4] Werner Heisenberg, *The Physical Principles of the Quantum Theory* (Chicago, The University of Chicago Press, 1930), p. 3. Cited in Ernest Nagel, *The Structure of Science* (New York, Harcourt, Brace and World, Inc., 1961), p. 295.

[5] Nagel, *op. cit.*, pp. 297-305.

making about reality and examine them carefully for contradictions. If our assumptions are implicit, then the likelihood of unwitting contradictions is great. In this regard, when the scientist says that he develops laws and theories to explain the "real world," what does he assume about the relationship of these laws to the "real world"? Does he asssume that the "laws" discovered constitute a part of the "real world," or does he assume that they are constructions of the human mind which describe with some ascertainable precision aspects of the real world?

This issue is well illustrated in an anecdote about three baseball umpires who were arguing about their job.

> Each called balls and strikes; each was bragging as to who did the best job. Said one: "I call them as I *see* them—and no one can do better than that." The second retorted, "That's nothing; I call them as they *are*." The third paused a moment, and finally added: *"They ain't nothing until I call them*—and then that's what they are." [6]

Each umpire illustrates a different metaphysical assumption.

The late professor Albert Einstein contended that "all knowledge about reality begins with experience and terminates in it." [7]

This is also a basic assumption of this book and it is argued that man has only *experiences* and *interpretations* of reality and consequently never knows "reality" with a capital R, although as a model he strives toward this end. In a very real sense, as man's knowledge of "reality" grows, then his understanding of "reality" and his relations to it are always changing.

> The kind of cause and effect relationships that we in modern society think of as "real" or "empirical" relationships are, for one thing, extremely hard to discover. What is amazing is how man ever did figure out such a relationship as that between planting seeds, for example, and months later seeing crops grow. Or, for another example, the relationship between sexual intercourse and pregnancy. Certainly, there is nothing self-evident about those relationships. Often seeds are planted and crops do not grow; often intercourse is practiced and pregnancy does not result. Is it really any more "reasonable" to connect these crops with those earlier seeds than it is to connect them with that omen which some wise man remembered? Is it really very obvious that this birth is a result of that coitus nine months ago, rather than a result of the woman's prayers, or a result of the intercourse's having taken place in the dark of the moon? [8]

---

[6] Doby, Francis *et al., op. cit.*, pp. 16-17. Italics added.
[7] Albert Einstein in Edward H. Madden, *The Structure of Scientific Thought* (Boston, Houghton Mifflin Co., 1960), p. 81.
[8] Harry C. Bredemeier and Richard M. Stephenson, *The Analysis of Social Systems* (New York, Holt, Rinehart and Winston, Inc., 1962), p. 254.

It is perhaps easy to note relationships between antecedent conditions and consequences when the time span between them is very brief and the relationship subject to direct observation. But so few instances of such occur that it is amazing that man ever formulated cause-effect logic in terms of antecedent conditions and subsequent consequences. A very good case can be made for the contention that the invention of this mode of reasoning, sometimes loosely called the scientific method, is the most significant contribution of the human mind in perhaps two thousand or more years.

The problem of validating the connection between antecedents and consequences is difficult because there are many antecedents that may be postulated as causes, and the "real" causes are highly elusive under the best of circumstances. While the concepts and theories which explain the empirical realities are freely chosen and constructed, the liberty of choice is of a special kind. Einstein says that the choice

> . . . is not in any way similar to the liberty of a writer of fiction. Rather, it is similar to that of a man engaged in solving a well-designed word puzzle. He may, it is true, propose any word as the solution; but, there is only *one* word which really solves the puzzle in all its forms. It is an outcome of faith that nature—as she is perceptible to our five senses—takes the character of such a well formulated puzzle. The successes reaped up to now by science do, it is true, give a certain encouragement for this faith.[9]

With this note on "faith" the fact that science is undergirded with a metaphysical foundation should by now be clear.

With the foregoing discussion of the metaphysical assumptions of science it should be easier to comprehend the essential characteristics of science per se.

5. THE CHARACTERISTICS OF SCIENCE

We have indicated previously that the goal of science is the development of theory or general principles which will systematically account for a wide range of empirical regularities. Science also possesses several methodologies for realizing or achieving this goal. Thus science includes both a goal and the means for obtaining it.

In considering the goal of science to be the development of theory, it should be noted that this consideration refers to the goal of the scientist as *scientist*. For example, when the scientist is researching to ascertain

---

[9] Madden, *op. cit.*, p. 84.

the factors which determine opinion formation and change, he is functioning as a scientist. On the other hand, if he is using the methods of science simply to find out what opinion prevails on some issue, then he is functioning as a technician or applied scientist. These distinctions are, of course, arbitrary since each endeavor contributes to the other. However, it is important to distinguish between the roles of the scientist as the *creator* of new knowledge or the user of *existing* knowledge to solve old difficulties. The former leads to an increase in society's stock of basic knowledge and the other to an implementation of this knowledge. The scientist as consumer of his own products becomes then a producer of more scientific theory. Ultimately, of course, science exists to help solve human difficulties and facilitate human problem-solving. One might say that primarily science exists to enable members of society to "know," but that ultimately it exists to enable society to "do." These two sets of activities when properly balanced enrich each other. Certainly in modern times theoretical science is the primary source of applied science or technology. However, applied science can and sometimes does generate problems of a theoretical nature. Thus the "knowing" and "doing" aspects interact.

In pursuing the primary goal of science it should be noted that there are two interrelated aspects to scientific discovery. The first aspect concerns the ascertaining that something or some relation *exists*. This might be called the problem of establishing that something *is*. This is a very complex matter itself because even the existence of the "thing" or "relationship" is often inferred through a chain of logical steps and confirmed or denied by indirect observation. The history of science affords many examples of this fact. The existence of bacteria was inferred quite some time before Pasteur demonstrated their existence.

Once something or some relationship has been shown to exist, then the second aspect concerns the matter of determining *what* it is. The latter is a matter of interpretation or theory. Carbon deposits recognized for some time now as fossil remains were observed by the people of medieval Europe, but they were not interpreted by observers of that time as fossils. Thus it may be fairly easy to establish that something *is* present, but it is not so easy to establish "what it is" that is present and is being observed. Back to our fossil fish example, it is important to note that these carbon imprints were not conceived by the people of this general era as fossils. They were not so conceived because there did not exist at that time an adequate geology which provided theories and evidence about the shifting of the earth's surfaces and the inundation by water of portions of the earth in the past, which at a much later point in time are free of water. Since they could not imagine water ever being over such places, they in turn could not imagine fish ever being in such places. Therefore, they interpreted the imprint remains in terms of what made sense to them at the time.[10]

In simplest form the fundamental structure of scientific research involves the following sets of steps: first, the statement of a physical problem; secondly, the translating of the physical problem into a mathematical problem; thirdly, the solving of the mathematical problem; and, fourthly, the interpreting of the mathematical results and the translation of these back into the physical problem. This can be diagrammed as follows:

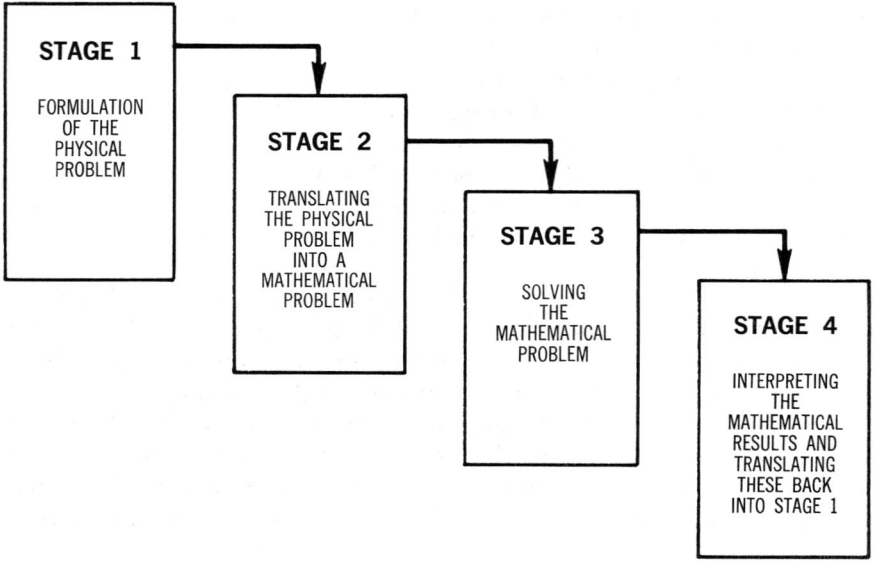

FIGURE 11:1. Schematic Diagram of the Stages of Scientific Problem-solving. See O. G. Sutton, *Mathematics in Action* (Harper & Row, Publishers, Inc., 1960), p. 15, for further elaboration.

A simple illustration should help clarify the meaning of this formulation.

(a) *An Illustration: The Physical Problem.* If at every moment the rate of increase of population is proportional to the population at that moment, then what is the *annual* rate of increase of a population during a given time span? Suppose the time span in question is ten years and that the population at the beginning of the ten-year period was 5 million and at the end of the period it was 7 million.

In obtaining a solution to this problem, as with any problem, certain

---

[10] For an interesting discussion of concept formation and experience the student should read Albert Einstein and Leopold Infeld, *The Evolution of Physics* (New York, Simon and Schuster, Inc., 1938), esp. pp. 235-238.

assumptions must be made. Obviously, population increases are represented by positive integers. That is, there are no fractions of people. However, we are going to assume that population increases as a *continuous* function. We are doing this because it is an observational fact that population growth is best described as an exponential function. Thus we are able to describe the population of an area at the end of a projected period of time by the equation

$$(1) \quad P_n = P_0(1+r)^n$$

where r is a nonzero real constant, the rate of growth. It can be found by solving Equation (1) for r:

$$(2) \quad r = \left(\frac{P_n}{P_0}\right)^{\frac{1}{n}} - 1.^{[11]}$$

P_0 equals the population at the first point in time and P_n at the second or later point in time and the exponent, $\frac{1}{n}$, represents the fractional time interval and the exponent n in formula (1) represents the total time from P_0 to P_n.

Formulas (1) and (2) are simply mathematical statements of the physical problem which was described earlier.

If, as before, $P_0 = 5.0$ million, $P_n = 7.0$ million, and $n = 10$, we have as the measure of the constant *annual* rate of increase

$$r = \left(\frac{7.0}{5.0}\right)^{\frac{1}{10}} - 1 = (1.40)^{\frac{1}{10}} - 1.$$

By logarithms,

$$\log (1.40)^{\frac{1}{10}} = \frac{1}{10} \log 1.40 = \frac{1}{10}(0.14613) = 0.014613.$$

The antilogarithm of this is 1.034, so

$$(1.40)^{\frac{1}{10}} = 1.034$$

and

$$r = 1.034 - 1 = .034.$$

That is, the population increase from 5 to 7 million over the ten-year period was at the average rate of 3.4 percent per year. Thus we now have the solution to the mathematical problem and all that remains is to translate and interpret these results in terms of the initial statement

---

[11] For a derivation of equations (1) and (2) see Thomas C. McCormick, *Elementary Social Statistics* (New York, McGraw-Hill Book Company, Inc., 1941), pp. 113-114.

of the physical problem. It is perhaps unnecessary to add that few scientific problems will be as easy to solve as was the foregoing example, but this example well illustrates the sequence of major stages.

The discussion which follows on the general characteristics of science should now be more meaningful. It was indicated earlier in this chapter that science contained both an end and the means for attaining the end. The end was stated as the development of principles and theories and the means are logic, mathematics, and methodology. Thus the characteristics of science discussed here refer to both means and ends.

(b) *Some Characteristics of Science:* (1) *Science is Propositional.*[12] It formulates statements of relationship about aspects and properties of nature which have ascertainable truth-value. The behavioral sciences deal with *propositions* about human behavior. Much of chemistry is composed of a set of symbols which describe the relations among molecules.

There are two kinds of errors which may occur in the formulation of scientific propositions. These are (1) errors in *logic* or logical fallacies, and (2) errors in *fact* or material fallacies. Logical errors can be avoided or ascertained by a correct use of the rules of symbolic logic.[13] In order to determine whether a material fallacy has been committed, we must have rules connecting propositions with the world of experience. We may accept a proposition as true when in fact it is false or we may conclude that it is false when in fact it is true. In other words, a scientist may accept a statement which is false, or he may reject a statement which is true. Scientific rules and procedures enable him to minimize these errors. The adequacy of one's research design is the principal means for minimizing errors of a material sort. Scientific methodology constitutes the set of rules or code by which the adequacy of one's research operations is judged.[14]

It should be emphasized that the changes in a science occur through the *addition, modification,* or *subtraction* of new propositions to its existing body of propositions. Generally, in any specific research situation, this involves choosing from a logically derived set of alternative propositions. This, of course, requires the use of a research design to enable a scientific choice to be made. Furthermore, the foregoing statement about

---

[12] The basic source for this list of characteristics is R. G. Francis in John T. Doby, ed., *An Introduction to Social Research* (Harrisburg, Pennsylvania, Stackpole Books, 1954), pp. 6-9.

[13] If the student has not already had a course in symbolic logic, then it is strongly recommended that one be taken.

[14] It would necessitate an extensive digression to attempt to discuss these rules and procedures here, but as an example of an approach to the problem the student is invited to read Chapter 13 in Allen L. Edwards, *Statistical Methods for the Behavioral Sciences* (New York, Holt, Rinehart and Winston, Inc., 1954). Especially relevant are pages 255-271 on the "Two Types of Error" and tests of significance.

"addition, modification, or subtraction" of propositions suggests that once a proposition has been accepted into the body of a science, it is always subject to subsequent revision or questioning. That is, *all* scientific propositions which have been accepted are accepted tentatively. This means that a statement that is acceptable at a given time may be modified or rejected in the future. This propositional control which science exercises applies to all levels of abstraction of theories as well as to methodology.

(2) *Science is Empirical.* The propositional characteristic of science refers to and rests on sense data. This in no way excludes abstract concepts and theories. It simply means that these abstract concepts and theories are formulated with a concern for the real or empirical world. In fact, these abstract concepts and theories are formulated to explain the observed patterns of the empirical world. These formulations are in the form of a hypothetical solution to the empirical problem. From the hypothetical solution predictions are deduced of other observable phenomena. Observations are then made to test these predictions. If the outcomes occur as predicted, then the hypothesis is accepted. If the predictions are only partially fulfilled or not at all, then the hypothesis is modified or rejected.

(3) *Science is Logical.* A system of logic, particularly symbolic logic, is not a theory (that is, a set of propositions about things or relations); it is instead a system of signs and the rules for their use. While science is logical, logic is not science. Hence logic is analytically separable from science. However, science is not independent of logic. Its conclusions and inferences regarding the acceptance or rejection of propositions are justified by the rules of logic. The rules and language of logic provide the structure of a science. In fact, modern science consists of a set of symbolic statements which have been given physical interpretations, and these interpreted signs then serve to designate the basic concepts of the theory or theories in question.

(4) *Science is Operational.* Logic refers to the formal structure of an argument and its correctness depends upon the rules of logic. In other words, the formal correctness of an argument does not depend upon the empirical content of an argument. In fact, one may construct a formal argument which has no empirical content. That is to say, one may develop logical classes, but this does not insure that there will be empirical members in these classes. For example, we could argue about the behavior of leprechauns and the argument could be formally correct, but from the point of view of science where are the leprechauns?

The operational characteristic of science is primarily concerned with the means or steps which one follows to generate or obtain empirical content for the theoretical classes. Specifically, it is the mathematical formulation of a physical problem. A simple illustration using the elementary concept of *density* in physics should suffice to show what we mean by an operational specification. The concept of density arises from the need to take into account the fact that objects are found to have different weights for the same volume or different volumes for the same weight. To describe this property of objects, physicists employ the concept *density*. To be sure, any student who has had any elementary physics is familiar with all this. Our purpose in describing the concept is to illustrate the operational characteristic of science. *Density* is defined as weight divided by volume. This, of course, presupposes that weight and volume have already been defined. Volume is defined as the product of three lengths which are mutually perpendicular, that is, in terms of cubic feet (ft^3) or cubic centimeters (cm^3). Weight is simply measured in terms of pounds or grams. Thus, density is defined as weight divided by volume. Suppose an object weighs 84 grams and is placed in a partly-filled graduated cylinder. Let us assume that the water surface rises from 120 cubic centimeters to 160 cubic centimeters. The volume of the object is 40 cubic centimeters. Since Density = $\frac{Weight}{Volume}$, then the density of the object in this example is $\frac{84}{40} = 2.1 \frac{g}{cm^3}$. The operational specifications were the procedures used to determine volume and weight, and density was then specified as the ratio of weight to volume.

(5) *Science is Public.* We have stated before that symbolic and propositional logic provided the structure of a science. When this structure is formalized, it is completely communicable and hence public. It is, of course, obvious that a scientific discovery cannot be incorporated into the body of a science until it has been disseminated to other scientists in the field and confirmed by them.

The standardized aspect of scientific procedure and the symbolic structure of science make it possible for specific studies to be reproduced by others and previous results to be tested.

(6) *Science is Problem-Solving.* In general, we mean by problem-solving the explanation of an empirical pattern or regularity. The absence of an explanation may be due to an incorrect formulation of the problem or to the inadequacy of existing theory. The solutions to problems which add to our stock of explanations about behavior in the real world result in the growth of theoretical or basic science. The application of this knowledge to human difficulties and needs results in the growth of technology. Problems of applied science or technology can and do give rise to basic scientific considerations, but it is important to keep in mind that the *goals* of technology and science are different. The goals of science are fundamentally concerned with the development of new theory and the goals of technology with its application to problems of living and adaptation.

(7) *Science is Systematic and Tends Toward a System*. It has been indicated before that two of the principal components of science are logic and theory. Logic provides the rules for inference and hence tends toward a system of closure. That is, it tends toward completion of the system and thus excludes propositions that are logically not a part of the system. But new discoveries may force a revision of the system of theory and thereby enable it to incorporate the new propositions.

As scientific knowledge increases, scientific concepts, laws, and hypotheses become more and more abstract and general. It is in this way that science can incorporate more and more new knowledge and still retain its basic body or structure intact. This characteristic of science is easily recognizable when one reads the history of a science and notes the growing abstractions from very concrete and common-sense type observations to highly abstract and indirect observations such as in the case of atomic physics. The tendency for a science to become more and more systematic is facilitated by the translation of its concepts and propositions into mathematical form. This adds not only to the precision of the statements but also to the flexibility in manipulation of the logical relations among statements. It also enables one to more easily and quickly discover contradictory statements and errors in reasoning.

(8) *Science is Open-Ended or On-Going*. Ideally, science seeks to develop a unified logical structure which will reduce all of its conceptual elements to a single unified system. That is, science is constantly striving for a higher logical unity. This results in concepts which appear more and more to be less compatible with the observations made by our senses.

It is doubtful if such unity of structure in science will ever be achieved. It nevertheless remains a scientific ideal. While science strives for a unified logical and theoretical system which will incorporate every single datum of scientific experience, in order to do so it must constantly improve its powers of generalization. In other words, science is constantly on-going. Sense data still are and always will remain the sole criterion for determining the adequacy of a system to explain and predict. While sense data determine the adequacy of the logical and theoretical structure, they are not necessarily the source of this structure. Much of the creative part of the structure comes from mathematics.

6. THE ROLE OF PREDICTION IN SCIENCE

Logically, the processes of making predictions and deriving explanations in science are the same. Consequently, what we have said about explanation is also applicable to prediction. There is an important difference in the time order of making predictions and formulating explanations. Obviously, prediction implies that the predictive statement or prediction is made *before* the outcome occurs. Explanation occurs after the outcome. Ordinarily, the term *prediction* is reserved for controlled experiments where the investigator arranges the antecedent conditions in a manner which will enable him to determine which one produced the outcome. The term *forecast* is usually reserved for statements about future outcomes under uncontrolled conditions.

It is clear that in certain kinds of experimental procedures the logical order of explanation and the temporal order of empirical events are the same. That is, the structure of the argument parallels the time order of events. This is the case with a prediction design. This arrangement allows for clear and convincing results. However, not all experimental procedures are of this "before-and-after" variety. A geologist drawing upon current theory may formulate a new theory which, if correct, would predict the location of a currently unknown geological phenomenon. The geologist would then check the predicted location to see if the phenomenon is present as predicted. If he finds it as he predicted, then his new theory is confirmed. But the event predicted in this case had occurred many years before. What difference does it make from the point of view of the rigor of scientific inference whether the event occurred before or after the prediction? Logically, of course, it would not be *pre*diction, but aside from semantics of this sort, what difference would it make for the logic of inference?

The answer is that it makes a vast difference in the scientist's ability to make a clear and unambiguous interpretation and explanation. Why? In the after-the-event or *ex post facto* situation one is often required to reason from *effects* to *cause*, whereas in the prediction type experiment one has more rigorous control over the antecedent conditions and can, therefore, systematically vary these conditions and observe their effects on the various outcomes.[15] In other words, in the prediction type of experiment he reasons from *cause* to *effect*.

However, the *ex post facto* design is *not* necessarily of the traditional effects-to-cause variety. One can formulate an "if . . . then" type of argument, that is, assert that if these conditions are true, then these results would be expected. The empirical problem would then be to carefully identify the asserted "if" conditions and then follow through to see if the expected results were present in a sample population. To be sure, as in the geology example, the outcome has occurred, but the investigator did not know the outcome distribution beforehand in respect to the particular subjects under investigation. This type of control of variables is sometimes called "symbolic control." It has interesting possi-

---

[15] For a good discussion of cause-to-effect and effect-to-cause experiments the student is invited to read Ernest Greenwood, *Experimental Sociology* (New York, Kings Crown Press, 1945), ch. 9.

bilities, but the basic difficulty is in knowing when you have an adequate and representative sample.

In the early part of Section 4 above we discussed the problem of identifying and determining *what* a thing or a relationship is once it has been noted by an observer. Those scientific discoveries which were predicted in advance from existing scientific theory pose no problem for determining *what* they are. This follows from the fact that the scientist knew in advance what to look for. The filling of the empty places in the periodic table in chemistry is an example of this kind of prediction. It is those discoveries that were not predicted which are so difficult to interpret or correctly recognize at the time of discovery.[16]

The electric current and the X-ray are well-known examples of discoveries which were not predicted in advance from existing theory. It is also well known that investigators earlier observed the presence of these properties, but without attaching any significance to them, much to their chagrin later. Thus it is that scientific concepts and theories are guides to scientific research and hence determine what the investigators take to be significant or not significant.

It should be clear that the predictive type scientific design, when it can be employed, is a powerful means of enabling the researcher to give an unambiguous interpretation to his experimental results. Let us remind ourselves again of the purpose of presenting this brief overview of the scientific perspective. The purpose was to help provide the reader with an orientation for viewing and analyzing human behavior. It is hoped that this orientation will stimulate the student to read further in the field of the philosophy of science and on scientific methodology. To the student who does, it will be a rewarding experience, and to the extent that he integrates this experience into his thinking about the nature of man he will find new glimmers of light filtering through the cracks in the walls of ignorance.

We will deal with some of the specific principles of experimentation and some related techniques in the next chapter.

7. SUMMARY

Science is viewed as an evolving body of knowledge about relationships in nature and the further evolving means for continually extending our understanding of nature.

The method of science was treated as principally a creative process, where the scientist maintains complete control over his propositions and manipulates these by means of the rules of symbolic logic, and checks

---

[16] For an excellent article which deals with the historical aspect of this matter the student should read Thomas S. Kuhn, "Historical Structure of Scientific Discovery," *Science*, Vol. 136 (June 1, 1962), pp. 760-764.

his interpretations by means of prediction and empirical observation. Hence, science is portrayed as fundamentally hypothetical-deductive-observational in nature.

Following this, certain basic metaphysical assumptions of science were discussed. Three basic assumptions were given. These were: (1) that the real world consists of ascertainable recurring regularities; (2) that this world is not changed by our knowledge of it; but (3) that our relations to the world about us may be changed by that knowledge. In regard to these assumptions, it should be noted that some authorities today would doubt whether number two above is altogether true. Some would argue that the world of reality would not be changed by our knowledge of it but that an application of this knowledge may change aspects of it. For example, radiation changes in the atmosphere are traced to atomic testing, and new sociological theories on the development of social behavior may lead to new child-rearing practices. But whether all this changes reality or simply the appearances of reality is still something of a moot question.

Finally, the characteristics of science were discussed. Eight characteristics were derived. These were: (1) science is propositional; (2) science is empirical; (3) science is logical; (4) science is operational; (5) science is public; (6) science is problem-solving; (7) science tends toward a system; and, (8) finally, science is ongoing.

Further References

1. Richard B. Braithwaite, *Scientific Explanation* (Cambridge, England, Cambridge University Press, 1955).
2. Herbert Feigl and May Brodbeck, eds., *Readings in The Philosophy of Science* (New York, Appleton-Century-Crofts, 1953), especially "Causality and the Science of Human Behavior," by Adolf Grünbaum, pp. 766-777.
3. Ronald A. Fisher, *The Design of Experiments,* 4th ed. (Edinburgh, Oliver and Boyd, 1947).
4. Abraham Kaplan, *The Conduct of Inquiry* (San Francisco, Chandler Publishing Co., 1964).
5. Melvin H. Marx, Editor, *Theories in Contemporary Psychology* (New York, The Macmillan Company, 1963).
6. John H. Mueller and Karl F. Schuessler, *Statistical Reasoning in Sociology* (Boston, Houghton Mifflin Company, 1961).

12
Some Principles and Methods of Experimentation

•

1. *Purpose of the Chapter*
2. *Introduction to the Problem*
3. *Sets and Functions*
4. *Bases for Establishing the Existence of Relationships*
    (a) *Concomitant Variation*
        1. Simple Linear Correlation and Simple Regression
    (b) *Analysis of Variance*
        1. Introduction
        2. The Concept of Variance
        3. Analysis of Variance: One-Way Classification —The Basic Problem
        4. Analysis of Variance: One-Way Classification —The Required Sums of Squares
        5. Analysis of Variance: Two Variables of Classification
5. *Methods of Inference and Interpretations of Research Results*
    (a) *Basic Types of Experimental Designs*
        1. Method of Concomitant Variation
        2. Method of Difference
        3. Method of Agreement
        4. Joint Method of Agreement and Difference
    (b) *Some Measures of Relationship*

6. *Difficulties and Pitfalls in the Use of Laboratory Experimental Designs in Social Psychological Research*
7. *Summary*

1. PURPOSE OF THE CHAPTER

THE CONTENTS OF THIS chapter as well as that of Chapter 11 seem to be out of place in the customary text on social psychology. For that reason alone it is important that its specific purpose be made clear.

It is not assumed by the writer that this is the first time the student has encountered materials on principles of experimentation. Rather, it is assumed that the student has already learned a good deal about this subject in introductory psychology and in introductory courses in the natural and physical sciences. Then why is the subject treated here by way of a single chapter if the student has already been exposed to many of the ideas? The answer comes from the writer's experience in teaching the subject. First, the training in principles of experimentation which the student receives in all the other courses which represent empirical science are principally aimed at orienting the student for *those* disciplines, but somehow the student fails to get the idea that the logic of science and the general principles of experimentation are common to *all* empirical science and what is different are the *techniques* of application of these principles. In other words, transfer of training does not successfully occur. In fact, what seems to occur is that most students appear to think that these principles of research are peculiar to the fields in which they are specifically encountered.

Secondly, a given field of science tends to *emphasize* particular aspects of the general principles of experimentation and therefore some specific attention must be given to the principles and techniques which will help the student better understand the empirical procedures and findings of the field under study at the moment.

In summary, then, this chapter is not intended as the student's first introduction to the subject, but instead it aims (1) to remind the student that what he has already learned in this area is relevant but must now be refocused to the context of social psychological behavior, and (2) to provide selected techniques which will be helpful in understanding the empirical procedures and findings of social psychology.

It will not be necessary to absolutely master all the statistical techniques presented in Sections 4 and 5 of this chapter, but it will be helpful to give these materials a good try.

2. INTRODUCTION TO THE PROBLEM

The experimental method more nearly approximates the ideal application of the logic of science than any other method in scientific use.

METHODS OF EXPERIMENTATION

Loosely speaking, it can be said that the experimental method is the concrete embodiment of the ideal logical structure of science. This, of course, does not mean that any particular experiment is necessarily good or even well designed or that only experimental data contribute to the advancement of science. The adequacy or degree of approximation of a given experimental design to the ideal logical model of experimental inference depends upon many things. Among these are the state of development of the theory and the adequacy of the instruments of observation within the field. These instruments may range all the way from paper-and-pencil tests to elaborately contrived hardware. It might also be added that the most important ingredient is the imagination and cleverness of the scientist himself. Furthermore, the methods and procedures for experimentation are themselves constantly undergoing evolution and improvement. For example, the classical form of the ideal experiment was to hold constant all the independent variables except the one which the investigator was interested in testing. He would systematically vary it and observe the effect on the dependent variable or outcome factor. Usually, the method of holding constant was by means of direct manipulation, such as controlling the temperature of a gas or the amount of certain chemicals included in a solution.

It does not take much imagination to detect the shortcomings of this early idealized form of experimentation. Suppose that a factor under study functions jointly with another factor. The investigator would probably conclude that it was not significant. Why? If his procedures only allowed for varying one factor at a time, then it is unlikely that he could have discovered joint effects since to do so would assume that he could simultaneously vary at least two factors. Thus one of the major shortcomings of the traditional experimental model was that it could not deal successfully with multiple factors.[1]

Another difficulty was the implicit assumption that control of the variables depended upon some form of direct manipulation. For example, this sort of reasoning suggests that one would have to manipulate the moon *itself* in order to observe its effects upon the earth.

Why not simply assume that it is not necessary for the investigator to control the moon in order to scientifically study its effects on the earth. Why not, as a beginning, simply observe the properties of the moon and the earth, say the tides, which vary together. This is commonly called *concomitant variation*. It simply means the degree to which two factors or a set of factors vary together in a way predicted by an hypothesis. Such occurrences are the basic raw materials of any science. In Chapter 2 we labeled such occurrences as empirical regularities or uniformities. These regularities are the realities of nature with which the scientist is concerned. For example, temperature (X) varies with

---

[1] It should be pointed out that one of the principal reasons for this was that the mathematics necessary for multiple factor analysis were not available in that era.

altitude (Y) and human attitudes (A) vary with amount of education (B). In other words, the fundamental basis for experimental inference is that one must first have established a concomitant relationship between two variables or among three or more variables.

In order to establish concomitant variation it is not necessary to attempt direct manipulation as in the oversimplified classical notion. All that is necessary is for the relationship to be so defined as to enable the investigator to at least *count* the instances of occurrence or preferably measure the units of observation.

3. SETS AND FUNCTIONS

The units under observation are determined by the variables under investigation. One variable may be deviant behavior and the researcher may be trying to connect this variable with some environmental property, let us say, social stress. The units under observation would be the specifications of deviant behavior and the specifications for stress. With two factors under observation the units will be in pairs or sets of two. A collection of objects or items is designated in the language of mathematics as a *set*. A set is usually represented by the capital letter S. There exist *infinite* sets the number of whose elements is unbounded. Our concern, however, will be with *finite* sets, namely those having exactly n elements for some nonnegative integer n. For example, consider the set of four aces in a deck of cards {diamonds, hearts, spades, clubs} or the set of two letters in the alphabet {a, b}. These sets have *four* elements and *two* elements, respectively. Some finite sets are very small and some are very large. The set of all housewives in America is quite large and the set of all living presidents of the United States is very small. In statistical theory as well as general mathematics we find considerable use for a subset called the *empty* set or *null* set. By way of illustration let us consider all subsets of the five-element set of five true-false examination questions. One among these is the empty subset (no question answered correctly). It is generally designated by ϕ. This set should not be confused with the set {0} which contains one object, namely, the integer 0. There are 5 subsets consisting of one element (one question answered correctly). There are 10 subsets consisting of two elements, that is, two questions answered correctly, and so on. The total number of possible elements or ways would be 2^5 or 32. Let S be the total set of 32 ways. The empty set would be the subset of five questions all of which were answered wrong, that is, the subset where none is answered correctly. There is obviously only *one* such subset. The students who remember the binomial theorem will recognize that these numbers are the coefficients of the powers of x from 0 to 5 in the expansion of $(1+x)^5$.

A set B is a subset of a set A if every element of B is an element of A.

METHODS OF EXPERIMENTATION

This is symbolized as: $B \subset A$. This may be read as "B is contained in A." If $A = \{a, b, c\}$ and $B = \{b, c\}$ then $B \subset A$. But, every set is a subset of itself, $A \subset A$, since each of its elements is contained in the set. In scientific research we are more likely to be concerned with a subset that does not contain all of the elements of the other set. Such a set is called a *proper* set and is defined as follows: A set B is a *proper* subset of a set A if every element of B is an element of A, but not every element of A is an element of B.

Thus, in the true-false test example above, the set of no correct answers, the empty set, ϕ, is a subset of A.

Sets may be combined in several ways. Let $X = \{X_1, X_2, \ldots, X_{10}\}$ and $Y = \{Y_1, Y_2, \ldots, Y_{10}\}$. These two sets may be arranged in a square table such as Table 12:1.

TABLE 12 1

Schematic Representation of a Two-Way Classification Table Illustrating a Set of Ordered Pairs

X SET (ROWS)	Y SET (COLUMNS)								ROW MEANS
	1	2	3	...	j	...	k		
1	X_{11}	X_{12}	X_{13}	...	X_{1j}	...	X_{1k}		$X_1.$
2	X_{21}	X_{21}	X_{23}	...	X_{2j}	...	X_{2k}		$X_2.$
3	X_{31}	X_{31}	X_{33}	...	X_{3j}	...	X_{3k}		$X_3.$
.	.	.	.		.		.		.
.	.	.	.		.		.		.
i	X_{i1}	X_{i2}	X_{i3}	...	X_{ij}	...	X_{ik}		$X_i.$
.	.	.	.		.		.		.
.	.	.	.		.		.		.
R	X_{R1}	X_{R2}	X_{R3}	...	X_{Rj}	...	X_{Rk}		$X_R.$
Column means	$\overline{X}_{.1}$	$\overline{X}_{.2}$	$\overline{X}_{.3}$	...	$\overline{X}_{.j}$	...	$\overline{X}_{.k}$		$\overline{X}$

The pair of elements, (X_i, Y_j), formed as indicated in Table 12:1 is an *ordered pair*. It is ordered in the sense that the first member of the pair is always an element of X and the second is always an element of Y. Such a subset or ordered pair is a *relation*. The relation will be called a function if it is *single-valued*, that is, if to each first coordinate there corresponds one and only one second coordinate. The set X is the *do-*

main of the function and the range of the function is contained in Y. The range of elements or values contained in Y may or may not consist of the whole set Y. Let us assume that Y refers to a population of people and X refers to intelligence quotient; then for a given set of X values there is a given number of people with these IQ values, but this number may not be all the people with these IQ values.

Referring again to Table 12:1, R is the number of rows and k is the number of columns. Let us assume that the X variable refers to persons or individuals and that the Y variable refers to experimental conditions; then the score for the ith subject in the jth condition is X_{ij}. The mean score for the ith subject is represented by $X_{i.}$, and the mean score for the jth experimental condition is represented by $X_{.j}$. The mean of all observations is represented by $\overline{X}$.

We accept the notation (X_i, Y_j) as representing an *ordered pair* in which X_i is called the *first coordinate* and Y_j is called the *second coordinate*. The set of all *first* coordinates (in the ordered pairs) is called the *domain* of the function. The set of all *second* coordinates is called the *range* of the function. As indicated before, this assumes that for each first coordinate there is one and only one second coordinate. A look at Table 12:1 will show that this is the case in that table. This does not mean that any given pair must have only one frequency. For example, if the pair (X_{12}) represents an IQ of 100 and age 10, then there may be a large number of children in a given population who have an IQ of 100 and are age ten, but each child has one and only one IQ.

Recall that in Section 1 of this chapter we introduced the notion of concomitant variation. From the point of view of social psychology our interest in concomitant variation is in determining if the variation in Y is *dependent* on a variation in X.

4. BASES FOR ESTABLISHING THE EXISTENCE OF RELATIONSHIPS

How does a researcher determine if the variation in one variable is *dependent* upon one or more *independent* variables? As the preceding statement implies, we are using the term *dependent variable* to refer to the effect or outcome to be explained and the independent variables as the factors for explaining the effect or dependent variable.

To answer the question that was just posed, let us begin by noting that there is no means of direct observation by which one can demonstrate that Y depends on X. Rather, we are *always* in position of *inferring* a relation between a set of problematic data and a set of explanatory data. The degree of confidence in the inference may approach certainty. In fact, the scientist may be certain that X produces Y. Let us say that he has by *controlled* observation demonstrated this over and over again.

Suppose we know that a certain virus, A, produces a certain kind of cold, B. But does it produce it every time it is present in a person? No, not necessarily; in other words, it produces it only under certain conditions and bodily states of the person. Maybe he has just suffered a psychological trauma which has affected his general level of resistance to disease. Hence the existence of a relationship is dependent upon the *conditions* which contribute to or intervene in connection with the relationship. Thus for these reasons alone, if we observe enough cases, there will always be some discrepancy between actual outcomes and theoretically expected outcomes. In other words, there is always some error to be expected in prediction because the conditions of functioning are never *exactly* the same and there is, therefore, always some error in measurement. This is true irrespective of the field of science in question. Hence, one really can only say that the degree of confidence in a scientific inference can only *approach* certainty.

It might be added that there are other reasons by which such a conclusion is justified. One of these additional reasons is that irrespective of how refined a measuring instrument the scientist may have there are always further refinements that can be made. Another reason is that there is always some variation which results from sampling fluctuations. Therefore, one may always expect errors due to crudeness of measurement. But given whatever confidence we have in our inferences, then what evidence is necessary to justify such inferences? In other words, if one wishes to test the hypothesis that the behavior of variable Y depends on the behavior of variable X, then what does he have to establish in order to conclude that it does?

Concomitant Variation

Perhaps the first and most obvious bit of necessary evidence is whether a change in X is accompanied by a change in Y. Assuming that it has been shown that a change in variable X is accompanied by a change in variable Y, then at least four important questions may be asked about the covariance. (1) Does the variation in Y *depend* on the variation in X? (2) Is the variation in Y independent of the variation in X in the sense that both X and Y depend on some other variable or variables? (3) Are the variations in Y and X *joint functions*, that is, do they interact? (4) Maybe Y and X are not related at all and the covariation observed in the sample is a chance event? How do we decide which of these four is correct? The answer to this question is a matter of experimental design and control. We shall now discuss a few ways which will enable us to answer these questions.

Let us first take up the question of whether there is in the first place a covariation, and if so, how much?

Simple Linear Correlation and Simple Regression. Suppose that we have a set of n pairs of values, that is, we know each value of Y that is associated with each value of X and that both measures are on the same individual or object. Therefore we know that Y_1 and X_1 go together, Y_2 and X_2, and so forth.

Suppose we have the following ten (10) hypothetical observations:

X	Y
0	1
1	3
2	5
3	7
4	9
5	11
6	13
7	15
8	17
9	19
10	21

It is noted that X and Y increase together and that the points with (X_i, Y_j) as coordinates form a straight line.

From any two points on the line, we can find the *rate of change of Y for a change in X*. This is generally called the *slope* of the line in analytic geometry and the *difference quotient* in calculus.

It should be clear that if Y is related to X, then a change in X should be accompanied by a change in Y. The slope or difference quotient is a measure of such change. This is given by:

$$\text{Slope} = \frac{Y_2 - Y_1}{X_2 - X_1}$$

In the case of the hypothetical data indicated by the coordinates in Fig. 12:1 below, the slope is

$$\frac{15 - 11}{7 - 5} = \frac{4}{2} = 2.$$

This means that for a given unit change in X, Y changes two times this amount.

The equation is $Y = bX$ and the student should recognize this as the straight-line equation when the line passes through the zero-point of origin of both the X- and Y-axes. b is a constant and is called the *regression coefficient* or *slope* as defined above. From now on we shall refer to it as the regression coefficient.

When the point of origin or line of intercept of the Y-axis is not at

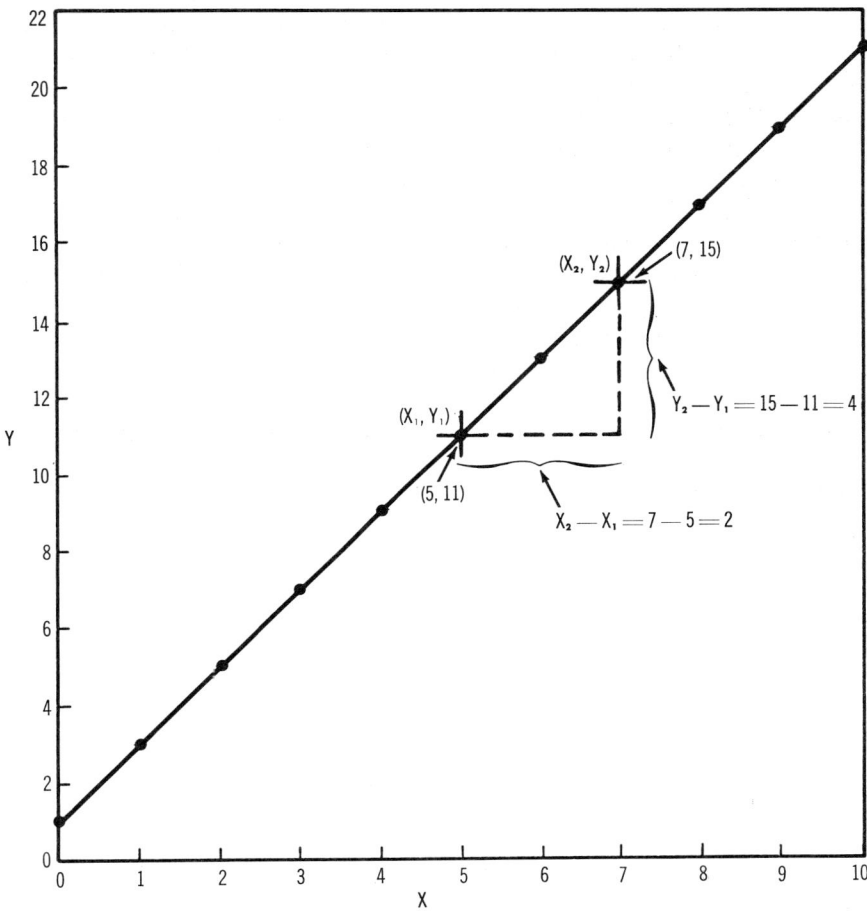

FIGURE 12:1. The Graph of a Linear or Straight Line Relationship.

zero, the effect will be to introduce an additive constant into the formula $Y = bX$. This constant is denoted by a and is called the *Y-intercept*. In such a case we have two constants and the relation is described by the equation $Y = a + bX$.

Such is the case in the hypothetical data shown above. The student will note that when $X = 0$, $Y = 1$. Therefore, the formula which describes the relation between X and Y above is: $Y = 1 + 2X$.

The above data are *positively* related as Fig. 12:1 indicates; that is to say, as X increases Y increases and the regression coefficient, b, is positive. Sometimes the regression coefficient, b, is *negative* which means that as X increases Y decreases.

The same general reasoning may be extended to include additional or multiple variables. This, of course, presupposes that the linear assumption still holds. If the relationship is curvilinear, then other techniques are called for.[2]

Notice in Fig. 12:1 above that the curve completely describes the relationship in that all the points fall on the line. This is not often the case. Generally there is error or scatter around the line and the problem then is to determine the line of *best fit*. That is to say that the constants a and b must be calculated in such a manner that the error variance will be at a minimum. A suitable method for doing this is the method of *least-squares*.[3] This will not be illustrated here. However, a method for calculating a and b whether there is or is not error around the line will be given for *ungrouped* data, that is, data which have only one value in an interval. This is the case with the data given above, except that there were not any errors in these data; that is, the curve represents a perfect fit of the data.

Suppose we have the following ten pairs of scores:

X	Y
6	11
4	8
3	2
7	15
8	17
2	7
5	4
4	7
3	4
5	9

Let us plot these data and the degree of scatter or departure from a straight line will be apparent.

Obtaining a line of best fit for the above data involves a process of curve fitting which will minimize the quantity

$$\Sigma(Y - \tilde{Y})^2$$

where Y denotes the observed values of the dependent variable and $\tilde{Y}$ denotes the estimated values of the dependent variable as given by the regression equation

$$\tilde{Y} = a + bX$$

---

[2] For the student who is interested in multiple variable relations he might begin with Philip H. DuBois, *Multivariate Correlational Analysis* (New York, Harper & Row, Publishers, Inc., 1957) and Mordecai Ezekiel, *Methods of Correlation Analysis*, 2nd ed. (New York, John Wiley & Sons, Inc., 1949).

[3] Ezekiel, *ibid.*, p. 64.

METHODS OF EXPERIMENTATION   351

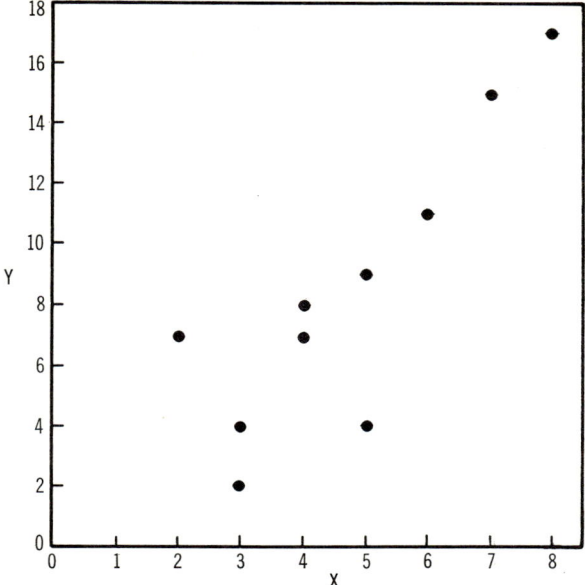

FIGURE 12:2. Estimating Regression from Imperfect Data.

The constants a and b may be calculated directly from the raw scores of the X and Y variables.

For b, we have

$$b_{YX} = \frac{\Sigma XY - \frac{(\Sigma X)(\Sigma Y)}{N}}{\Sigma X^2 - \frac{(\Sigma X)^2}{N}}$$

where N is the total number of observations, which in the above example is ten.

For a we have

$$a = \frac{\Sigma Y - b\Sigma X}{N}.$$

Obviously, if we divide Y and X by N we get the mean of Y and the mean of X, which yields the equivalent formula $a = \overline{Y} - b\overline{X}$.[4]

It is clear that when the value of b has been obtained, a can then be derived, so we will calculate b first. To do so we will need the following table:

---

[4] A more detailed presentation of these is found in most introductory statistics textbooks. See, for example, Morris Zelditch, *A Basic Course in Sociological Statistics* (New York, Henry Holt & Co., 1959), pp. 96-98.

TABLE 12:2

Calculating Table for Regression Constants a and b for Ungrouped Data

X	Y	X²	Y²	XY
6	11	36	121	66
4	8	16	64	32
3	2	9	4	6
7	15	49	225	105
8	17	64	289	136
2	7	4	49	14
5	4	25	16	20
4	7	16	49	28
3	4	9	16	12
5	9	25	81	45
47	84	253	914	464

$$b = \frac{464 - \frac{(47)(84)}{10}}{253 - \frac{(47)^2}{10}} = \frac{69.2}{32.1} = 2.15,$$

and

$$a = \frac{84 - 2.15(47)}{10} = -1.71$$

Recall the main idea of the regression coefficient as being the amount of change which occurs in a dependent variable, Y, per unit change in an independent variable, X. Let us take a further look at the intuitive meaning of the terms in the b formula in relation to the basic definition of b. Let $x = X - \overline{X}$ and $y = Y - \overline{Y}$, that is, letting x and y be *deviates from their respective means*, where the mean is defined as $\frac{\Sigma X}{N}$, then the point of intercept of the X on the Y axis is no longer at X equals zero, but shifts to the point of intersect of the means of the X and Y axes. On the basis of these definitions of x and y we can set up the following algebraic equalities of b_{YX} where the subscript YX means the regression or dependence of Y on X.

$$b_{YX} = \frac{\Sigma XY - \frac{(\Sigma X)(\Sigma Y)}{N}}{\Sigma X^2 - \frac{(\Sigma X)^2}{N}} = \frac{\Sigma XY - N(\overline{X})(\overline{Y})}{\Sigma X^2 - N(\overline{X})^2} = \frac{N\Sigma XY - \Sigma X \Sigma Y}{N\Sigma X^2 - (\Sigma X)^2}$$

$$= \frac{\Sigma xy}{\Sigma x^2}.$$

It is helpful to think of Σxy as the amount of covariance or varying together of X and Y. The term Σx^2 is the sum of the squared deviations from the mean which represents the variation of the independent variable alone, and $\dfrac{\Sigma xy}{\Sigma x^2}$ is the ratio of the varying together of X and Y to the variation of X alone; hence b is the measure of the amount of variation in Y which corresponds to a unit change in X.

Perhaps it should be recalled that the fact that two variables tend to increase or decrease together does not imply that one necessarily has any direct or indirect effect on the other. Both may be influenced by other variables so as to produce a strong mathematical relationship. The presence of a strong mathematical relationship is necessary to establish a functional dependence between two variables, but it is not sufficient. In other words, more information about the nature of the covariation is necessary before such a decision could be made. Of particular importance is information concerning the time order of the events. That is, does the independent variable always precede the dependent variable in time, and when it does is it followed by the dependent variable or outcome? Also, when it is absent, is the effect also absent? These questions imply a one to one relationship. This is almost never the case. If more than one independent factor is involved or if interfering factors are uncontrolled, then, obviously, the one independent factor could not account for all the variation. In the case that multiple factors are involved, then a multiple correlation and regression analysis would be called for.[5]

Another method for establishing concomitant variation is called the *Analysis of Variance* and was developed by the late professor Sir Ronald A. Fisher.

Analysis of Variance

Introduction. In most cases there are several variables in addition to the ones which the investigator has controlled which need to be controlled if the research design is to yield fruitful and valid results. In some cases these interfering variables can be controlled by laboratory means, but others can be controlled, and are often only possible to control, through the use of statistical designs. We wish to briefly introduce two principles which are fundamental to statistical designs which have as their aim the drawing of inferences from experimental results. These

---

[5] For the student who is interested and has the necessary mathematical background he is invited to read the section on Multiple Linear Regression in Paul G. Hoel, *Introduction to Mathematical Statistics*, 2nd ed. (1954) or 3rd ed. (1962) (New York, John Wiley & Sons, Inc.). Also, Mordecai Ezekiel, *Methods of Correlation Analysis*, 2nd ed. (New York, John Wiley & Sons, Inc., 1949).

principles are called *randomization* and *replication*. Let us now consider their meaning.

A good example of the use of these is provided by Hoel:

> Consider an agricultural experiment in which two different seed varieties are to be tested on a piece of land. If the piece of land were divided into two equal pieces and one variety planted on each, the difference in yields could not be used as a valid estimate of the differential effect of the two seed varieties, because of the possible difference in the soil fertility of the two pieces.
>
> Experiments can often be made valid by applying the principles of *randomization* and *replication*. Thus, in the present illustration, if the piece of land were divided into a number of small plots of equal size, and if one variety of seed were planted on half of these plots and the other variety on the remaining half, with the selection of the plots for each variety determined by a random process, then the varying fertility of the land would affect the two varieties approximately equally and therefore the difference in varietal yields would represent a valid estimate of the differential effects of the two seed varieties.
>
> Randomization by itself is not necessarily sufficient to yield a valid experiment. For example, if one merely tossed a coin to determine which half of the original piece of land should be planted with one of the seed varieties, the selection would be random but it would not permit the two seed varieties to be equally affected by any varying soil fertility. If the two seed varieties were equally productive but the two halves of land were markedly different in fertility, then regardless of which seed variety was selected for each half, the conclusion would invariably be that the seed varieties differed in productivity. In order to insure validity, it would be necessary that the piece of land be divided into a sufficiently large number of similar plots so that the probability of having one of the seed varieties largely located on the more fertile plots will be very small. This repetition of an experiment or experimental unit is called replication. Thus, to insure validity in an experiment, randomization should be accompanied by sufficient replication.[6]

Randomization and replication are useful in enabling a clear interpretation of experimental results. It is also an essential part of most statistical models. We shall now consider one basic model for which randomization is a fundamental assumption.

The model which was discussed in the section of this chapter entitled Simple Linear Correlation and Simple Regression has been called a "linearity model." The hypothesis underlying that model implies that the relationship between the two variables takes the form of a *straight line*. If this is not actually the case, the linear correlation coefficient will

---

[6] Hoel, *op. cit.*, pp. 246-247.

underestimate the degree of relationship. In other words, it will measure only the amount of straight-line relationship between X and Y.

The basic problem in the linear correlation model is to determine the amount of relationship about a geometric line.[7] In the analysis of variance model the fundamental purpose is to separate the total amount of variance into individual parts, each part assignable to a known source, factor, or condition. This allows one to assess the relative magnitude of variation resulting from different sources and to determine whether a particular part of the variation is greater than chance expectation. There are many forms of the analysis of variance and the particular form used depends upon the particular research problem and its related experimental design.[8]

The Concept of Variance. Perhaps the simplest and quickest way to indicate the meaning of the concept of variance is by way of an example. Suppose we have a set of test questions and that we administer the test to a sample of subjects with the following distribution of right answers.

TABLE 12:3

Calculating Variance for Frequency Distribution of Test Scores

(1) TEST SCORE X_i	(2) FREQUENCY OF RIGHT ANSWERS f_i	(3) $f_i(X)$*	(4) DEVIATION FROM THE MEAN $X_i - \bar{X} = x_i$	(5) FREQUENCY TIMES THE DEVIATION $f(X_i - \bar{X}) = f_i x_i$	(6) FREQUENCY TIMES THE DEVIATIONS SQUARED $f(X_i - \bar{X})^2 = f_i x_i^2$
0	1	0	−2.64	−2.64	6.97
1	2	2	−1.64	−3.28	5.38
2	3	6	−0.64	−1.92	1.22
3	4	12	+0.36	+1.44	.52
4	3	12	+1.36	+4.08	5.55
5	1	5	+2.36	+2.36	5.57
	14	37			25.21

* Frequency multiplied by X.

[7] The correlation model can for some purposes be more clearly presented in the form of a variance ratio. See T. C. McCormick, *Elementary Social Statistics* (McGraw-Hill Book Company, Inc., 1941), pp. 182-183, and Philip H. DuBois, *op. cit.*

[8] For a clear and fundamental introduction to some of these designs see George A. Ferguson, *Statistical Analysis in Psychology and Education* (McGraw-Hill Book Company, Inc., 1959), chapters 15 and 16. For a more advanced and more complete set of techniques see B. J. Winer, *Statistical Principles in Experimental Design* (McGraw-Hill Book Company, Inc., 1962).

The above table is a frequency distribution with a class interval of 1.[9] The symbol f_i denotes the frequency of occurrence of the particular value X_i. Multiplying each value X_i by its frequency and adding together the products, $f_i X_i$, we obtain the sum of 37. The arithmetic mean, $\overline{X}$, is then 37 divided by 14, or 2.64.

In general, where $X_1, X_2, X_3, \ldots, X_i$ occur with frequencies $f_1, f_2, f_3, \ldots, f_i$, and k is the number of different values of X (in Table 12:3 this is 6), then the weighted arithmetic mean, X, equals

$$\frac{f_1 X_1 + f_2 X_2 + f_3 X_3 + \ldots f_i X_i}{N} = \frac{\sum_{i=1}^{k} f_i X_i}{N}$$

where

$$N = \sum_{i=1}^{k} f_i$$

and the summation is over k terms, i.e., the number of different values of X. Also

$$\sum_{i=1}^{N} = \sum_{i=1}^{k} f_i X_i.$$

Our immediate interest is in the concept of variance, but in order to understand it we need to understand the mean. The notion of variation or deviation assumes knowledge of a point or characteristic around which the variation occurs. In respect to the concept of variance the point around which the variation is measured is the mean. In other words, variance is a particular measure of departure from the mean or central tendency.

Let us symbolize variance by the symbol s^2.

$$s^2 = \frac{\Sigma f(X - \overline{X})^2}{N}$$

We see that variance is the mean of the squared deviations from the mean. Another way of saying this is to note that it is the sum of the squared deviations from the mean divided by N or the total number of observations. The square root of the variance is known as the *standard deviation*.

Let us now calculate the variance in Table 12:3 above.

$$s^2 = \frac{\Sigma f(X - \overline{X})^2}{N} = \frac{\Sigma f x^2}{N}, \text{ where } N = \sum_{i=1}^{k} f_i$$

Now $s^2 = \dfrac{25.21}{14} = 1.80$.

---

[9] See any elementary statistics text for calculating the mean when the class interval is greater than one.

Keeping in mind the foregoing concepts of the *mean* and *variance*, let us now turn to a consideration of the *analysis of variance*.

The term *analysis of variance* is somewhat ambiguous since its application is primarily concerned with procedures for testing hypotheses about the *means* of populations. This technique is used to test the significance of the differences between the means of three or more different samples. It can be applied to two means but other more conventional techniques are generally used when only two means are involved.[10]

Analysis of Variance: One-Way Classification—The Basic Problem. The problem is to explain the variation among a set of means from k different sample populations. The method is to divide the sum of squares $\Sigma(X - \overline{X})^2$ into two additive components. These are then used to test whether the k samples have been drawn from the same or different populations.

We may wish to test the different effects of k treatments on some dependent variable. These may be different ways of instructing, different ways of memorizing, different types of childhood training, or different dosages of a drug. A different treatment is applied to each of the k samples and each sample contains n members. The members are assigned to the treatments by means of some randomizing process. The means of the k samples are calculated. The null hypothesis asserts that the samples are drawn from populations having the same mean.[11] In other words, the hypothesis of equal means is stated, which is a way of saying that the differences among treatments are not statistically significant. If the variation cannot be attributed to sampling error, we reject the null hypothesis and accept the alternative hypothesis that the treatments applied were significant in their effects.

Consider a psychological experiment to compare success of learning at three different levels of difficulty of materials to be learned. Suppose that we randomly assign ten subjects to each of the three levels; then we have a grand total of thirty experimental subjects. Thus $k = 3$ treatments and $n = 10$ subjects per treatment. Assume that the subject matter differs only by level of difficulty and that the subjects were assigned randomly to each experimental level. The mean number of right answers is computed for each sample of ten subjects for each level of difficulty. Differences in rate of learning are reflected in the variation among the three means. If this variation is of such magnitude that it could arise in random sampling in less than 5 percent of the cases, then we normally reject the null hypothesis and accept the alternative hypothesis that the amount of learning varies with the level of difficulty.

[10] See, for example, the "*t*" test in Ferguson, *op. cit.*, pp. 131-156.
[11] For the student who is interested in the whys of the null hypotheses he is invited to try his hand with Karl R. Popper, *The Logic of Scientific Discovery* (New York, Basic Books, Inc., Publishers, 1959).

The basic table for a one-way classification problem using analysis of variance may be represented as follows:

TABLE 12:4

Illustration of General Notation of a One-Way Classification Table for Analysis of Variance

Category

	GROUP A		GROUP B		GROUP C		GROUP k	
(1)	X_{11} X_{21} X_{31} $\vdots$ $X_{10\,1}$		X_{12} X_{22} X_{32} $\vdots$ $X_{10\,2}$		X_{13} X_{23} X_{33} $\vdots$ $X_{10\,3}$		X_{1k} X_{2k} X_{3k} $\vdots$ $X_{10\,k}$	
(2)	Total T_A	...	T_B	...	T_C	...	T_k	T = Table Total
	Mean $\overline{X}_{.1}$		$\overline{X}_{.2}$		$\overline{X}_{.3}$		$\overline{X}_{.k}$	$\overline{T}$ = Table Mean

$T_A = X_{11} + X_{21} + X_{31} \ldots X_{10\,1}$ and the same for groups B, C, and so on.
T (Table Total) $= T_A + T_B + T_C + T_k$.

$$\overline{X}_{.1} = \frac{T_A}{10}\,;\ \overline{X}_{.2} = \frac{T_B}{10}\,, \text{ and so on.}$$

$$\overline{T} = \frac{T}{40}.$$

Element X_{32} in category B designates an observation on the third person in treatment class B. In general, this is designated as X_{ij} or an observation on element i or subject i in treatment class j. Notations for the totals required in the computation of the sums of squares appear in part (2) of the above table. For example, T_A designates the sum of all observations in treatment class A, and $X_{.j}$ designates the mean of a particular treatment class.

What basic computing formulas are needed? Let us attempt to logically deduce the kinds of formulas needed. Recall that the basic idea underlying the analysis of variance is that the *total sum of squares* may be partitioned into independent and additive parts, each part resulting from an identifiable source of variation. The null hypothesis specifies the nature of the relationship among these components.

Let us begin by calculating the total sum of squares.

Analysis of Variance: One-Way Classification—The Required Sums of Squares. We have denoted the sum of all the observations in a particular group by T_j:

$$T_j = \sum_{i=1}^{n_j} X_{ij}.$$

The sum of *all* the observations in all the k groups is denoted by T:

$$T = \sum_{j=1}^{k} \sum_{i=1}^{n_j} X_{ij}.$$

This may be read as the sum of the sums of the j categories.

The computation formulas are now readily obtainable. The formula for the *total* sum of squares is

$$\sum_{j=1}^{k} \sum_{i=1}^{n_j} (X_{ij} - \overline{X})^2 = \sum_{j=1}^{k} \sum_{i=1}^{n_j} X_{ij}^2 - \frac{T^2}{N}; \quad N = \sum_{j=1}^{k} n_j.$$

We simply find the sum of squares for all the observations and subtract T^2/N.

Recall that in a table involving a single variable or one-way classification our interest is in assessing the treatment effects and their differentials, if any, as these are reflected in the column means. Hence the principal interest is in *between-treatment variation*. Since the different columns or categories represent different treatments, it is presumed that the column means will show significant differences if the different treatments do in fact produce different effects. Thus, another sum of squares of principal interest is the *between-group* sum of squares. The formula is

$$\sum_{j=1}^{k} n_j (\overline{X}_j - \overline{X})^2 = \sum_{j=1}^{k} \left(\frac{T_j^2}{n_j} \right) - \frac{T^2}{N}$$

Obviously, if there is not significant variation of the column means around the total or grand mean, then the different treatments did not produce statistically significant differences. In such a case all the variation except random column variation would be found to be *within* the columns. This leads us to the final sum of squares for consideration in a one-way classification table and it is generally labeled the *within-groups* sum of squares.

$$\sum_{j=1}^{k} \sum_{i=1}^{n_j} (X_{ij} - \overline{X}_j)^2 = \sum_{j=1}^{k} \sum_{i=1}^{n_j} X_{ij}^2 - \sum_{j=1}^{k} \left(\frac{T_j^2}{n_j} \right).$$

The fraction

$$\sum_{j=1}^{k} \left(\frac{T_j^2}{n_j} \right)$$

is the sum of squares of the columns totals divided by the corresponding number of cases.

The above formulas are also applicable to treatment groups of unequal or equal sizes.

A numerical example should help clarify the foregoing formulas. Suppose an experimenter is interested in evaluating the effectiveness of three methods of teaching a given course. A group of thirty subjects is available to him. This group is assumed by the investigator to be a random sample from the population of interest. Three subgroups of ten subjects each are formed at random; the subgroups are each taught by a different one of the three methods of teaching. Upon completion of the course, each of the subgroups is given the same test covering the material in the course. The symbol n designates the number of subjects in a sub-group and k the number of treatments, in this case the number of teaching methods employed.

The hypothetical scores are given in the table below:

TABLE 12:5

Computation Procedures for the Analysis of Variance:
One-Way Classification

	Teaching Method			
	1	2	3	
	6	4	8	
	8	4	10	
	5	3	12	
	9	8	14	
	7	7	13	
	4	5	10	
	6	2	11	
	7	3	9	
	5	6	15	
	8	5	7	
T_j	65	47	109	$\sum_{1}^{3} T_j = T = 221$
n_j	10	10	10	$\sum_{1}^{3} n_j = N = 30$
$\bar{X}_{.j}$	6.5	4.7	10.9	$\dfrac{T^2}{N} = 1628.03$
$\sum_{i=1}^{n_j} X_{ij}^2$	443	253	1249	$\sum_{j=1}^{k} \sum_{i=1}^{n_j} X_{ij}^2 = 1945$
$\dfrac{T_j^2}{n_j}$	422.5	220.90	1188.10	$\sum_{j=1}^{k} \dfrac{T_j^2}{n_j} = 1831.50$

METHODS OF EXPERIMENTATION

Referring now to the formulas for calculating the sums of squares and substituting the appropriate numerical results from the foregoing table will give us the required sums of squares. First, the total sum of squares is:

$$1945 - 1628.03 = 316.97$$

The between-group sum of squares is $1831.50 - 1628.03 = 203.47$. The within-group sum of squares is $1945 - 1831.50 = 113.50$.

Notice that the between-group and within-group sums of squares for a one-variable table must necessarily, when added together, equal the total sum of squares or a computational error exists.

The computational results of the analysis of variance are usually displayed in summary form as indicated in the table below.

TABLE 12:6

Summary of Analysis of Variance for the Data of Table 12:5

SOURCE OF VARIATION	SUM OF SQUARES	DEGREES OF FREEDOM	MEAN SQUARE OR VARIANCE ESTIMATE	F VALUE
Between-Groups	203.47	$k - 1 = 2$	101.74	
Within-Group	113.50	$N - k = 27$	4.20	24.22
Total	316.97	$N - 1 = 29$		

The within-group variation is the pooled variation within each of the subgroups. When divided by the appropriate degrees of freedom (which will be defined below), it may also be thought of as the experimental error or mean square error.

The hypotheses about the equality of the population means can be tested by the F ratio (after Professor R. A. Fisher, who originated the test). For a one-variable table the F ratio is the ratio of the between-group variance to the within-group variance or the experimental error; hence in this case:

$$F = \frac{\text{Between-group variance}}{\text{Within-group variance}}$$

We now need to refer to a table of theoretical F values in order to evaluate the above obtained F. <u>See</u> Appendix for Table 1. The table is first entered at the degrees of freedom associated with the numerator and next for the denominator; in this case, at 2 and 27 degrees of freedom respectively. The critical F value at the 5 percent level for 2 and 27 degrees of freedom is 3.35. The observed F value for the above data is 24.22. Since it is *larger* than the critical value of 3.35, we tentatively reject the hypothesis that the column means are equal and accept the hypothesis that they are unequal. This means that the different methods of teaching presumably made a real difference in mean results per method. We emphasize the tentativeness of the conclusions, since they are based on a chance probability of .05. The critical value chosen was at the .05 chance level. This means that with a greater mean square of 2 degrees of freedom and a lesser mean square of 30 degrees of freedom, an F value as large as 3.35 can occur by chance not more than five times in a hundred cases. Since the observed F value in the foregoing illustration is much larger than 3.35, it would be expected to have a chance value considerably smaller than 5 per cent. Obviously, the smaller the probability of chance, the greater the probability of a real or systematic effect.

If we wanted to increase our confidence in the results, we could choose a more stringent critical value, say, the 1 percent level. In this case, with the same degrees of freedom the critical F value is 5.49 and the probability of such an F value occurring by chance is only one in a hundred times. Of course, as we decrease the probability of accepting a relationship as significant when in fact it is *not*, we also increase the probability of rejecting it as false when in fact it is real. In other words, there are two kinds of errors which one should beware of in testing statistical hypotheses. These are sometimes called type I and type II errors. The *rejecting* of a true hypothesis is a type I error and the *acceptance* of a false hypothesis is a type II error. Suppose one sets the null hypothesis as the hypothesis to be tested, and the test results in the decision to reject the null hypothesis when in fact it is true; this is a type I error. On the other hand, if one accepts the null hypothesis as true when in fact it is false, this is a type II error. Of course, in regard to any given hypothesis one can make only one of these errors. The only way to guard against both of these kinds of possible errors is to increase the degrees of freedom by increasing the number of observations or sample size.

We have used the term *degrees of freedom* without defining it and we will now attempt to show its meaning. In the first place, the term *degree of freedom* refers to the number of *independent* observations on a given source of variation—independent in the sense that a subsequent observed result is not dependent upon the previous one. Suppose we have the following column of observed values and its resulting total:

$$\begin{array}{c} 1 \\ 2 \\ 3 \\ 4 \\ \underline{5} \\ 15 \end{array}$$

The concept of degrees of freedom may be illustrated as follows:

METHODS OF EXPERIMENTATION

Given a fixed sum, how many of the numbers may be assigned arbitrarily? That is, how many are free to vary? In the case of the above column of values with the sum of 15, exactly four can be assigned arbitrarily; the fifth number has to be such that the total is fifteen.

In other words, the degrees of freedom is the number of independent observations minus the number of constants or fixed values used in estimating the variance. The number of degrees of freedom for each subgroup or column in the teaching methods experiment is $n-1$ or $10-1=9$. The number of degrees of freedom for the within-group variation or all the subgroups pooled is $k(n-1)$ or $N-k$ which is $3(9)=27$ or $30-3=27$.

The problem in the foregoing one-way classification illustration was to determine whether the three treatments were equally effective in respect to the mean result. This assumed that the subjects who were randomly assigned to the subgroups did not differ in respect to previous background in the course subject matter. In other words, if the subgroups differed significantly in respect to past training in the subject matter, then this would obscure or depress any actual effects of the teaching methods. To prevent this interference with the experimental results, the factor of previous training would need to be taken into account. This would involve a two-factor or two-variable analysis of variance design.

Analysis of Variance: Two Variables of Classification. The variations in the observations in the analysis of variance experiment in the section of this chapter entitled *Analysis of Variance: One-Way Classification* were, as we saw, caused by different methods of teaching. But the variations may also have been due to a difference in the background training of the subjects.

The development of the analysis of variance procedure for a two-way classification with single observations per cell may be illustrated in the following table:

TABLE 12:7

Illustration of Two-Variable Classification with Single Observation per Cell

		First Variable			Row Mean
		A	B	C	
Second Variable	a	X_{11}	X_{12}	X_{13}	$\overline{X}_{1.}$
	b	X_{21}	X_{22}	X_{23}	$\overline{X}_{2.}$
	c	X_{31}	X_{32}	X_{33}	$\overline{X}_{3.}$
	Column mean	$\overline{X}_{.1}$	$\overline{X}_{.2}$	$\overline{X}_{.3}$	$\overline{X}_{..}$

In this table the double subscripts identify the row and the column. The first subscript identifies the *row;* the second identifies the *column.* Thus X_{12} is the score in the first row and the second column. In general, X_{rc} denotes the measurement in the rth row and the cth column. The dot notation in the row and column totals is used to designate means. The symbol $X_1.$ refers to the mean of the first row, $X_2.$ to the mean of the second row and so on. Similarly, $X._1$ refers to the mean of the first column, and $X._2$ to the mean of the second column. The grand mean, the mean of all N observations, is X without any dot designations although some designate the mean of all observations by $X\ldots$

In the previous case of a single variable classification an estimate of the variance was obtained for the column means. Here we shall also obtain an estimate for the row means because we are interested in seeing if both factors affect the variance. The computation is illustrated for the following hypothetical data for three treatments A, B, C and three background levels or types a, b, c.

TABLE 12:8

Illustration of Two-Variable Classification with Single Observation Per Cell, Using Hypothetical Data

	A	B	C	T_r
a	5	8	11	24
b	7	10	13	30
c	10	14	18	42
T_c	22	32	42	96

The procedure for obtaining the desired sums of squares is the same as before. The sum of squares used in estimating the population variance from column means is computed as before and is

$$\frac{(22)^2}{3} + \frac{(32)^2}{3} + \frac{(42)^2}{3} - \frac{(96)^2}{9} = 1090.66 - 1024.00 = 66.66.$$

Similarly, the sum of squares for estimating the population variance from the row means is

$$\frac{(24)^2}{3} + \frac{(30)^2}{3} + \frac{(42)^2}{3} - \frac{(96)^2}{9} = 56.00.$$

The total sum of squares is

$$5^2 + 7^2 + 10^2 + 8^2 + 10^2 + \ldots 18^2 - \frac{(96)^2}{9} = 1148 - 1024 = 124.$$

The student should note that the denominator in each term used in computing the foregoing sums of squares is the number of items which have been added in the total which appears in the numerator.

The sum of squares which corresponds to the experimental error in a two-way analysis of variance is sometimes called the *remainder or residual sum of squares* and is equal to the total sum of squares minus the sum of the column and row sum of squares,[12] in this case, $124 - 122.66$ or 1.34.

The above results may be viewed more clearly if we summarize them in a table.

TABLE 12:9

Summary Table for Two-Way Analysis of Variance, Single Observation Per Cell

SOURCE OF VARIATION	SUM OF SQUARES	DEGREES OF FREEDOM, df	MEAN SQUARE OR VARIANCE ESTIMATE	F VALUE
Column means	66.66	2	33.33	98.03
Row means	56.00	2	28.00	82.35
Residual	1.34	4	.34	
Total	124.00	8		

The total degrees of freedom is $N - 1$ or $9 - 1 = 8$. The degrees of freedom for the residual sum of squares is obtained by subtracting the sum of the degrees of freedom for the columns and rows from the total degrees of freedom. In this case, that would be $8 - 4$ or 4.

The F test for the hypothesis that the row means are equal can be made by comparing the variance estimate for rows with the residual variance estimate.

The F ratio is: $F = \dfrac{28.00}{.34} = 82.35$. The critical F value at the 5 percent level with 2 and 4 degrees of freedom is 6.94. Since our obtained value is 82.35, we conclude that the three groups differ in subject-matter background. The test for column means is

$$F = \frac{33.33}{.34} = 98.03.$$

Hence we conclude that the column means also differ. The theoretical F value which will not be exceeded by 95 percent of the samples is 6.94 for 2 degrees of freedom associated with the numerator of the F ratio

---

[12] This applies to two-way analysis of variance with one observation per cell. The case would be different with repeated observations per cell or with repeated observations per cell with unequal n's.

and for 4 degrees of freedom associated with its denominator.

In order to appreciate the increased sensitivity obtained by eliminating the variation due to differences in background training when testing the hypothesis that the treatment or column means are equal, consider how the hypothesis would have been tested if the row classifications were not available. This would be the situation, for example, if the three treatments had been assigned to the nine cells at random. This, of course, would be a one-variable or one-way analysis of variance. The table below summarizes the results when the row classifications are not available.

TABLE 12:10

Summary of Analysis of Variance of Data in Table 12:8 without Row Classification Information

SOURCE OF VARIATION	SUM OF SQUARES	df	MEAN SQUARE OR VARIANCE ESTIMATE	F RATIO
Column means	66.66	2	33.33	$F = \dfrac{33.33}{9.56} = 3.49$
Within groups	57.34	6	9.56	$F_{.95}(2, 6) = 5.14$*
Total	124.00	8		

* To be read as "the theoretical F value which will not be exceeded by 95 per cent of the samples is 5.14 for 2 degrees of freedom in the numerator of the F ratio and for 6 degrees of freedom in the denominator."

It is interesting to note that when the row classification was not available, the F value for the column means or treatment effects is *not* significant. Thus, failure to control for background effects in the above case totally obscured the real effects of the treatment variable. The important principle in experimental design which this result points to is that, in addition to the randomization process in assigning subjects to treatments, it is also necessary to *control* as many interfering variables as one can. From this point of view the one-way analysis of variance is much like the simple correlation coefficient in that it may not be sensitive enough to discover the relationships which are actually present.[13]

A comparison of the F ratio for column means when the second variable was controlled with the F ratio for the same when the second variable was *not* controlled is very striking. The F ratio for the column

[13] It is beyond the scope of this text to consider the more complex designs but the student should begin now to read a text like Allen L. Edwards, *Experimental Design in Psychological Research*, rev. ed. (New York, Holt, Rinehart and Winston, Inc., 1960).

METHODS OF EXPERIMENTATION

means with the second variable taken into account was 98.03 and it fell to 3.49 when the second variable was *not* taken into account. We thus see the increased sensitivity of the test as additional related variables are controlled.

A thorough treatment of the "bases for establishing relationships" would require a detailed analysis of all the major types of experimental design as well as an analysis of the logic and methods of inference. This itself would require the space of a very large textbook. Our analysis of simple linear correlation and one- and two-way analysis of variance represented statistical techniques for establishing relationships, but by *themselves* they are not sufficient to determine the precise nature of the relationships. That is to say that further evidence and conditions must be established before one can show that X *produces* Y rather than simply *varies* with Y. Some of these conditions and methods of inference will be discussed in the next section.

5. METHODS OF INFERENCE AND INTERPRETATIONS OF RESEARCH RESULTS

Suppose that a researcher has established by either an appropriate correlation analysis or an appropriate analysis of variance that two factors are related. What does such a concomitant relationship mean? To answer this question one needs to know *how* the variables are related. Are they *positively* related or *negatively* related? A relationship may be described as positive when an increase in X is accompanied by an increase in Y or a decrease in X is accompanied by a decrease in Y. A negative relationship means that an increase in X is accompanied by a decrease in Y, or a decrease in X is accompanied by an increase in Y. Another question is: are they *jointly* related, that is, do they interact? Recall the discussion of the regression coefficient in Section 4. It was conceived as the ratio of the covariation of the two variables to the variance of the independent variable or $b_{yx} = \frac{\Sigma xy}{\Sigma x^2}$. This, of course, is a measure of the amount of change in Y per unit of change in X. It can also be reversed. In this case, we would consider X as the dependent variable and Y as the independent variable, and we have $b_{xy} = \frac{\Sigma xy}{\Sigma y^2}$, when $\Sigma xy = \Sigma XY - \frac{(\Sigma X)(\Sigma Y)}{N}$ and $\Sigma y^2 = \Sigma Y^2 - \frac{(\Sigma Y)^2}{N}$ when X and Y refer to raw scores.

If b_{yx} and b_{xy} are each significant, this means that Y and X are affecting *each other;* in other words, they are intercorrelated. The same question could be asked and answered by using an analysis of variance technique. For example, is the effect of the columns and rows in combination different from the sum of their separate effects? If the effect in combination is significantly greater than the sum of the separate effects, then there is interaction present.

The task of determining *how* a set of factors is related in terms of a sequence of cause-and-effect relationships is sometimes very complex. All we can hope to do in this regard at the introductory level is to present some of the more common research designs used to clarify research results.

BASIC TYPES OF EXPERIMENTAL DESIGNS

The classical statement of experimental methods is by John Stuart Mill (1806-1873) who was able to systemize the logic of research of his day within the framework of five methods.[14] As much as I am tempted, I shall not present Mill's methods and canons in his own words; however, it is strongly recommended that the student read them in the reference cited. We will list his methods and discuss them in relation to our general question of how to explain an observed relationship. Mill derived five methods which he used to describe all the types of logical procedures required in ordering data. These are: *Method of Difference; Method of Agreement; Joint Method of Difference and Agreement; Method of Concomitant Variation; Method of Residue.*

This text stresses the idea that a research problem exists when a researcher observes an empirical regularity which existing knowledge will not adequately explain. This empirical distribution we have designated operationally as a *dependent variable.* Assuming that the investigator has determined by theoretical and/or empirical means which variables are to be defined as the independent variables, which are the intervening variables, and which the dependent variable, then the beginning phase of the process of explanation is to relate by some correlation or variance analysis technique an independent variable to the dependent variable. If the dependent variable varies in any manner whenever the independent variable varies in some particular way, then the researcher concludes that the two are at least statistically related and probably functionally related. This is the basic idea of concomitant variation.

Since we have conceived of the research process as beginning with a problem of variation, we shall now discuss more fully concomitant variation designs.

Method of Concomitant Variation. The fundamental idea of concomitant variation should already be clear to the student from the discussion of correlation analysis earlier in the chapter. Nevertheless, it will

[14] John Stuart Mill, *A System of Logic,* 8th ed. (New York and London, Harper & Bros., 1900), ch. 8, pp. 278-291.

METHODS OF EXPERIMENTATION

not be out of order to restate some of the ideas. The usual concomitant variation design involves the following:

(1) A range of measures, scores, or frequencies of an independent variable are systematically obtained.

(2) Corresponding measures, scores, or frequencies are obtained on a dependent variable.

(3) If the dependent variable varies systematically in relation to the independent variable, then the researcher concludes that the two variables are related.

An illustration of this method is as follows: An experimenter was interested in discovering what relationship existed between high school grade average and college grade average. To do this he might select a random sample of college seniors and calculate the average grade of each for the four years in college. He would also, of course, have to obtain the corresponding high school grade averages for each student. These scores would then be arranged in terms of a set of ordered pairs and the amount of correlation calculated.

Suppose he discovered that there was a positive relationship which indicated that the students with the highest high school averages also obtained the highest college average. This indicates one kind of concomitant relationship. Let us symbolize it by + +.

A relationship may be of the sort that the dependent variable decreases as the independent variable decreases; this would also be a positive relationship and we will symbolize it by − −. This may be illustrated by noting that as the strength of an attitude decreases, the interest of the person in the object of the attitude also decreases.

A third type of concomitant relation is where the independent variable increases and the dependent variable decreases. A study at Indiana University showed that as per capita income (X) increased, this was accompanied by a decrease in the suicide rate (Y).[15] This type of relationship we shall symbolize as + −.

A fourth type is when the independent variable decreases and the dependent variable increases. This is symbolized as − +. This is simply the reverse of the third type. An illustration of the fourth type would be: As the amount of information on vital issues (X) decreases, rumor production (Y) increases.

Take the frequent statement that crime and divorce rates vary concomitantly with urban areas. This statement is often contrasted with such rates in rural areas. The inadequacy of such a statement is evident

[15] Unpublished Master's thesis reported in John H. Mueller and Karl F. Schuessler, *Statistical Reasoning in Sociology* (Boston, Houghton Mifflin Company, 1961), pp. 282-283.

if we find crime and divorce in *both* areas since under such conditions area could hardly be considered the cause. This is like saying that age is correlated with knowledge. Age is a time index. The fundamental question is what happens during time that is actually related to an increase in knowledge. The same is true about the statement which contrasted rural and urban areas. What *processes* and *conditions* are present in the urban areas that are not present in the rural areas which also vary concomitantly with crime? This requires an extension of our method to include additional methods.

In conclusion, it can be said that the Method of Concomitant Variation is not a method of proof of cause-and-effect relationships, but it can suggest such when the degree of concomitant variation is high. It is certainly true that nothing can be the cause of an effect if the effect does *not* vary when the alleged cause varies. The method of correlation analysis and the method of analysis of variance treated earlier are the two main methods for dealing with data collected under the Method of Concomitant Variation.

We indicated above that the Method of Concomitant Variation needs to be supplemented by other methods. We shall deal next with the *Method of Difference* as supplementary to the Method of Concomitant Variation.

Method of Difference. In some of the examples which dealt with concomitant variation we noted the difficulty of the independent factor varying not only with the effect but also with its opposite. Obviously, this makes for difficulty in interpretation. For example, suppose the independent variable is the order of birth of children and the hypothesized dependent factor is high anxiety of the firstborn. Suppose that by actual observation or check it turned out that half of the firstborn are classifiable as being anxious and half are not. In such a case it is unlikely that birth order is related to the production of anxiety, although it still might be a contributing factor, but this would have to be ascertained through additional information. The *Method of Difference* is useful in enabling us to gain a more precise picture of the relationships involved and to disentangle such confusing results.

Perhaps this is a good place to point out that generally a researcher does *not* use just one of these methods at a time, and if it does not work, then he tries some other. More often in any good research design many different methods are *combined* into one major research design. This is always the case in any research beyond a simple exploratory description of the problem. We are here treating the various methods separately only for purposes of exposition.

The modern application of the Method of Difference is best illustrated by the use of an experimental group and a control group.

The researcher proceeds as follows:

(1) Two groups of subjects are selected by matching, by randomization, or by both and are presumed to be equal in all relevant respects except for measurable chance differences.

(2) One group is designated the control group and the other the experimental group. The experimental group is properly exposed to the independent variable or variables, and the same is withheld from the control group.

(3) If a change occurs in the dependent variable in the experimental group, but such a change does not occur in the control group, then the researcher attributes the change to the independent variables he manipulated in the experimental group.

The social psychologist may make use of this method as illustrated below:

He selects a population of subjects and divides them into two or more subgroups which are equal in regard to relevant variables. The equalizing of the groups in regard to relevant factors is achieved by random selection and factor matching or measurement matching. Suppose we wanted to match the groups by sex; then we would simply have an equal number of males and females per group. If it were relevant to match for education and IQ, then they would be matched by number of years of education and IQ score. The principal idea is to compose the groups so that they are as nearly equal as possible on all factors known to influence the dependent variable. By "equal as possible" we mean that the groups are the same except for random sampling differences. The experimenter would then introduce the treatment variable to one or more of the groups and withhold it from the other group or groups.

The literature of psychology and social psychology is replete with such experiments.[16] A classical example in social psychology is Sherif's experiment on the formation of group norms. Among the questions which interested Sherif was one about group effects on individual response to an objective but unstable stimulus. In his study of group effects on judgment he employed the well-known autokinetic effect phenomenon to obtain the objective unstable stimulus situation. In complete darkness or in a closed, unlighted room when there are no lights visible, a single small light seems to move, and it may appear to move erratically in all directions. This is an example of the autokinetic phenomenon. If the point of light is presented repeatedly to an individual, it will seem to appear at different places in the room. The position of the point of light is at all times constant.

[16] See Gardner Murphy *et al.*, *Experimental Social Psychology* (New York, Harper & Row, Publishers, Inc., 1937) and Eleanor Maccoby *et al.*, *Readings in Social Psychology* (New York, Holt, Rinehart and Winston, Inc., 1958); also, the *Journal of Social Psychology* and the *Journal of Abnormal and Social Psychology*.

Sherif asked the subjects to judge the distance which the light appeared to move. Since the light actually did not move but was perceived to move, then the estimated distance was a function of subjective factors. The experimental problem dealt with the question of whether one's judgment of the perceived movement was affected when rendered with the knowledge of others' judgment of the perceived movement. To answer this question it was necessary to study the perceived movement in two situations. First, the subjects responded to the experience movement when *alone*, except for the experimenter, and then a second time when the individual was in the *group situation*. The control group, of course, responded both times under the *alone* condition.

The experimental group was divided into two subgroups. One was exposed to the *group situation* after being experimented upon when *alone*. The other was first introduced to the *group situation* and was afterwards exposed to the *alone* situation. This was done to determine whether the effects produced under the group situation would persist in the alone situation.

Other controls were utilized in the study but the above should suffice to illustrate the Method of Difference. This method is not a method of discovery, since in its application it is necessary that the researcher have knowledge beforehand of the factor or factors that he varies. That is, Sherif, for example, believed that the "social situation" would produce significantly different responses than the "alone" situation. To test this assumption he had two groups that differed in respect to the "social situation" and observed their responses in regard to the same dependent variable or outcome.

It is, of course, difficult to adhere strictly to the requirements of the Method of Difference. For example, it is very difficult to find or to create conditions which are "exactly" alike except for the factor or factors in which one is testing. Mill recognized this and provided this rule of application: "But to determine whether this invariable antecedent is a cause, or this invariable consequent an effect, we must be able, in addition, to produce the one by the means of the other: or, at least, to obtain . . . an instance in which the effect 'a' has come into existence, with no other change in the pre-existing circumstances than the addition of 'A.'" [17] In the above example, a change in judgment was capable of being produced by the introduction of the responses of other subjects, while other pre-existent circumstances were kept as stable as possible.

The principal value of the Method of Difference is that it can help a researcher decide whether a given variable could *not* be the cause of a given effect. *The principal rule is that no variable can be the cause of a phenomenon if it is absent when the phenomenon occurs.* It should

---

[17] Mill, *op. cit.*, p. 282.

now be clear that the advantage of this method is that it permits the use of a control group.

Its principal weakness centers around the fact that it is not a method of proof in the sense that it can show that A causes B. It can show that A is one of the factors or conditions which will produce B, but suppose that there are multiple factors which will produce B. In such a case, the application of the Method of Difference gives only a partial answer and does not conclusively establish proof.

At this point it should be noted that experimental methods or any other research methods can only establish whether a relationship exists between some antecedent factor or condition and some subsequent outcome or effect. It cannot determine *what* event or outcome is important for investigation or *what* antecedent factors or conditions are *relevant* to examine in connection with the effect. Knowledge about the relevant conditions and alleged causal factors has to come from previous research experience and from the theorizing of the researcher.

Returning now to the Method of Difference, suppose that a researcher has found in one instance that when he introduces antecedent factor A, effect B occurs and when factor A is not present, B does not occur. He now recommends his treatment to his friend and his friend tries it, but he does not get the effect B. Assuming that the researcher in the first instance was correct, then we are forced to conclude that other factors may also affect B. This necessitates a closer examination of the alleged relationship between antecedent A and effect B. A modern interpretation and application of Mill's *Method of Agreement* will help clarify the results.

Method of Agreement. In the immediately preceding section we saw that the Method of Difference was principally a means for determining the contribution of a given factor to a particular effect. But if the one factor only partially explains, then we need to look for other factors. Suppose that we hypothesize that some other factor is also related. Let us see how the Method of Agreement would enable us to test this.

The basic ideas of the Method of Agreement are:

(1) The researcher observes two or more instances of an effect or outcome.

(2) Each time the effect occurs he notes the factors present which seem to be related to the outcome or effect.

(3) He makes repeated observations using different combinations of the independent factors until he ascertains the one or ones which are always present when the effect or dependent variable occurs.

(4) He infers that the factor or factors that are always present when the effect occurs are related to the effect.

Suppose a sociologist or a psychologist were studying the factors related to occupational success. He could examine the college and professional school records of a sample of practitioners in a number of occupations. In addition, he might follow up the leads provided by a study of the records with interviews of the sample subjects. Suppose he found that in each case of a successful practitioner, he had known early in life what he wanted to become. The application of the Method of Agreement would suggest a relationship between early occupational commitment and occupational success. Likewise, the investigator might find a number of other factors held in common by successful occupants of occupations, such as high intellectual ability and strong motivation. Each of these may actually be related.

If the investigator finds that there are multiple factors involved, then the research problem becomes one of determining the individual effects of each variable, the joint effects of variables, if any, and finally the combined or total effects of all the variables under investigation.[18] However, the basic logic still remains that of the two-variable analysis discussed in connection with the Method of Concomitant Variation, Method of Difference, and the Method of Agreement.

We will not discuss the Method of Residue, but will conclude the presentation of methods with a discussion of the Joint Method of Agreement and Difference.[19] It should be clear to the reader that the Methods of Agreement and Difference are complementary.

Joint Method of Agreement and Difference. This type of research design utilizes the following procedure:

(1) The experimenter determines whether two or more instances of the occurrence of an effect have only one factor in common.

(2) He then tests to determine if, in two or more instances where the common factor is absent, the effect does not occur.

(3) The conclusion is that since the two situations only differed with respect to the presence and absence of one factor, then that factor is related to the effect.

We will borrow an example from Searles to illustrate concretely the Joint Method. The problem concerns the determination of the cause of a case of ptomaine poisoning. Searles says:

> Suppose that we have a party of six people who eat at a cafeteria and that afterwards three develop ptomaine poisoning. An inquiry is made into the details of their menus, and it is found that every item of their meals

---

[18] Such an undertaking is sometimes called "multiple factor analysis." Students are introduced to such techniques in intermediate and advanced statistics and courses in advanced experimental designs.

[19] For a discussion of the *Method of Residue* the student may refer to Mill, *op. cit.*, Ch. 8 or Herbert L. Searles, *Logic and Scientific Methods* (Copyright, 1948, New York, The Ronald Press Company), pp. 203-205.

METHODS OF EXPERIMENTATION 375

differed with the exception of chicken. All of those stricken with the poisoning had eaten this one thing, and only this, in common. According to the Method of Agreement, the chicken would be regarded as the cause of the poisoning. But if we wished to make a check in order to be doubly sure, we would supplement our inquiry by comparing those afflicted with the three who were not afflicted. We find that the negative cases, that is, those not poisoned, have alone in common the absence of chicken on their menus. Combining the symbols with the concrete illustration, we have the following:

Positive Instances	Chicken A	Potatoes B	Bread C	Olives D	followed by ptomaine poisoning pqrs
	Chicken A	Salad E	Pickles F	Fruit G	followed by ptuv
	Chicken A	Peas H	Rolls I	Nuts J	followed by pwxy
Negative Instances		Potatoes B	Bread C	Steak K	followed by qro
		Salad E	Pickles F	Beef L	followed by tuv
		Peas H	Rolls I	Duck M	followed by wxz

Hence chicken "A" is causally related to ptomaine poisoning "p."[20]

As indicated earlier in the separate discussion of these methods, great care must be exercised in the choice of "relevant factors." A strict application of the rule requires that the negative instances have nothing in common save the absence of the alleged causal antecedent. If this rule were taken literally, it would be impossible to apply and could lead to ludicrous results. For instance, in the foregoing illustration by Searles there were such factors in common as the roof, the furniture, the kitchen, and so on, but these factors were presumably irrelevant. The method, however, does not tell us what is relevant or irrelevant. The matter of relevancy of factors, both for control and for testing, must be decided by the researcher on the basis of past research facts and a logical application of existing theory in regard to these facts and the problem under consideration.[21]

It would be helpful if the logic of the Joint Method of Agreement and Difference were summarized by means of a 2×2 classification table.

Let us denote the dependent variable by D and its negation by $\bar{D}$ or "not D." The independent variable we will denote by the capital letter I and its negation by $\bar{I}$. If it is helpful to have the D's and I's refer to specific content, then the student might imagine that the independent variable refers to "broken homes" and the dependent variable to "emo-

---

[20] Searles, *ibid.*, pp. 202-203.
[21] For a general discussion of the procedures in theory testing, see William H. Sewell, "Some Observations on Theory Testing," *Rural Sociology*, Vol. 21 (March, 1956), pp. 1-12.

tionally ill." Suppose we make a hundred observations and apply the logic of the Joint Method of Agreement and Difference. In this case, there would be fifty cases involving the I variable and fifty involving the "not I" variable. The table would look like the following:

TABLE 12:11

Table Illustrating Joint Method of Agreement and Difference

	I	$\overline{I}$	Total
D	(a) 50	(b) 0	50
$\overline{D}$	(c) 0	(d) 50	50
Total	50	50	100

If such a distribution were to result from a sample of one hundred cases, we would have demonstrated as best one can that the dependent variable D occurs "if and only if" the independent variable I occurs. It is the assumption in this text that the values in cells (b) and (c) will only approach zero but never empirically reach zero. There are at least two major reasons why this is true. First, scientific measurement is never so completely refined or error-free; and, secondly, we are always, in the sense of "all possible" cases, only dealing with a sample population and there is error due to sampling fluctuation. Therefore, on the basis of these two reasons alone we could expect to find positive values greater than zero in these cells.

Assuming that there will always occur values greater than zero in cells (b) and (c), that is, the minor diagonal of the table, then the problem becomes one of determining whether the proportion in the major diagonal [cells (a) and (d)] is significantly different statistically from the minor diagonal to warrant inferring a relationship between I and D. In other words, the argument becomes a probability argument.

It should now be easy to see that since we are conceiving of the values in the minor diagonal as representing the "error" in the research (that is, sampling error and measurement error and perhaps error due to inadequate conceptualization), then, if there exists a theoretically exact way to measure this error, this allows a basis for deciding whether a relationship exists between the independent and dependent variables. The argument is very simple, but the mathematical proof is very complex and is not appropriate to be introduced here.

Intuitively, the arguments may be seen as follows: Let us take a

METHODS OF EXPERIMENTATION

boundary case, one where there is complete explanation. Referring to the foregoing table of one hundred cases with zero error in cells (b) and (c), in this case we would have established a "causal" or invariant relationship between the independent variable and the dependent variable, that is, there is no error in this case. Let us now take the opposite extreme in which case there would be zero values in cells (a) and (d); hence any implied relationship between the independent variable I and the dependent variable D would be completely contradicted. In this case, there is nothing but error. Normally, as indicated previously, we find that the actual results are somewhere in between these extreme possibles and hence the evaluation becomes a matter of determining the probability that such a proportion or mean could occur by chance.

Assuming that we have values or frequencies in cells (b) and (c), then, if we can measure the error that we would expect to occur by chance, we are then in a position to state exactly what the probability is that the difference between the two groups under comparison might be the result of chance. Methods for exactly measuring the amount of variation in a research design that is due to random error or chance are given in textbooks on statistics or experimental design and will not be presented here.[22] Here it is only desired to establish the fact that such techniques exist and to indicate in a very simple way their role in experimental designs.

As the foregoing discussion indicates, we are arguing that we have actually established the existence of a relationship when we have successfully displaced chance or experimental error in a research design. Thus, one of the major outcomes of scientific research in a given field is the reduction of error in the establishing of relationships. For example, if we find that the correlation between two variables is .50, this means that the percent of the total variance *accounted for* by the independent variable is 25 percent, that is, r^2, or in this case .50 squared. With 25 percent of the variance accounted for the researcher's problem then is to explain the remaining 75 percent.[23]

All research decisions in respect to hypothesis testing are fundamentally an elaboration or modification of the logic expressed in the foregoing 2 × 2 table. The discussion of the 2 × 2 table was aimed at showing how to establish that a relationship exists. Once it has been established that a relationship exists, the next step is that of determining the *degree* of the relationship or association present.

[22] See, for example, Paul G. Hoel, *Introduction to Mathematical Statistics*, 2nd ed. (New York, John Wiley & Sons, Inc., 1954) or Hubert M. Blalock, *Social Statistics* (New York, McGraw-Hill Book Company, Inc., 1960).

[23] For a discussion of the statistical basis for this example see any elementary text on statistics. Example, T. C. McCormick, *Elementary Social Statistics* (New York, McGraw-Hill Book Company, Inc., 1941), pp. 182-183.

Some Measures of Relationship

There are many measures by which the *degree* of relationship can be measured in a 2 × 2 table. The choice of the measure depends upon the theoretical argument and the nature and distribution of the data within the table. It is only necessary to point out this matter here. The student will be confronted with this problem in detail in courses in statistics and research designs.[24]

One measure will be given here, but without consideration of mathematical proof. The measure is Yule's Q. The formula is:

$$Q = \frac{ad - bc}{ad + bc}$$

where the letters a, b, c, and d refer to the particular cells noted in Table 12:11, which illustrated the Joint Method of Agreement and Difference. Substituting the values for the letters, we have:

$$Q = \frac{50(50) - 0(0)}{50(50) + 0(0)} = \frac{2500}{2500} = 1.00$$

It is clear that we have perfect association. Q would show zero association if the cell frequencies represented a purely random distribution of the table totals. The student should substitute various values in the four cells, being careful, of course, to maintain the same marginal totals, and observe the effect on Q.

Another measure which is more commonly used to measure the amount of association in a 2 × 2 table is the phi coefficient, or ϕ. One formula for calculating the phi coefficient where a, b, c, and d represent the usual cell frequencies is

$$\phi = \frac{ad - bc}{\sqrt{(a+b)(c+d)(a+c)(b+d)}}$$

Like Q, the statistic ϕ is applicable only to 2 × 2 tables of true dichotomies that have no scale of values, or to continuous variables that can be logically dichotomized. ϕ does not perform exactly the same as Q under all conditions. If we apply ϕ to the table used for computing Q, we will note that ϕ also yields 1.0. However, Q will also yield a coefficient of 1.0 or −1.0 with only one cell with zero frequency. Under such a condition ϕ will be less than 1.0. Let us illustrate. Suppose we have the following table of results:

---

[24] For a good discussion of alternative measures, see Roy G. Francis, *The Rhetoric of Science: A Methodological Discussion of the Two-by-Two Table* (University of Minnesota Press, 1961), chapters 3-7.

TABLE 12:12

Delinquency by Home Condition (Hypothetical Data)

	BROKEN HOMES	NONBROKEN HOMES	
Delinquent	30	0	30
Nondelinquent	30	40	70
	60	40	100

From the foregoing table,

$$\phi = \frac{1200 - 0}{\sqrt{30 \cdot 70 \cdot 60 \cdot 40}} = \frac{1200}{2245} = .53,$$

and

$$Q = \frac{ad - bc}{ad + bc} = \frac{1200 - 0}{1200 + 0} = 1.0.$$

Q is necessarily unity or 1.0, since *all* the delinquents come from broken homes. However, the converse, that all children from broken homes are delinquents, obviously does not hold. Thus it appears that there is a fundamental difference in what ϕ and Q measure. So a ϕ value of 1.0 implies both necessity and sufficiency of conditions in explanation.

If the reader will recall the discussion of the Method of Difference and Agreement as separate methods and then compare them with the Joint Method of Agreement and Difference, then the difference between ϕ and Q becomes clear. The formula for Q does *not* take into account joint or mutual relationships. ϕ is designed to measure the degree of two-way association between two sets of attributes. In a perfect two-way association, where the minor diagonal, that is, cells b and c, add to zero, then ϕ and Q will both equal unity.[25]

The discussion of ϕ and Q is only intended to give a clearer picture of the ideas involved in research designs which apply the *Joint Methods of Agreement and Difference*. At this point in the student's consideration of research designs it is not necessary to become involved in considerations of which measure to use. In general, where one has a 2 × 2 table involving true dichotomies the phi coefficient provides a clearer measure than Q of the degree of association. However, where the marginal totals

---

[25] Q is not a wholly unambiguous measure. For a technical discussion of its meaning see L. A. Goodman and W. H. Kruskal, "Measures of Association for Cross Classification," *Journal of the American Statistical Association*, Vol. 49 (1954), p. 730. For an excellent general discussion of measures of association the student should read G. U. Yule and M. G. Kendall, *An Introduction to the Theory of Statistics*, 14th ed. (New York, Hafner Publishing Co., Inc., 1950), pp. 1-68.

or subtotals are *unlike*, we still have a problem of *evaluating* the degree of relationship present. It has been proposed that an escape from this difficulty is to express the observed or obtained ϕ as a proportion of the maximum possible ϕ under a given set of marginal totals. But as Mueller and Schuessler say, "By that technique, an observed ϕ of .2 and a ϕ_{max} of .2 would yield a 'corrected' ϕ of unity! This would certainly be an overstatement of the existing association.

"In any event, it is not clear whether a low value of ϕ is due to the inhibiting force of the marginal frequencies or to a weak intrinsic relation between the variables as evidenced by cell frequencies." [26]

There are many measures designed to determine the degree of relationship among a set of variables. We shall mention two additional measures since they are also based on the phi coefficient, but in this case, the phi coefficient *squared*.

The first of these measures is Tschuprow's T, which is defined as:

$$T^2 = \frac{\phi^2}{\sqrt{(r-1)(c-1)}}$$

The coefficient varies between 0 and 1 for any square table, that is, when the number of rows and columns is equal. Rows and columns are designated in the above formula as r and c respectively. All that is necessary to determine T^2 for a 2 × 2 table is to calculate phi square and then determine the square root of the product of $(r-1)(c-1)$ and divide this result into ϕ^2. Suppose $\phi = .50$ and we have a 2 × 2 table, what is T?

$$T^2 = \frac{\phi^2}{\sqrt{(r-1)(c-1)}} = \frac{.50^2}{\sqrt{1.0}} = \frac{.25}{1.0} = .40$$

$T = \sqrt{.40} = .63$.

When the number of rows and columns is larger than 2 × 2, ϕ^2 can attain a value larger than unity. Therefore, some other measure for the numerator of T^2 becomes necessary. The general measure for this purpose is χ^2 (chi square), where

$$\chi^2 = \Sigma \frac{(f_o - f_t)^2}{f_t}$$

To obtain χ^2, we subtract each expected frequency (f_t) from the corresponding observed frequency (f_o), divide the squared difference by the expected frequency, and sum these ratios. Suppose we have the following 3 × 3 table.

---

[26] John H. Mueller and Karl F. Schuessler, *Statistical Reasoning in Sociology* (Boston, Houghton Mifflin Company, 1961), pp. 256-257. For a logical formulation of this problem see Roy G. Francis, *op. cit.*, pp. 97-103.

METHODS OF EXPERIMENTATION

TABLE 12:13

Illustrating the Calculation of χ^2 (Chi Square)

		SOCIAL CLASS			
		High (1)	Middle (2)	Low (3)	
DEATH RATES	High (1)	15 (1)	30 (2)	50 (3)	95
	Medium (2)	25 (4)	20 (5)	30 (6)	75
	Low (3)	35 (7)	10 (8)	20 (9)	65
		75	60	100	235

Table 12:13 provides the observed frequency (f_o) values and by use of the subtotals from this table and an application of certain probability rules we can calculate the needed expected, or f_t values. On the basis of the marginal totals in Table 12:13 the probable or expected value for row (1) (high death rates) and column (1) (high social class) is $\frac{75(95)}{235}$ or $\left(\frac{75}{235}\right)\left(\frac{95}{235}\right)$ or 30.32. For cell (2) or row (1) and column (2) we have $\frac{60(95)}{235}$ or 24.25. Following the same procedure for the remaining seven cells, we come up with the following table of expected frequencies.

TABLE 12:14

Expected Frequencies for the Observed Frequencies in Table 12:13

		SOCIAL CLASS			
		High	Middle	Low	
DEATH RATES	High	30.32	24.25	40.43	95.00
	Medium	23.94	19.15	31.91	75.00
	Low	20.74	16.60	27.66	65.00
		75.00	60.00	100.00	235.00

It should be observed that if the computations used in calculating the expected frequencies are correct, the marginal totals will sum to the same as the related observed frequencies; otherwise, an error has been made.

To obtain χ^2, we subtract each expected frequency for the corresponding observed frequency, divide the squared difference by the expected frequency, and sum these ratios. These calculations are shown in Table 12:15.

TABLE 12:15

Chi Square (χ^2) Test for Table 12:13 and 12:14

(1) DEATH RATES	(2) SOCIAL CLASS	(3) f_o	(4) f_t	(5) $f_o - f_t$	(6) $(f_o - f_t)^2$	(7) $\dfrac{(f_o - f_t)^2}{f_t}$
High	High	15	30.32	−15.32	234.70	7.74
High	Middle	30	24.25	+ 5.75	33.06	1.36
High	Low	50	40.43	+ 9.57	91.58	2.26
Medium	High	25	23.94	+ 1.06	1.12	0.04
Medium	Middle	20	19.15	+ 0.85	0.72	0.03
Medium	Low	30	31.91	− 1.91	3.65	0.11
Low	High	35	20.74	+14.26	203.34	9.80
Low	Middle	10	16.60	− 6.60	43.56	2.62
Low	Low	20	27.66	− 7.66	58.67	2.12
				0.00		$26.08 = \chi^2$

It was seen above that the expected frequencies used in Table 12:15 were calculated from the row and column totals of the observed frequencies in Table 12:13. This means that the expected frequencies are the random expectations, given these observed marginal totals; but with different marginal totals one would get different expected values. Therefore, in evaluating the χ^2 of this table, it is necessary to take into account the degrees of freedom, that is, the number of independent cells. In any $r \times c$ table, like Table 12:13, it is clear that if the row totals and the column totals are given, the number of cells that are free to vary are $(c-1)(r-1)$ or in this case $(3-1)(3-1) = 4$, so that a 3×3 table has 4 degrees of freedom. This follows from what we have already learned about the degrees of freedom for a given column with a fixed sum. It will be recalled that, given a fixed sum, there were $N-1$ values which could be assigned arbitrarily and still add up to the given sum. If we have *both* columns and rows with fixed sums, then the degrees of freedom would be $(c-1)(r-1)$.

If now the value of χ^2 obtained, that is, 26.08, is referred to a table of χ^2, such as Appendix Table 2, and the table is entered at 4 degrees of freedom and at the 5 percent level of significance, it is seen that a χ^2 as large as 9.48 could occur by chance five times in 100 times. Our χ^2 is 26.08, which is much larger, and would occur by chance less often than five in 100 times. Since it is customary to reject chance as the explanation of an event that can happen by chance no oftener than five

METHODS OF EXPERIMENTATION

times in 100, we conclude that one's life expectancy is related to one's social class position.

Now that we have established by the χ^2 test that life expectancy and class position are related, the next question is how much are they related? It was this question which caused us to introduce the notion of χ^2 as a substitute in the numerator of T^2 when the table is larger than a 2 × 2 table. Since we now have the needed χ^2 value, we are in position to calculate T^2 for the 3 × 3 table or any other square table so long as we have the χ^2 value for that table. The new formula is: [27]

$$T^2 = \frac{\chi^2}{N\sqrt{(r-1)(c-1)}} = \frac{26.08}{235\sqrt{(3-1)(3-1)}} =$$

$$\frac{26.08}{235\sqrt{4}} = \frac{26.08}{235(2)} = .06 \text{ and } T = \sqrt{.06} = .24.$$

T^2 has the defect of underestimating the relationship present for tables that are *not* square. A measure that is free from this defect is preferable. Such a measure has been developed by Cramér, and Blalock denotes it by the symbol V.

$$V^2 = \frac{\chi^2}{N \text{ Min}(r-1, c-1)}$$
$$V = \sqrt{V^2}$$

where Min $(r - 1, c - 1)$ refers to either $r - 1$ or $c - 1$, whichever is the smaller. In other words, the smaller is chosen as the denominator and is multiplied by N. If they are equal, either is chosen. V and T are equivalent whenever $r = c$; otherwise, V will always be somewhat larger than T. Both measures are the same as ϕ for 2 × 2 tables.[28]

6. DIFFICULTIES AND PITFALLS IN THE USE OF LABORATORY EXPERIMENTAL DESIGNS IN SOCIAL PSYCHOLOGICAL RESEARCH

One of the major points which we have emphasized is the notion of multiple factors and joint effects in the functioning of social behavior. We have seen in previous parts to this book that human behavior always occurs in a complex network of relationships. This fact produces difficulties for research design formulations. The principal difficulty centers in the ever-present possibility of oversimplifying reality or in combining variables or separating variables in ways which provide

---

[27] See Blalock, *op. cit.*, p. 229, or Yule and Kendall, *op. cit.*, p. 56, for a slightly different form of this equation.
[28] Blalock, *op. cit.*, p. 230.

misleading results. The principal task is to build a design which allows for a balanced interplay of factors which approximates reality to a determinable degree. The complex analysis of variance designs and the multiple and partial correlation designs are steps in this direction.

Particularly the latter methods, that is, the multiple and partial correlation procedures, can be very effective in establishing joint or separate relationships in a natural context providing that the researcher is sufficiently clever in measuring the variables and in designing the sample or series of samples.

No particular research procedure or strategy is adequate by itself for the disentangling of the matrix of relationships in social and psychological reality. The strategy which I would suggest is one of utilizing interlocking levels of complexity of particular behavior variables in an expanding context of social organization in both laboratory and natural settings. Take the phenomenon of prejudice as an example. Prejudice may be studied as it manifests itself in an interpersonal situation such as in the case of two people or a dyad. Does its manifestation vary as the number of people in interaction increases? What happens when you change interacting partners? The interpersonal situation can be extended to include an organizational context such as a business firm, factory, or the permanent staff of a school system, and so on. The context may still be expanded to include the interlocking organizations and institutions within a community. All the time, we are keeping under observation the same sample of people but under the condition of an expanding context or matrix of natural relationships. Such an approach is complex and is fraught with great difficulties in the control of variables, but if these can be measured they can be controlled mathematically. The probable successes are well worth the efforts.

7. SUMMARY

We have attempted to show that the narrow classical view of experimentation is not only not sufficient but can be misleading in its results. This is true of the behavioral sciences and it was and is also true of the physical sciences.

We speak of experiments today in outer space. Certainly these procedures are not of the classical type of relating an independent variable to a dependent variable while other interfering variables are controlled. The controls are not of a direct form of physical manipulation, but the manipulation is indirect by means of mathematical measurement and symbolic control. The same is true of modern studies on social and psychological behavior. In fact, systems of social behavior are now being simulated on computers and the results checked against empirical situations.

The research endeavor was conceived as beginning with an observation of an empirical regularity either from the laboratory or the field that was not explainable from existing knowledge. Efforts to explain this regularity focused *first* on the establishment of concomitant variations —in other words, the finding of other empirical factors which indicated that they were related to the factor to be explained or the dependent variable. Toward this end, two major methods were presented and analyzed, namely, linear correlation and analysis of variance.

Following this a *second* set of considerations was introduced to assist in determining how the variables under consideration were connected. This involved a discussion of Mill's methods and modern modifications and uses of these. It also took into account the question of differing combinations of variables under different contexts and the varying approximations of the outcomes to "reality."

Also, the matter of the degree of relationship was considered and several measures of association were presented. Finally, some of the pitfalls of a too narrow view of the meaning of experimentation were discussed.

Further References

1. Ernest Greenwood, *Experimental Sociology* (New York, Kings Crown Press, 1945).
2. Paul G. Hoel, *Elementary Statistics* (New York, John Wiley & Sons, Inc., 1960).
3. G. Udny Yule and M. G. Kendall, *An Introduction to the Theory of Statistics*, 14th ed. (New York, Hafner Publishing Co., Inc., 1950).

APPENDIX: TABLES 1 AND 2

APPENDIX

TABLE 1 Table of F

5% (Roman Type) and 1% (Bold Face Type) Points for the Distribution of F

(Values of F at 5 percent points lightface type, and 1 percent points boldface type)

Reproduced by permission from *Statistical Methods* (Table 10.5.3), 5th edition, by George W. Snedeco, Copyright ©, 1956, by the Iowa State University Press, Ames, Iowa.

n_1	1	2	3	4	5	6	7	8	9	10	11	12	14	16	20	24	30	40	50	75	100	200	500	∞	n_2
14	4.60 8.86	3.74 6.51	3.34 5.56	3.11 5.03	2.96 4.69	2.85 4.46	2.77 4.28	2.70 4.14	2.65 4.03	2.60 3.94	2.56 3.86	2.53 3.80	2.48 3.70	2.44 3.62	2.39 3.51	2.35 3.43	2.31 3.34	2.27 3.26	2.24 3.21	2.21 3.14	2.19 3.11	2.16 3.06	2.14 3.02	2.13 3.00	14
15	4.54 8.68	3.68 6.36	3.29 5.42	3.06 4.89	2.90 4.56	2.79 4.32	2.70 4.14	2.64 4.00	2.59 3.89	2.55 3.80	2.51 3.73	2.48 3.67	2.43 3.56	2.39 3.48	2.33 3.36	2.29 3.29	2.25 3.20	2.21 3.12	2.18 3.07	2.15 3.00	2.12 2.97	2.10 2.92	2.08 2.89	2.07 2.87	15
16	4.49 8.53	3.63 6.23	3.24 5.29	3.01 4.77	2.85 4.44	2.74 4.20	2.66 4.03	2.59 3.89	2.54 3.78	2.49 3.69	2.45 3.61	2.42 3.55	2.37 3.45	2.33 3.37	2.28 3.25	2.24 3.18	2.20 3.10	2.16 3.01	2.13 2.96	2.09 2.89	2.07 2.86	2.04 2.80	2.02 2.77	2.01 2.75	16
17	4.45 8.40	3.59 6.11	3.20 5.18	2.96 4.67	2.81 4.34	2.70 4.10	2.62 3.93	2.55 3.79	2.50 3.68	2.45 3.59	2.41 3.52	2.38 3.45	2.33 3.35	2.29 3.27	2.23 3.16	2.19 3.08	2.15 3.00	2.11 2.92	2.08 2.86	2.04 2.79	2.02 2.76	1.99 2.70	1.97 2.67	1.96 2.65	17
18	4.41 8.28	3.55 6.01	3.16 5.09	2.93 4.58	2.77 4.25	2.66 4.01	2.58 3.85	2.51 3.71	2.46 3.60	2.41 3.51	2.37 3.44	2.34 3.37	2.29 3.27	2.25 3.19	2.19 3.07	2.15 3.00	2.11 2.91	2.07 2.83	2.04 2.78	2.00 2.71	1.98 2.68	1.95 2.62	1.93 2.59	1.92 2.57	18
19	4.38 8.18	3.52 5.93	3.13 5.01	2.90 4.50	2.74 4.17	2.63 3.94	2.55 3.77	2.48 3.63	2.43 3.52	2.38 3.43	2.34 3.36	2.31 3.30	2.26 3.19	2.21 3.12	2.15 3.00	2.11 2.92	2.07 2.84	2.02 2.76	2.00 2.70	1.96 2.63	1.94 2.60	1.91 2.54	1.90 2.51	1.88 2.49	19
20	4.35 8.10	3.49 5.85	3.10 4.94	2.87 4.43	2.71 4.10	2.60 3.87	2.52 3.71	2.45 3.56	2.40 3.45	2.35 3.37	2.31 3.30	2.28 3.23	2.23 3.13	2.18 3.05	2.12 2.94	2.08 2.86	2.04 2.77	1.99 2.69	1.96 2.63	1.92 2.56	1.90 2.53	1.87 2.47	1.85 2.44	1.84 2.42	20
21	4.32 8.02	3.47 5.78	3.07 4.87	2.84 4.37	2.68 4.04	2.57 3.81	2.49 3.65	2.42 3.51	2.37 3.40	2.32 3.31	2.28 3.24	2.25 3.17	2.20 3.07	2.15 2.99	2.09 2.88	2.05 2.80	2.00 2.72	1.96 2.63	1.93 2.58	1.89 2.51	1.87 2.47	1.84 2.42	1.82 2.38	1.81 2.36	21
22	4.30 7.94	3.44 5.72	3.05 4.82	2.82 4.31	2.66 3.99	2.55 3.76	2.47 3.59	2.40 3.45	2.35 3.35	2.30 3.26	2.26 3.18	2.23 3.12	2.18 3.02	2.13 2.94	2.07 2.83	2.03 2.75	1.98 2.67	1.93 2.58	1.91 2.53	1.87 2.46	1.84 2.42	1.81 2.37	1.80 2.33	1.78 2.31	22
23	4.28 7.88	3.42 5.66	3.03 4.76	2.80 4.26	2.64 3.94	2.53 3.71	2.45 3.54	2.38 3.41	2.32 3.30	2.28 3.21	2.24 3.14	2.20 3.07	2.14 2.97	2.10 2.89	2.04 2.78	2.00 2.70	1.96 2.62	1.91 2.53	1.88 2.48	1.84 2.41	1.82 2.37	1.79 2.32	1.77 2.28	1.76 2.26	23
24	4.26 7.82	3.40 5.61	3.01 4.72	2.78 4.22	2.62 3.90	2.51 3.67	2.43 3.50	2.36 3.36	2.30 3.25	2.26 3.17	2.22 3.09	2.18 3.03	2.13 2.93	2.09 2.85	2.02 2.74	1.98 2.66	1.94 2.58	1.89 2.49	1.86 2.44	1.82 2.36	1.80 2.33	1.76 2.27	1.74 2.23	1.73 2.21	24
25	4.24 7.77	3.38 5.57	2.99 4.68	2.76 4.18	2.60 3.86	2.49 3.63	2.41 3.46	2.34 3.32	2.28 3.21	2.24 3.13	2.20 3.05	2.16 2.99	2.11 2.89	2.06 2.81	2.00 2.70	1.96 2.62	1.92 2.54	1.87 2.45	1.84 2.40	1.80 2.32	1.77 2.29	1.74 2.23	1.72 2.19	1.71 2.17	25
26	4.22 7.72	3.37 5.53	2.98 4.64	2.74 4.14	2.59 3.82	2.47 3.59	2.39 3.42	2.32 3.29	2.27 3.17	2.22 3.09	2.18 3.02	2.15 2.96	2.10 2.86	2.05 2.77	1.99 2.66	1.95 2.58	1.90 2.50	1.85 2.41	1.82 2.36	1.78 2.28	1.76 2.25	1.72 2.19	1.70 2.15	1.69 2.13	26

n_1 degrees of freedom (for greater mean square)

APPENDIX

n_1 degrees of freedom (for greater mean square)

n_2	1	2	3	4	5	6	7	8	9	10	11	12	14	16	20	24	30	40	50	75	100	200	500	∞	n_2
27	4.21 **7.68**	3.35 **5.49**	2.96 **4.60**	2.73 **4.11**	2.57 **3.79**	2.46 **3.56**	2.37 **3.39**	2.30 **3.26**	2.25 **3.14**	2.20 **3.06**	2.16 **2.98**	2.13 **2.93**	2.08 **2.83**	2.03 **2.74**	1.97 **2.63**	1.93 **2.55**	1.88 **2.47**	1.84 **2.38**	1.80 **2.33**	1.76 **2.25**	1.74 **2.21**	1.71 **2.16**	1.68 **2.12**	1.67 **2.10**	27
28	4.20 **7.64**	3.34 **5.45**	2.95 **4.57**	2.71 **4.07**	2.56 **3.76**	2.44 **3.53**	2.36 **3.36**	2.29 **3.23**	2.24 **3.11**	2.19 **3.03**	2.15 **2.95**	2.12 **2.90**	2.06 **2.80**	2.02 **2.71**	1.96 **2.60**	1.91 **2.52**	1.87 **2.44**	1.81 **2.35**	1.78 **2.30**	1.75 **2.22**	1.72 **2.18**	1.69 **2.13**	1.67 **2.09**	1.65 **2.06**	28
29	4.18 **7.60**	3.33 **5.42**	2.93 **4.54**	2.70 **4.04**	2.54 **3.73**	2.43 **3.50**	2.35 **3.33**	2.28 **3.20**	2.22 **3.08**	2.18 **3.00**	2.14 **2.92**	2.10 **2.87**	2.05 **2.77**	2.00 **2.68**	1.94 **2.57**	1.90 **2.49**	1.85 **2.41**	1.80 **2.32**	1.77 **2.27**	1.73 **2.19**	1.71 **2.15**	1.68 **2.10**	1.65 **2.06**	1.64 **2.03**	29
30	4.17 **7.56**	3.32 **5.39**	2.92 **4.51**	2.69 **4.02**	2.53 **3.70**	2.42 **3.47**	2.34 **3.30**	2.27 **3.17**	2.21 **3.06**	2.16 **2.98**	2.12 **2.90**	2.09 **2.84**	2.04 **2.74**	1.99 **2.66**	1.93 **2.55**	1.89 **2.47**	1.84 **2.38**	1.79 **2.29**	1.76 **2.24**	1.72 **2.16**	1.69 **2.13**	1.66 **2.07**	1.64 **2.03**	1.62 **2.01**	30
32	4.15 **7.50**	3.30 **5.34**	2.90 **4.46**	2.67 **3.97**	2.51 **3.66**	2.40 **3.42**	2.32 **3.25**	2.25 **3.12**	2.19 **3.01**	2.14 **2.94**	2.10 **2.86**	2.07 **2.80**	2.02 **2.70**	1.97 **2.62**	1.91 **2.51**	1.86 **2.42**	1.82 **2.34**	1.76 **2.25**	1.74 **2.20**	1.69 **2.12**	1.67 **2.08**	1.64 **2.02**	1.61 **1.98**	1.59 **1.96**	32
34	4.13 **7.44**	3.28 **5.29**	2.88 **4.42**	2.65 **3.93**	2.49 **3.61**	2.38 **3.38**	2.30 **3.21**	2.23 **3.08**	2.17 **2.97**	2.12 **2.89**	2.08 **2.82**	2.05 **2.76**	2.00 **2.66**	1.95 **2.58**	1.89 **2.47**	1.84 **2.38**	1.80 **2.30**	1.74 **2.21**	1.71 **2.15**	1.67 **2.08**	1.64 **2.04**	1.61 **1.98**	1.59 **1.94**	1.57 **1.91**	34
36	4.11 **7.39**	3.26 **5.25**	2.86 **4.38**	2.63 **3.89**	2.48 **3.58**	2.36 **3.35**	2.28 **3.18**	2.21 **3.04**	2.15 **2.94**	2.10 **2.86**	2.06 **2.78**	2.03 **2.72**	1.98 **2.62**	1.93 **2.54**	1.87 **2.43**	1.82 **2.35**	1.78 **2.26**	1.72 **2.17**	1.69 **2.12**	1.65 **2.04**	1.62 **2.00**	1.59 **1.94**	1.56 **1.90**	1.55 **1.87**	36
38	4.10 **7.35**	3.25 **5.21**	2.85 **4.34**	2.62 **3.86**	2.46 **3.54**	2.35 **3.32**	2.26 **3.15**	2.19 **3.02**	2.14 **2.91**	2.09 **2.82**	2.05 **2.75**	2.02 **2.69**	1.96 **2.59**	1.92 **2.51**	1.85 **2.40**	1.80 **2.32**	1.76 **2.22**	1.71 **2.14**	1.67 **2.08**	1.63 **2.00**	1.60 **1.97**	1.57 **1.90**	1.54 **1.86**	1.53 **1.84**	38
40	4.08 **7.31**	3.23 **5.18**	2.84 **4.31**	2.61 **3.83**	2.45 **3.51**	2.34 **3.29**	2.25 **3.12**	2.18 **2.99**	2.12 **2.88**	2.07 **2.80**	2.04 **2.73**	2.00 **2.66**	1.95 **2.56**	1.90 **2.49**	1.84 **2.37**	1.79 **2.29**	1.74 **2.20**	1.69 **2.11**	1.66 **2.05**	1.61 **1.97**	1.59 **1.94**	1.55 **1.88**	1.53 **1.84**	1.51 **1.81**	40
42	4.07 **7.27**	3.22 **5.15**	2.83 **4.29**	2.59 **3.80**	2.44 **3.49**	2.32 **3.26**	2.24 **3.10**	2.17 **2.96**	2.11 **2.86**	2.06 **2.77**	2.02 **2.70**	1.99 **2.64**	1.94 **2.54**	1.89 **2.46**	1.82 **2.35**	1.78 **2.26**	1.73 **2.17**	1.68 **2.08**	1.64 **2.02**	1.60 **1.94**	1.57 **1.91**	1.54 **1.85**	1.51 **1.80**	1.49 **1.78**	42
44	4.06 **7.24**	3.21 **5.12**	2.82 **4.26**	2.58 **3.78**	2.43 **3.46**	2.31 **3.24**	2.23 **3.07**	2.16 **2.94**	2.10 **2.84**	2.05 **2.75**	2.01 **2.68**	1.98 **2.62**	1.92 **2.52**	1.88 **2.44**	1.81 **2.32**	1.76 **2.24**	1.72 **2.15**	1.66 **2.06**	1.63 **2.00**	1.58 **1.92**	1.56 **1.88**	1.52 **1.82**	1.50 **1.78**	1.48 **1.75**	44
46	4.05 **7.21**	3.20 **5.10**	2.81 **4.24**	2.57 **3.76**	2.42 **3.44**	2.30 **3.22**	2.22 **3.05**	2.14 **2.92**	2.09 **2.82**	2.04 **2.73**	2.00 **2.66**	1.97 **2.60**	1.91 **2.50**	1.87 **2.42**	1.80 **2.30**	1.75 **2.22**	1.71 **2.13**	1.65 **2.04**	1.62 **1.98**	1.57 **1.90**	1.54 **1.86**	1.51 **1.80**	1.48 **1.76**	1.46 **1.72**	46
48	4.04 **7.19**	3.19 **5.08**	2.80 **4.22**	2.56 **3.74**	2.41 **3.42**	2.30 **3.20**	2.21 **3.04**	2.14 **2.90**	2.08 **2.80**	2.03 **2.71**	1.99 **2.64**	1.96 **2.58**	1.90 **2.48**	1.86 **2.40**	1.79 **2.28**	1.74 **2.20**	1.70 **2.11**	1.64 **2.02**	1.61 **1.96**	1.56 **1.88**	1.53 **1.84**	1.50 **1.78**	1.47 **1.73**	1.45 **1.70**	48

n_2	1	2	3	4	5	6	7	8	9	10	11	12	14	16	20	24	30	40	50	75	100	200	500	∞	n_2
50	4.03 7.17	3.18 5.06	2.79 4.20	2.56 3.72	2.40 3.41	2.29 3.18	2.20 3.02	2.13 2.88	2.07 2.78	2.02 2.70	1.98 2.62	1.95 2.56	1.90 2.46	1.85 2.39	1.78 2.26	1.74 2.18	1.69 2.10	1.63 2.00	1.60 1.94	1.55 1.86	1.52 1.82	1.48 1.76	1.46 1.71	1.44 1.68	50
55	4.02 7.12	3.17 5.01	2.78 4.16	2.54 3.68	2.38 3.37	2.27 3.15	2.18 2.98	2.11 2.85	2.05 2.75	2.00 2.66	1.97 2.59	1.93 2.53	1.88 2.43	1.83 2.35	1.76 2.23	1.72 2.15	1.67 2.06	1.61 1.96	1.58 1.90	1.52 1.82	1.50 1.78	1.46 1.71	1.43 1.66	1.41 1.64	55
60	4.00 7.08	3.15 4.98	2.76 4.13	2.52 3.65	2.37 3.34	2.25 3.12	2.17 2.95	2.10 2.82	2.04 2.72	1.99 2.63	1.95 2.56	1.92 2.50	1.86 2.40	1.81 2.32	1.75 2.20	1.70 2.12	1.65 2.03	1.59 1.93	1.56 1.87	1.50 1.79	1.48 1.74	1.44 1.68	1.41 1.63	1.39 1.60	60
65	3.99 7.04	3.14 4.95	2.75 4.10	2.51 3.62	2.36 3.31	2.24 3.09	2.15 2.93	2.08 2.79	2.02 2.70	1.98 2.61	1.94 2.54	1.90 2.47	1.85 2.37	1.80 2.30	1.73 2.18	1.68 2.09	1.63 2.00	1.57 1.90	1.54 1.84	1.49 1.76	1.46 1.71	1.42 1.64	1.39 1.60	1.37 1.56	65
70	3.98 7.01	3.13 4.92	2.74 4.08	2.50 3.60	2.35 3.29	2.23 3.07	2.14 2.91	2.07 2.77	2.01 2.67	1.97 2.59	1.93 2.51	1.89 2.45	1.84 2.35	1.79 2.28	1.72 2.15	1.67 2.07	1.62 1.98	1.56 1.88	1.53 1.82	1.47 1.74	1.45 1.69	1.40 1.62	1.37 1.56	1.35 1.53	70
80	3.96 6.96	3.11 4.88	2.72 4.04	2.48 3.56	2.33 3.25	2.21 3.04	2.12 2.87	2.05 2.74	1.99 2.64	1.95 2.55	1.91 2.48	1.88 2.41	1.82 2.32	1.77 2.24	1.70 2.11	1.65 2.03	1.60 1.94	1.54 1.84	1.51 1.78	1.45 1.70	1.42 1.65	1.38 1.57	1.35 1.52	1.32 1.49	80
100	3.94 6.90	3.09 4.82	2.70 3.98	2.46 3.51	2.30 3.20	2.19 2.99	2.10 2.82	2.03 2.69	1.97 2.59	1.92 2.51	1.88 2.43	1.85 2.36	1.79 2.26	1.75 2.19	1.68 2.06	1.63 1.98	1.57 1.89	1.51 1.79	1.48 1.73	1.42 1.64	1.39 1.59	1.34 1.51	1.30 1.46	1.28 1.43	100
125	3.92 6.84	3.07 4.78	2.68 3.94	2.44 3.47	2.29 3.17	2.17 2.95	2.08 2.79	2.01 2.65	1.95 2.56	1.90 2.47	1.86 2.40	1.83 2.33	1.77 2.23	1.72 2.15	1.65 2.03	1.60 1.94	1.55 1.85	1.49 1.75	1.45 1.68	1.39 1.59	1.36 1.54	1.31 1.46	1.27 1.40	1.25 1.37	125
150	3.91 6.81	3.06 4.75	2.67 3.91	2.43 3.44	2.27 3.14	2.16 2.92	2.07 2.76	2.00 2.62	1.94 2.53	1.89 2.44	1.85 2.37	1.82 2.30	1.76 2.20	1.71 2.12	1.64 2.00	1.59 1.91	1.54 1.83	1.47 1.72	1.44 1.66	1.37 1.56	1.34 1.51	1.29 1.43	1.25 1.37	1.22 1.33	150
200	3.89 6.76	3.04 4.71	2.65 3.88	2.41 3.41	2.26 3.11	2.14 2.90	2.05 2.73	1.98 2.60	1.92 2.50	1.87 2.41	1.83 2.34	1.80 2.28	1.74 2.17	1.69 2.09	1.62 1.97	1.57 1.88	1.52 1.79	1.45 1.69	1.42 1.62	1.35 1.53	1.32 1.48	1.26 1.39	1.22 1.33	1.19 1.28	200
400	3.86 6.70	3.02 4.66	2.62 3.83	2.39 3.36	2.23 3.06	2.12 2.85	2.03 2.69	1.96 2.55	1.90 2.46	1.85 2.37	1.81 2.29	1.78 2.23	1.72 2.12	1.67 2.04	1.60 1.92	1.54 1.84	1.49 1.74	1.42 1.64	1.38 1.57	1.32 1.47	1.28 1.42	1.22 1.32	1.16 1.24	1.13 1.19	400
1000	3.85 6.66	3.00 4.62	2.61 3.80	2.38 3.34	2.22 3.04	2.10 2.82	2.02 2.66	1.95 2.53	1.89 2.43	1.84 2.34	1.80 2.26	1.76 2.20	1.70 2.09	1.65 2.01	1.58 1.89	1.53 1.81	1.47 1.71	1.41 1.61	1.36 1.54	1.30 1.44	1.26 1.38	1.19 1.28	1.13 1.19	1.08 1.11	1000
∞	3.84 6.64	2.99 4.60	2.60 3.78	2.37 3.32	2.21 3.02	2.09 2.80	2.01 2.64	1.94 2.51	1.88 2.41	1.83 2.32	1.79 2.24	1.75 2.18	1.69 2.07	1.64 1.99	1.57 1.87	1.52 1.79	1.46 1.69	1.40 1.59	1.35 1.52	1.28 1.41	1.24 1.36	1.17 1.25	1.11 1.15	1.00 1.00	∞

n_1 degrees of freedom (for greater mean square)

APPENDIX

TABLE 2 Distribution of χ^2 Probability

n	.99	.98	.95	.90	.80	.70	.50	.30	.20	.10	.05	.02	.01	.001
1	.000157	.000628	.00393	.0158	.0642	.148	.455	1.074	1.642	2.706	3.841	5.412	6.635	10.827
2	.0201	.0404	.103	.211	.446	.713	1.386	2.408	3.219	4.605	5.991	7.824	9.210	13.815
3	.115	.185	.352	.584	1.005	1.424	2.366	3.665	4.642	6.251	7.815	9.837	11.345	16.268
4	.297	.429	.711	1.064	1.649	2.195	3.357	4.878	5.989	7.779	9.488	11.668	13.277	18.465
5	.554	.752	1.145	1.610	2.343	3.000	4.351	6.064	7.289	9.236	11.070	13.388	15.086	20.517
6	.872	1.134	1.635	2.204	3.070	3.828	5.348	7.231	8.558	10.645	12.592	15.033	16.812	22.457
7	1.239	1.564	2.167	2.833	3.822	4.671	6.346	8.383	9.803	12.017	14.067	16.622	18.475	24.322
8	1.646	2.032	2.733	3.490	4.594	5.527	7.344	9.524	11.030	13.362	15.507	18.168	20.090	26.125
9	2.088	2.532	3.325	4.168	5.380	6.393	8.343	10.656	12.242	14.684	16.919	19.679	21.666	27.877
10	2.558	3.059	3.940	4.865	6.179	7.267	9.342	11.781	13.442	15.987	18.307	21.161	23.209	29.588
11	3.053	3.609	4.575	5.578	6.989	8.148	10.341	12.899	14.631	17.275	19.675	22.618	24.725	31.264
12	3.571	4.178	5.226	6.304	7.807	9.034	11.340	14.011	15.812	18.549	21.026	24.054	26.217	32.909
13	4.107	4.765	5.892	7.042	8.634	9.926	12.340	15.119	16.985	19.812	22.362	25.472	27.688	34.528
14	4.660	5.368	6.571	7.790	9.467	10.821	13.339	16.222	18.151	21.064	23.685	26.873	29.141	36.123
15	5.229	5.985	7.261	8.547	10.307	11.721	14.339	17.322	19.311	22.307	24.996	28.259	30.578	37.697
16	5.812	6.614	7.962	9.312	11.152	12.624	15.338	18.418	20.465	23.542	26.296	29.633	32.000	39.252
17	6.408	7.255	8.672	10.085	12.002	13.531	16.338	19.511	21.615	24.769	27.587	30.995	33.409	40.790
18	7.015	7.906	9.390	10.865	12.857	14.440	17.338	20.601	22.760	25.989	28.869	32.346	34.805	42.312
19	7.633	8.567	10.117	11.651	13.716	15.352	18.338	21.689	23.900	27.204	30.144	33.687	36.191	43.820
20	8.260	9.237	10.851	12.443	14.578	16.266	19.337	22.775	25.038	28.412	31.410	35.020	37.566	45.315
21	8.897	9.915	11.591	13.240	15.445	17.182	20.337	23.858	26.171	29.615	32.671	36.343	38.932	46.797
22	9.542	10.600	12.338	14.041	16.314	18.101	21.337	24.939	27.301	30.813	33.924	37.659	40.289	48.268
23	10.196	11.293	13.091	14.848	17.187	19.021	22.337	26.018	28.429	32.007	35.172	38.968	41.638	49.728
24	10.856	11.992	13.848	15.659	18.062	19.943	23.337	27.096	29.553	33.196	36.415	40.270	42.980	51.179
25	11.524	12.697	14.611	16.473	18.940	20.867	24.337	28.172	30.675	34.382	37.652	41.566	44.314	52.620
26	12.198	13.409	15.379	17.292	19.820	21.792	25.336	29.246	31.795	35.563	38.885	42.856	45.642	54.052
27	12.879	14.125	16.151	18.114	20.703	22.719	26.336	30.319	32.912	36.741	40.113	44.140	46.963	55.476
28	13.565	14.847	16.928	18.939	21.588	23.647	27.336	31.391	34.027	37.916	41.337	45.419	48.278	56.893
29	14.256	15.574	17.708	19.768	22.475	24.577	28.336	32.461	35.139	39.087	42.557	46.693	49.588	58.302
30	14.953	16.306	18.493	20.599	23.364	25.508	29.336	33.530	36.250	40.256	43.773	47.962	50.892	59.703

For larger values of n, the expression $\sqrt{2\chi^2} - \sqrt{2n-1}$ may be used as a normal deviate with unit variance. Table 2 is taken from Table IV, Distribution of χ^2, Fisher and Yates, *Statistical Tables for Agri-cultural and Medical Research* (Edinburgh, Oliver & Boyd, Ltd.). By permission of the authors and publishers.

NAME INDEX

Adams, Donald K., 17, 35, 37
Allport, Floyd H., 124
Anderson, Poul, 40, 129
Arsenian, J. M., 230
Atkinson, John W., 262

Back, Kurt, 268, 274
Baitsell, G. A., 25
Baldwin, James M., 5-6, 25
Banfield, Edward C., 243
Barnes, H. E., 3, 27, 50, 137
Barnett, H. G., 319
Beach, F. A., 68
Beadle, George Wells, 70
Beardslee, David C., 117, 121, 132, 147
Becker, Howard, 3, 27, 37, 50, 137, 319
Benedict, Ruth, 239
Berelson, Bernard, 146, 267, 270
Bergmann, Gustav, 42
Berkowitz, Leonard, 159, 160, 161, 242
Bevan, William, 115
Blalock, Hubert M., 377, 383
Blau, Peter M., 252, 254, 284
Bohannan, Paul, 54
Boring, Edwin G., 3
Boskoff, Alvin, 319
Bowlby, J., 207, 230, 232
Braithwaite, Richard B., 340
Bredemeier, Harry C., 53, 202, 239, 289, 290, 329
Britt, S. H., 23
Brodbeck, May, 38, 42
Bruner, Jerome S., 132
Brunswik, Egon, 115, 156, 177
Burtt, E. A., 24
Butler, R. A., 231

Cannon, Walter B., 71
Cantril, Hadley, 142
Carnap, Rudolf, 32
Carpenter, C. R., 230
Cartwright, Dorwin, 275, 284
Chapanis, Alphonse, 310
Chapanis, Natalia P., 310
Charlesworth, James C., 33
Childe, V. Gordon, 64
Cicourel, Aaron V., 254, 257
Cloward, Richard A., 281
Cohen, Yehudi A., 243
Collins, Barry E., 195

Collins, Mary E., 270
Conant, James B., 325
Cooley, Charles H., 6, 25
Coombs, C. H., 304
Cooper, Eunice, 161, 162
Count, Earl L., 71
Crutchfield, Richard, 16, 107

Darwin, Charles, 49
Davis, Kingsley, 24, 34, 84
Deese, James, 168, 175, 187
Deutsch, Morton, 270
Dickson, William J., 196
Dingle, Herbert, 32
Doby, John T., 24, 38, 155, 329, 334
Dobzhansky, Theodosius, 53, 66, 71, 82, 84
Dollard, John, 230
DuBois, Philip H., 350, 355
Duncker, Karl, 193
Durkheim, Émile, 253

Edwards, Allen L., 334, 366
Einstein, Albert, 329, 332
Etzioni, Amitai, 263
Ewert, P. H., 123, 124
Ezekiel, Mordecai, 350, 353

Fabricius, E., 230
Faris, Ellsworth, 28
Faris, Robert E. L., 17, 28
Feigl, Herbert, 38, 42
Ferguson, George A., 355, 357
Festinger, Leon, 243, 268, 306, 307
Fisher, Ronald A., 340, 361
Foley, J. P., 230
Ford, C. S., 68
Francis, Roy G., 24, 325, 328, 329, 334, 380
Frank, Philipp, 33
French, J. R. P., Jr., 275
Fritts, Paul M., 141

Gage, N. L., 164
Garfinkel, Harold, 255
Gerard, Ralph, 65, 98
Gerth, H. H., 275
Getzels, Jacob W., 105, 106
Gewirtz, J., 236
Gilbert, W. S., 266

395

NAME INDEX

Gillin, John, 8
Goodman, L. A., 379
Greenwood, Ernest, 338, 385
Gruber, Howard E., 105, 207
Guetzkow, Harold, 195

Hallowell, A. Irving, 126
Harlow, Harry F., 72, 101, 115, 120, 206, 230
Harrison, G. A., 72
Hartley, Eugene L., 8, 16, 99, 127
Hartley, Ruth E., 8
Hebb, D. O., 139, 192, 230
Heider, Fritz, 159, 301
Heisenberg, Werner, 328
Helson, Harry, 115
Hempel, C. G., 38, 42, 340
Henderson, A. M., 275
Hess, Eckhard H., 145, 230
Hilgard, Ernest R., 168, 171, 179, 180
Hinde, R. A., 230
Hoagland, Hudson, 86
Hoel, Paul G., 353, 354, 377, 385
Hoffman, Lois W., 233, 238
Hoffman, Martin L., 233, 238
Hollander, E. P., 30, 159
Holmes, F. B., 230
Holz, A. M., 84
Homans, George C., 196, 259, 268, 276
Hovland, Carl I., 151, 152, 159, 166, 256, 302, 319
Howells, William, 26, 51, 67, 72
Hull, Clark, 198
Hulse, Frederick S., 72
Hunt, J. McV., 98, 100, 109
Hunt, Raymond G., 30, 159
Huxley, Julian, 89

Infeld, Leopold, 332

Jackson, Philip W., 105, 106
Jahoda, Marie, 161, 162
James, William, 25, 157
Janis, Irving L., 319
Jasper, Herbert, 120
Jaynes, J., 230
Jennings, Helen H., 261
Jersild, A. T., 230
Johannsen, Wilhelm, 78
Jones, Edward E., 259

Kagan, Jerome, 238, 240, 241
Kahn, Robert L., 284
Kaplan, Abraham, 340
Karpf, Faye B., 6
Katz, Daniel, 299, 301, 313
Kelley, H. H., 259, 260, 276, 284, 319
Kelman, H. C., 310, 311, 312

Kendall, M. G., 379, 383, 385
Koch, Sigmund, 45, 299, 301
Kohler, W., 230
Komarovsky, Mirra, 264, 265
Krech, David, 15, 16
Kruskal, W. H., 379
Kuhn, Thomas S., 339

Lambert, Wallace C., 30, 235
Lambert, William W., 30, 235
Langer, Susanne, 62
Lawrence, Douglas H., 243
Lazarsfeld, Paul F., 8
Lazarus, Richard S., 144
LeBon, Gustave, 4
Lecky, Prescott, 261
Lewin, Kurt, 15
Li, Ching Chun, 109
Lindzey, Gardner, 10, 30
Linton, Ralph, 10, 11, 12, 18, 54, 181, 200, 201
Lippmann, Walter, 137
Litwin, George H., 262
Lorenz, K., 230
Lumsdaine, A. A., 319
Lynd, Robert S., 23

Maccoby, E., 244, 371
Madden, Edward H., 329, 330
Magoun, H. W., 75
Mandeville, Bernard de, 137
March, James G., 284
Marquis, D. M., 171
Marx, Melvin H., 340
Mason, Marie K., 34
McCleary, Robert A., 144
McClelland, David C., 177, 178, 182, 183, 184, 185
McCormick, Thomas C., 155, 333, 355, 377
McDougall, William, 4-5, 28
McKinnon, Donald W., 194
Mead, George H., 6, 18, 25
Mead, Margaret, 136, 202
Mednick, Martha T., 243
Mednick, Sarnoff A., 243
Mendel, Gregor, 78
Merton, Robert K., 8, 10, 156, 270, 289
Mill, John Stuart, 368, 372, 374
Miller, Daniel, 244
Miller, N. E., 230
Mills, C. Wright, 275
Mills, Theodore M., 258
Moltz, H., 230
Moore, Wilbert E., 319
Morgan, Lewis H., 89
Morgenstern, Oskar, 33
Mueller, John H., 340, 369, 380

NAME INDEX

Muller, H. J., 27
Mundy, D., 259
Murphy, Gardner, 100, 115, 120, 132, 139, 147, 317, 371

Nagel, Ernest, 328
Newcomb, T. N., 8, 17, 99, 127, 270
Newell, A. J., 102, 316
Newman, H. H., 99
Nietzsche, Friedrick, 132
Nolte, A., 230

Odum, Howard W., 93
Ohlin, Lloyd E., 281
Oppenheim, Paul, 38, 42, 340
Orth, Charles D., 266
Osgood, Charles E., 159, 162, 258, 301

Parsons, Talcott, 10, 44, 249, 275
Pasteur, Louis, 3
Penfield, Wilder, 72
Petrillo, Luigi, 166
Piaget, Jean, 8, 102, 103, 104
Polt, James M., 145
Polyak, S., 67
Popper, Karl R., 357
Postman, L., 41

Quinn, Olive Westbrooke, 273

Radloff, R., 259
Raven, B. H., 275
Razran, Gregory, 198
Redfield, Robert, 63, 64
Rheingold, H. L., 236
Ribble, M. A., 230
Riesen, Austin H., 117, 118, 119
Roberts, Lamar, 72
Roe, Anne, 66, 72
Roethlisberger, F. J., 196
Rose, Arnold, 3, 26
Rosenberg, M. J., 302, 303, 305
Rosenblum, L., 230
Rosenzweig, M. R., 41
Ross, Edward Alsworth, 4, 28
Ross, H., 236

Shalins, Marshall D., 74, 75, 89, 91, 95
Saltzman, I. J., 187
Sampson, Edward S., 30
Sarbin, T. R., 10, 18
Schachter, Stanley, 268
Schein, E. H., 235
Schlosberg, Harold, 138, 143, 168
Schuessler, Karl F., 340, 369, 380
Scriven, Michael, 72
Searles, Herbert L., 374
Sears, Robert, 244

Service, Elman R., 74, 89, 91, 94, 95, 93
Sewell, William H., 129, 130, 375
Shaw, J. C., 102, 316
Sheffield, F. D., 319
Shepard, Samuel, 191
Shepherd, Clovis R., 284
Sherif, Carolyn W., 126, 132, 277, 279, 280, 284
Sherif, Muzafer, 7, 126, 132, 151, 152, 159, 166, 256, 277, 279, 280, 284
Shibutani, Tamoutsu, 157, 244
Shils, Edward, 10, 44
Simon, H. A., 102, 284, 316
Simpson, George G., 66, 72
Skinner, B. F., 170, 172, 173, 198
Smelser, Neil J., 45
Smelser, William T., 45
Smith, Homer W., 72
Smith, Karl U., 121, 122, 123, 188, 190
Socrates, 12
Solley, Charles M., 132, 139, 147
Sorokin, Pitirim A., 5, 45
Spence, Kenneth W., 14, 42, 179
Spuhler, J. N., 65, 66, 68, 69
Stein, Morris I., 194
Steiner, Gary A., 146, 276, 270
Steiner, Ivan D., 163
Stephenson, Richard M., 53, 202, 239, 289, 290, 329
Stevens, S. S., 141, 149, 198
Stotland, Ezra, 299, 301, 313
Stouffer, Samuel A., 21, 263, 266, 270
Strauss, Bernard S., 81
Suci, George J., 258
Sumner, William G., 4
Swanson, Guy, 244

Tagiuri, Renato, 166
Tannenbaum, Percy H., 258, 301
Tarde, Gabriel, 28
Tarski, Alfred, 32
Tax, Sol, 56
Terrell, Glenn, 105, 107
Thibaut, John W., 259, 260, 279, 284
Thomas, W. I., 6, 25, 155
Thorpe, W. H., 230
Tolman, Edward C., 15
Tomilin, M. I., 230
Trotsky, Leon, 89, 91, 92
Turgot, Jacques, 49
Turner, Ralph H., 156, 166

Upshaw, Harry S., 152

Veblin, Thorstein, 89, 92
Vince, M. A., 230
Von Bertalanffy, Ludweg, 109
Von Mises, Richard, 33

Wagenen, G. van, 230
Weber, Max, 275
Weiner, J. S., 72
Weiss, W., 319
Wertheimer, Michael, 105, 107, 117, 121, 132, 147
White, Leslie A., 56, 58, 59, 60, 62
Whiting, Beatrice B., 244
Whorf, Benjamin L., 128
Winch, Robert F., 261
Winer, B. J., 355
Wohlwill, Joachim F., 116
Woodruff, L. L., 25

Woodworth, Robert S., 138, 143, 168
Woolsey, Clinton N., 72, 120

Yarrow, Leon J., 232
Yerkes, R. M., 230
Yule, G. U., 379, 383, 385

Zelditch, Morris, 351
Zimbardo, P. G., 308
Zimmermann, Robert R., 206
Znaniecki, Florian, 6, 7
Zuckerman, S., 230

SUBJECT INDEX

Abstraction, levels of, 14, 34 ff., 42
Acceptance-rejection of items, 151, 152
Accommodation, 103, 104
Achievement
   IQ and, 106
   motivation, 178, 262
   physiological, potentiality and, 88
Activity, units of, 126
Actual behavior, 87, 135
Actual frame of reference, 159
Adaptability
   general, 89, 92
   physical bases of, 66 ff.
Adaptation, 52, 53, 54-55
   perceptual, 120
Adaptive function of interaction, 102, 103
Affective behavior, 206 ff.
   attitude and, 17
   contact comfort and, 208 ff.
   fear and, 211 ff.
   retention of, 221 ff.
Affective-cognitive consistency theory, 301 ff., 313
Agreement, method of, 373-374
   joint method of difference and, 374 ff., 379
Alleles, 81-82
Ambiguous face, 141-142
Ambiguous figure, 138
Ambiguous situations, 252-253, 256-257
American Soldier, The, 8
Analysis, 31 ff., 323 ff.
   conceptual level of, 35 ff.
   units of, 14 ff., 42
   of variance, 353 ff.
Aniseikonia, 143
Anthropoidea, 73-74
Anxiety, social change and, 288-290
Apes, 74
Army rank, attitudes and, 8
Arunta, 87
Aspiration, level of, perception and, 126-127
Assimilation, 103, 104, 159, 160
Association, perception and, 116
Attitude, 16-17, 43, 299-301
   change, 297 ff., 315-317
   Festinger's theory of, 306
   generalization of, 17
   judgment and, 152-153

Attitude—*Continued*
   Kelman's theory of, 310
   learning of, 273
   norms and, 135
   rank in Army and, 8
   Rosenberg's theory of, 301
   toward values, 296
Auditory feedback, delayed, 121
Auditory inversion, 124
Authority power, 276
Autokinetic effects, 128, 256, 371-372
Automation, 316
Autonomic discrimination, 144
Autonomous group, 267
Autosomes, 78
Awareness, perception and, 144

Backward society, development of, 90 ff.
Becoming, 99
Belief, attitude and, 300
Behavior
   actual, 87, 135
   analysis, 31 ff., 323 ff.
   patterns of, 250
      difficulties in understanding, 324
      early experience and, 206, 232
   persistense of, 54
   personal *vs.* social, 163, 165
   potential limits of, 87
   social context of, 235 ff.
   systems of, 39, 196
Berdache, 239
Bigotry, 162
Biological evolution, 50-52
Biological foundation of man, 26-27, 251-252
Biological potentialities, 76 ff.
Biological prerequisites to culture, 65 ff.
Biological specialization, 89-90
Bipedal locomotion, 67
Body cells, 51, 79
Brain
   evolution and size of, 69-70
   learning and function of, 101-102
   sexual control by, 68
   visual perception and, 120
Bull Dogs, Red Devils and, 277 ff.

Carnivorous diet, 68
Cataracts, perception and, 116-117

Categorization, 133, 151
Cause-effect logic, 329-330, 338
Cell differentiation, 79
Cells, 51, 79
Cerebral cortex
  expansion, 69-70
  sexual behavior and, 68
Chimpanzee, visual perception of, 117 ff.
Chi square, 380, 381, 382, 383
Chromosomes, 78, 79-80, 81
Cicourel's model for norms, 254 ff.
Clinging contact, 229
Coercive power, 275
Cognitive-affective consistency theory, 301 ff., 313
Cognitive dissonance theory, 306 ff., 313
Cognitive element of attitudes, 299, 300
Cognitive style, 107
Cognitive system, 288
Cohesiveness, group, problem-solving and, 274
Collective wisdom, 70
College plans, community influence and, 130
Combined development, law of, 90
Committees, 196, 267
Common-sense observation, 31 ff.
Communication
  ideas and, 86
  vocal, evolution and, 68-69
Communist desocialization, 233-235
Community variables in perception, 129
Comparison levels, 260
Competence in interpersonal behavior, 163, 164
Compliance, 256
  attitude change and, 310-311
Conceptual level of analysis, 14, 35 ff.
Concomitant variation, 343, 347 ff., 368-370
Conditioning, 169
  classical, 169-170, 171, 172
  distinction of two types of, 171-172
  instrumental or operant, 170, 171, 172, 187 ff.
  interpersonal response, 236
  responses, 56, 57-58
Conformity, creativity and, 107
Consequences, perception of, 158
Consonance, cognitive, 306
Constitutive expectancies, 254-255
Contact comfort, 208 ff., 231
Continuity, perception and, 141, 154
Contrast, perception and, 141, 159, 160
Coordinates, 346
Coordination of action, 250
Correlation, linear, 348
Covariation, 347, 353

Cramer's V, 383
Creativity, 104 ff.
  conformity and, 107
  imagination and, 105, 107
  learning and, 193-194
  parental security and, 108
  in science, 327, 331
Cross-pressures, 271
Cues, social, perception and, 133, 154
Cultural attitudes, learning of, 273
Cultural deprivation, 232-233
Cultural potentialities, 86 ff.
Culture, 9n., 18, 52 ff., 134
  adaptations and, 53, 55
  biological prerequisites to, 65 ff.
  contradictions in, 264-265
  evolution and, 49 ff., 63-64, 76 ff., 89 ff.
  perception and, 125 ff.
  system of, 76
Cytoplasm, 79

Danireans, 16
Data
  conceptual level of analysis of, 35 ff.
  explanatory, 38, 39
  objectiveness of, 36
  problematic, 38, 39
  scientific language and, 31 ff.
  social psychology problems and, 39-41
Death rate, social class and, 381, 382
Definition, social, 150, 166
Delinquency, home conditions and, 379
Density, concept of, 336
Deoxyribonucleic acid, 81
Dependence on others, 200
Deprivation, social and cultural, 232-233
Description, 31 ff.
Design, experimental, 368 ff.
  difficulties in, 383-384
Desocialization, 233-235
Development, law of combined, 91
Diet, evolution and, 68
Difference, method of, 370 ff.
  joint method of agreement and, 374 ff., 379
Difference quotient, 348
Differentiation of response, 180
Diffusion, 54, 55-56, 77, 91-92
Diploid sets, 80
Discontinuity of progress, 92
Discrimination, 146, 151. See also Perception.
  autonomic, 144
  learning, 171
  partial reinforcement and, 175, 178
  relational, 178
  of stimuli, 180
Dissonance, cognitive, 306 ff., 313

SUBJECT INDEX

Distance, physical, interaction and, 268-269
Distasteful materials, perception and, 145-146
Distribution, frequency, of scores, 355-357
DNA, 81
Domain, 345-346
Dominant alleles, 82
Drive, 203-205
Dyads, 80

Education, IQ and, 99
Efficiency in group behavior, 163, 164, 165
Egg, 82
   cleavage, 79
Emotionality index, 213, 218, 219, 225
Empirical regularities, 326, 343-344
Empiricism, scientific, 335
Empty sets, 344
Energy resources, 76-77, 203
Environment, 79
   behavioral, 134
   change, 286, 297, 298, 317
   cognitive elements of, 308-309
   evolution and, 50
   genes and, interplay of, 98
   irregularity of, 181
   neural organization and, 102
   spatial and temporal patterns of, 122
   visual perception and, 119
Epistemological principle, 35
Error in research, 376
Esteem, 19-20
Ethnic prejudice, 270-271, 273
Evaluation of behavior. See Judgment, social.
Evolution, 26-27
   concept of biological, 50-52
   culture and, 49 ff., 63-64, 76 ff.
   general, 74, 76, 89
   phylogenetic, 72, 73-74
   potential of culture and, 89 ff.
   specific, 74-76, 89, 92
Exchange theory, 259 ff., 276-277
Expectancies
   constitutive, 254-255
   individual, role and, 21
   of others, response and, 150
   partial reinforcement, 175
Experience, 98
   cumulative nature of, 291
   early, behavior and, 206 ff.
   figure and ground factors in, 139-141
   intelligence and, 99 ff.
   past, perception and, 116 ff.
   science and, 326-327

Experimentation, 341 ff.
   design, 368 ff., 383-384
   difficulties in social psychological, 383-384
   establishing existence of relationships in, 346 ff.
   introduction to problem in, 342-344
   results, inference and interpretations of, 367 ff.
   sets and functions in, 344-346
Expert power, 275-277
Explanation
   learning and, 35
   scientific, 31 ff.
Explanatory data, 38, 39
Extinction of response, 176 ff., 184-185
Eye color, genetics and, 83
Eye disuse, perception and, 117

F ratio, 361, 365-366
Fable of the Bees . . ., 137
Fact, errors in, 334
Family
   learning and, 202-203
   nuclear, 202
Father, identification with, 240-242
Fear, affective development and, 211 ff.
Feedback, sensory, 121-123, 187
Feelings, attitudes and, 299
Femininity, 239, 241-242
Fertilization, 78, 80
Festinger's theory of cognitive dissonance, 306 ff., 313
Figure factors in experience, 139-141
Film Technique and Film Acting, 162
Finite sets, 344
Foot evolution, 67
Forecasting, 338
Freedom, degrees of, 362-363
Frequencies, expected and observed, 380 ff.
Frequency distribution of scores, 355-357
Friendship, 236
   in-group formation and, 277 ff.
   physical distance and, 268
Functions, experimental, 344-346

Galileo, 32
Galvanic skin responses, 144
Game, norms and, 254-255
Gametes, 79-80, 82
Giftedness, 105
Generalization of attitude, 17
Generalized person, 137, 154-156, 256
Generalized threats, 183
General problem-solver, 316
Genes, dominant and recessive, 82-83
Genetic mutation, 50-51

Genetic potentiality, 76 ff., 100
Genetic resources, physical basis of culture and, 66
Genius, genetics and, 85
Genotype, 81 ff., 98
Germ cells, 51, 78, 79-80
Gestalt, 102, 127, 179
Goal attainment, desired response and, 237
Goal directedness, 203
Goals, society's potential and, 91
Gonadectomy, 68
Gonads, 79-80
Ground factors in experience, 139-141
Groups, 10, 247 ff.
  autonomous, 267
  biological aspects of, 251-252
  cohesiveness of, and problem-solving, 274-275
  conditions underlying formation of, 249 ff.
  delayed feedback in, 122
  exchange theory and, 259 ff.
  imaginary, 16
  influence on individual, 272 ff.
  in-group formation, 277 ff.
  institutionalized, 267
  meaning and, 258 ff.
  mediating, 267
  "mind" concept, 4
  norms and, 135, 371-372
  performance, 194 ff.
  power and, forms of, 275-277
  problem-solving, 267
  self-esteem and, 20
  small, interaction and, 267 ff.

Habit, 19
  extinction, 176 ff.
Hands, evolution and, 67-68
Haploid set, 80
Harlow and Zimmermann, "Affectional Responses in the Infant Monkey," 206 ff.
Heisenberg's uncertainty principle, 328
Heredity, 26-27, 51. *See also* Genes; Genetic.
  visual perception and, 119
Heterogametes, 82
Heterozygote, 82
Hominoidea, 73, 74
Homogametes, 82
Homosexuality, 146, 161, 239
Homozygotes, 82
Human rights revolution, 316
Hypnotic suggestion, attitudes and, 304-305
Hypotheses, errors in, 362

Idealized frame of reference, 159
Ideas, communication and, 86, 91-92
  obsolescence of, 289
Identification, 240-242
  attitude change and, 311
Ideology of groups, 248
Imagination, creativity and, 105, 107
Independent assortment, 80
Individual behavior, 4-5
  creativity and, 104 ff.
  expectations, role and, 21
  intelligence and, 99 ff.
  performance, 194 ff.
  potentialities in, 97 ff.
  small group influence on, 272 ff.
Indo-European language, 129
Industrialization, 95-96, 237
  retirement and, 293
Infancy
  biological helplessness in, 249
  frequency of vocalization in, 236
Inference, methods of, 367 ff.
Infinite sets, 344
Information feedback, 123
Ingratiation, 259, 260
In-group formation, 277 ff.
Inhibition, proactive and retroactive, 316
Instinct theory, 4, 28
Institutional discipline, 237
Institutionalized group, 267
Institutions, social, change and, 291 ff.
Integration
  of action, 250
  adaptation and, 53
Intelligence, 99-100
  achievement and, 106
  college plans and, 130, 131
  creativity and, 105 ff.
  experience and, 99 ff.
  Piaget's concept of, 103-104
  as problem-solving, 102
  quotient (IQ)
    education and, 99
    increase in, 100
Interaction, social, 17, 21-22, 44, 266 ff.
  intelligence and, 102-103
  patterns, 53-54
Intercorrelation, 367
Interdependence, 10, 248, 250, 277
Interindividual action, 12, 16
Internalization, attitude change and, 311-312
Interpersonal relations, perception and, 163
Interpersonal response conditioning, 236
Interpretation of research results, 367 ff.
Invention, 54, 77
Irresponsibility, obsolescence of, 289

SUBJECT INDEX

Is-ought problem, groups and, 250
Item discrimination, 151

Joint functions, 15, 21, 347
Joint method of agreement and difference, 374 ff., 379
Judgment, social, 148 ff.
   ambiguous situations and, 252-253, 256-257
   attitudes and learning and, 152-153
   perceptual, 159 ff.
   role-taking and, 156 ff.
   stereotype and, 154-156
Just noticeable difference (jnd), 149

Karyotype, normal, 83
Kelman's three-process theory of attitude, 310 ff.
Kuder Preference Record, 164

Labor, division of, 238
Language
   generalized responses and, 182
   meaning and, 258
   perception and, 128-129
   scientific, 31 ff.
   thinking and, 40
Larynx, 69
Leadership, exchange theory and, 261
Learning, 167 ff.
   analysis of variance and, 357
   brain function and, 101-102
   complexity of situation of, 186-187
   definitions in, 168-170
   distinctions of two types of conditioning and, 171-172
   early childhood, 182-183, 185-186
   evolution and, 52, 63
   explanation and, 35
   family and, 202-203
   feedback and, 187 ff.
   group and individual performance in, 194 ff.
   irregularity of original conditions in, 184-185
   judgment and, 152
   norms and, group, 272
   partial reinforcement and, 179
   perception and, 114, 115, 116, 123-125
   potentiality release and, 190 ff.
   punishment, 183
   reinforcement of operant and, 172 ff.
   response generality and, 181 ff.
   sets, 101, 124
   symbolic control and, 182-183
   threats and promises and, 183
   unreproducibility of conditions of, 185-186

Least-squares, method of, 350
Legitimate power, 276
Linearity model, 348, 354-355
Local structures, 205-206
Locomotion, bipedal, 67
Logic, 335
   errors in, 334

Manipulation, 67-68
   fine, accommodative vision and, 66-67
Man Makes Himself, 64
Manual labor, 237-238
Marmosets, 74
Marriage, 292
Masculinity, 239 ff.
Materiality, 36
Maternal separation, 231-232
Mean, 356
Meanings, 258 ff.
   perception and, 125n.
   symboling behavior and, 62
Mediating group, 267
Meiosis, 79-80
Mendel, Gregor, 78
Metaphysics of science, 328-330
Methods
   analytic, 323 ff.
   experimental, 341 ff.
Militarism, 93-94
Miller-Lyer illusion, 133
Mitosis, 79
Model
   building, perception and, 132
   identification with, 240-242
Molar and molecular units of behavior, 15
Monkeys
   affective behavior of, mothering and, 206 ff.
   evolution and, 73 ff.
   learning sets in, 101
Mother
   attitude toward role of, 17
   identification with, 240, 241-242
   retention of affectional response to, 221 ff.
Mothering, affective behavior and, 206 ff.
Motivation, 203-205
   achievement, 178, 262
   learning and, 168
   perception and, 132
Motor activities, institutional discipline and, 237
Mutation, 50-51

"Natural," meaning of, 37
Natural selection, 51
Negroes, prejudice toward, 270-271, 273

Nervous system
  evolution and, 51
  feedback and, 121-123
  learning and, 101-102
  perception and, 130, 132
  sexual behavior and, 68
Nonsense syllables, perception and, 144
"Normal," meaning of, 37
Normative behavior, 148-149
Norms, social, 10-11, 248, 250, 253 ff.
  anxiety and, 288
  biological aspects of, 251-252
  Cicourel's model for, 254 ff.
  compliance to, 256
  formation of, 371-372
  judgment and, 150-151
  learning of, 272
  perception and, 130 ff.
  role-status and, 20
  sex role and, 238-239
  vagueness of, 257-258
Nuclear family, 202
Null set, 344
Number system, 90
Nystagmus, 117

Objects, perception of, 132, 159
Obligations, 10
Observation, 14
  controlled, experimental, 346-347
  scientific vs. common-sense, 31 ff.
Obsolescence, anxiety and, 289
Omnivorous diet, evolution and, 68
Open-field tests, 218, 219, 222 ff.
Operant, reinforcement of, 172 ff.
Operational nature of science, 335-336
Opinion, attitude and, 300
Organization, perceptual
  change in, 141 ff.
  delayed sensory feedback and, 123
  figure-ground in, 139
  stereotyping and, 154
Organization, social, 205-206, 248. See also Groups.
  attitude change and, 297 ff.
  interaction function and, 102, 103
  meaning and, 262 ff.
  social change and, 291 ff.
  values and, 292-294
Other-enhancement, 259
Others, dependence on, 200

Pairs, ordered, 345
Paranoia, 161
Parents
  creativity and, 108

Parents—*Continued*
  identification with, 240-242
  learning and, 202-203
  power of, 275
  separation from, 231-232, 241
Past experience, perception and, 116 ff.
Pavlov, 57
Perceived instrumentality, attitudes and, 303, 305
Perception, 113 ff. *See also* Judgment, social.
  attitudes and, 17
  autonomic discrimination in, 144
  behavioral and cultural influences in, 125 ff.
  cues and, social, 133, 154
  definition, 115
  exchange theory and, 262
  experience and, 116 ff.
  figure-ground factors in, 139-141
  interaction and, social, 7
  judgment and, 159 ff.
  language and, 40, 128-129
  learning and, 114, 123-125, 155
  norms and, social, 130 ff.
  organization in, 120, 141 ff.
  performance and, 126-127
  problem areas in, 116
  role and, 21, 157-158
Performance
  group and individual, 194 ff.
  perception and, 126-127
  potential and, 87
Perseveration, 120
Personal *vs.* social behavior, 163, 165
Personality, 19
  restructuring of, 233-235
  system, 262
Phenotype, 81 ff., 98
Phi coefficient, 378, 379, 380
Phylogenetic evolution, 73-74
Phylogenetic discontinuity of progress, 92
"Physical," meaning of, 36-37
Piaget's concept of intelligence, 103-104
Placement of items, 151
Pleasurable materials, perception and, 145-146
Population increase, 314, 332-333
Populations, 53
  performance of, potentialities and, 88
Positions, social, 9, 10, 18, 19
Posture, upright, 67
Potentialities, 73 ff.
  biological, 77 ff.
  cultural, 86 ff.
  individual, release and development of, 97 ff.
  learning and release of, 190 ff.

SUBJECT INDEX

Power
 forms of, 275-277
 influences, status and, 274-275
Practice, perception and, 132
Preconception, learning and, 193
Predictability of social behavior, 250, 251
Prediction, role of, in science, 337-339
Predispositions, attitudes and, 299
Prejudice, 162
 racial, 270-271, 273
 stereotyping and, 154, 155
Pireneans, 16
Primates, 73-74
Principia Mathematica, 316
Principles, values and, 296
Probabilistic theory, Brunswik's, 156
Probabilities, 36
 partial reinforcement and, 177
Problem, introduction to experimental, 342-344
Problem areas in social psychology, 39-41
Problematic data, 38, 39
Problem-solving, 267, 332-333, 336
 cohesiveness of group and, 274
 creativity and, 104
 intelligence and, 102
 learning and, 192
Progress, 315
 phylogenetic discontinuity of, 92
Promises, generalized, 183
Propaganda, 234
Propositions, scientific, 334-335
Prosimians, 73
Protoplasm, 79
Proximity, perception and, 140
Pseudophones, 124
Psychology *vs.* sociology and social psychology, 3 ff., 41 ff.
Punishment, 259
 cross-pressures and, 271
 learning and, 183, 185
 social institutions and, 292
Pupil size, pleasant and unpleasant stimuli and, 145-146
Purposes of investigation, 39

Q measure, 378, 379

r^2, 377
Racial prejudice, 270-271, 273
Radiation, species, 89
Randomization, 354
Rank, attitudes and, 8
Reality, social, 134
 concept of, 328-330
Reason, science and, 326-327
Recessive alleles, 82
Reciprocal acts, 10, 250

Red Devils and Bull Dogs, 277 ff.
Reference, frame of, perception and, 127-128, 135, 159, 162
Reference scale, 153
Referent power, 276
Referents, terms and, 31 ff.
Reflex response, evolution and, 56-57
Reflexive schemata, 103
Regression, 348 ff.
Reinforcement, 172 ff.
 feedback and, 187 ff.
 interval, 174
 partial, 173, 174 ff.
 perception and, 114, 115, 116, 123
 ratio, 174
 regular, 172
 secondary, 187
Relation of pairs, 345
Relationships, 10, 22, 44
 establishing existence of, 346 ff.
 measures of, 378 ff.
 perception and, 133
Remainder or residual sum of squares, 365
Replication, 354
Reproductive cells, 79-80
Research. *See also* Experimentation.
 scientific theory and, 327
Residence, perception and, 129-130
Residual sum of squares, 365
Resocialization, 200 ff., 233-235
Response
 complexity, 56 ff., 75
 definition of, 169
 differentiation of, 180
 emission frequency, 172
 generalization, 103, 178, 181 ff.
 interpersonal, conditioning and, 236
 of others
  perception and, 128
  as stimulus, 150
 partial, 176
 patterns, 54, 150
  retention of affectional, 221 ff.
 specificity, 178
Retinal image inversion, 124
Retirement, 293
Reward, 259-260
 cross-pressures and, 271
 power, 275
 social institutions and, 292
Ribonucleic acid (RNA), 81
Rights, 10
Rocking motion, 229
Role, 10-11, 18-19
 concept of, 11, 16 ff.
 cultural contradictions and, 264-265
 mental image of, 21

SUBJECT INDEX

Role—*Continued*
  motivation and, 204
  multiple, 265-266
  norms and, 135
  prescribed, 20-21
  psychological counterparts of, 19 ff.
  set, 10
  sex, identity and, 238 ff.
  taking, judgment and, 156 ff.
  Rosenberg's affective-cognitive consistency theory, 301 ff., 313
Rubin's Goblet, 139-140
Rules of preferred play, 255

Saulteaux Indians, 126
Schemata, 103, 107
Science, 325
  characteristics of, 330 ff.
  description, 31 ff.
  metaphysics of, 328-330
  prediction in, 337-339
  theory and, 4
  understanding nature and, 325-327
Selection, natural, 51
Self-esteem, 19-20
Self-image
  attitude change and, 311
  sex role and, 239
Self-other judgments, 160
Self-presentation, 259
Self-reliance, conformity, creativity and, 107
Sensorimotor period of development, 103
Sensory feedback, 121-123, 188
Sensory perception, experiences and, 116 ff.
Service's law of evolutionary potential, 89 ff.
Sets, 107
  experimental, 344-346
  learning, 101, 124
Sex cells, 79-80
Sex chromosomes, 78
Sex determination, 82
Sex differences in behavior, 199-200
Sex role identity, 238 ff.
Sexual behavior control, 68
Sham behavior, 137-138
Sign behavior, 58, 62, 75
  meaning and, 258
Similarity, perception and, 141
Skinner, B. F., 170, 171
Slope, 348
Social change, 285 ff.
  affective-cognitive consistency theory and, 301 ff.
  anxiety and, 288-290
  attitude change and, 297 ff., 313-315

Social change—*Continued*
  cognitive dissonance theory and, 306 ff.
  definition of, 288
  institutions and, 291 ff.
  three-process theory of attitude change and, 310-312
  values and, 294 ff.
Social deprivation, 232
Social interaction, 7, 12, 16, 21-22
Socialization and resocialization, 200 ff., 263
Social *vs.* personal behavior, 163, 165
Social planning, 315-317
Social psychology, 3 ff.
  applications of, 22-23
  basic units of analysis of, 14 ff.
  conceptual level of analysis, 35 ff.
  data and problems of, 39-41
  definition of, 12
  difficulties in research in, 383-384
  general approach to, 23 ff.
  importance of studying, 12-13
  psychology, sociology, and, 3 ff., 41 ff.
Social Psychology of Modern Life, 22-23
Social Security, 293
Social system, 9
Society, 18
  potentiality of, 90 ff.
  structures of, 205-206
Socioability, 24
Socioeconomic status, college plans and, 130, 131
Sociology, social psychology, psychology, and, 3 ff., 41 ff.
Somatic cells, 51, 79
Space, absolute, 129
Spatial frame of reference, perception and, 128
Spatial patterns of environment, 122
Speech
  evolution and, 68-69
  response and, 60-61
Sperms, 79, 82
Squares, sums of, 358 ff.
Standard deviation, 356
Standards, values and, 296
Status, social, 10, 18-19
  obsolescence of, 289-290
  power influences and, 274-275
  psychological counterparts of, 19 ff.
Stereoscope perception, 143
Stereotyping, 137, 256
  judgment and, 154-156
Stimulus
  conditioned, 189
  creativity and, 107
  discrimination and, 180
  generalization, 103, 116, 170, 179

SUBJECT INDEX

Stimulus—*Continued*
  monotonous, 121
  others' responses as, 150
  partial reinforcement and, 174-175
  perception and, 114, 116, 145-146
  positive and negative, 145-146
  setting, 127
  unconditioned, 169, 189
Straight-alley tests, 214-215, 225-226
Subception, 144
Symbol, 7-8, 56
  meaning and, 258
Symbolic control, 338-339
  lack of, generalized responses and, 182-183
Symbolic imitation, 103
Symboling behavior, 61 ff., 75, 258
Synapsis, 80
Systems of behavior, 9, 39
Systems, scientific, 337

T measure, 380
Teaching evaluation, 360 ff.
Technological development, 237-238, 290, 293, 316
Temporal patterns of environment, 122
Terms, referents and, 31 ff.
Tetrads, 80
Theory
  interdependence of fact with, 32
  science and, 4
Thought
  attitudes and, 299
  development of, 104
  language and, 40
  learning and, 192
Threats, generalized, 183
Three-process theory of attitude, 310 ff.
Transfer of learning, 116
Transposition, 179-180
Trotsky, Leon, 91, 93
Tschuprow's T, 380

Twins
  behavior patterns of, 87-88
  intelligence of, 99

Uncertainty principle, 328
Underachievement, 93
Units of analysis, 14 ff., 42
Upright posture, 67
Urban change, 286-287

V measure, 383
Values
  attitudes and, 303, 305
  social change and, 294 ff.
Variables
  dependent, 38, 42, 43, 346, 368, 369
  independent, 38, 43, 346, 369
  symbolic control of, 338-339
Variance, 355-357
  analysis of, 353 ff.
Variation, concomitant, 343, 347 ff., 368-370
Veblen, 92
Visual exploration, 220
Visual feedback, delayed, 121-122
Visual inversion, 124
Visual perception, 116 ff.
Vision, accommodative, 66-67
Vocal communication, evolution and, 68-69
Vocalization, frequency of, of infancy, 236

Wallonians, 16, 17
Weaponry, revolution in, 316
Word usage
  response and, 60-61
  scientific, 31 ff.

Yerkes Laboratories, 117
Yule's Q, 378

Zygote, 78, 80

९